MOONLIGHT MELODY

*A Path of Faith and Acceptance from Seoul to a
US Oncology Practice to Prison and Release*

VICTORIA GATES, MD

BALBOA.PRESS
A DIVISION OF HAY HOUSE

Copyright © 2020 Victoria Gates, MD.

All rights reserved. No part of this book may be used or reproduced by any means, graphic, electronic, or mechanical, including photocopying, recording, taping or by any information storage retrieval system without the written permission of the author except in the case of brief quotations embodied in critical articles and reviews.

Balboa Press books may be ordered through booksellers or by contacting:

Balboa Press
A Division of Hay House
1663 Liberty Drive
Bloomington, IN 47403
www.balboapress.com
844-682-1282

Because of the dynamic nature of the Internet, any web addresses or links contained in this book may have changed since publication and may no longer be valid. The views expressed in this work are solely those of the author and do not necessarily reflect the views of the publisher, and the publisher hereby disclaims any responsibility for them.

The author of this book does not dispense medical advice or prescribe the use of any technique as a form of treatment for physical, emotional, or medical problems without the advice of a physician, either directly or indirectly. The intent of the author is only to offer information of a general nature to help you in your quest for emotional and spiritual well-being. In the event you use any of the information in this book for yourself, which is your constitutional right, the author and the publisher assume no responsibility for your actions.

Any people depicted in stock imagery provided by Getty Images are models, and such images are being used for illustrative purposes only. Certain stock imagery © Getty Images.

Print information available on the last page.

ISBN: 978-1-9822-5937-2 (sc)
ISBN: 978-1-9822-5939-6 (hc)
ISBN: 978-1-9822-5938-9 (e)

Library of Congress Control Number: 2020923376

Balboa Press rev. date: 11/18/2020

Contents

Introduction vii

Chapter 1   East versus West (Rabbit in the Moon) 1
Chapter 2   New Kid on the Block... 10
Chapter 3   Fish out of Water.. 18
Chapter 4   A Penny Saved Is a Penny Earned 25
Chapter 5   Useless as Tits on a Boar Hog................................... 32
Chapter 6   Shoot for the Moon and Reach for the Stars (Haste
             Makes Waste) 37
Chapter 7   Let Tomorrow Take Care of Itself............................. 50
Chapter 8   Shark Fin Soup and Sweet Bread 61
Chapter 9   That Sounds Like a Good Plan 67
Chapter 10   Uncle Pie of America 78
Chapter 11   Where There's a Will There 's a Way 86
Chapter 12   My Decision to Become an Oncologist (Moonlighting)........ 98
Chapter 13   Dr. Gates Is Coming 113
Chapter 14   Sharks Follow the Smell of Blood (Be Careful, Dr. Gates) 121
Chapter 15   All Is Well... 129
Chapter 16   The Enchanted Garden (Looking for His Help Was
             Useless) 138
Chapter 17   I Should Not Have Married Dr. Lemon.................. 147
Chapter 18   One Step at a Time.. 158
Chapter 19   What Medicare Fraud? This Is Where the Story Unfolds... 166
Chapter 20   My Pizza Party (I Love Them All).......................... 175
Chapter 21   Pure Americanism (I Should Have Packed My Stuff
             and Left Town) 185
Chapter 22   I Think You Love Your Patients More Than You Love Me ... 196

Chapter 23	Everybody Knows Everybody's Business	205
Chapter 24	Busier Than a Fast-Food Restaurant (Trojan Horse)	217
Chapter 25	My Throat will be burning	227
Chapter 26	Bigger Snowballs (Do Not Eat Your Meal)	236
Chapter 27	"She's Here, and She's a Big Fish" (Richard, the Money-Grabbing Attorney)	244
Chapter 28	Innocence Equals Ignorance (Victoria Gates v. America)	253
Chapter 29	Closing My Clinic My Money Too and No One to Trust	263
Chapter 30	Where Did You Go to Law School? Nothing but a Stage Show	272
Chapter 31	A Sitting Duck (Dr. Lemon was a Perpetrator)	285
Chapter 32	He Was a Culprit So Be It!	291
Chapter 33	Ready to Go through the Fire (Detestable and Nefarious Misogyny)	296
Chapter 34	Too late, Like Water under a Bridge (You Do not Look Like a Prisoner)	302
Chapter 35	Rock Bottom	311
Chapter 36	The School of Suffering (Lessons We Could Learn in No Other Classroom)	323
Chapter 37	I Had to Save My Own Life	336
Chapter 38	We Thought You Were Dead (Coming out of a Fiery Furnace without a Burn)	346

Introduction

To everything, there is a season, and a time to every purpose under the heaven: A time to be born, and a time to die; a time to plant, and a time to pluck up that which is planted; A time to kill, and a time to heal; a time to break down, and a time to build up; A time to rend, and a time to sew; a time to keep silence and a time to speak.
—Ecclesiastes 3: 1–3, 7 KJV

God not only wanted to bring me out of my confinement, but also wanted to bring me out better than I was before. There was a set time for me to receive his blessing and a set time for favor, to share my experience and story with the others. I struggled with the near death and went into the midst of the fiery furnace of prison, I came out without a burn which was a miracle. My truth would prevail through my book, there was a purpose behind every problem. It was the fire of the suffering that brought forth the gold of a godliness.
—Madame Guyon

My desire is to share the difficult experiences I have lived and my faith and to bring the stories of my life to the lives of others so that they will be encouraged. When people are discouraged, I want to assure them that a new season of their favorite time is coming. There were times when I had lost so much, I did not see a way out—when finding a way forward looked impossible. But to God, everything is possible. Through our adversity, we became stronger, wiser, more creative, more appreciative, and happier.

All things begin to happen.

I was not shocked or surprised when I was sentenced to serve nearly two decades in a federal prison. If that was my new mission, I was willing to walk by faith, not by sight.

For me, life had long presented a series of problems. Every time I solved one, another was waiting to take its place. Who said life was fair? But faith, perseverance, wisdom, hope, and love would change my destiny.

I would like to share my survival skills with others. It would be beneficial to learn from my mistakes, as it is always wise to learn from the experiences of others.

I acknowledge one who was forgiven much and one who was loved the most and loved best.

Through my daily meditation and yoga practice, God planted a new seed in my heart so that I could see things differently. I trusted in faith that, with men, it may be impossible, but with God, all things were possible. We should never underestimate a supernatural power. And we must know that God can change anything and everything in a heartbeat.

I declared my determination, knowing that if I had faith, nothing would defeat me. I had lost many things. However, God's restoration was manifoldly greater than my losses. He had already brought me out and left me better off than I was before. We must focus on God when we go through fiery trials, maintaining faith and staying the course. Even if we are tired, discouraged, and frustrated, we must not give up on our future. It may be taking a long time, but your dream will come true, and you will receive true peace and joy. We must endure and persevere, even though it is difficult and tiring. We must believe, even though we do not see anything happening and feel hopeless. God will step in, and the Holy Spirit will assist us.

This is my confession and my genuine experience through the many adversities and trials I have faced. We can develop a healthy, robust community when we live with God and enjoy the results of that community. All that is required is that we do the hard work of getting along with each other and treating each other with dignity and honor.

As the Bible tells us:

> The wisdom that is first pure, then peaceable, gentle, and easy to be entreated, full of mercy and good fruits without partiality and without have hypocrisy. The fruit

of righteousness sown in peace of them that makes peace.
(James 3:17–18 KJV)

Discrimination is nothing but narrow-minded intelligence. When conflict is handled correctly, we grow closer to each other, and that brings peace and harmony.

CHAPTER 1

East versus West (Rabbit in the Moon)

On a chilly February night in 1975, I arrived at LAX with a one-way ticket and $110 sealed in my pocket. I was twenty-one when I landed in Los Angeles, California.

The shimmering lights of LA as seen through the windowpane of the airplane before it touched down on the tarmac were a magnificent sight. I felt that the beautiful, twinkling city was welcoming my adventurous new journey toward an American life. Youthful, zealous motivation and unrestrained ambition allowed me to challenge the unknown future without fear. I did not have any immediate family, distant relatives, or friends in the United States.

I had met an American chief of priests during my Catholic retreat in Korea. We were spiritually connected due to my serious faith. He was willing to support my goal to be a doctor in the United States. My only connection was a married couple, who had revered the director of the priests in America for decades.

This priest had introduced me to the couple via a letter, sending them my photo so that they would recognize me when they picked me up from LAX. I had not met the couple previously. Nor had I spoken with them by phone. They had only the photo to help them identify me upon my arrival.

They were there when I exited the plane. Several individuals were holding signs for various hotels, trying to find their incoming guests. I saw a beautiful couple holding a sign bearing my name in the mass of people. They were looking for a young Asian woman among the disembarking passengers. Fortunately, we did not have any trouble finding one another.

A professionally dressed, lovely young woman approached me and asked me, "Are you Victoria Gates from Seoul, Korea?"

"Yes! I am the person you are looking for!" I was so excited.

She introduced herself. "I am Mariana, and this is my husband, Raymond." Mariana had big brown eyes and sandy hair. She appeared to be intelligent and kind and had an assertive voice.

My heart filled with joy and enthusiasm. We embraced warmly, and they led me toward their car.

A huge five-lane highway and numerous swiftly moving vehicles intimidated me and made me feel even smaller than I already had.

Mariana asked, "Are you hungry?"

"Not really," I quietly responded.

She smiled. "Well, we are taking you to a restaurant. We haven't had dinner."

Raymond guided us to an exotic restaurant. The waiters and waitresses were attractively attired, especially the blond women, who wore bright red flowers on their heads. The bathroom was clean, and everything was automatic. I was amazed at the toilet that had no flushing device, the faucet with no handle, and the hands-free paper towel dispenser.

We enjoyed the evening together after the delicious dinner. Mariana was a professor at UCLA and described California well. She explained about Beverly Hills and Hollywood in detail, giving me a very heartwarming impression of my new environment. She told me that California had been dubbed the Golden State because, during the gold rush, many people had swarmed to California from different states in search of gold. The sky was a deep turquoise blue, which is my favorite color. The dry, warm breeze gently caressing my face and arms made me feel happy and blessed in February 1975.

The gorgeous weather was one of many reasons California continued to be one of the most populous states and an attractive tourist destination. The variety of colored skyscrapers, the many electronic devices, and the advanced society astonished me. Two gigantic amusement parks, Disneyland in Anaheim and SeaWorld in San Diego, drew millions of tourists to the fascinating Los Angeles area each year.

Mariana and Raymond took me to Disneyland during my first weekend in California. I enjoyed the Disney theme park, the original magic kingdom, Animal Kingdom, the water park, the roller coaster through the cave, and more. We had a great day. From early in the morning until sundown, it was nothing but thrills, laughter, and fun.

I found California to be vastly different from my childhood home, Korea. I arrived in LA in February and found a warm dry climate. In contrast to Korea's cold and snowy weather in February and four distinct seasons, Los Angeles had mild winters. The weather in Korea was like what you would experience in West Virginia.

At the end of World War II, Korea was divided at the 38th parallel north latitude into two zones, with the troops from the Soviet Union in the north and the troops from the United States in the south. By 1948, two separate governmental bodies had emerged—the communist People's Republic of Korea in the north and the Democratic Republic of South Korea.

American and Soviet troops were withdrawn by 1949. Nonetheless, the Americans were quickly drawn back in with the onset of the Korean War, which was fought between 1950 and 1953. It began when North Korea invaded South Korea. United States troops, under General Douglas McArthur, helped South Korea, and the Chinese forces aided North Korea.

I spent a relaxing and pleasant week with Mariana and Raymond. They had two beautiful children, a boy, and a girl. Their son was three years old at the time, and their daughter had just turned one. They were a successful couple, and they had built an additional extra room onto the original house, including a spacious playroom for the kids. They were frugal but kind and generous to others, with a strong Catholic faith.

Through Mariana, I got a job at the hospital assisting medical personnel. Once I started working, I quickly became a workaholic. First, I had one job, but that soon turned into two jobs and, later, almost three full-time jobs without any days off. I saved every penny I earned for my future education.

Three years later, through one of the nurses at the hospital where I worked, I met an old couple at a Methodist church. Their last name was Fisher. Both were in their sixties. The wife was called Anna, and the husband's name was Arthur. They were active churchgoers and faithful Christians. They asked me to live with them in their genuinely nice, three-bedroom house. I loved their garden, which was brightly filled with colorful flowers.

Arthur was still working as a supervisor at the Broadway Department Store. Anna had retired and stayed home. They had three grown-up children, two daughters and one son. This was my golden opportunity to grow, to learn, and even to create a wonderful family with incredible people, but my naivety and youth were unable to recognize the value of precious family ties at the time.

I was young and restless with unstructured ambition. Certainly, hindsight is better than foresight. Anna and Arthur coming into my life was not an accident; it was God's grace. The couple originated from the Netherlands, in northwestern Europe, known also as Holland. The Dutch Empire's settlement of Amsterdam later became New York.

Margaret was the older daughter among the Fishers' three children. Their second child was Peter, and the youngest daughter was Dana. Margaret and Dana loved to cook a big meal, and we would celebrate each holiday together. Margaret's husband, Roy, played banjo and ukulele well. We jumped in his swimming pool, splashing water at each other and had a carefree fun time.

I remembered we were singing a song all together, "A Tiny Bubble in the Water," after an elaborate Thanksgiving Day meal. What a cherished moment of pleasure! I did not know the pricelessness of a loving family union at the time, due to my unknown future and irresistible desire to be a successful doctor, which haunted me all the time.

My thought process changed as I got older. What I had once valued as important was no longer purposeful. In the past, a successful title and money were awfully meaningful—or so I had thought they would be. It was as if we lived our lives based on the carnal mind, without the love of God, not bearing in mind that he said that wealth in this life cannot be guaranteed:

> Let not the wise man glory in his wisdom, neither let the mighty man glory in his mighty let not the Rich man glory in his riches: But let him that gloried glory in this, that he understands and knows me, that I am the Lord which is exercise loving kindness, judgment, and righteousness, in the earth: for in these things I delight, saith the Lord. (Jeremiah 9: 23–24 KJV)

My mother loaned millions of dollars to her dearest business associate, and her friend was unable to pay the money back. The lack of cash flows quickly damaged my mother's department store. At the same time, the Korean economy was declining and fallen almost to recession level.

Consequently, my father's architecture business went down as well. My parents were suddenly suffering from a financial crisis. My father was a well-respected gentleman and a self-reserved, quiet man. He never scolded or grounded us. In contrast, my mother was gregarious, impulsive, and outspoken. During my school years, miniskirts were popular, and I often wore a suede beige jacket with a fur collar, which matched my knee-high boots.

My father must have noticed when I bent to pick up a textbook. He told my mother, "Victoria's skirt is too short."

This was among the only such comment that I heard from my father throughout my entire childhood back home. He generously complemented and praised us, kids when we were doing well at home or school.

My mother's character was opposite that of my father. She was very affectionate. However, she complained frequently and got upset easily.

At age four, I became a serious Christian and always admired Catholic nuns when they solemnly prayed to God. I imitated them and prayed to God just as the nuns did. I was a good child and tried to obey God's law.

When my parents were struggling with money, all my earned money went to my parents. I skipped dinner at times to save money for them. I did not miss Sunday Mass throughout grade school, focusing on God, which help me to concentrate my goals. By my faith and the grace of God, finally, I decided to be a doctor in America. That was my dream.

Prior to my parents' financial problems, my mother had betrothed my sister to the son of a multimillionaire, who had graduated from the most prestigious university. My sister's father-in-law was a Mayo. He owned a coal mining company, was part owner of a university hospital, and owned many business buildings in different cities.

My sister was extremely beautiful and charming. On the other hand, I was a tomboy. She was selected to be in a Miss Korean beauty pageant. Contemporaneously, she got engaged. Not knowing my sister's situation, one of the most famous movie stars at the time, Hang Jung Shoon, gave my sister the opportunity to be a TV talent. When she became betrothed to the son of the wealthy business owner, she would subsequently not be permitted to exposed herself in that way in public.

Previously, my sister had had a close friend who was a pharmacist, and they had fallen in love with each other. They had dated until she graduated from the university. My mother was not allowed my sister to marry her boyfriend, Kim Shawn, because she thought he was not rich enough to ensure that my sister's life would be comfortable.

> For many reasons, I did not care for Korean traditional culture. In my opinion, it seemed too narrow and driven by a controlling mentality. Coming to the United States with my ambition, I felt free from the rigid ethnic culture I had been raised in—so free I could even fly like a bird: Nevertheless, there are good things found in thee, in that thou hast taken away the groves out of the land, and hast prepared thine heart to seek God. (2 Chronicle 19:3 KJV)

Yes, God had blessed me. I was born into a wealthy family. My father was an architect, and he built a two-story house for our family. My mother owned a department store and managed several employees on Main Street downtown. Money was not a subject of concern when we were growing up. My parents were not highly educated during the Korean War. And like many parents who found themselves in the same situation, they were eager to educate us and to provide their best for us so that we could be happy.

We had a live-in maid and a home tutor. We were spoiled and did not have much motivation at the time. My sister, Daisy Gates, and I participated in many different lessons, including piano and ballet, which we practiced together. Neither of us liked to study. When the tutor came to teach us at home, we frequently lied to him, telling we had gone to have paid lessons to skip his tutoring sessions. The chalkboard against the wall upstairs was rarely occupied.

My sister and I would sneak out for Chinese food at a restaurant. Daisy did not like to eat food at home or at the restaurant. She admired my good appetite and stared at me while I enjoyed the Chinese food. My favorite dish was a deep-fried, glazed empanada with succulent, colorful vegetables, such as snow peas, large mushrooms, carrots, and slender green onions.

Our delightful enjoyment was sneaking out of the house and smelling the stimulating aroma from the sizzling hot food in the Chinese restaurant. Whenever I smell food wafting from the kitchen, it brings back my childhood memories with my sister. Surely, my childhood was great!

My sister was an excellent and popular ballerina at her Christian school. The curriculum of grade schools was quite different in Korea than that in America. We had a mandatory break time after lunch for all students. We were required to stretch and increase the blood flow to our brains in the commons of the school. Daisy was chosen to be the leader to demonstrate the exercises. She stood on a tall platform. Students loved her graceful instruction. She was always proud of herself and was often the center of attention since she won many ballet contests.

In the early '60s, after the Korean War, many people were trying to make ends meet. My sister wore high-priced sunglasses, rolled-up Western style T-shirts, and khaki pants. Many of her friends came to celebrate her birthday party at our home. She showed off her agility and how far she could bend backward by performing limbo dancing. Her friends clapped their hands and were amazed by her stable balance.

Daisy had to be the best and the first in whatever she did. Even though, my parents were wealthy I paid my school tuition on the last day of the deadline. On the other hand, my sister was invariably first in line to pay her tuition. If any new or sophisticated items were displayed in stores, my sister wanted them first. A Parker fountain pen was just released, and she purchased it immediately. On the contrary, I bought a low-priced but practical pen. I did not care for expensive tailor-made clothes. In contrast, she preferred an extravagant tailor-made wardrobe. Most of the time, I ended up wearing hand-me-down clothes of her, as I was younger than her. I liked simple clothes, in any event, and did not value fancy clothes at all.

Despite our vastly different lifestyle preferences, though, she was my best friend. And respected her and followed her advice faithfully.

One day, we were given money to order tailored clothes. Since my sister was very fastidiously selective about her attire and because she was six years older than me, I obeyed her decisions. Consequently, she designed our outfits, with layers of ruffled skirts in soft pink fabrics—outfits that were not casual or appropriate to wear to school. She sketched them for ballerinas, just as she desired.

Regardless of their inappropriateness for school, we were quite excited and proudly showed off, wearing our fancy dresses, and posing in front of our mother. My sister asked, "Do you like these dresses that I personally designed?"

"Oh my God, where do you think that you will wear them?" my mother answered unexpectedly.

My mother's face suddenly turned red, and she got terribly upset. She complained that we had wasted her money on clothes that were not practical. Mother was extremely angry with us. In the aftermath, we were kicked out of the house. We spent the night in the backyard.

In the face of my mother's punishment, we looked at each other and said, "Oops! Sorry, Mom." We spoke quietly like church mice as we made our way out the door.

Nonetheless, we still thought the dresses were beautiful, and we giggled about it. That night, while outside, we talked for hours. My sister told me a mysterious fairy tale regarding a white rabbit that went to the moon. She pointed out the shadow on the moon as we looked at the bright full moon surrounded by twinkling stars. My eyelids got heavier and sleepier, and then I fell asleep on her shoulder.

It was getting late in the night when our live-in maid finally opened the door for us. I hit the pillow and dreamed about the white rabbit in the moon.

Recollecting my childhood, I saw that I had so many precious memories. Whenever we would go on picnics, my mother would prepare for us her excellent sushi and serve small snacks. My sister, tutor, and I would wade through freshwater streams, trying to catch tiny fish in our cupped hands. We had so much fun when we were coming down the mountain from the temple. We would run around the hiking path catching lighting bugs. Frequently, we would collect a bag of lightning bugs and use it as a fairy light.

"The fairy light will scare tigers and chase them away because they do not like any light," my mom said.

We picked up holly berries, and Daisy painted the red berries with a glossy coating using fingernail polish, giving them a smooth, shiny surface. Then she decorated her bookcase with them. I loved to stare at the delightful red holly berries instead of studying my homework.

My mother was Buddhist, my sister was a Protestant, I was Catholic, and my father did not involve himself in religion. No one voiced any objections to our freedom of religion. Our childhood was innocent and full of joys, hopes, and dreams.

CHAPTER 2

New Kid on the Block

What a blessing from God that I had the opportunity to live with Anna and Arthur. They were filled with love, zealous faith, caring, and altruistic spirit. Arthur had broad living experiences around the world, and Anna was an outstanding cook. Anna enjoyed feeding her family and made marvelous tender pot roasts in a large iron kettle, which was too heavy to lift with my two hands. She made simple peeled potatoes into fluffy, ambrosial, white-blossomed mounds that were testier than any potatoes I had ever eaten. She then poured succulent roast beef gravy over the softly busted white potatoes. Most of her side dishes were freshly steamed green vegetables and salads with homemade dressings. She enjoyed cooking a variety of fish and chicken dishes as well.

Anna and Arthur were truly two of the most delightful and wonderful people I had ever known. They frequently brought homemade dinner to my workplace. The dinner would be placed in Pyrex glassware, which was wrapped with a kitchen towel and accompanied by a small stainless-steel thermos. Then they would carry my hot dinner in a large bag. Anna and Arthur would sit with me in the hospital cafeteria and tell me jokes and the news about what had happened that day to their neighbors, the people at work, and their family. They laughed frequently with affectionate and happy smiles. I was genuinely loved by their kindness.

Anna with white hair

> By whom also we have access by faith into this grace wherein we stand and rejoice in hope glory of God. And not only so, but we glory in tribulations also: knowing that tribulation worketh patience; And patience, experience; and experience, hope. We have also obtained access by faith into this grace in which we stand, and we rejoiced in hope of the glory of God. (Romans 5: 2–4 KJV)

Even though I was experiencing this sheer happiness with my adopted family in the United States, occasionally, my mind drifted back to the past—to what had happened in the beginning of my life in America, prior to meeting Anna and Arthur.

My determination had brought me to a new country all alone to be a doctor. Additionally, I wanted to save enough money to help my parents. These desires propelled me to study hard and focus on my future success.

After my arrival in California, my friend Mariana found a job for me. During my day off from the job, I studied for the MCAT (Medical College Admission Test) so I could attend medical school. One day, the CEO of the City Library came to where I was studying. He introduced himself, saying, "My name is Rick. What's your name?"

"My name is Victoria Gates, and I have been here for only one month," I told him.

Thereafter, he asked nonstop questions. What are you studying? Do you have a family? How do you spend time on your day off?

Later, Rick gave me some advice on how to take the MCAT and which books to use to study. After a few weeks passed, he brought several different MCAT books and loaned them to me. I appreciated him greatly and was excited about my future in med school. Not knowing him very well, I thought that I was a lucky person.

Time went on, and he visited me regularly where I was studying. One weekend, he unexpectedly came to my apartment and a knocked on the door in the evening. "I brought a box of Kentucky Fried Chicken for your dinner."

I thanked him deeply. What a sweet and kind man he was! Rick did not stay in my apartment after he dropped off the fried chicken.

As time passed—nearly six months—I became confused, puzzled, and dumbfounded by his presence. He continuously followed me everywhere I went. I did not understand why he was stalking me.

Back home in Korea, most of the college students were less interested in studying and more interested in their dating partners. They shared experiences of dates among themselves. Our classmates' dating stories were popular on the school campus and in the schoolroom. But I did not follow suit. Even when I had reached the age to join the campus, I was not interested in dating. Rather, I was involved in learning arts, such as painting, playing piano, singing, and dancing. Different learning activities filled my daily life. As a child, I was busy playing mandolin or drums, playing tennis, and writing poems. The beauty of arts and a busy schedule gave me a total satisfaction. There was no time to yearn for dates, and I had no desire to go out with any schoolboys.

I was innocent and had no experience with men and no understanding of their behaviors. Consequently, I could not figure out the CEO of the department. I perceived that something was not right and felt a creepy sensation, but I thought this was simply my distrusting people and my naivety. Again, and again, I noticed Rick following me everywhere, even to the grocery store, like a dark shadow. When I attempted to see him, he would hide against the wall. Obviously, he was not shopping. He did not carry a basket or push a cart in the store.

One day when he came to my table in the library, I asked him directly, "Why have you been following me everywhere?"

"You are new here, and I wanted to make sure that you are safe," he told me.

I was becoming increasingly uncomfortable as he continued to follow me everywhere and came to my table without missing a day. I wanted to stay away from him.

Two months later, he bought a necklace with a hanging heart-shaped pendant. He asked me, "I wanted to have your opinion. Do you like this necklace?"

"It is very pretty, especially the small diamonds around the heart shape," I said. "I am sure your wife will love it. Did you buy it for her birthday?"

"No, it's for you," he said.

I was completely taken aback and repeated, "You mean you bought this necklace for me? I hardly know you."

A few moments later, he offered me the necklace and tried to put it around my neck. I gently refused to accept the necklace and blocked his approach. His behavior induced chills up and down my spine. My discernment was no longer dubious, and I questioned his mental status.

He then, as he had time and again, tried to persuade me that I was too religious and pure—that I would not fit into American culture. For a moment only unspoken silence answered his comment.

When I finally found the words to respond, I told him, "Yes, I am a faithful Catholic believer and want to live by God's law. I love Jesus. He is my savior."

One day, before I had come to the United States, Jesus had appeared clearly in my dream. He had descended from heaven. Radiant beams of light shone down from his palms and luminous aura of radiation surrounded his presence. Additional rays of light shone gently down through his white robe. Little winged cherubs were playing tiny trumpets and joyously flying around Jesus. At the same moment, the vast land of earth cracked and created a bottomless abyss. A mass of panicked people fell from the cliff into the immeasurable black depths of the pits. Amid this unspeakable, sudden, and calamitous disaster, my raptured heart burst without fear. I jumped with joy and praised and exalted Jesus as my savior. This mystical experience and vision of Jesus showed me I had an amazing spirit. I ran to my school dormitory, a red brick building covered with the abundantly clustered flowers of tall acacia trees, their green leaves decorating the window frames. I shouted emotionally to the students in the dorm to go and praise Jesus.

> The buzzing of the alarm clock woke me from my unforgettable dream. Truly, my dream, the vision of Jesus, gave me everlasting pleasure and a complete peace. As the Bible tells us: I have come a light into the world, that whosoever believeth on me should not abide in darkness. He that rejected me, and received not my words, hath one that judged him: the word that I have spoken, the same shall judge him in the last day. (John 12: 46, 48 KJV)

I was not ashamed to proclaim that I loved Jesus. Rick was a wolf in sheep's clothing. He was certainly disruptive and disguised his ruthless nature through an outward show of kindness, innocence, and false generosity.

Suddenly a light bulb turned on, and my understanding of his behavior as stalking became clear. It was unsettling that he desired to make me his prey because I was a "new kid on the block"—young and naive.

One night, Rick showed up on my doorstep after midnight and knocked on my apartment door.

I looked through the peephole and saw that, indeed, it was Rick standing behind the door. I asked anyway, "Who is it?"

He answered, "It's Rick." His voice was hesitant and parched sounding. "I came to see you because I could not sleep. May I come in a few minutes?"

I told him, "It's extremely late, and I will see you tomorrow. Good night!"

Rick continuously knocked on the door for nearly an hour, as if he did not hear my repeated requests for him to leave. I was afraid he would wake the whole neighborhood. His voice was desperate and restless.

I got upset and finally opened the door. I angrily whispered, "What in the world do you want from me? It's late at night."

Rick said, "I've been thinking about you all day long and then tossing and turning in my bed. I could not sleep. A chain of thought drove me crazy, and I came here to talk with you."

Then he slowly approached me, moving closer and closer and getting right into my personal space. I saw the sheen of tears in Rick's eyes. I racked my brain and tried to figure out what was wrong with him. How had he become the CEO of a department? As he was a married man, did he have any moral commitment? was this an American lifestyle? Was he going through a midlife crisis?

He stood close, in my face, and told me, "I want to marry you." He did not ask, would you marry me?

My eyes got bigger, and I wondered whether I was having a nightmare or if this was real. At that very astonishing moment, he grabbed my arms and tried to kiss me. He must have been dreaming.

Thank God I had learned Tae Kwon Do during my grade school years with two American

door. I was able to get away from his gripping hands. Luckily, he was weak, tired, and appeared emaciated. I easily got out of his reach, as he was exhausted by his own emotional torment.

I ran for my life. Now, the best thing I could do was go into the empty laundry room, which was located next to my apartment. A large, tall tin trashcan stood up against each corner in the laundry room. I noticed immediately that they had broad-mouthed tops and narrow bottoms. That was the perfect place to hide myself. I squeezed in behind one of the cans against the wall. My whole body was immediately frozen with terror of what had happened that night. I could hardly breathe or move. It was as if I were immobilized like the Tin Man in *The Wizard of Oz*. I was lucky to be able to hide behind a can, as I was very skinny. I weighed barely over a hundred pounds and was a reasonably tall five foot five.

I curled my body up in a fetal position and pressed myself tightly between the floor and the wall. Sounds of stomping in and out of my apartment could be heard. I also heard Rick walking quickly up and down, pacing, as if he were a crazy maniac suffering from a mental breakdown. I thought that he was out of his mind!

Eventually, Rick came to the laundry and turned on the light. I barely breathed, terrified by this unexpected madness. I felt as if my heart might stop beating. Rick opened the lid of every trash can and dug out the garbage, searching for me inside the cans. He could not find me anywhere. Disappointed, he let out a long sigh and started to put the lids back on, one at a time.

Finally, he turned off the light and stealthily left the room. The sound of his gradually fading footsteps allowed for peace and the protection of God's love to return to the laundry room, sheltering me under his wings. Quietly, I stretched my legs and back and took a deep breath, sighing in relief that this attack was over.

I stayed in the small corner of the laundry room until the soft beams of the early day broke the darkness, the first light of the morning shining through the small windows and into the room with a soft pink glow. The early morning dawn transformed the navy-blue sky to cobalt blue. The sun rose and chased the dark shadows of impurity slowly away and banished them from the room through the rising of the glorious bright morning sun.

Apartment residents must have been getting up, as I began to hear the daily hustle and bustle. I looked around the laundry room. And giving thanks to God for helping me through this experience, I quickly entered my apartment.

I took a hot shower and packed some of my possessions. It was a live-and-learn experience, teaching me not to trust men, especially strangers. Rick surely had a tainted and unscrupulous morality and defiled the character. It was a disgusting experience.

The true color of his carnal desire blinded his judgment. Perhaps, a person cannot change his character once it has been formed. As it is said, "A leopard cannot change his spots."

I called one of my female friends, who had been studying with me for the MCAT in Los Angeles. I shared my nightmare experience of the past evening with her. She was just as shocked as I was and came over to pick me up at once. My friend wanted to report the incident to a police department, but I decided not to complicate the matter. I left a brief letter to the apartment manager, and we drove to a Korean church.

A friend in need is a true friend indeed. I learned that day that a friend who helps us when we are in trouble is real friend, unlike others, who disappear when trouble arises.

The Korean church was located next to the MCAT prep school. In previous years, an extremely wealthy Korean family had owned the huge estate. But as time went on, the patriarch of the family had developed a serious physical ailment and had eventually passed way. As a result, this Korean dynasty had fallen, and the estate had been turned into a bare Korean church. Sometimes, we used one of the church classrooms for the MCAT prep classes, and the pastor of the church knew me very well.

When Pastor Park heard the story of what had happened in my apartment, he offered for me to stay in one of the empty rooms next to the church.

The church did not have many parishioners, and it hardly made ends meet. I helped with their evening meals and shared a small portion of Chinese noodles. The house was old and damaged. The windows were broken, and the church did not have enough money to repair them. I observed the poor circumstances; the broken windows were patched with old newspapers to keep out the wind and cold.

I had never been exposed to such a poor living condition. These experiences were imprinted on my brain. I determined to never be poor like this.

The church members were genuinely kind and down to earth. They did not have money, but they were happy. One day, they invited me to a Korean restaurant. We enjoyed some delicious *bool go gi*. This is a dish made of thin strips of tender beef with a special Korean sauce that was sautéed with sesame seeds, sesame oil, minced garlic, ginger, and glazed soy sauce. Then the meat is grilled in a special wok on a dining table while you are eating the meal. There were many side dishes, including fresh long leafy lettuce and hot kimchi, which is a fermented cabbage, like German sauerkraut.

I lodged at the pastor's residency for about one month. Rick discovered me at the Korean church and came there to try to see me every day. The church family members knew Rick after he visited the church constantly looking for me.

I refused to see him. When he came through the front door, I would go out the side door. I wished he would not come to church. Rick was a well-educated and intelligent stalker. One Saturday afternoon, Rick found me while I was studying in the church classroom. As soon as I saw him, I ran to the pastor's house. Subsequently, he took all my MCAT books. Yet he continued to come to the church daily. Then I left the church.

CHAPTER 3

Fish out of Water

No doubt, I was homesick and wished to be with my family and friends in Korea. My mother used to make a homemade wine and wonderful food. When I was a child, my mother, my sister, and our live-in made would prepare mouthwateringly delicious food for the family. Being sociable, my mother loved having frequent parties. Having special meals was not important to us because my mother cooked all the times.

After I came to America, of course, my daily life was not the same as before. For that reason, my parents and sister were utterly disappointed when I decided to immigrate to the United States by myself. My sister said, "Even if somebody were waiting for me with a million dollars at LAX, I would not betray my family and leave my own country at such a young age. Why don't you reconsider your endeavor?"

It had taken a long time for me to make my decision. But once I made up my mind, it turned into a steel trap of ironclad determination. My sister was a mama's girl and a homebody, while I was a carefree tomboy.

Eating Korean food with Korean people flashed me back to my golden childhood and made my mind drift back home. I missed my family and friends. As we know, absence makes the heart grow fonder.

I prayed to the Lord for protection under God's shield and asked him to keep Rick away from me. This was my prayer: "We all go through dark nights of the soul when God has abandoned us. As with David, our aching can give way to joy when we approach God honestly, plead for help, and reaffirm our trust in a God, whose love for us will never ignore or change."

Christ is the answer to heartache. Christ answers our pain. Though by all others we are forsaken, he will at our side remain.

My prayer was answered when I met Anna and Arthur. I moved into their place and lived with them. Rick would not be able to find me since I was a well protected under the haven of their home. Rick would not dare come to their house looking for me. That was the end of the harassment by Rick. I finally awoke from an unpleasant and scary nightmare.

Anna and Arthur provided me a large bedroom. It had a queen-size bed with a nice comforter and a bay window with a beautiful drape over the white sheer curtain. Both nightstands matched the large dresser against the wall. There was a large bathroom with a vanity.

When I lay on the bed, through the window, I was able to see the front entrance with its colorful flower garden. The garden was a showcase for delicate and lovely flower blossoms. The bright yellow butterflies and a couple of hummingbirds flew toward the feeder filled with sweet red nectar that dangled below the roof in front of the bay window. I had found a haven away from Rick.

Anna and Arthur enjoyed traveling with their new fancy camper, which had many amenities, such as a cooktop, a shower, three large pullout couches for beds, and a bedroom. Inside, the camper was climate controlled with air and heating systems.

The most exciting adventure was a trip to Las Vegas. We planned to stay within a budget. Thus, Anna decided to spend sixty dollars, Arthur planned to spend a hundred dollars, and my spending limit was only twenty dollars to play the casinos' slot machines. Arthur quickly lost fifty dollars, Anna also lost forty dollars, and I immediately lost the twenty I had allotted myself and gave up playing.

Anna hesitantly put in her last twenty dollars. And guess what happened to her? She was shocked with joyful surprise when sirens went off, along with red flashing lights. Ton of coins dropped into the metal pan attached to the machine. Anna jumped up and down, hugged Arthur, and watched the continuously dropping coins. She had a hard time not screaming with excitement. Many casino gamblers looked at her and smiled and cheered on her winning. Arthur grinned widely and patted her back proudly. I looked at the dropping coins and covered my open mouth with both hands.

Anna won $680. We did not lose any money after all, because Anna compensated all our losses. She then treated us to entertainments such as circus shows, restaurant meals, and small souvenirs. She also paid for the gas.

Indeed, we had a great fun together. Arthur preferred to drive at night, being that there was less traffic. Anna sat next to him carrying on conversations, and I got to sleep on the pullout couch bed in the camper.

We also spent a few weekends at the Big Bear and Lake Arrow resorts in California. Sometimes, we enjoyed wading in the stream, and sunbathing on the sand, and looking at the beautiful and expensive houses along the lake. Occasionally, we would purchase small gifts. However, most of the time, we just pleased window-shopping. There were many fantastic pancake houses along the lake. I did not realize how carefree a time we were having and how I would cherish those memories.

During my summer vacation, Anna and Arthur took me to different picturesque locations. Yosemite National Park was breathtaking, with its lush woods and amazing waterfalls. We went to Redwood National Park, with its well-known gigantic trees, some so huge the three of us could not wrap our six stretched arms around the trunks. We roasted marshmallows and hot dogs over the campfire with a view of a serene Lake Mead. These memories are precious and unforgettable moments. Anna and Arthur had compassion to share their love with me. Their kindness and faith made my situation be happier and safer.

Dana, their youngest daughter, loved to cook as much as her sister Margaret. Dana brought a new guest, Richard, to her parent's home where I was living with them. She introduced Richard to me. He was a handsome, tall, and well-built American manager at Wells Fargo Bank. Richard was a young bachelor and an attractive beach boy with incredible surfing skills. He owned a nice contemporary condominium next to the affluent Newport Beach.

We had an amusing time. Richard and I shared stories while we sipped tea and ate homemade chocolate cookies. Afterward, Richard and I went out several times on dates. Dana knew we liked each other, and she secretly invited him to her Thanksgiving dinner party with her family.

Dana had a lively character and a very entertaining personality. Even the meal reflected her style, with a beautifully decorated Turkey dinner. Her crunchy freshly made cranberry sauce boasted mixed nuts. There were many different pies; my favorite, caramel cake; and pineapple upside-down cake. The red cherries inside of the round pineapple on the top were well displayed. The Thanksgiving decorations and flower arrangements on the table welcomed all—family and friends—who had joined. I felt that I was walking on seven heavens. I had a contented life with Anna and Arthur and their children for about two years.

Their son, Peter, was a president of a pipe organ company and supplied pipes for the Mormon Church and other congregations in Utah. He looked like a movie star and was charismatic. Peter visited his parents several times a year, along with his son and daughter. His wife was a professor at a college.

I had just celebrated twenty-third birthday with them when I met Darlene while I was working at the hospital. She was an exceptionally pretty head nurse in an operating room at the local hospital. After we had been acquainted several times in the hospital cafeteria, she invited me to her house. We became close friends and went out to parties, movies, and to eat out together. Sometimes she rented a beach house for us. One day, I tried to windsurf—without skill.

My unsuccessful attempt at windsurfing

One day, I was staying with Darlene at the beach house. Darlene loved to watch beach boys who were surfing in the moonlight. It was magnificent to watch the sparkling, silvery, ruffling surface of the ocean, which embraced the peace and tranquility of the night. The surfers danced skillfully and rhythmically back and forth over the huge gushing waves. Their balance and agility displayed unimaginable talent. We enjoyed nights of excitement and loved the smell of the salt breeze. The caressing droplets made us forget the time of night. This type of excitement was different from a routine daily life. It was rewarding and purely enjoyed.

Darlene was a partygoer and a social butterfly. With her striking blue eyes, flattering blond hair, and perfect figure, she knocked out many men with her beauty. She had two beautiful daughters, who were seven and ten years old at the time.

Oftentimes, Darlene invited me to go to parties with her. However, I preferred to be a babysitter for her daughters. We went to one party together, and I felt like a fish out of water. I was allergic to alcohol, and the cigarette smoke made me cough. It was a loud dancing party filled with smoke, joking, laughter, drinking, and flirtation.

Over the following months, I met another nurse. Her name was Dianna, and she had an angelical face with big dreamy blue eyes and thick long eyelashes. She was about five foot six and had a slender body. Both Darlene and Dianna look like magazine cover girls or Hollywood movie stars. They had typical Southern California looks and were beachgoers. They liked parties, dancing, shopping, eating out, boat outings, and dating. They both lived a vibrant lifestyle. They were not afraid of trying new friendships and challenging the status quo. Everything was exciting with them, and they introduced me to many different friends. But they were not academically motivated. They spent days full of pleasure and did not have any dull moments.

Many times, Darlene and Dianna teased me that I was too conservative and lived as if I was under parental protection. They said, "We know that Anna and Arthur love you very much, and you are comfortable. But you are now twenty-three years old. Soon, you will be twenty-four. They are old folks. Don't you want to get married and have your own life, before you get too old? You should have a husband and children."

They encouraged me to get my own place. Darlene was born and raised in a suburb of Los Angeles County. She knew many people and was familiar with most of the areas in the county. She liked to drive everywhere. She checked out the real estate and found a cozy three-bedroom house, located fifteen minutes from Anna and Arthur's place.

She repeatedly asked me to purchase the house that she had found. Darlene was overly enthusiastic and persuaded me to have my own place.

I was not sure about the quick decision; Anna and Arthur were like my parents. They were also my parents' age. Living with them was like living with my parents, under the umbrella of their unconditional love. After the previous terrifying experience with Rick, I really felt comfortable and happy living with them.

I needed some time to think about this matter carefully before I decided. Meanwhile, Dianna continued her attempts to convince me to buy the house. She was very persistent. She said, "I will help you move and decorate your house. Let us go see it again."

The house had a two-car garage next to a small living room, separated from the dining room by sliding glass doors. The kitchen was medium-sized, but it had three bedrooms and two baths, like Anna and Arthur's house. However, the house was much smaller than theirs. It was also much older. In the yard was a peach tree next to the fence, climbing vines, morning glories, and two flower beds, along with a small vegetable garden. The grass was overgrown in some places, and in other area, there were bare patches. It required a lot of work to be done.

The house was located on a cul-de-sac in a quiet neighborhood. In the early 1970s, the market price of a house was more than reasonable in California. As time went on, I began to agree that it might not be a bad idea to have my own place. After seven months, I decided to purchase the house. I felt that I could do this, since I had been saving some money while working three jobs.

The down payment was only $5,200, and the monthly mortgage payment was about $350. The new house was within seven minutes of Dana's house, five minutes from Dianna's apartment, fifteen minutes from Anna and Arthur's, and twenty minutes from Darlene's house.

Arthur replaced the entrance with a sturdy wooden door that had a peephole. Anna, Arthur, Dana, and I changed the kitchen floor to a nice subtle linoleum tile that immediately brightened the house. We added ready-made sheers over the sliding door and installed curtains from Sears. I had a happy life before medical school.

Five days later, I had a painting party. Over the course of two days, Anna, Arthur, Darlene, Dianna, and other friends helped to paint the inside and outside of the house. The carpets were shampooed. Anna made a beautiful comforter and bedroom window treatment, with the assistance of Arthur and Dana. It was lovely, a soft and silky pinkish fabric pleated over the surface of the bed with graceful ruffles that hung below and coordinated gracefully with the window treatment.

CHAPTER 4

A Penny Saved Is a Penny Earned

The real estate market went up, and six months later, the house was valued at $27,000 more than when I had purchased it. My real estate investment had made me money more quickly than my income from my regular job.

My flashback back briefly stayed in the room at the church, where I had discovered tough living conditions in poverty. Unshakable determination to work hard not to be poor and to diligently prepare for future prosperity. I started to save every penny. I lived by the adage, "A penny saved is a penny earned."

The downside of my hard work and frugal lifestyle was diminished social exploits. I had not gone to a party with Darlene for a long time.

Even so, Dianna often dropped by my house on her bicycle as part of her routine regular exercise. Dianna's apartment was close to my house. One sunny afternoon, she brought some snacks and homemade popcorn balls, which were one of my favorites. Her face was flushed with excitement, and her impatient manner suggested that she had to tell her secret immediately. Dianna's exuberant expression was aglow with what she wanted to tell me.

She said, "I met a guy, Wagner. He is incredibly handsome. I have a crush on him. He is very sexy, and my dream man. I want to go on a date, but I do not know how to approach him."

"Who is he?" I asked her. "Where did you meet him? Is he single? Where does he live?" My barrage of questions continued. "How old is he?" I wanted to know. "What has attracted you to him so quickly?"

Dianna continued her story about Wagner. "His father had a surgery and was admitted. Wagner has been visiting his father every day. I was his father's nurse, and I saw Wagner when he came to visit. The first moment he looked at me, I felt a lightning bolt penetrating my heart, and I felt a sudden heat flush my body. My soul melted. I wanted to get to know him. Will you help me?"

"Really!" I replied. "How could I contact him? What would I say to him?"

Dianna had just turned twenty-one and was still young and inexperienced in life. She described her crush in detail. "Wagner has blue eyes and dresses stylishly. He has dark hair with a few streaks of silvery highlights falling over his forehead. His dark hair, blue eyes, and charismatic gentle manner bewitched me at once."

She went on and on about her feelings like a broken record. As I listened to her desperate story and beseeching for help, I picked at her delightful homemade popcorn balls.

"Oh boy! You are infatuated with him," I said, adding, "Dianna, it sounds like love at first sight. I will do my best to look for him tomorrow. Let us see what I can do for you, okay?"

She squeezed my hands, and I could see deep gratitude on her face. Her trembling hands were sweating with nervousness. I wondered whether she had lovesickness or if she was just extremely lonely. Most of the time, we get confused and want to have love for love's sake. We fall in love with love, picturing a romantic fairy tale. Why can't we be content and happy without desiring to receive love from others? Are we not perfect by ourselves? We can receive absolute peace and joy if we focus on God, no matter what happens in our surroundings, environment, and circumstances. However, we must be disciplined. It takes daily practice to reach the goals God has set for us.

With those thoughts in mind, the next day, I walked toward the nursery at the hospital. A man was staring through the window at the many infants in their beds. He appeared to fit the description of the man Dianna had told me about with such an emotion. I approached him very carefully and politely.

When I was next to him, he shifted his focus from the infants to me and courteously moved toward the corner of the window. "Would you like to see the precious babies?" he asked.

I whispered, "Thanks! They are innocent and cute. Look at the second baby from the right. He is smacking his lips and smiling with lovely dimples. All of them are adorable. By the way, are you Wagner?"

His face lit up and reddened with pleasant surprise. "How do you know my name?" he asked.

"One of my friends, Dianna, spoke to me about you," I told him. "She was a licensed nurse caring for your father a few days ago. She has big blue eyes, an athletic build, and shoulder-length blond hair."

Wagner rubbed his temple above his right eyebrow. He squinted in concentration and appeared to be trying to remember his visitor of a few days before. After a few seconds, he declared, "Yes, I remember an attractive young nurse. What about her? What is her name?"

I was momentarily speechless and excited that I had done it—I had broken the ice. "Well, she was extremely impressed by your kind, charming, and charismatic manner," I said, adding, "She was hoping to get to know you outside the hospital."

"Is that so?" Wagner smiled. He then pulled out one of his business cards. "Would you please tell her to call me after 4:00 p.m.?"

"This is very sweet of you; I greatly appreciate your generosity," I exclaimed. "It was a pleasure meeting you, and I will give your business card to Dianna. I am sure she will be thrilled."

"When Dianna contacts me," he asked, "would you like to come with Dianna to my favorite Mexican restaurant? Does Dianna like Mexican food?"

"I love Mexican food, and so does Dianna."

"Sounds good. Let us have a fantastic time and get to know each other."

The wonderful message was promptly delivered to Dianna as soon as I got off work.

Dianna could not believe that I had been able to communicate with Wagner and open the door for her relationship. She hoped to be his sweetheart. She was extremely thrilled and screamed with joy. She almost cried. Dianna thanked me profusely, hugged me, and then jumped up and down, dancing.

On Friday evening, the three of us went out to a popular Mexican restaurant. The waiter greeted us pleasantly and guided us to a nice corner booth. Workers were wearing Mexican dancing clothes, white shirts under huge black sombreros with gold piping on the brim and black strings under their chins. Many of the waiters had moustaches. The waitresses wore long lacy dancing dresses.

There were many lit Mexican lanterns softly dangling by strings affixed to the ceiling. Here and there, Mexican flags and their historical pictures were displayed on the walls. The restaurant was filled with loud mariachi dancing music, which propelled the workers to move faster as they served food from table to table.

My favorite Mexican food is chile relleno, which is cheese stuffed inside a large green pepper. Dianna enjoyed taco al pastor with chalupas. Wagner relished a combination Mexican dish including chalupas, rice, beans, and sour cream with avocado.

A large burro piñata was oscillating gently, which accentuated the mood of an authentic Mexican lifestyle. I felt briefly as if I were in Mexico, having Mexican food in a restaurant.

All of us savored chips and hot salsa. The fresh homemade chips were delicious. We had a marvelous time.

After eating out that evening, Dianna, and Wagner dated for several months. I never knew what happened between Dianna and Wagner, but their relationship was not successful. It was only a flash in the pan.

If I knew then what I know now, I would never have accepted Wagner's invitations go out after his relationship with Dianna ended. My decision to see Wagner socially changed the course of my life.

The carefree status of being single is not so bad. However, our traditional fairy tale of romance and our respect for pro-social culture have cultivated a certain "normality" of lifestyle. For women, this principally includes the goals of marriage and having children. For me, this was reinforced by others' happiness and inspired me to carry out similar joyful interpersonal relationships that mirrored the common yearning among people.

My mind was filled with romantic images, such as walking together gracefully with a beloved, holding hands and exchanging stories, smiling, laughing, teasing, chasing each other. Along a seashore, discovering beautiful seashells and creating cherished memories. I saw couples and families, full of surprises during birthday celebrations, having babies, decorating a new home, and cooking delicious meals together. They shared their children's graduation; together, they received good news about the new job, a promotion, or being elected to lead a group with new ideas.

Up to this point, my lifelong dream had been to become a compassionate doctor. I yearned to help others to be well, happy, and healthy and, possibly, to cure individual's ailment. However, when I met Wagner, my dream changed to my personal romantic thoughts, at least for a while. Wagner persistently asked me over the phone to meet him as soon as possible.

Finally, we went out to a small quiet restaurant to discuss his frustration. While Wagner and I were eating a simple meal, he unceasingly vented his frustration. Wagner wanted to confess to me his feelings toward me.

"Okay," I said, connecting with him while I sipped tea.

"When I saw you for the first time, I was attracted to you. Remember we talked to each other looking at the infants in the nursery through the window," Wagner said.

He recalled how I had asked him to go out with Dianna. At the time he invited Dianna and me together because he wanted to know me and share my interests. "I went out with Dianna," he added, "but she's too young for me, and there is no challenge. We had some childish fun. During the short time we dated, less than three months, she had many different boyfriends. Yet she was jealous of me having female friends."

Wagner continued, noting that Dianna had many goals but lacked a tenacious discipline. She changed her mind like the weather. She was quite capricious and moody. "We decided not to see each other. She wanted to move to her aunt and uncle's house in Colorado," he explained, "Is there any possibility I can see you again soon? I would like to settle down. I want to get married and have children."

At that moment, Wagner appeared to be sincere. His motives came across as decent and based on integrity. It seemed he had a virtuous and respectable, wholesome side.

Wagner continued expressing his feelings and declared, "I've been searching to find my soul mate. I am attracted to you because you're motivated, ambitious, and a hard worker. You have resilient discipline to achieve your goals. I think you will be successful, and I want to be your friend. May I see you again soon?"

We went out to see several movies, went window-shopping, and shared a simple picnic, just the two of us. One day, when I had just gotten off work, Wagner said he wanted to rent a charter plane.

Wagner was affectionate to me and charming. He only worked one job, as an assistant computer engineer, but I worked nonstop. He repeatedly talked about how much he wanted a charter plane; however, he did not have enough money to pay the $120 for the thirty-minute flight. I, on the other hand, worked three jobs and did have money saved. I went to the bank and withdrew $250 from my account and paid $120 for the charter plane. The private pilot took us from West Covina to Catalina Island.

The charter plane had only three seats—one for a pilot and two passenger seats in the back. I did not enjoy high altitudes, even though looking over the shimmering blue ocean and the beautiful houses gave me a sense of affluence and I felt rewarded after all my hard work.

The plane suddenly descended as if it was a diving in the air when the air currents changed. That scared me to death. The feeling of falling without safety protection which made me nervous.

The day was pleasant, and we enjoyed sightseeing over La Jolla's white sand beach, red soil cliffs, clusters of ground cover flowers, and hillside houses. It was a breathtaking view.

After a short flight, we landed at a private airport, where there were small souvenir stores, restaurants, and fast-food vendor markets. Several bulls ran around the empty field behind the fence. The area where they grazed was guarded by a wire fence, the barrier intended to prevent the bulls from getting close to tourists. Wagner took pictures of me standing next to the charter plane. He also took pictures of private fancy jets. We had a simple lunch and snacked on pink, puffy cotton candy.

Mr. Wrigley's residential Mansion stood prominently on the top of the hill as if it were a magnificent castle. You may have heard about Mr. Wrigley. He was the genius who produced Juicy Fruit and Double Mint chewing gums, which are my favorites. Close to Wrigley's Mansion, there were many stores, markets, and restaurants at the bottom of the hill. Among the stores in this strip mall was a stand offering submarine tours.

Wagner and I decided to explore underwater sightseeing. Looking through the submarine's thick windowpane, we were amused to see the white sand seabed under the water. There were many sea corals; bright blues and yellows; and large and small fish, some with stripes. It was a gratifying trip.

Wagner held my hand gently. I felt a warmth and pleasurable contentment as I dreamt about our romantic relationship. Our personal relationship grew. We went on dates when I had day offs. Wagner wanted to be a computer engineer. He built computers and had enjoyed working with electronic devices since he was in junior high school.

He built my stereo cabinet and created a touch function to turn the music on and off by touching the outside of the glass door of the stereo cabinet. He was able to invent a sound system to turn on and off the lights as well.

His computer knowledge grew more toward academic theory. My love for him also grew, and my feelings of affection for him progressed as time passed. As time went on, we caressed hands while watching movies. We hugged and kissed good night.

Creating a family with a handsome engineer through dedicated caring for each other was not a bad decision.

After six months of dating, Wagner was promoted. He was recruited by an industrial corporation that was larger than the company he had previously worked with.

CHAPTER 5

Useless as Tits on a Boar Hog

I visited Anna and Arthur and passionately informed them that Wagner proposed to me. They were thrilled. They wanted to shop for a beautiful wedding gown and plan a reception.

Dana had a gorgeous wedding gown, which was still in mint condition. Dana suggested that I wear her gown that was in its original plastic bag. It had been stored and was without wrinkles. She volunteered to take care of flower arrangements, bouquets, and a garter.

Anna and Arthur planned guest lists for a reception and meals. Dana was slightly taller than me, but we were both slender, and her wedding gown fit me perfectly. Wagner and I bought two simple gold wedding bands without any stones. We got married at a small church with only a few guests. The reception, dance, and dinner were also modest, but all of us had a great time.

Our wedding presents were like housewarming gifts. Wagner and I had planned to go to Las Vegas for our honeymoon. I called one of the hotels and the paid for a suite in advance. The day before the trip, Wagner decided not to go to Las Vegas. I cancelled my reservation. Unfortunately, the hotel had a no-refund policy, and I lost $150, which made me unhappy. I wondered why he was suddenly acting so differently. I thought I might have offended him.

He started to drink, and his mood changed. Wagner and I did not agree on trivial issues. We were not able to compromise to solve problems. Wagner watched television every evening. I still worked hard, and I was tired after I got off work. As soon as I got home, he wanted to make love, like a sex maniac.

I did not get married for sex. For me, marriage was about commitment and sharing hobbies, life missions, principles, and philosophies of life.

One afternoon, I did not feel well. I got off work early. The phone rang, and a woman wanted to speak with Wagner. She left a message, saying that she would be at her apartment after work. She did not say who she was. Nor did she ask who had answered the phone. I thought, *that was unusual*. But I was exhausted and did not feel well, so I did not ask who I spoke with the caller. Obviously, the woman did not know who I was. Wagner expected me to get off work much later. The woman might have thought I was his cleaning lady.

One day, I followed him using my friend's car. Subsequently, I found him holding a woman's hand in the same Mexican restaurant where he had taken both Dianna and me. The place was noisy. To my surprise, Wagner was going out with his secretary.

Wagner came home late that night. He appeared to be happy and acted like he had been working hard. I did not show my anger, despite having discovered his affair. I could not believe Wagner's behavior. We were still newlyweds and not even over the honeymoon period. Now, his behavior made me to think back to what had happened between Dianna and Wagner. Dianna was crazy about him, yet the relationship did not last long. Wagner broke Dianna's heart. Dianna was proud and a pretty girl, who had not told me the truth. She might have perceived that she was not pretty enough for Wagner, who had cheated on her.

Ironically, Wagner had blamed Dianna for her childishness and immaturity. I do not believe Dianna was immature; rather, Wagner was childish. He was a womanizer. He could not keep his pants on. He hopped from woman to woman, like a little kid wanting new toys. He was disgusting and an imbecile! He was useless as tits on a boar hog.

Wagner's handsome face was like a movie star. His deep blue eyes did no good for anyone but, rather, misled women's hearts and trampled on their love.

Wagner may have been abused as a child. He seemed to have some type of a chemical imbalance. That could explain his abnormal behavior. Nevertheless, I was not sure how to deal with the peculiar behavior. I had thought marriage would bring me fulfillment and happiness. Instead, my romantic imaginary marriage was far from reality. This abnormal marriage gave me heartaches and brought tremendous frustration and stress. I convinced myself that I had hastily jumped to conclusions about Wagner. I believed he was a man of principles and a genuinely kind person. My naive, wishful thoughts were truly fallible. I had a false impression of Wagner at first—until I detected his true color.

I was looking at a mirror image as if it were real. However, it reflected an optical illusion, like a mirage. What I thought about Wagner was my inaccurate judgment of him. Perhaps I loved the love of fairy tales. I wanted a respectful marriage and unconditional compassion. He was not a dignified husband but was behaving like an American gigolo.

I regretted having been attracted to his skin-deep, good-looking face without having accurately discerned his value, honesty, and ethical integrity. Surely, all that glitters is not gold. How could anyone cultivate an intimate relationship on a sandcastle without a solid foundation?

"Are you hungry?" I asked Wagner. "I waited for you so we could have dinner together."

"I am not hungry," he replied. "I had meetings with the executives of different departments and had dinner with them. I am sorry. I should have called you to say that I would be late tonight. It is stressful to adjust to a new system that is not yet familiar to me. However, I'm proud of myself and becoming a computer engineer in my new job."

"Oh yeah?" I said. His lying was so obvious. Still, I let him continue to make excuses.

"I was busy doing the upgrades for the computer networks," he told me. "I had to connect each department to the central hub. It's a lot of work, and it gave me a headache."

I smelled alcohol on his breath. "By the way, how is your secretary?" I asked him.

"She is nice, but very young," he replied.

Then he wanted to have sex with me.

"I'm very tired and have a headache," I told him.

I turned my back against him, but he forced me to have sex with him, which made me angrier. He lost my respect. How could I cultivate a trustful relationship if there was no trust or integrity? How could I depend on this man to pick me up if I stumbled? Would he still be attracted to me when my face was wrinkled and when I got weak and old?

He had a double standard. His mind was tainted, valuing simple pleasures, lust, and superficiality. His charm and charisma conquered many women. His handsome facial structure and well-built body captured the hearts of vulnerable women. His slick lip service enticed and extracted sexual favors from them. He trapped many women in his web of deceit. Wagner knew how to throw darts at women's heart and misled many women into false romantic fairy tale dreams.

His unacceptable behavior was the turning point that created a crack in our intimate personal relationship. A few weeks later, I discovered love letters from many women, declaring their love and saying they wanted to be with him again. I also found hidden pornographic books in his cabinet drawer at home. I realized that he was not capable to love anyone truthfully and unconditionally. He could only dole out selfish and abusive behavior. I hoped that no one else would fall for his squandering and deceitful ways.

"Forget Wagner!" I mumbled to myself. "Forget all the nonsense."

I worked even harder than before to shake off his betrayal and unfaithfulness that caused my aching pain. I could not hold back my tears. They would not stop rolling down my face while driving, cooking, and working. The pain and hurt tortured me very, as if I were stricken by lovesickness.

Wagner was extremely kind, polite, and super nice to me to compensate for his guilt. He tried to be pacifying and placated my irritable and wounded emotions. I felt like a severely injured bird. He still did not know what I had found in his file cabinet, including the letters and the books.

I wanted to prove to myself that I was the worth something. I deserved an accomplishment. After awhile, I purchased another house. I had been working like a workaholic and saving funds. During that time, Wagner offered his credit card to help me buy some furniture. Of course, he expected me to pay him back with the cash, which I did immediately.

In less than three months of marriage, I again found him at his secretary's apartment. I decided to knock on the door. He unexpectedly opened the door while pulling up his trousers. He was shocked to see me at the door, full of surprise and embarrassment. I was convinced that it was over—that there was no way to patch our marriage. A man who could not keep his pants on was not my husband. His act defiled our marriage, and that could not be changed by him kneeling or pleading to be forgiven. Initially, I had believed that marriage would be a haven of protection from other men's harassment; now, my husband was my harasser.

One week later, he was drunk and angry with me. I had decided to file for divorce. A few days after we agreed to divorce, he took all my new furniture and tricked the judge into awarding it to him by showing his credit card receipts for the purchases, even though I had reimbursed him in cash directly.

Wagner then rented the room next to his secretary's apartment. I thought that was good riddance! He could have all my new furniture. It had been my poor decision to marry him in a hurry; I had no one to blame but myself. I was glad that he had moved out of my house.

Not only Wagner did steal my furniture, but he also wanted half of my assets, including the new home which I had purchased in California.

I endured the growing pains because of my unwise decision to marry him. This taught me to appreciate the value of making wise decisions.in the future. We are often confused about sex. Lust is not unconditional love. Nowadays, our school curriculums teach safe sex and prevention of teen pregnancy. However, schools do not guide students on how to choose their partners wisely. Perhaps students are too young to know the value of this important lesson and would reject the guidance. But it would be worth sharing.

I had not had much experience with the opposite gender when I met Wagner. My innocence was nothing more than ignorance. After all, my inexperience could not justify my unwise decision.

My feelings of love for Wagner were gone, and my hatred grew rapidly. I lost a substantial amount of weight. For awhile, I had many sleepless nights that made me sick to my stomach.

Thank God, I had been prepared to protect my new house. I had added my friend's name on the deed after I secured a notarized promissory note stating that, once the divorce was finalized, the house would revert to solely my name.

My dream and plan for my family quickly faded after three months of marriage. Long ago, I had known that I wanted to have a stable and safe life. Now I promised myself I would not be taken advantage by anybody again. If this was the American style of modern society, then so be it. I would not be fooled ever again.

CHAPTER 6

Shoot for the Moon and Reach for the Stars (Haste Makes Waste)

I kept an extra job, along with my full-time work. I enrolled in a modeling school called Studio Seven in Covina, California. Several supermodels from Studio Seven were chosen to be cover magazines stars. This modeling school interviewed only a few candidates, who had to meet the school's high standards. Admission was determined based on snapshots, height and weight measurements, and evaluation of personal characteristics to determine who possessed the qualities needed to be a professional model. The cost of modeling training was $2,500 for six months under professional instructors.

Once we were selected as students for modeling, classes started with makeup sessions, runway step classes, and classes on how to pose and turn gracefully. Then professional photographers took many pictures for our portfolios.

Sometimes, Hollywood actresses came and taught us acting classes. One of our guest trainers who came for a session was apparently a well-known actress. All the modeling trainees except me knew the actress. They told me she had played opposite Christopher Reeve as his girlfriend in *Superman*.

She instructed the trainees to be seated in two rows in the front of a huge mirror. "Everyone closes eyes," she told us. "Fantasize that you've just received a huge, beautiful flower bouquet from your boyfriend.

"Now open your eyes in surprise. How are you going to react?"

We had to show her our facial expressions and practiced reacting in the most attractive and elegant manner. Likewise, the actress instructed us how to gracefully eat grapes from a bowl, expressing with our face that the grapes were remarkably succulent and mouthwatering.

In another acting class, our trainer announced that we were to show excitement while eating Kentucky Fried Chicken for a television commercial.

The training course was entertaining. Finally, after six months of training, we wore glamorous long dresses like professional models and performed delightfully, walking on a red-carpet runway at a country club. There was a full house, and the audience included friends and family, who had come for our graduation. We received professional certificates and a long-stemmed red rose, followed by a reception party.

Right after the graduation, a Los Angeles garment factory contacted Studio Seven, requesting a few models to display their new line of clothes at their fashion show. Studio Seven chose me for the fashion show, and the clothing company offered $150 per every fifteen minutes for displaying and advertising new outfits. I turned the offer down. For me, the modeling was just to get my mind off the pain induced by Wagner's betrayal. I never wanted to be a model for a living.

My goal was to study medicine. I tried to enroll at UCLA—unsuccessfully; I had a mediocre MCAT score. Besides, I was not younger than twenty-five years old. Additionally, I did not have financial support. The UCLA medical school administrators expressed that it would be difficult for me to be admitted to UCLA. I acknowledged that becoming a doctor was not an easy goal. Nevertheless, I decided to shoot for the moon and reach for the stars.

The empty house, without furniture, was silent and peaceful since Wagner was gone. He had taken my furniture and disappeared like smoke in the wind.

Once again, I reaffirmed my mission and dream. I would learn continuously until my last breath during this journey. In the meantime, I needed to learn to be a skillful acrobat, adept at the swiftly changing roles and adopting a position or viewpoint in this different American culture. My mind was set; I was determined to be a winner. That would require more discipline, and I would need to learn how to balance in a perfect storm. I would train like an acrobat who walks on a narrow rope high in the sky, as if gliding through space.

In 1980, I turned twenty-six years old. It had been five years since I had first arrived at LAX all alone. Time seems to fly quickly in life, regardless of what happens, and I found I was no exception. I had good times and bad times. I had happy and sad times. I recalled a Bible passage:

> To everything, there is a season. A time to weep, a time to laugh, a time to mourn and a time to dance; A time to cast away stones, and a time to gather stones together; a time for embracing, and a time to refrain from embracing. A time to love, and a time to hate, a time of war, and a time of peace. (Ecclesiastes 3:1, 4, 5, and 8 KJV)

Surely, I had lived a life of lighthearted happiness and carefree childhood, without toils or snares under my parents' care. In America, though, my selection of friends (or to the point, and my lack of ability to discern their characters) was not prudent. As a result, I had to bear much suffering and pain.

Even so, God still loved me and blessed me to own three houses during my twenties in California. Further, I was able to obtain American citizenship after I lived in the United States for five years. I thanked God for my blessings.

People want friends so they will not be lonely. Even though I enjoyed being alone and free without Wagner, I needed friends. New furniture, in my favorite color and style, came to replace what he had taken. The arrangement of the new furniture and decoration of the house transformed it into a better atmosphere. The once echoing, empty space became cheerful, attractive, and cozy. It made me comfortable, helped me recover from my wound, and provided a superficial happiness.

I suddenly realized that I had a beautiful house and was blessed. The previous owner had designed this house thoughtfully, and it was a lovely home. I loved the double gates with the arched doors on both sides of driveway. The driveway's front had a flowery ground cover. It was beautiful when the flowers opened as the sun shone. The front courtyard was paved with red bricks. The center of the courtyard had an outdoor water fountain, with an adorable sculpture of boy and girl.

Clustered purple and white lilac stood against the wall of the courtyard next to the cherry blossom tree, which always appeared to be welcoming me home. There were different colored roses along the brick fence. The sumptuous pomegranates showed off their ruby red seeds when fully ripened and enticed me to taste their unique sweetness. Two tall fruit trees—one an apricot tree in the other a plum tree—stood prominently, both covered with abundant fruits. The right corner of the wall had bundles of oranges and lemons. There was also a pear tree. Here and there were circular flowerbeds filled with colorful, charmingly arranged flowers. A large hammock was placed between covered patio poles. An elongated slender hummingbird feeder filled with delicious red nectar swung nearby, bringing birds whose presence gave me a peaceful serenity.

Sitting at the desk in the corner of the open glass door, I could look out at the beauty of arching rainbows with sprinkled droplets of water from the lawn. I could take in the mixture of soft, mild fragrances wafting from the roses, lilacs, and Jasmine blooms. It was all enchanting, filling me with joyous inner peace, and I felt my contentment returning.

I welcomed all my friends and neighbors to help themselves to the variety of fruits from my backyard, as I was still busy working many jobs. They brought grocery bags and enjoyed the free harvest. When the fruit ripened, birds picked the fruits, making it fall off from the trees to the lawn. The fallen fruit ruined the gardeners' lawn mower, and they complained.

I took care of myself and tried to reduce my work schedules. After a while, one of the hospital employees introduced me to Dr. Louis, who was extremely wealthy. I met him at a special event in the hospital. At the time, my self-confidence had somewhat improved, as had my overall appearance. I carried myself gracefully since I had had the modeling training. I socialized with people comfortably and could express myself enthusiastically.

The brief acting class at Studio Seven certainly benefited my social interaction. I sensed that Dr. Louis was interested and attracted to me, just by looking at his sharp and fiery eyes. Dr. Louis was a bachelor and had never been married. He owned part of the hospital, ten cabins in Big Bear and twenty Lake Tahoe condos, a Huntington Beach shopping mall, and three mansions. Two were located at the top of Huntington Beach, and the third was across from the *Time* magazine house in Los Angeles, California.

"What's your name?" Dr. Louis asked me.

"My name is Victoria Gates."

He extended his right hand with a big smile and shook my hand firmly. His hand was warm and soft. "Do you like downhill skiing?" he challenged.

"Yes, I love skiing," I replied, adding, "I'm not a good skier. But ski trips revitalize me."

"Would you like to go on a day ski trip with me?"

"That sounds exciting! I am looking forward to skiing with you. Thank you very much."

Dr. Louis wanted to make sure that I had a day off on Saturday. "Are you working this Saturday?"

"No."

"That's perfect," he said. "I'll pick you up early Saturday morning."

"That sounds great! I will be ready for the trip."

I had only gone skiing a few times. Many years ago, I had gone on ski trips to resorts in Park City, as well as Snowbird and Alta in Utah, with Dianna. At the time, I had bought top-of-the line ski clothes, including gloves, a sweater, a jumper, and a jacket.

"I don't have the equipment, such as skis, poles, and boots," I told him. "I have only ski clothes. I wanted to let you know that I am not a skillful skier."

"Don't worry," he assured me. "I will be happy to teach you how to ski. We will rent ski equipment. That is easy to do. I will pick you up early Saturday morning. I want you to be rested." He looked at me and smiled.

It took a couple of hours to drive to the ski resort in Big Bear from where I lived. My mind drifted to the past, while Dr. Louis drove his Mercedes. His car was comfortable, and he was concentrating on driving. This allowed me to go back in time to the first time I had gone skiing.

In Utah, I had not known how to ski. Dianna and I had taken some lessons on the beginner ski course. There I was, just learning and taking beginner lessons. I should have stayed on the novice slopes. But I had managed to descend the slope quickly without falling. So, I challenged myself to ski on the intermediate slope—before I had trained or practiced slalom. I did not learn schussing, which was the fastest technique. Although I did well use the wedge or snowplow technique, I was still a beginner and hardly an expert.

I came down very quickly, not knowing how to control my speed.

I shouted to the skiers in front of me to watch out. Haste makes waste! Rushing is one of my biggest flaws.

Sure enough, a short time after I started down the intermediate ski slope at that resort and Park City, I fell badly on an icy spot. Luckily, I did not break any bones. Although, my ego was wounded. The velocity yanked the right thumb by the hook of the ski pole when I fell on my buttocks. My right thumb was swollen, red, and tender to touch. Thank God, it was not broken.

The ski club arranged the hotel rooms for the skiers. Dianna and I, along with two middle-aged white females, shared a large Hilton Hotel room. The other two women in the room were expert skiers and had been skiing every year in Utah. Both women had broken a leg or arm in the past. Nevertheless, they would not give up skiing because they loved the sport. I might have given up skiing if I had broken bones that required me to be immobilized for more than a month. So far, I had not had an adverse experience, and that led to me fearlessly embracing the challenge of the intermediate slope.

I really should have learned to look before I jumped into a situation. To this day, impatience is one of my biggest weaknesses. Sometimes, I wonder whether I like to challenge myself by taking on difficult tasks instead of taking an easier route. It is better to choose a safe course of action than a risky one.

I think skiing is an excellent sport. I clearly remembered looking down at the white snow-covered mountains, the snow ensconced trees, and the sprawling ski slopes from up high in the ski lift. The entire area was white with snow, revealing its purity. The scenery was breathtaking and the magnificent view, a marvelous sight to behold. This incredible beauty made me feel as if I was in a mystical wonderland. What a masterpiece of God's creation!

The dangling icicles on the tree branches seemed like perfectly decorated Christmas trees with sparkling crystal ornaments. Rays of colorful lights were reflected in the sunlight, as if icicles were bright, multifaceted diamonds radiating prisms. Here and there, water dripped from the icicles.

In general, the skiers were friendly, kind, and courteous. They truly had a sense of sportsmanship and were willing to help people in need. For example, when my mind was once again caught up far away from the present, I forgot to get off the lift and wound up at the top of the line—on the most expert slope. When I got off the lift, I found myself on the top of the mountain. Only a few skiers were going down. It took tremendous skill to maneuver the narrow, steep cliff.

There was no way I could ski down. I could not have even made my way down walking, as the narrow course was a shiny, slippery slope. Looking at the cliff made me dizzy. I stood on the top of the mountain and completely broke down.

One young man had just gotten off the lift and saw my frantic facial expression. "Are you okay?" he asked. "Is there something wrong? Do you have a problem?"

I explained my problem.

The kind and fine-looking young man told me to hold his ski poles. I could not even maintain a standing position. Consequently, I squatted close to the ground while I held his ski poles. There were no tree roots or rocks to grab onto. There was only snow on the glossy, icy narrow downhill ramp.

Finally, I got down to a wide-open and more level hillside. I thanked Young man profusely for saving me from danger. He smiled at me and then jumped back on the lift and skillfully skied down at a higher speed, making sharp turns as if he were in a race. He must have been a ski champion.

Dianna met a young male skier who invited us to a fancy seafood restaurant and drove us around the city to see a Mormon church. Later, Dianna and I back to the Hilton. As we sat in the lobby drinking coffee, a young gentleman in a formal executive suit was next to us, telling someone to get his private jet ready. There were many wealthy people around the ski resort. I was impressed by wealth.

After the Utah ski trip, I had gone to the Big Bear ski resort several times with one of the hospital administrators who worked at the same hospital. Surprisingly, at the time, I had managed these few experiences downhill skiing without falling.

The resort in Big Bear made great artificial snow. The Southern California sun is hot. Sunlight or not, looking at the snow made me cold. I wore a ski mask. In contrast, athletic young female skiers were downhill skiing in bikinis at high speeds, as if they were racing. I stared at them in astonishment. At the same moment, I felt like I had just gotten out of the boat. What liberation, what carefree freedom. Skiing is certainly an exciting and vibrant sport.

Dr. Louis drove to Big Bear in less than two hours, and we skied all afternoon. The weather was excellent, and the artificial snow conditions were superb. After lunch, I came down too fast and fell on my buttocks on an icy spot again. Fortunately, my ballet lessons helped me to get my balance, and I quickly pushed the ground with the heels of my hands. This time, I bumped my tailbone, although it was not broken.

Dr. Louis came down rapidly and lifted me up when I fell. He appeared overly concerned about my fall and repeatedly asked me whether I had injured myself or had any pain anywhere on my body.

"Did you get hurt? Are you okay?" he asked me several times.

"Nope! Sorry, Dr. Louis. I am fine." I smiled at him.

We shortened our day of downhill skiing and decided to go home. We had dinner at a restaurant. He was a multimillionaire, but his mannerisms were gentle and modest. He respected others, including me, and he was far from a womanizer. After I fell, my tailbone was strained, and I felt discomfort in my lower back, especially when I bent to pick up anything up from the floor. I also had mild bruises on the edges of my palms. Nevertheless, it healed within two weeks.

Dr. Louis' mother wanted to have dinner together. "Would you like to come join us? I will pick you up. When do you have day off?" Dr. Louis invited me to his mother's house and asked me.

"I will be free next week," I told him.

"That's perfect," he replied.

I prepared a beautiful flower bouquet for his mother to thank her for the dinner invitation.

Dr. Louis had a huge house across from the *Time* magazine house in Los Angeles. There were two large statues, placed on pedestals, on each side of the circular drive. The driveway was unusually long and wide. Inside were two separate formal dining rooms and casual dining areas. He explained that there were four bedrooms upstairs, though I did not go to see his private rooms.

After dinner, we walked around the back. He had a large swimming pool and gazebo. On the side of the house was a large guesthouse toward the corner of the property. The landscape looked like a British Royal garden.

Dinner was delicious, and his mother appreciated my flower bouquet.

While we were having desserts, she sat next to me and whispered, "My son loves you very much."

The house was a mansion. For holidays, Dr. Louis entertained and welcomed ambassadors, doctors, the Los Angeles mayor, and other politicians at his house. What a fortunate blessing. Yet I was not ready to marry anyone, even someone extremely wealthy. Materialism did not attract me at the time. Deep inside my subconscious, my passionate longing was a quest for healing. My fervent desire to be a doctor governed my life.

I introduced one of my friends to Dr. Louis. My friend loved him at first sight. He, on the other hand, did not pay her any attention at all.

This stage of my life was a turning point and a transitional period. I enjoyed my nice houses, and I had saved enough money to be comfortable. I had a prestigious circle of friends. I was amused by his material success.

He took me to a movie that I did not care for. We exited the theater before the movie was over. Later, we went to a beachfront seafood restaurant in Huntington Beach, close to his beach houses. I loved seafood—lobsters, oysters, abalones, you name it. My favorite fish dish was broiled sea bass. He took me to many seafood restaurants in Huntington Beach.

We dated more frequently. I still worked extra shifts. Knowing my nonstop working schedule, he offered to pay me three times more than I could ever make by working additional jobs. I could spend his money and buy whatever I wanted because he was extraordinarily rich. He indirectly implied his proposal that we get married.

"Do you know how many women would like to have your position?" he asked. "We will travel the world. You can buy whatever you want, live in a luxurious house, enjoy sailing yacht, and drive expensive cars. Besides, you will never need to work again. I'll help your family and I will support them as well."

Dr. Louis was genuine and generous, quite the opposite of Wagner. He was tall; well built; and had an executive appearance, dark hair, and brown eyes. He was twelve years older than I was, and he was not an America gigolo. He had a down-to-earth personality. He was humble and respectable. He was also a hard worker with an excellent work ethic. He was honest and did not deceive anybody.

Early one afternoon, he took me to Huntington, a gated community beach house, which was one of his two big houses there. Each was worth more than $1 million at the time. Before driving to his own oceanfront house, he took me to the home of his friend, a famous psychiatrist who owned property in the same gated community, not far from Dr. Louis's house. At the entrance of his friend's house, there was a gigantic waterfall decorated with a variety of flowers and a small circular pond.

The psychiatrist's wife came to greet us and informed he was not home. We thanked her and left.

Dr. Louis had two oceanfront houses, one located on the shallow oceanfront and another newly built house alongside the deep ocean. He gently directed me, placing his arm around my back. The facade of the house was paved with ceramic tile, and a bright colorful flowerbed formed a semicircle around the house.

In the entrance stood a huge grandfather clock. Next to it was an authentic suit of Spanish armor, including helmet, gorget, shoulder piece, breastplate, gauntlet, and a skirt of tassels. Every piece was still intact. Looking at the walls, I saw many original paintings and felt as if I were inside a museum.

A short distance from the front entrance was a huge separate living room with extremely high ceilings, which appeared to be more than fifty feet height. The massive, lightly tinted glass windows stretched from floor to ceiling. The elegant window treatments, with exquisite, ornate French lace curtains, were eye-catching. I was looking at the most beautiful fabric I had ever seen. I kept staring at the pattern of the lace with amazement. He stood next to me, holding a remote control. And when he pushed a button, the gorgeous long curtain opened gracefully, displaying a magnificent blue ocean view with no obstruction.

At the back of his property, there was an open deck with outdoor furniture and a brightly colored beach parasol in the center of the glass tables. The wooden deck extended to a short narrow pier and anchored there was a fancy yacht.

"Is this the typical American upscale lifestyle?" I mumbled to myself.

He held my hand. He wanted to show me his art collection. We stepped out into another spacious room, next to an enormous living room. The chamber was filled with priceless art collected from all over the world. His assortment included several alabaster statues; marble dolphins; and a glass showcase that exhibited ivory, jade, rubies, pearls, and much more. I saw a crystal piece that had three-dimensional etching with a beautiful lady inside. The crystal was delicately carved into a unique piece of art.

One of his many paintings was different from the others. Its texture was smoother, and it depicted a fairy tale image.

"Wow! I loved this painting," I said, my enthusiastic admiration bubbling over.

"Do you like this painting? I literally stole a pair of paintings at an exceptionally good bargain."

"How much did you pay?" I asked him.

"I only paid $35,000 a piece, and $70,000 for both. If you are nice to me, I will give them to you."

I beg your pardon. I thought but kept silent. He paid $70,000 for paintings. That could be a down payment for a house. "Really?" I said. "Those are expensive."

"Most original paintings are usually worth more than $200,000," he replied.

However, his money did not attract me. Tangible material possessions could come and go quickly.

He had four bedrooms, each tastefully decorated with expensive furniture. They were surrounded with the exquisite, modern bathrooms. All the drapes automatically opened and closed by remote control.

Dr. Louis and I shared personal stories, future goals, and missions. I learned he had donated many paintings, along with providing funds to the local schools, as well as to governments. He disclosed that his father was French. My father had worked as a waiter to put Dr. Louis through medical school. Dr. Louis's interest in real estate had led him to become a business tycoon. He also generated large sums of income from his family practice in medicine. He understood people who were suffering from poverty. This made him humble. He did not boast about his wealth and was sympathetic toward the needy.

There were four large tennis courts in this gated community. We played tennis one day, and my gold bracelet fell off my wrist. I could not find it, but I did not ask him to look for it. The tennis courts were exceptionally large, and my bracelet was very thin.

Later that day, he drove me to a Huntington Beach restaurant. It was the ambrosia of seafood and was succulent.

After he dropped me off at my house, he stayed for a while. I played

"Maiden Prayer" and "Fur Elise" on my piano for him. He enjoyed it tremendously and praised me for being cultured.

The following week, he took me back to his beach house and introduced me to his neighbors. One of his neighbors was a popular female lawyer, who had married another attorney. They had a large sailboat, which was anchored next to their deck. Almost all the neighbors had some type of sailboats, yachts, ski boats, motorboats, or jet skis. His neighbors were mainly business tycoons, restaurant chain owners, and lawyers, along with the state governor. But there were only two doctors.

The lawyer couple liked Dr. Louis and insisted that we go sailing, since the weather was perfect. I agreed, even though, I was not prepared for the outing. The couple prepared lunch and drinks. We enjoyed sailing in gorgeous weather that day.

Another neighbor invited us for dinner after the boating outing. It was the typical American meal, including appetizers, fish and chicken entrees, and apple and peach pies. We mutually exchanged our personal stories, discussed breaking news and politics, and shared gossip and many witticisms. Everyone was happy and laughed. Though I did not understand some of the jokes, I laughed with them anyway to get along with the group.

Thank God it was Saturday night, and I was off on weekends. Dr. Louis's neighbors suggested that I should stay at his beach house because it was awfully late after the dinner. They offered me toothpaste, a toothbrush, a comb, and a pair of large underwear that were three times bigger than mine.

I knew Dr. Louis would not hurt me, not like Rick. Still, I felt awkward. Eventually, I decided to stay at his house. Everything there was in mint condition, with fresh sheets and a nice comforter. The room was beautiful with paintings, flowers, plants, and a private bathroom. Surprisingly, I slept well, and I did use that extra pair of underwear, though they came down to my hips, refusing to stay on my waistline and practically falling off.

I came downstairs, after I had taken a shower and changed back into my clothes from the previous day. He was studying at the table.

He looked at me with his benevolent smile. "Good morning! Did you sleep well? Were you comfortable? Are you hungry? We'll go out for breakfast when you're ready."

He was such a gentleman. Even though, I had iron-clad determination to follow my dream of going to medical school. I no longer wished to get married.

We had a good conversation at the breakfast. He mentioned marriages several times. He was noticeably quiet when I stated that I had come to America to be a doctor.

CHAPTER 7

Let Tomorrow Take Care of Itself

Later, Dr. Louis and his lawyer friends flew to the Himalayas on his friend's private jet. The Himalayas are home to the word's highest mountain, Mountain Everest, and extend from the east of Pakistan through India, Tibet, China, Nepal, and Bhutan.

Dr. Louis called me right after he returned from his trip and began to share his experiences. He told me about some young Himalayans who walked in deep snow in their bare feet, without socks or shoes, while carrying a bundle of twigs and tree branches to use for firewood. He talked about how he had warned his friends about altitude sickness, experienced at elevations above 10,000 feet (300 meters) and caused by insufficient oxygen in the air. If it is severe, altitude sickness can result in death. Thus, he and his friends had to acclimate their bodies gradually by adjusting their physiological conditions to environmental changes as they were climbing higher.

He told the story of a woman who was struggling with labor pains on the side of the mountain while they were climbing to the mountain. Apparently, her husband was unable to assist her to deliver their baby. Fortunately, Dr. Louis was a family medical doctor. He communicated this by sign language to bridge the language barrier. He then successfully delivered a cute and healthy baby boy. Grabbing a towel from his backpack, he wrapped the newborn and handed him to the woman. The couple graciously appreciated Dr. Louis's skillful delivery of the baby and they rejoiced in their newborn.

Dr. Louis and his friends continued to climb until they reached a temple and saw a skinny man who sat in the same spot for many days. According to the local Himalayans, the man had been sitting in the one spot for nearly one month without food or water, which, in America, could not be understood.

This man practiced astral projection, a form of deep spiritual meditation that enabled his soul to transcend his body while sitting in one spot. People had reported seeing a mysterious elongated light leaving the body during this spiritual proceeding, and the light was moving from mountain to mountain.

I was fascinated by his story. I wished to learn more about astral projection.

Dr. Louis and his lawyer friends visited a village where the king and queen resided. They met the royal tailor who made the king and queen's wardrobes. Dr. Louis kindly asked the tailor to make a nice vest for me. The local people already knew that Dr. Louis had saved the woman by delivering her baby successfully on the side of the mountain.

The tailor respected Dr. Louis and was willing to make me a special long throw over vest with a soft fur lining. The vest was a colorful soft suede mosaic with beautiful embroidery. One of Dr. Louis's friends, who lived in Beverly Hills, wanted the same vest in a different size for his wife. Dr. Louis explained that the king's tailor had made only two such vests—one for me and another for his friend's wife.

They had an amazing voyage, and they returned home safely from the Himalayas.

As I look back, I realize that Dr. Louis was a decent and proper gentleman. However, my audacious hope and fervent determination could not be relinquished easily. My focus remained on becoming a doctor, and I no longer yearned for marriage with the same fascination that had filled my dreams of romance in my youth.

Dr. Louis called me on my birthday and told me he had reserved an opera house restaurant for our dinner in Beverly Hills. Prior to dinner, he took me to his LA house. His mother wished me a happy birthday and unexpectedly gave me a big flower bouquet, which was wonderfully arranged. Then, Dr. Louis gave me the suede vest, a special royal necklace, and a large art museum picture book from Himalayas.

We celebrated my birthday at the opera house restaurant, which featured a stage where short versions of operas were performed. As we started to eat, a group of famous opera singers circled our table and sang "Happy Birthday" and wished me the best on my birthday. All the diners and singers applauded cheerfully.

I had an incredible private birthday celebration with Dr. Louis. This cherished memory made my twenty-seventh birthday unforgettable. He was a reliable, trustworthy, and honest aristocrat.

Still, I did not have romantic feelings for him. Perhaps I was too young to know any better—to fully appreciate the preciousness of his character.

As time went on, a few months later, another member of the hospital staff introduced me to a single cardiologist who had never been married. His name was Dr. Neal, and he worked at many different hospitals in Los Angeles, California. He lived in Westwood near UCLA and Hollywood's Sunset Boulevard.

Soon after I was introduced to him, this cardiologist became extremely interested in me. He followed me during my lunch breaks and eagerly gave me his beeper, cell, and home phone numbers and his home address.

His house was far from mine, a two-hour drive. Nevertheless, he invited me for dinner in Hollywood soon after he met me. He picked me up, and we had a delicious dinner at a fancy restaurant.

During dinner, he asked, "Would you like to see a play? *Evita* is playing at Dorothy Chandler Performance Center, and we're right next to the theater after all."

I gladly responded, "I love to see plays and especially love *Evita*. I know her story pretty well."

Dr. Neal purchased orchestra seats for us. During the intermission, he asked, "Are you enjoying the performance?"

"I love the history in *Evita*, as well as the singing and dancing," I gushed. "And the aria and choreography are charming."

Dr. Neal sincerely, "I am so glad you're having a good time. I am also enjoying myself. Just sitting next to you and watching you is better then watching the play itself."

I thought that was an unusual comment, and I received it as a flattering. I did not say anything but smiled.

The play tells the incredible story of a woman who was a singer and dancer in a cabaret bar and yet knew how to interact with the many politicians. Eventually she married the president Peron in Argentina. Evita surely shot for the moon and reached for the stars, and she achieved her goals.

California is a vast land of opportunity. Californians spend a great deal of time driving to get from one place to another place. Dr. Neal spent more than half a day to go out on a date with me. I assumed that he did not mind at all. When he dropped me off after the pleasurable evening, he told me, "I would like to see you soon. Would you like to have dinner with me at the Seven Seas restaurant in Hollywood? The stage features colorful Polynesian hula dancers and ukulele players. I think you'll enjoy it."

When I nodded, he continued, "I'll pick you up early Saturday."

"Thanks for invitation! It sounds terrific," I replied, adding, "Drive carefully. Good night."

That weekend, Dr. Neal came to my house to pick me up. I usually slept for four hours, and the remainder of my days was spent in the hospital working. I maintained a full-time and a per diem job. I was tired. Consequently, I was resting on the outdoor hammock and had fallen asleep.

Dr. Neal rang the doorbell several times, getting no response. After a while, he walked along the sidewalk and discovered me sound sleep. When he called my name, I opened my eyes and found him standing next to the hammock holding a large bouquet of red roses.

He looked happy. "I hope I'm not disturbing your sleep. I rang the doorbell many times without answer, which made me seriously worried. Are you okay? Here," he said, handing me the flowers. "These are for you. Are you ready to go out? Let us have a wonderful time together."

We went out on dates for a few months to see movies, plays, or ballets. We visited several ocean-view art galleries at Laguna Beach or New Port Beach and attended music festivals, social gathering with friends, and dinner parties with his colleagues and family members. We tasted a variety of ethnic foods at different restaurants.

Dr. Neal who was only four years older than I was, but he was much younger than Dr. Louis.

One day at an art gallery, he enquired, "Have you been to Paris?"

"No. I haven't been there," I answered, adding, "Everybody wants to travel around France, especially Paris."

"My parents have a nice house located awfully close to Champs Elysees," he told me. "It takes only five minutes to get downtown. I am sure you would be pleased be the lively city and by staying in the center of Paris. Would you like take a trip to Spain and France?"

"That sounds great!" I replied.

"Is there any possibility that you would cover your own airfare?" he asked. "My parents are old, and they follow a traditional culture of respect, like you, which is one reason I adore you so much. If you do that, I will take care of the other expenses including hotel reservations, meals, vouchers for entertainments, and tours."

He explained that we would stay in Spain for a while before flying over to Paris and asked, "Do you like that idea?" He also wanted to know if I had any other recommendations and informed me that his parents, who were kind, were excited to meet me.

I told him that it all sounded awesome. I was thrilled and could hardly wait to take a trip to Europe with him.

Two weeks later, we flew to Madrid, Spain. We stayed in separate rooms at the Hilton Hotel.

I was surprised to see an American Hilton Hotel in the center of Madrid. A few people spoke English, and most of the hotel staff spoke Spanish. The hotel lobby was huge, and a smattering of booths displayed information on a diverse variety of tours. Across from the Hilton was a towering shopping mall, which displayed many advertisements in colorful neon signs. Surprisingly, I even saw a Sears sign on the building.

Madrid was a busy city with many tourists. Its historical buildings were populous, marvelous, and elaborate. Here and there, gigantic fountains were sprinkled about the city, along with many sculptures.

As I looked at the signs for the Hilton and for Sears, I had a moment of confusion whether I was in Europe or in New York or California. The Madrid shopping mall offered excellent products, such as leather boots, purses, and a backpack. I enjoyed the shopping in Madrid.

That night we took off to see a stage performance of an exotic flamingo dance at a popular restaurant. During the performance, we relished a wonderful Spanish meal.

The next morning, we got up early and walked down to Prado Museum, a popular museum in Madrid. We greatly appreciated the precious collections of Pablo Picasso, El Greco, and Bartolomé Esteban Murillo' paintings, delicate sculptures, and modern art. We then joined a bus tour to visit a famous monastery and La Sagrada, the great church in Barcelona.

On the fourth day, we went to a bullfighting stadium called a *plaza deteros* (bullring). I wore white parachute pants, knee-high Spanish leather boots, a parachute sweater, and the throw over Himalayan vest to see the bullfight. As we walked down the steps of the stadium, many people stared at me and complimented my vest.

A couple of women even asked, "Where did you buy the vest?"

I thanked them for their compliments and told them the vest was a gift from my friend.

The first part of the bullfighting was a fun and thrilling game, although when the bullfighter got injured, my stomach clenched and I was ashamed that I could not help the injured bullfighter but instead could only sit and watch his suffering. Because of this, I did not want to watch the game any longer. Violent games are not my favorite sports, and we left early.

That night, we walked down the main street and collected a few souvenirs. The street was a narrow, steep, and lined with strip malls and fast-food restaurants. Again, I was surprised when I saw a McDonald's, where youngsters socialized with their peer groups, just like in America.

The outdoor cafés were popular spots in Spain. We had a light dinner and coffee at one of the sidewalk cafés and enjoyed watching the Spaniards and relaxing.

The next day, we flew from Spain to Paris. I enjoyed the exotic sound of the French stewardesses welcoming us on board. The airplane flew at an exceptionally low altitude, and I could see the beautiful architecture of the French buildings and houses and the geometrically arranged landscape, distinctively different from the layout of an American city. The flight to France did not take long time—only thirty minutes to get from Spain to Paris.

Dr. Neal's parents were waiting for us, and we met them as soon as we exited the plane. They were very polite. His father drove us to their home, where I refreshed myself and shared stories with him about the trip to Spain.

In the interim, his sister and mother were preparing a big meal in honor of our visit to Paris. The large, elongated dinner table was filled with a variety of great, pleasurable food. We relaxed and had a delightful evening together.

Afterward, we checked into separate rooms at a small hotel near his parents' house. I felt good and very privileged to have flown from Spain to Paris in such a respectful and sweet atmosphere. His parents' welcome was remarkable, and I could feel their genuine love.

Nevertheless, this sense of fortune did not last long when I spoke my broken French. I had a hard time communicating with the front desk clerk to get my room key. At last, I settled in my room and took a nice warm shower. Then the real trouble started.

I tried to dry my hair, and my dryer did not work. Nor did my curling iron and steamroller set. I had not had any problems using the dryer at the Hilton in Madrid. My hair was wet, but I could not communicate with the front desk clerk. Dr. Neal had gone to his room after he had said good night sometime earlier. I spent time trying to fix the nonfunctioning hair apparatus. Well, I did not have any choice but to sleep with wet hair, which guaranteed my hair would look like I'd just gotten out of a wind tunnel or had put my fingers in a socket in the morning.

I was tired and decided to use the toilet before getting into bed. Next to it was another toilet without a seat, which was not familiar to me. I pushed the button at the back of the toilet. Instantly, shooting water splashed me. Moment before, I had been catered to and honored by Dr. Neal's parents. Such treatment quickly vanished. Well, that was too bad!

I chose not to worry about today and to let tomorrow take care of itself. I would later learn that the shooting water was from the bidet, and Paris had a different voltage, which meant an adapter was required to run electrical appliances. All my problems were fixed the following day, which put a smile on my face once again.

The huge wrought iron skeleton of the Eiffel Tower is a landmark of Paris. The engineer, Alexander Gustavo, initially designed the 984-foot (300-meter) tower for the world fair of 1889—the Exposition Universelle. It has been used to transmit television programs.

We rode the elevator, went up to the top-floor restaurant, and had lunch. Dr. Neal stopped by the information center, and meanwhile, I went to use a washroom. I could not use the restroom because I did not have French francs, so I had to get a proper coin from him. A woman in the restroom did not expect a tip, but she charged me an exact number of francs to use a bathroom. This was just one of the many cultural differences I would encounter on this trip. Now I understood why tourist books and guides were popular, even in airport bookstores.

In Paris, we visited the Louvre, one of the world's largest art museums. Dr. Neal loved the paintings. Paris had long been a world capital of art, and the museum provided historical information about the arts for tourists. But he and I were appreciative and observed the famous paintings of Gauguin, Monet, Matisse, and Pissarro and the fine sculptures.

The front of the Louvre had a beautiful, bright flower garden, where Dr. Neal took many pictures of me. There were also walking paths, small stores, ice cream shops, and many roaming tourists surrounding small trees.

The excursion boat of Bateau-Mouche was a nice tour, and we learned much as we traveled along the Seine River. We delighted in the boat outing and enjoyed listening to the music and songs of French bands.

The masterpiece of Gothic architecture, the cathedral of Notre Dame was next to the excursion boat entrance. I went to Notre Dame and lit a candle and wished to become a doctor. Notre Dame stands on a small island in the Seine River and is also the center of Paris.

Not far from Notre Dame, there were strip malls and vendor markets selling inexpensive sculptures, ceramic statues, and many smaller souvenirs. I bought a large statue of Jupiter holding an adored lady. It was a delicately carved sculpture, which I got for the amazingly low price of $250. I had an elongated square leather bag. The sculpture fit in the bag perfectly, but it was heavy to carry.

We stayed for one week, mainly at Champs Elysees. There were many perfume stores; it seemed tourists loved Paris perfume. I bought several perfumes, and they were captivating. I was surprised once again when I saw a Sears department store near the famous Paris Opera House.

Dr. Neal's sister was a lawyer and was married to an architect. They had a daughter who was five years old. The little girl spoke English and French without an accent. When we were shopping in Champs Elysees, his sister and her daughter joined us. We strolled from one store to another while I held the daughter's hand.

Many young Frenchmen asked me, "Parle vouz Francis?" (Can you speak French?)

I answered, "No parle vouz Francis. Parle vouz Anglaise?" (I cannot speak French. Can you speak English?)

A few people stopped me and asked me questions, but I did not understand them. The people appeared to be elated and showed me pleasant smiles. I assumed they were asking amiable questions. I told them again, "Pardon, no parle vouz Francis." What else could I say? I did not speak French.

The quality of leather was excellent in Paris as well as Spain. I bought knee-high boots, high-heeled shoes, and a lovely kidney bag that I wore over my chest. I felt that I could fit in in fashion-forward Paris when I wore tight pants with a turtleneck sweater, my new knee-high boots, and the new suede kidney bag. I walked confidently with my head up. I was young and enjoyed the high-fashion city of Champs Elysees.

There were sidewalk cafés, where we stopped to eat, drink, and observe the Arc de Triomohe, an impressive monument at the western end of Champs Elysees in Paris, which is on a well-known avenue. As I recall, it was there that Napoleon ordered all to honor his military victories.

We then stopped by a place called Place de la Concorde, which stands at the eastern end of Champs Elysees. There were many historical fountains and statues and an Egyptian pillar known as Obelisk of Luxor. The tour was informative, and I also adored the colorful flowers of the Luxembourg Garden.

Next, we toured the Palace of Versailles, which was amazingly impressive. I can only imagine the palace as the royal residence for more than a hundred years. The palace contained a magnificent royal chapel and a private theater. I loved the open garden with its historical fountains at Versailles.

After the tour, we roamed the hillside of the famous Sacro Sancta Church freely. Young people played guitars on the cement bleachers, and a group of their peers sang as if they had spectators while they looked down at the picturesque landscape. I sat next to the group and joined their melody. They were happy when I joined them and clapped their hands and smiled. I did not know French, but I flowed with their melody and hummed with their rhythm. That was fun!

Sacro Santa was next to the region of Montmartre, known as a home for many Parisian artists. Display after display offered paintings for sale all throughout the Montmartre vicinity. We each bought at least one painting. Dr. Neal's sister got the largest painting, and I purchased the most economical painting, but I loved it.

He invited his family to join us at the finest Japanese restaurant in Paris. The waiter guided us to a semiprivate room with a large steel cooktop. The cook came and grilled shrimp, scallops, pineapples, vegetables, and onions on the cooktop. The food was delicious, even though he had not added much seasoning. The chef chopped up a chunk of beef into small pieces. Again, he did not add much seasoning. He flipped the meat once, juggled his knives over his white hat, and then tossed the meat once more. He repeated his show as if he were a circus entertainer until the meat was ready to eat. My eyes got bigger each time he threw his knives in the air over his head and I stared as he juggled them until they landed perfectly on the cooktop. The sumptuous and tender meat just melted in my watery mouth. The food was succulent.

I asked, "What is the secret to making such delicate and delicious meat?"

"The secret is that the staff goes to the butcher shop early in the morning," he told me. "The meat is fresh, which makes a difference."

Dr. Neal's father and mother, along with his sister and her husband and their daughter, Dory, joined us. And we all enjoyed watching the hibachi cooking and had a delightful meal.

The following night, Dr. Neal's friend, the foreign minister, invited us, along with his sister and her husband, to Club 76 in the center of Champs Elysees. The club is an exclusive place, and no one can enter without a membership. We all went to the club because the foreign minister had a private membership. It featured an extravagant restaurant and had a huge dance floor, a stage, and a white sheer screen that hung close to the wall inside the club. All of us greeted each other in French. My French was not fluent and made the others laugh.

I meant to say, "Good evening, gentlemen. But the word *gentleman* in French sounded like the word *mouse*. So, my, 'Good evening, gentlemen' turned out to be, 'Good evening, mouse.'" Oops!

Thank God, they thought I was cute, and my embarrassing mistake was accepted as an entertainment.

We were pleased to watch an excellent French dancers' performance while we ate fantastic French delicacies. I was especially astonished to observe the exotic setting of the dancing stage. Suddenly, the floor was filled with white smoke like a fluffy cloud. At that instant, a fairy-looking lady with long blond hair appeared on a white horse. The smoke encircled her as she rode gracefully and performed sensual dancing that I had never seen before in America. A few minutes later, half naked women appear behind the white screen, dancing to the music under the dim light.

French wine is known to be excellent, and Dr. Neal offered me a lavish glass of wine.

"Thank you, but no thanks," I told him. "I cannot drink wine. I am allergic to any alcohol because of an alcohol dehydrogenase enzyme deficiency. Drinking just a drop of alcohol makes me extremely sick."

"That's okay," he said. "You can have fresh juice."

We toasted our future and our blessed friendship. We shared personal stories and reminisced about our pleasant experiences. The night was an extraordinary occasion, and we all had a splendid time together.

Before I left the club, I went to the washroom. This time, I was prepared with my francs, and the coins allowed me to use the restroom. I was surprised that even the exclusive private club had the same setup.

The next day, Dr. Neal and I flew back to California. It took over sixteen hours to return home from France.

CHAPTER 8

Shark Fin Soup and Sweet Bread

Dr. Neal was a cardiologist, and he had several close friends who were open-heart surgeons. One of the heart surgeons invited us for dinner at his house in Beverly Hills. The house was located on the top of the hill and had a gorgeous view. His property boasted a few running streams and small waterfalls, and the surgeon guided us along the steppingstones on the side of his house.

He showed us two unique sitting rooms inside gazebos, where he usually meditated in the morning. Heart surgeons have a crucial responsibility, dealing with imminent life-and-death situations. All doctors, particularly open-heart surgeons, need to incorporate stress-free times in their lives.

Everyone has his or her own lifestyle and choice of house setting and decoration. This surgeon owned an enormous hillside property, where he meditated surrounded by creeks and waterfalls. Dr. Neal's friends and relatives lived in the wealthy atmosphere of Beverly Hills.

At this stage of my life, I refocused on my goal to study medicine. I still had a great time going out with different people before I involve myself in studying at a medical school. I knew that, once I had started school, tremendous discipline would be required to get me through. My dream to become a doctor was set in stone and imprinted on my heart.

I occasionally dated an intensive care unit doctor, Dr. Ricardo, from the local community hospital. He was a first-generation American, whose family came from Argentina. He loved playing tennis and took me to a couple of tennis tournaments. He was fond of European food, and we went to French restaurants regularly. He knew most of the local restaurant employees.

One day, he invited me to a popular restaurant that served the best French cuisine. We had a fantastic shark fin soup that I loved more than the entrée itself. He worked hard and lived his life to the fullest.

"Did you like the French food?" Dr. Ricardo asked. "French food is one of my favorites."

"I loved the shark fin soup. I had never tried it before," I told him, adding, "At first, I wasn't sure about having shark. But I found it unexpectedly delightful."

"I'm glad that you like French food."

We talked about French restaurants in downtown Los Angeles, and he asked if I had been to Buena Ventura, where there were different restaurants, stores, and hotels. "It's a pretty awesome place," he told me.

I told him that I had seen the tall fancy building downtown that appeared to be one of LA's landmarks but that I had not been there.

"Can you get off early on Thursday? If you are interested, we could have dinner at a French restaurant in Buena Ventra. I'll call for a reservation."

"That sounds brilliant," I replied. "I'm excited."

The dazzling thirty-five story Buena Ventra was as magnificent as I expected. It had an enclosed tinted glass elevator connected to the outside of the building. One of the first skyscrapers, the building was well known for its distinctive and elegant construction.

I was scared to ride the glass elevator because it was difficult to look down or look out. I had phobia of heights, acrophobia, which made me nervous. My peripheral nerve transmitted abnormally, and my entire nervous system was highly stimulated. I automatically pressed my body close to the inside wall of the elevator, as if this would somehow make me safer. The glass elevator ride was challenging. Thankfully and gradually, I overcame my fear of heights.

The foyer of the French restaurant was attractively decorated with colorful flowerpots lined along both sides of the entrance, which was impressive. Several water fountains gave the entryway next to the open-air restaurant an affluent atmosphere.

Our dinner reservation was fabulous, and many diners appeared to be enjoying French cheese and wine. I had a bottle of Perrier and was contented. After eating freshly baked sesame crackers with cheese, I was not hungry. I wanted to have a light dinner and ordered sweet bread. The sweet bread dish looked different than what I had thought it would be. When the waiter brought the food, it hardly looked like bread to me.

"What is sweet bread?" I asked to the waiter

"It is made of cow thalamus, which is a part of the cow brain," the waiter explained. "Have a lovely dinner, madam!"

"What?! A cow brains. No way will I eat this," I murmured to myself. I stared at the dish and pushed it quietly to the side of the table.

"Are not going to eat your dinner?"

"I ate too much appetizer, and I'm not hungry," I replied. "Will you not mind if I rather eat my chocolate torte?"

In any event, we had a fantastic time, sharing thoughts about classical music and sports. After dinner, we went to another restaurant that had a rotating thirty-fifth floor, offer a spectacular view of the downtown LA night view. The fantastic panorama reminded me how great America is.

The following weekend, Dr. Ricardo invited me for dinner at his house. His niece worked as a manager at his clinic. She came to his house and prepared Argentinian food, and we ate the delicious meal. He had an opulent house on the hillside. It included a huge swimming pool with a diving board and two fancy Jacuzzis on each side of the pool, which embellished his house with colorful lights at night. A low hedge of iron railing next to the pool opened to a lush golf course landscape. A huge sliding glass door in the front of the formal dining room revealed an astonishing view. On the Fourth of July, we gazed at the splendid fireworks as we dined.

Dr. Ricardo had a passionate and romantic personality, and he treasured sports cars. He had recently bought a red convertible Ferrari. He even had a matching pair of gloves. He surely cherished his car.

"Do you like my new car?" he wanted to know and also, "Have you been to Palm Springs?" He explained that he had a condo in a gated community in Palm Spring. There were many four-star restaurants, excellent spas, boutique shops, and a variety of other activities available in the exclusive city. He proposed that we visit when I was not working, noting that it was not far, only an hour and a half by car, and that I would enjoy riding in his Ferrari.

"That sounds remarkable," I say.

Palm Springs was a perfect place to unwind daily stress. I appreciated his amazing condo in a gated community. It was encircled by a man-made pond and beautifully arranged flower gardens. There were tennis courts, an indoor racquetball court, and a gymnasium. Plus, a few Hollywood movie stars resided in the community. The weather in Palm Spring was sunny and hot but dry.

After lunch, we went shopping. Many shoppers and pedestrians stared us while he drove his car to a store. We wore tennis outfits and sun visors. We were visible in his convertible Ferrari. The people on the street might have thought we were tennis pros.

Various strip malls displayed exotic clothing and unique collectible items. I found several sundresses that I loved.

Dr. Ricardo saw that I adored the dresses and asked, "Do you like those sundresses?"

"Yes, they are lovely."

"I will buy them for you if you do not mind."

"Thanks!" I told him.

On the way back home, he bought a bouquet. He adored seeing me with colorful flowers. "You are so pretty like a flower," he said.

Briefly, I felt like I was one of the celebrities. I loved this lifestyle.

A few weeks later, we decided to drive up to Monterrey Park. There, we cherished the Pacific Ocean view and savored superb seafood at an oceanfront restaurant. We enjoyed a relaxing weekend, leisurely roaming around the ocean-view offerings and watching a monkey performing tricks to earn a few dollars. The roasted pistachios from a vendor tasted better than they ever had. I was happy.

Driving along the coastline afforded a breathtaking view through the woods. The sweet aroma of a bakery wafted into the car, and I realized we had reached the city of Carmel, where the movie star Clint Eastwood was serving as the mayor.

I had never seen the city, which was jam-packed with bakeries, and so the appetizing scents of fresh pastries filled the air. The residents were friendly, and the city attracted many tourists. The food was first-rate, and the pastries were indulgently scrumptious. There was no way I could try all the different pastries if I still desired to fit into my date's small sports car. The city was small but lovely, especially with its white beach.

The next day, we went to see the Golden Gate Bridge in San Francisco. Emery Hotel was located at the top of the hill. I could see the Golden Gate Bridge perfectly through a huge windowpane in the room. The hotel had many amenities, including lavish restaurants. We had an exquisite dinner next to a Polynesian dance show that took place on a boat in a man-made, decorative pond inside the restaurant. Clusters of flowers hung from the roof of an artificial hut, and there were tropical trees on the boat. I admired the special effects, which created rainfalls over the boat as the performers, clad in Polynesian dress, sang, and danced.

The young couple next to us was cursing at each other and causing a scene. Dr. Ricardo immediately requested a change in the seating arrangement. The waiter politely escorted us to another table close to the front of the showboat.

"When I was in medical school," he said, "I sacrificed everything to focus on studying, often eating only bananas for lunch. I worked hard to be successful. I do not need to hear this type of nonsense while I'm having dinner with you."

"Okay then," I whispered to myself.

The new Ferrari got people's attention. But in truth, the seat was small, hard, and extremely uncomfortable for a long trip. Comparison is a thief of joy. Some people envy others who have something like a Ferrari. However, once you have such a possession, it does not mean much.

We returned home safely after the pleasurable trip to San Francisco. After that, we revisited Palm Springs several times. Palm Springs was not as far from our houses, and it was an entertaining city to enjoy a weekend in. At one place we visited, we enjoyed Moroccan food and were fond of watching the belly dancers, whose performance was the highlight of the evening. The dining tables were as low as coffee tables, and most diners savored the exotic Moroccan food while in sitting positions on floor mats or low couches. The restaurant did not have cutlery. The waiter, who wore traditional Moroccan clothes, brought over a massive kettle and basin, poured water from the kettle over my hands above the basin while I washed them, and then provided a large towel from his shoulder.

We had seven delicious entrées, along with a heavenly, delicate apple pie for dessert, which was nothing like American pie. The fluffy piecrust and uniquely sweetened, stuffed apple melted in my mouth, and I craved more. Dr. Ricardo and I went to many different restaurants for dinner, but the Moroccan food remained my favorite.

Was I dreaming or had I died and been reincarnated? Unusually, many wealthy men wanted to marry me at the time—when I was not interested getting marry but determined to study medicine.

Unlike my destiny, I was blessed for a while, being catered to and experiencing affluent lifestyle and rich surroundings. I knew this romantic relationship would soon end, and I was ready to start medical school. Indeed, I did enjoy the dazzling entertainments I was afforded in the period leading up to my medical school enrollment.

CHAPTER 9

That Sounds Like a Good Plan

I had taken several courses toward a Master of Science in critical care, studying the legal aspects of care, statistics, and anthropology at California State University. The subjects were interesting, and I received good grades. I learned stories of witchdoctors, witchcraft, and excavation, which propelled my fervent desire to be a real doctor and to heal sick people. As a result, I decided to go to medical school, instead of obtaining a master's degree.

I met Jim, a young laboratory supervisor, at a small hospital in California.

"What are you studying? Is that the MCAT book that you're looking at?" he curiously asked. "Are you trying to go to medical school?" He was sweet and a good-looking young man, who had blond hair and deep blue eyes. He resembled the movie star Robert Redford.

"Yes," I told him. "I would like to study medicine. However, it is not easy to get into medical school here in California. I already applied to UCLA and spoke with a school administrator, who explained that UCLA medical school selects students who have high MCAT scores and sufficient financial support. The school prefers younger students, under the age of twenty-five. I am almost twenty-eight years old, and my MCAT scores aren't that high. One of the school faculty members informed me that the medical school tuition is expensive, and I don't have a sufficient funds."

"Wow, what a coincidence!" he exclaimed. "Likewise, I tried to get into medical school, and I don't have enough money either." He acknowledged that medical school tuition was extremely expensive. Even though he had two undergraduate degrees in biology and chemistry, getting into UCLA was difficult. His father was a licensed doctor working as a missionary, and his mother was a registered nurse. They were nice and loved Tim very much, but they were not rich.

"Are you interested in getting information about overseas schools?" he asked.

"Of course, yes! What and incredible pleasure meeting you here and sharing the same goal."

"I have a friend who went to medical school in Mexico and is currently working as a doctor in California. He is visiting me for a few days. He will be more than happy to share some insight about medical school overseas. Would you like to have dinner together? My condo has a swimming pool, and we can cool off in the pool after dinner and discuss school. How does that sound to you?"

"That sounds like a good plan," I told him.

His friend advised us that we would have to study harder than students attending an American school to get a medical license in the United States.

At the time, my family and friends persuaded me not to go to medical school overseas. They repeatedly reminded me that I was blessed to have good job, money, and a circle of wealthy doctor friends. "Many prestigious doctors profoundly love you and want to marry you," many of my friends persuade me to reconsider my schooling. They did not understand why I declined to settle down with a wealthy man and have children.

Regardless of their advice, I had a burning desire to be a doctor; that was my lifetime dream. I had lived with myself for twenty-eight years, and I knew myself better than others did. It was not easy to make the right decision and to relinquish my comfort zone.

I would wear armor to fight for the difficult field of medical school that lay ahead. I was willing to discipline to study and be ready to take test after test—all of which required careful thought processes. Certainly, it was a challenging time.

This meeting was not by accident. I found out that, synchronously Jim was also twenty-eight years old. He shared my faith in God. He, too, was independent, and he had the same ambition to be a doctor. We reviewed our future endeavors and talked about going to medical school together. We had two options—one option was to attend a Caribbean school, and the other choice was a school in the Dominican Republic.

We finally received an answer, thanks to our unceasing efforts. Jim was able to locate the medical school administrator and recruiter's office near his condo in California.

A few weeks later, Jim called me, saying, "We will be interviewed soon by the school administrator. Please prepare your undergraduate school transcripts and MCAT results."

Subsequently, we went to see the school administrator, who requested that I bring more documents and said he would let us know the outcome and whether we had been accepted into the program soon.

Jim and I were overjoyed when the news came. We had both been approved and would be admitted to the medical school in Santo Domingo. We promptly researched the Dominican Republic and gathered information. Fortunately, the school administrator had already arranged our apartment close to the medical school in Santo Domingo.

Dominica is a small island in the Caribbean Sea. The city lies on the country's southern coast in an island north of the Venezuelan coast. The Dominican became independent in 1978 after being ruled by Great Britain. Most Dominicans have African or mixed African British and French ancestry and dress in Western-style clothing. Their main foods include bananas, crabs, frog legs, lobsters, and sweet potatoes. Many Dominicans live in cities where English is spoken, and some speak the nation's official language. The villagers chiefly speak a language called French Patois, which is a mixture of African and French. About 80 percent of the people are Roman Catholics, and the rest are Protestants.

Dominican history is interesting because on November 3, 1493, one Sunday, Christopher Columbus became the first European to sight the island. He named it Dominica, the Latin word for Sunday. Some historians believe he is buried on the island in the cathedral of Santo Domingo. Santo Domingo was the first city in the Western hemisphere found by Europeans. The University of Santo Domingo, which was established in 1538, is the oldest university in the Western hemisphere.

"Are you sure you want to move to Santo Domingo to study medicine?" Jim asked.

"I will move there regardless of what happens in my future," I assured him. "I cannot give up on my dream of becoming a doctor."

Jim, just my age and a Christian, was in a similar situation.

After being accepted at CIFAS medical school, we had only a few months to get ready for school. We had to sell or rent our houses before leaving for Dominica.

We were both excited and apprehensive about going to live in a foreign country. Jim sold his condo, and I rented my house. All my household items were sold to friends or given away.

Dr. Ricardo was heartbroken, as we had grown close by this point. He also attempted to prevent me from going to medical school overseas. I made my final decision without a second thought and fully anticipated a new journey ahead of me.

He threw me a big party and invited his friends and relatives. A special Argentinian chef cooked, grilling a baby pig, along with preparing many other traditional foods, which were displayed around the swimming pool. I was introduced to his family and friends. We sang popular songs together and smiled each other. He whispered to me that I should try the well-cooked delicacy while I was sitting next to him. He cut a piece from the piglet, which was unfolded after it was cut in the middle, showing its snout. Looking at the poor piglet gave me goose bumps. I felt sorry for the cute piglet. I politely refused to eat the roasted pig and preferred to have salad, cakes, mixed fruits, Argentinian empanada, and my favorite pistachios.

He displayed ambivalence when it came to his feelings toward me; one minute, he wanted to take a trip to Hawaii with me, and the next minute, he realized that I would leaving him right after Hawaiian trip. He wished that I would stay with him, but he could not convince me to give up my dream. My ironclad determination to go to medical school was not breakable by any means.

The night before my adventure in a new world was to unfold, Dr. Ricardo took me to his favorite French restaurant. One last time, I had delicious, boiled sea bass with rich French sauce and my favorite shark fin soup. He held my hand under the table, and he appeared to be sad.

"I am sorry, Dr. Ricardo," I told him. "I have to leave in the morning. Jim and I are going to the medical school in Santo Domingo."

He stared at me without a word or smile for a while. A few minutes later, he broke his stillness. "Are you going to be okay and safe?" he said. "I am worried about your new venture. If you need anything, please do not hesitate to call me. I will pick you and Jim up from your house and take you both to the airport."

This time, he drove his Cadillac, not his Ferrari. Jim and I had a comfortable ride in his car. I wore jeans, a casual shirt, and flat shoes. Jim also wore comfortable clothes. We got out of the car, and I put on my backpack at the airport.

Dr. Ricardo had never seen me in casual clothes; nor had I dressed like a student around him. He looked at us deep in thought and then hugged me tight and gave me a kiss on my forehead.

"Be careful! Have a safe journey, study hard, and hope to see you soon."

Jim and I flew from California to the International Airport of Santo Domingo. Exiting the plane, we found a hugely different atmosphere at the luggage terminal than what we were used to. Dark-skinned police or people who appeared to be militias were standing everywhere, all of them armed with rifles and bayonets. I could barely communicate with the local people in Spanish. I much appreciated that some people at the airport spoke English.

We communicated that we needed to take a taxi to CIFAS University. Probably many Americans came to the Dominican Republic to study medicine, and some local people figured out our need immediately and called a taxi for us.

We saw a beautiful southern coastal view on the way to our new apartment in Santo Domingo. The treetops along the seaside were covered with bright red and yellow blossoms of tropical flowers. The blue ocean and tall palm trees were brilliantly intertwined in the fabric of the island.

The road was paved well for international tourism. There were no skyscrapers. Nor did I see many residential houses. The weather was warm, around 80 degrees Fahrenheit without humidity. The sky was a cloudless cobalt blue. It was a picturesque scenic view of a tropical island without the congestion of traffic or people. I loved the peaceful and quiet remote coastline.

Once again, I saw standing militias wearing rifles with bayonets strapped to their shoulders, which totally spooked us. The sight of the militias reminded us that we were in a foreign country with a different social structure, culture, and background. Still, we were pleased on the taxi ride to take in the scenery. The blue ocean view, the lovely colorful flowers, and the warm pleasant weather suppressed our subconscious fear of the unknown.

The administrator had arranged our residential situation ahead of time. The taxi driver dropped us off at our new apartment, in the Piazza Colon in Santo Domingo, capital of the Dominican Republic. We arrived safely without any problems, despite navigating solely by way of my broken Spanish and the driver's Spanglish.

The studio had three bedrooms, a spacious living room, and a kitchen on the second floor. Most apartments close to the school did not have air-conditioning. Favorably, we had three separate air-conditioning units in our dwelling. Jim chose the first bedroom close to the entrance. We reserved the second bedroom for a study room. And I had a third bedroom, which was tucked in and offered a little more privacy.

A marvelous statue of Christopher Columbus stands in the Piazza Colon. Our medical school, CIFAS University, was close enough to our residence—seven minutes by public transportation known as a *publico*. The publico is like a small taxi and usually jammed with local folks. Sometimes, natives were carrying piglets, chickens, bundles of bananas, or grocery bags inside the public, and students with their heavy books and backpacks often squeezed between the locals. Thank God it only took a few minutes to get to school.

Some students had money. They bought their own cars and refused to use a publico. CIFAS medical school was small, and 95 percent of the students were Caucasian male. The remaining few were either white females or natives. Lectures were in English. A cafeteria was in a separate building. The restrooms, dean's office, administrative offices, and the cadaver room were on the first floor, and the library and classrooms were on the second floor.

I was very anxious to excel at the basic science courses. I tended to study better in the classroom. I got permission from the administrator to use the classroom to study after lessons were finished. I could not eat heavy meals, as they put me to sleep. Generally, I ate one avocado and one banana for dinner. I was immobilized at the desk and frozen to my chair in the classroom so that I could get high scores on the exams. I lost substantial weight and slept less than four hours a day. Every day, I studied in the empty classroom and left school around midnight. I used to be scared to death when I was passing by the cadaver room

I made high scores for the first semester. Disappointedly, I acknowledged that CIFAS accreditation was not advantageous. Thus, I decided to transfer to UTESA University, which was better and larger than CIFAS.

The UTESA campus also had a separate cafeteria. The dean's office, the administration offices, and many of the classrooms were spread across two floors. There was a large library for students to study. In my opinion, UTESA University was more advanced and credible than CIFAS. Even though Jim, surprisingly, decided to stay at CIFAS, we still shared the apartment.

UTESA was farther from my residence. At the time, it was hard to catch a publico promptly, and I was late for lectures. The last thing I wanted to do was to be late and miss a lecture. Finally, I decided to purchase a motor scooter.

One weekend, my classmate Charleston drove me in his car to a large store that sold bicycles, motorcycles, and motor scooters. I purchased a scooter made in the United States and paid cash. A friendly salesperson from an insurance department promptly approached us and told us that I had to have insurance coverage for my new scooter, which was required by the Public Safety Department in Santo Domingo. Thus, I contracted for insurance coverage before I took my scooter out of the store.

I rode my new scooter without instruction on a quiet street near the store while Charleston watched. Riding a scooter was not quite the same as riding a bicycle. I rode without any problems—up until I hit a pothole. The unbalanced tires instantly threw me down on the ground, and my poor new scooter was immediately dented. My knees were scraped and bleeding.

Charleston took me and my scooter to the store to get some medical aid. I had already wrecked my new scooter. The salespeople were appalled and could not believe the scooter was damaged and that I was bleeding from my right knee and elbow. I had just purchased the scooter twenty minutes ago, and here I was back at the store with it crushed.

The man from the insurance division appeared in a hurry with his clipboard and conveyed to me in Spanglish. "Madam, please sign your name here. You do not need to have insurance for a scooter; it is not mandated by the government. We are cancelling your insurance coverage. In case you really wish to have some coverage for risk, here are some addresses for other companies."

In the interim, one of the salespersons provided me with gauze and bandages. The store technician adjusted my crooked scooter. Charleston put my scooter and me in his car, and we drove back home. The following weekend, I practiced riding the scooter on my neighborhood street, where there were not many potholes. This time, I wore a helmet and kneepads.

I soon discovered that, even with my scooter, the school was too far from my apartment. At the point, one of my classmates suggested I consider living in the former ambassador's residence—a huge house with a live-in maid much closer to UTESA, in which the ambassador's wife rented out a room for medical students. My friend added that from there, I could get to the school on my scooter in five minutes. I was excited and happy when I received this new information.

The following day, after school, I went to the ambassador's house and knocked on the front gate.

A live-in maid came out and asked, "How can I help you?"

"May I speak to the person in charge of renting a room for a medical student?"

"Would you please wait for a moment?" the maid replied. "I will ask the wife of the ambassador."

A middle-aged woman came out right after the maid had gone in the house. Pleasantly, she guided me inside. "What's your name?" she asked. "Are you a medical student?"

I showed her my school ID and told her my name. I explained that my nice apartment was too far away for me to get to school promptly. The landlord showed me one of the rooms. She was willing to provide more amenities if I needed them for my study. She promised me to make me as comfortable as possible and expressed her desire that I become a good doctor. I felt very blessed and profusely appreciated her kindness.

I would move to their home within two weeks. The house was extensive, with surrounding flower gardens and a covered patio toward the back of garden. I was happy and satisfied.

I returned to my apartment and took a cool shower and thanked God. I wrapped my naked body in a towel after the shower. I saw a wiggling creature moving across the mirror when I was applying facial cream. I was terrified by this unidentifiable slithering creature and ran out the washroom in such a hurry that I almost dropped my towel. Luckily, Jim was not there; he was still at the school.

I did not know what the creature was. Nor did I know what to do with it. I went back to the bathroom very cautiously and looked closely at the annoying creature. It was a baby lizard, which had made me think of a rattlesnake as it had come into my view—scaring me to death at the time.

Lizards did not come indoors in California, and I had no experience seeing one inside a bathroom. Santo Domingo was a tropical island; apparently bugs were in their native habitat here. I should expect to see them around.

I dressed carefully and decided to make myself be calm. I went to the kitchen to have a glass of cold mango juice and papaya. I started to cut the papaya and was removing the seeds to fill it with cottage cheese when a large, unfamiliar flying creature flew over my head. I jumped and jerked my hand, and the cottage cheese scattered all over the kitchen countertop.

The big brown water bug resembled like a gigantic cockroach as it flew over my head back and forth several times and then disappeared through the back door. I was much bigger than any beetles I had ever seen, and, unaccustomed to such bugs, its appearance chilled my spine. I loved animals but not bugs.

Nevertheless, nothing would make me depressed or deter me from my objective—to be a doctor. I told myself that neither lizard nor flying beetles would stop me from studying medicine in Santo Domingo. I would simply change my attitude to acceptance and ignore God's different creatures that resided here.

When I moved to the island, I brought nice clothes and shoes, but they were useless and not practical under the circumstances. I ended up wearing tennis shoes, long-sleeve shirts, and long pants to protect myself from mosquitos, which bit any and every exposed part of the body. They were thirsty and hungry, and I concluded these tropical mosquitoes must be starving.

Jim helped me move to the ambassador's house, and he took many pictures of me after I had moved to the new place.

Victoria Gates, MD

The horse was gentle, but I was scared in Dominica.

I knew Jim wanted to have a romantic relationship and settle down with me, but I was not interested in an intimate affair. We were just friends with the same goal, and my mind was only focused on medicine. I had not moved here to have a romance or to get married. I wanted to be a doctor.

The program swiftly progressed, exam after exam, without any breaks. Many of the American students gave up and returned home due to the brutally grueling schedules. There were many tragic accidents that occurred to students during the medical school.

One of students moved to Santo Domingo with his wife and children. He was involved in a car accident and became paralyzed, losing the use of both of his legs. Still, he never gave up his dream. He was able to overcome thanks to his family's devotion and his determination that, together, got him through the inconceivable ordeal.

I observed another unfortunate case. Many local natives knew that Americans had money. One of the locals stole from a student's tuition stash, which was hidden under the student's mattress. The native did not want to return the stolen money, and he ironically reported to a policeman an opposite story, saying that the student had committed the crime—stealing the native's money. The student could not speak Spanish. Nor did he have the time to defend himself and ended up imprisoned. Dominican jail was not comparable to America. The prisons did not have beds, and inmates slept on a dirt floor. There was no shower facility. Nor were the inmates provided meals.

Approximately, 45 percent of the American students in Santo Domingo dropped out the program and returned to the United States during the basic science courses. The entire curriculum had no semester breaks, shortening the overall course of education. My average sleep decreased to two to three hours to keep up with the tests. I was physically and mentally exhausted.

A few expensive local hotels had Sunday buffets, live band music, and huge swimming pools, where we unwound our stress from studying. One of the nice things about Santo Domingo was that it had excellent Spanish food available in many restaurants, and the price of the food was reasonable. Dominicans loved music with the pounding rhythm of African drums and the rattle of Spanish maracas. Dominicans enjoyed dancing the merengue, which is the national dance. The cost of living was inexpensive compared to America. I lived well, by God's grace.

The ambassador's family invited me to have meals with them on weekends. There was always a variety of food on the table, and the live-in maid served us. After the heavy lunch, we would all take a siesta.

CHAPTER 10

Uncle Pie of America

Charleston, one of my classmates and a close friend, who had a master's degree in space science and had graduated as an honor student, nevertheless struggled to keep up at the medical school. On the other hand, I was one of the most dedicated students. I was always eager to have a front seat so I could pay attention to the lectures. I left my book on the table during the lecture break to reserve the seat for the next lecture. That way I could listen well to the next lecture also. For the time being, I usually went to the library to review the lessons I had just learned.

Playful Charleston misbehaved to make me laugh. He took my reserved book from the classroom and returned it to me in the library. "Victoria, you forgot your book, and I brought it back from the seat." He grinned from ear to ear.

"Oh no!" My eyes got big. "I reserved the front seat for the next lecture," I told him.

Charleston burst out laughing and shouted, "Really? I am so sorry. Do you want me to take it back to the same seat?"

"It's okay, Charleston. I will take it back. Thank you for looking after my book. However, next time, I prefer you leave my stuff on the table, please."

Despite his mischievous behavior and goofing off, he did not seem to have any problems studying and understanding neurology. I struggled with the brain structure, nerves, veins, and nerve conductions. Charleston had built his own cabin, which gave him a geometric and three-dimensional vision.

He was an "Uncle Pie of America." His great-great-great-grandparents were from Europe and immigrated to the United States a few hundred years ago. The family had settled in Oil City, Pennsylvania, and his grandparents preserved their great-grandparent's house, which was almost three hundred years old. Charleston's father was a mixture of German and a Native American, and his mother's ethnic background was a mixture of British and French. His parents were slightly inclined toward white supremacy. In contrast, Charleston loved all races, and he was not racist.

I focused on my studies and was comfortable in the ambassador's house. One day, early in the morning, Charleston knocked on the back window of my room and whispered through the window from the street, "Victoria, it's Charleston. Would you like to play tennis with me? It's early enough. No one's at the tennis court. I have balls and two rackets. Could you come out please?"

I was in the middle of reviewing lectures. I really did not want to play tennis, but at his insistence, I left the house quietly. We played tennis for an hour and stopped at the small mall nearby and window-shopped. Afterward, we had breakfast together at a fast-food restaurant.

He was hilarious, and we laughed together. As time went on, he visited quite often, and we became close friends. We spent time together and occasionally went out for dinner or walked around the city, enjoying the native's dance on the street and the merengue music.

In my memory, I was devoted to nothing but study and used the empty classroom until late in the night. I will never forget how scared I was about passing by the cadaver room all alone at night. This was before I had taken my anatomy examination.

Some students were as diligent as I was and as focused on passing the test. They would do anything to pass the test and even broke into the cadaver room after the school hour to learn and memorize body structures in detail. I joined this group of students to enter the cadaver room without the school's permission. We studied, inspected, and quizzed each other on the cadaver parts to get better grades. Initially, I was fearful about the lifeless body, but my desperation to excel at the test eliminated the terrified feelings. We students analyzed the cold, dark body numerous times and repeatedly went over the anatomy. We studied hard and received good grades. Perseverance, hope, and purpose were the products of our determination to create a bright future.

Charleston and I both passed anatomy and neurology with high scores.

In general, we students were financially poor during our school days and lived on a budget. Despite that fact, Charleston loved to shop and buy trivial things and was fascinated by nonessential items sold at the street vendors' market.

When we had a clinical brain dissection with the professor, I was engrossed in learning the small parts of the brain and gave the professor my undivided attention. Out of the blue, Charleston brought painted feathers to the classroom. He gave them to me as a gift. I was flabbergasted. His humorous behavior in the middle of the class annoyed me. All our classmates laughed with him. His odd action made me think, why was he enthralled by these useless, colorful chicken feathers? I wondered about his mindset. I did not like the feathers, and I did not want to keep them.

A few days later, Charleston visited the ambassador's house while I was studying. He rang the bell at the crack of dawn and greeted me with a big smile and his typical lighthearted manner.

"What's up, this early morning?" I asked. "I hope you did not wake the ambassador's family?"

"I wanted to show you something cute." He slowly placed the wiggly creature on his bear arm.

I jumped up quickly and screamed. "Yuck! What is it?"

"I found a fuzzy caterpillar," he said. "It squirmed gradually from his arm toward his wrist. Instantly he stretched his arm to me.

I panicked; afraid the undesirable worm might move toward me. "Oh my God!" I cried out. "Charleston, that is not cute. I hate any slithering creatures. Please get rid of it."

He chuckled, standing in front of the house like a street loiterer.

As I had anticipated, the landlord, Mrs. Cantu heard us and was startled by my frightened voice. She was not happy about the commotion outside of her house or about Charleston clowning around with the caterpillar and ringing the bell before daybreak. Late in the morning, sure enough, Mrs. Cantu gently reprimanded me, saying that her husband had previously suffered a heart attack, and he was retired. He needed to be relaxed and have a quiet, peaceful environment.

I completely understood her concerns. "I am so sorry about the disturbance next to the house early in the morning. I admit my misdeed, madam. I will definitely mention to Charleston the ambassador's condition and remind him that he should not make noise and ring the doorbell that early."

The next day, I saw Charleston at school, and everything seemed to be normal again.

I studied hard, and it paid off. I received a scholarship, which helped me to save some money.

I told Charleston not to visit me at the house. Nevertheless, he came back early in the morning and rang the doorbell again.

I came out quietly and asked him, "Is there an emergency or something wrong with you? Are you okay?"

Looking like a little kid, he greeted me innocently. "Would you like to have breakfast with me? I was going to have breakfast and thought about you. Please, let us go together. I will drive you."

I sneaked out noiselessly. We went to a small fast-food restaurant. Freshly made mango juice was my favorite. We talked for a while and walked around the tennis courts without playing.

Later that morning, I returned to the ambassador's house, and Charleston followed me.

"See you later!" I said, speaking softly.

He still did not leave and insisted on seeing my room. He was curious about how I had been studying in that room.

"You cannot come inside this house," I told him sharply. "Mrs. Cantu is old school, and she is a serious Catholic believer. She does not want a man in my room."

Charleston insisted on seeing my room. "I will not touch or kiss you. You are paying rent. Why I cannot I see your room? I am not intruding on her house. I just want to see your room."

I explained to him about this family and that they had different cultural traditions that came along with their Roman Catholic background. Santo Domingo was not America, and they were not the same. We had to respect their culture and their beliefs.

He did not want to understand my explanation, and he seemed disappointed.

I felt uneasy about rejecting him.

"I am not a Dominican," he persisted. "I am American. What is wrong with seeing your study room? I am not going to do anything. I am curious how you have been studying. You were able to receive a scholarship, but I did not get it. Truly, I would like to see the former ambassador's house. He was popular in Dominica in the past."

"Gee whiz! You are acting like a child. What does it matter where or how I study, Charleston? You must be quiet. Will you promise?"

He nodded silently.

"All right, friend, we are taking a chance with this world tour. You must be unnoticeable like a church mouse. Please do not talk too much. Tootsie, hang onto your hat and follow me."

We tiptoed through the house and slithered into my study room. I should have known better. Charleston did not behave as he had promised he would.

He looked around the room and he sat at my desk. "This chair pumps the power that makes you study harder. Is this how you were able to get a scholarship?"

His clowning jests made me laugh, and we momentarily forgot to be quiet. Oops! We woke the big baby, the master of the house, Mrs. Cantu walked into the room without knocking on the door. Her facial expression was unfriendly. She immediately chased him out. As I expected, she told me to find a different house within a week. I knew that my sincere apology would not change her instant decision.

Shoot, Charleston! What am I going to do now?

I felt like Charleston had set a firecracker under Mrs. Cantu, and it was the kiss of death. My time living in the comfortable house next to the school was over. It was history now. Well, I decided not to cry over spilled milk.

The next day, Charleston was astonished to learn what had happened at the house. He felt terrible about what he had done and that his actions had contributed to my situation. We all live and learn. Living in the ambassador's house was not my cup of tea, anyway, so be it. There was no dull moment with him. Now I had to find a house to live in temporarily.

I was looking for a pleasant apartment, behind the school and next to the ocean. The apartment manager informed me that there would be a vacancy in three weeks. My dilemma was, where I would stay until then? Charleston was living in a one-bedroom, and I could not share a bed with him.

Within a week, Charleston discovered from his classmate that one of CIFAS students had an extra room, which was empty. It was perfect to rent for two weeks, before I moved to my new apartment. This Iranian student had rented a three-bedroom place. He was married to a Puerto Rican lady, who stayed at home. His old brother wanted to attend CIFAS and was preparing to enroll in class. Initially, they seemed polite and kind. Under the difficult circumstance, I paid the rental fee in cash and moved in the following day.

In the interim, my motor scooter driving had improved. I had been shopping and carrying groceries in its basket, which was attached to the front of the scooter. Frequently, I bought a roast chicken and made a quick sandwich for meals. I had been noticing my roasted chicken would be more than half gone when I had only had a little, and there would hardly any leftover meat in the bag. I asked my roommates about the disappearing chicken. "Have you seen my bag of chicken that I just bought and put in the communal refrigerator?"

Unpleasantly, the inhabitants answered in the negative tone of voice they knew nothing about the chicken.

The night before I moved into my own apartment next to the coastline, the couple forced me to pay them a whole month's rent instead of paying only for the two weeks of my lodging. I disagreed, as we had originally contracted only for two weeks. The couple became aggressive and attempted to push me against the wall. I was appalled at their dishonesty. You never could judge a book by its cover. I had thought they were courteous people, but they were behaving differently now to get more money from me.

As the pair literally attacked me to collect money we had not agreed on, I recalled how, just a week ago, they' tried to match me with his brother. Of course, I was not interested in becoming involved in a personal relationship. That perceived rejection might have triggered resentments.

That night was the end of the two weeks that I had agreed to stay with strangers. I was thankful that the morning dawn broke the dark side of the night in this weird place.

I went to the school next day early in the morning and left the lodging place. I told Lynn, my close friend, what had happened. She was distressed and shocked. She recruited more than a dozen handsome white medical school students, and they wanted to get justice against the Iranians' misconduct.

The fifteen students revved their motorcycles loudly and drove up and down in a line around the Iranians' place, like an angry mob. Meanwhile, Lynn and Charleston went into the room where I had stayed and removed my belongings. The Iranians quickly went inside their room, terrified by the unexpected mass agitation against them, and did not come out. Charleston wanted to show them his muscle. I recommended against it.

Finally, I moved to the seaside apartment. Lynn was interested in being my roommate, which was a good idea. She took the second bedroom. She had been a professional model in America before she'd enrolled in medical school. She had earned some money as a fashion model in Santo Domingo while she was studying medicine.

She had a striking figure, shiny blond hair, and twinkling blue eyes and attracted many students and professors. Kind and well dressed, she got good grades despite not being dedicated to studying. Lynn went out on dates with a current Dominican ambassador. She drove his Mercedes to school. She loved parties and enjoyed sunbathing around the hotel swimming pool. Her dresses were noticeably beautiful, and her swimming suit body caught people's attention. She wore professional makeup and usually decorated her hair with red Hibiscus flowers.

I purchased both indoor furniture and outdoor furniture for the balcony and shared them with her. She was accustomed to taking a nap and relaxing in her hammock in the corner of the living room after school.

Toward the last course of basic science, many more students dropped out of the program upon facing difficulties finding an accredited clinical training program in the United States to join. Two UTESA medical students passed the advanced basic science knowledge examination in America. They were able to transfer to US medical schools. As a result of the difficulty finding clinical medical training, some students went to Europe, either France or Germany, to be trained before they could take a medical licensing exam.

At the time, six Caucasian male students were selected by the American dean of the school to be trained in the United States under a sponsored program. Disappointingly, although I was among the top ten in the program and received a scholarship, I was not selected to be trained in America. I was obviously not a Caucasian. At that moment, my unknown future provoked anxiety.

Despite the reality I was facing, I assured myself with different affirmations:

"When the going gets tough, the tough get going."

As FDR stated, "The only thing we have to fear is fear itself."

"Rome was not built in a day." And to become a doctor was not an easy path.

"Where there is will, there is way."

I thought of Thomas Edison, who had made more than a thousand mistakes before he had invented the first successful light bulb, which changed our lifestyle and made our world a better place.

CHAPTER 11

Where There's a Will There 's a Way

My bravery and courage would lead me to become a doctor. I had the willpower to rise above my destiny. I heard students swear that, if no one else from this school became a doctor, Victoria Gates would be a doctor—by virtue of her dedication, commitment, and devotion. I also believed in myself. If any other student became a doctor, there was no reason I could not be a doctor. Furthermore, my ironclad determination and perseverance would help me accomplish my mission and goals. Along with the students whispering their predictions, I reminded myself often, "Where there's a will, there's way." I would go through either mountain or sea.

Charleston was charismatic, humorous, and lovable. He had a down to earth character and possessed excellent interpersonal skills. He knew the American dean's office address and St. Francis Hospital, where the six selected students would be trained in Milwaukee, Wisconsin.

When the basic science courses were completed at UTESA, our next turning point would be established based on where we were trained in clinical medicine. The basic sciences learning courses were simpler, based on the textbooks and the professors. The hands-on skills, on the other hand, were extremely important, and learning advanced, high-tech medicine would make or break our futures. At this juncture, another 10 percent of the students gave up and returned to the United States.

"No matter what happens to me, I will pack my books and belongings and move to Milwaukee. I will stay at the dean's office at the clinic until he accepts me to be trained at the St. Francis Hospital," I declared to Charleston.

Charleston knew me well enough not to argue with me.

I gave all my furniture in the seaside apartment to Lynn and left Santo Domingo. Jim was still studying at CIFAS, and I had not seen him for more than a year. I did not have the chance to say goodbye to him when I left Santo Domingo. I flew to Milwaukee by myself in the middle of the snowy winter months in Wisconsin.

I rented an apartment close to St. Francis Hospital and bought a car. Shortly after I settled in the apartment, I drove to the clinic. I spoke with the receptionist.

The receptionist, Martha, told me, "Dr. Jackson is seeing patients. I will let him know you are here. Would you like to wait for him in the lobby? May I get some coffee for you?"

"Thanks for your kindness," I said. "I had coffee earlier. I'll wait for him here."

Martha was polite and friendly.

In the intermittent time, my mind rushed through some negative thoughts. *What if he refuses to accept me? What will my next step be?*

I will knock on every door until one person opens a door for me, I told myself.

I sat there anxiously but quietly. The dean examined a couple of patients, who were there for follow-up visits.

When he came to the front office, he saw me in the lobby. He walked toward me with a surprised expression on his face. "Who are you?" he asked. "What's your name? What can I do for you?"

"Dr. Jackson, I am honored to meet you," I have began. "My name is Victoria Gates, and I've come here from UTESA University. I know you are the dean of UTESA for the clinical training program. I was one among the top 5 percent in the program and received a scholarship, but I was not selected for training in America. Before medical school, I worked in various hospitals in Southern California for many years. I am thirty years old. I came to America from Seoul, Korea, at twenty-one, all by myself, to become a doctor. Please accept me to be trained, along with the six selected students, at the St. Francis Hospital. I have packed my possessions and flown here from Santo Domingo. I have already rented an apartment near St. Francis. I hope you understand my daring behavior and audacious hope and that you recognize my fervent desire to be a doctor.

"Dr. Jackson, there is no choice. I must stay here until you can accept me to learn clinical medicine under your program. I promise you will not be disappointed in me. I will be a good student." I was sure of myself.

Dr. Jackson listened intensely to my story, a look of amazement crossing his face. "What is your name again?" He appeared to understand my unshakable dream. He smiled at me.

"My name is Victoria Gates, sir," I answered swiftly.

"You are quite different and do not back down with your tenacious determination. I like your perseverance," he said. "Did you say that you have a place to stay? How about a car? Do you have way to commute here?"

"I rented an apartment and purchased a car the day before yesterday. I am Roman Catholic, and I give thanks for Catholic hospitals, like St. Francis Hospital."

He stared at me and grinned. "My training program will be starting next week. I will see you here Monday at 8:00 a.m."

I could not believe that he had accepted me on the spot. I almost jumped up and down, but I calmly showed my gratitude. Thanks be to God! I was in the training program through God's grace. "You saved my dream and helped me tremendously," I told Dr. Jackson. "I will help others when the time comes. I thank you again from my deepest heart. I am looking forward to seeing you next week."

I had to release the ecstatic news that I had been accepted to his training program. I quietly cried out, "Yes, yes, yes!" I raised both of my arms and praised the Lord. I had confirmed for myself—whatever happened in my life, I should never give up my aspirational dreams.

The six selected students and I were blessed because of being trained under licensed physicians in Wisconsin. We did rotations and trained in clinical skills with Wisconsin Medical School students. Permission was granted for us to participate in faculty disciplinary meetings, lectures, and patient care. After finishing our clinical rotations, we went to Saint Luke Hospital to listen to teaching videotapes.

Charleston was a semester behind me, and he had no choice but to stay in Santo Domingo. Initially, he refused to stay there and quit studying. He would rather fly with me to Wisconsin.

"If you drop out of school, I will never see you again," I told him.

He then decided to finish the basic science courses in Santo Domingo. In the meantime, one of my classmates flew to Dr. Jackson's clinic and expressed a wish to join the clinical training at St. Francis Hospital. Unfortunately, she could not convince Dr. Jackson. Her ancestry was German, and she went to Germany for her clinical training.

A few months later, Charleston flew to my place in Wisconsin after he had completed his basic science courses.

"What am I going to do with you, Charleston? I think, Dr. Jackson may not accept you for his clinical training program, since he declined the female student who also has a scholarship."

I had been working hard and received good evaluations for my clinical knowledge and skills.

Favorably, Dr. Jackson was pleased with my dedication and often teased me with a few Korean words. He was an internationally well-known psychiatrist and had earned three PhD and spoke seven languages. Additionally, he had published books and had given speeches on television programs. Recently, he had finished a criminal law degree and passed his bar examination.

Dr. Jackson was kind, smart, and knowledgeable, yet stern. We were afraid of Dr. Jackson during the clinical training. All of us walked on eggshells and dared not violate the rules or regulations of the program. What if he terminated the program? We would be in a disastrous situation. The six handsome Caucasian students who had been initially acccepted for the program fit in well with the Wisconsin Medical college students, and Charleston would harmonize perfectly with them.

I went to see Dr. Jackson regarding my personal matter one week after Charleston arrived. Dr. Jackson was in his office. "Is there any possibility to see you briefly before you get off?" I asked.

"Are you having any problems at the hospital? Is it an urgent issue?"

"No, sir. I have a personal drawback."

"Would you wait for me here? I am almost done today."

When he returned to his office, I explained my difficult situation with Charleston, who needed to be encouraged. He had the potential to be an excellent doctor in the future. "Charleston is altruistic, selfless, and caring," I told him. "We studied together. Now, he is completed his basic science and has flown here to stay with me. I completely understand that I am asking a lot of you. I would like you to let Charleston be trained here with me. You are the person who can protect his future." I clasped my two hands tightly and silently prayed.

Dr. Jackson did not say a word for a few minutes. He appeared to be thinking about this unexpected student, who had come after he had declined to accept the female student from UTESA not long ago. He seemed to be taking this matter seriously for a while. I listened nervously as he finally said, "I want you come to my office with him, tomorrow at 9:00 a.m."

"Absolutely, sir. I will bring him at 9:00 a.m." I was excited.

I had rented a two-bedroom flat in Greenfield, Wisconsin. We converted the living room to a study area next to the dining room. We did not buy any fancy furniture. A large simple board was used for our study table, and we slept on mattresses with bed frames.

I informed Charleston what Dr. Jackson had said. I kept praying that Charleston would be accepted and join our training program. Unknown futures and waiting times were not the most comfortable phase. I reminded myself again that the only thing we had to fear was fear itself. I decided to do right and live one day at a time and not worry about the unknown tomorrow.

Our living expenses budget was tight, since we did not work for a couple years, except for a moonlighting job I took that brought in a small amount of income. Charleston was completely broke and worse off than I was. He did not have any formal suits and needed decent clothes for his interview with Dr. Jackson. We purchased an inexpensive suit and a couple of neckties for him.

Charleston had a warm heart, a kind nature, and a humble personality. He smiled often and had striking deep blue shiny eyes that attracted people.

The following morning, we sat anxiously in Dr. Jackson's office. Dr. Jackson walked into his lobby, where we were waiting for him. He greeted us and guided Charleston to his office for an interview.

A few minutes later, Charleston came out of Dr. Jackson's office, with an enthusiastic smile. "I am in, Victoria! We can train together."

"Thanks be to God! We are blessed."

We expressed our appreciation to Dr. Jackson profusely and left his office.

Some of the professors at the Wisconsin Medical School were our medical clinic preceptors. One was an expert neurosurgeon who performed incredible microscopic laser brain surgeries, which was amazingly impressive. His technic was far more advanced than that of other surgeons. He had wonderful leadership skills and was an amiable character who we respected greatly.

Charleston and I supported each other and went through hardship lightly. We finally completed clinical medicine together. After all, we had another obstacle ahead—another challenge to face. We would have to pass the ECFMG (the Educational Commission for Foreign Medical Graduates) to be accepted for a residency program. Even native US citizens who had studied overseas had trouble passing the ECFMG, and some students gave up.

Before we left Wisconsin, we invited Dr. Jackson for dinner. He initially did not accept our invitation, but we persuaded him to join us. We pinched our savings, and we were excited to go out for dinner. I gave my savings to Charleston. At the end of the delicious dinner, the waitress brought the bill with a smile, and Charleston joyfully received it. Suddenly, his expression changed. Charleston looked fearful when he discovered the total amount of the bill.

Dr. Jackson and I looked at Charleston's face and we tried to figure out what was wrong with him. Finally, Dr. Jackson asked Charleston. "What's wrong? Are you okay?"

Charleston humbly and honestly explained to Dr. Jackson. "I thought we had enough money to cover the expenses for dinner, but it won't cover the tip. I am so sorry. This is embarrassing."

Dr. Jackson laughed. "I will treat you and pay for the dinner and the tip," he told us.

"No, sir. We really want to do something to appreciate your support. You opened our future dreams. Would you just pay the tip, and we will be happy to take care of dinner?" Charleston implored.

Dr. Jackson liked Charleston's honesty. We had a lovely time and a wonderful meal together.

Dr. Jackson planned to attend our graduation as a clinical dean. Astonishingly, he went to a place to learn how to skydive. Unexpectedly, he landed in an incorrect position, and he broke his ankle. He was brave, but unfortunately, he had an accident. Despite the injury, he came and gave a speech during our graduation ceremony.

Charleston and I passed the ECFMG. We were accepted into a residency program for Internal Medicine at West Penn Hospital (West Pennsylvania Hospital).

I visited Charleston's mountain cabin, which he had built many years before our residency program started. It was on the top of a hill in Oil City, Pennsylvania. One of his Danish friends was renting his place while he was in school. His log cabin was peaceful. It had an open field surrounded by trees and populated by wild animals, such as deer, rabbits, pheasants, ducks, and many more.

His neighbors, farmers, visited his cabin at the crack of dawn. They shared morning coffee and toast with fried eggs. The freshly brewed aroma of coffee woke me up and made me join their daily rituals. The scenery rejuvenated my well-being.

The lifestyle was too slow for me. While Charleston did not mind becoming a house call doctor, there was no way I could be a physician in a small village. My mind drift to the past when we were studying for the ECFMG in Southern California. At the time, I decided to move with Charleston into one of my houses close to the Kaplan review examination center and two blocks from Loyola Law School.

The ECFMG was not a freebie, and it was hard to pass.

One UTESA medical student—a forty-two-year-old psychologist—came to Santo Domingo with his wife to study medicine. He struggled to learn basic science of medicine. He studied hard and, in the end, passed the ECFMG sooner than most of the students. Soon after he received the great news, though, he had a sudden heart attack and died, leaving his wife alone. It was beyond sad and tragic.

Many unimaginable stories weaved together the history of overseas medical school. Numerous unthinkable dramas intertwined a tapestry of ambitious adventures along the pathway to becoming a doctor in Santo Domingo or at other overseas medical schools.

During graduation, another bit of shocking news swept the campus and made us tearful. A smart student who had studied hard and was finally ready to graduate the following day had suffered a great loss. Her husband had flown to Santo Domingo to congratulate her on her great achievement. They had celebrated and made love on the night before the graduation. In the middle of making love, he had

had a heart attack and had died on top of her. I can only imagine the state of her traumatized, broken heart.

I personally witnessed, heard, and experienced many beyond heartbreaking narratives during medical school in Santo Domingo. Life was not fair. Nevertheless, life moved on, and again we were racing against a ticking clock. What to do or what not to do required my discernment.

My family plan was ignored, and having a child was not the priority at the time. My entire energy was consumed and focused on passing the exams. The ECFMG was difficult and required serious study. Charleston could not afford his payment for the course. I paid $1,500 for his review course at Kaplan.

We studied hard at Kaplan until the center closed. Afterward, we went to the library of Loyola Law School and tried to memorize what we had learned until midnight. There were many law students studying late at night. Some had group study sessions in the open library, and others used cubical areas.

There was a student who always studied in the library for a long time. Normally, he would fall asleep right before midnight, in a standing position, clenching his fists on the countertop. He snored loudly enough to wake the dead. This student's determination reminded me of us, and we believed that he would be an excellent lawyer soon. Even though he snored loudly, none of the students paid attention to his fatigued condition, mostly students were busy with their own assignments.

At the Kaplan center, Charleston would sit next to me and listen to the review course material on tape. Occasionally, he would send me a note with the cartoon character Charlie Brown floating over the water under the sun. He must have been daydreaming of the beach instead of concentrating on his test material.

We disciplined ourselves daily without taking a day off. And in the end, we both passed the difficult ECFMG exam. We visited a friend of his who worked at a law firm in South Carolina. He gave us information on where to go to apply for a residency position before we were accepted to West Penn Hospital. His friend was married. The couple lived on Myrtle Beach on the coast, and their yard was sandy. Charleston loved people, and he had friends in many different states.

We enjoyed our visit. Charleston wanted to live in Pennsylvania because he had his cabin there, along with all his family, including his mother, father, two sisters, and grandmother. That was one of the reasons we got our residency training in Pittsburgh. In the interim, I sold one of my California houses, in case we need place to live.

West Penn Hospital was affiliated with the Pittsburgh Medical School. The hospital faculty and preceptors were top-rated doctors. Among them were a nephrologist and a cardiologist who had graduated from Harvard Medical School. They had superb knowledge about their subspecialties and had made innovative, cutting-edge discoveries.

Shortly after our training started, Charleston lost his confidence in his ability to handle sick patients and quit internal medicine training in Pittsburg. He wanted to be a pediatrician.

Simultaneously, one of our classmates in UTESA was training in a pediatric residency program in Jacksonville, Florida. He recommended that Charleston apply at Heart Hospital in Pensacola.

Charleston wanted me to go with him for his interview for his pediatric residency program. We drove to Florida together. Most his books and belongings were packed into a small trailer attached to the back of my car. Night driving was safer because there was no traffic but getting there took all night long. We reached Jacksonville the following morning. We stayed at our classmate's apartment. Finally, we took showers and drove to Pensacola. He interviewed, and he was promptly accepted into the pediatric residency program.

Charleston wanted to live in a house. We contacted a realtor. The realtor showed us houses, and we chose one of the properties, which was located on a hillside next to a public park. The house was clean and had a basketball hoop in the driveway. It offered him some privacy, as it was some distance from the neighbors. Charleston loved this house, and we purchased the place for him. The house was located closed to Heart Hospital. I hoped he would become an outstanding pediatrician, while enjoying the cozy, quiet house. Charleston was happy living in a new home. He appreciated my efforts to support him unconditionally. He wanted to marry me.

I returned to Pittsburgh for my internal medicine training at West Penn hospital. I did not buy a house but, rather, rented a small apartment across from the hospital just for convenience.

Pittsburgh was one of the greatest steel manufacturers in the world and accounted for 10 percent of all steel producing in the United States. The air was contaminated with the smell of sulfur. A unique city, Pittsburgh lies in southwestern Pennsylvania, where the Allegany and Monongahela rivers joined and formed Ohio River. These rivers helped make the center of the state's inland waterway system. Pittsburgh's factories still lined the bank of the Allegheny, the Monongahela, and the Ohio. Approximately 95 percent of Pittsburgh's people were born in the United States. The city had many residents of German, Irish, Italian, and Polish ancestry.

The residency training was not easy, and our beepers constantly went off. Notably, when we were paged "Code Stat" or "Code Blue" (the codes were emergency alert systems to doctors and assigned health care staff), on-call residents immediately ran to the designated area. At the same time, everybody ran whenever a patient whose life was threatened—by heart attack, sudden unconsciousness, respiratory arrest, and other such dire circumstances—had been admitted. Residents were invariably sleep deprived during training.

Amid my residency year, one of the trainees in New York made a fatal mistake due to lack of sleep. After that incident, nationwide residency programs were changed, and our residency regulation improved. We were able to have extra sleep and rest after on-call duty.

My senior resident at West Penn Hospital, Lynn, had been raised in a wealthy father. She often invited me for dinner, and we enjoyed seeing a ballet performance of Tchaikovsky's *Swan Lake* and a play of Victor Hugo's *Les Miserable* at Heinz Hall, a performing arts center and concert hall located at 600 Penn Avenue. The historical Heinz Hall was still well preserved.

One day, Lynn took me to Mount Washington. From up on the hill, we looked down at the city of Pittsburgh. In front of a towering modern condominium called Tremont was Point State Park, with a large, beautiful water fountain, with multiple jets shooting up in the air and creating tall spectacular springs. The city's three rivers ran together below Tremont. The dignified building was remarkable, and its luxurious structure was better than most hotels. An unknown architect had developed the outstanding high-rise condo on Mount Washington. Unable to finish his project due to lack of sufficient funds, he'd ended up bankrupt, and the bank had taken over the building.

I was impressed by the shiny, tinted blue glass building and received some information about the condo from a local realtor. After I toured the building, I purchased a smaller unit in the Pavilion of Tremont. There were three main buildings. Building A was the tallest, and C was shortest of the three—though all three buildings still reached towering heights. Many units were not yet completed. The realtor was able to show me another unit that had been purchased by the former wife of Johnny Carson. This condo was located on the top floor of building B, which was surrounded with tall, blue-tinted glass windows from floor to ceiling.

The city view was magnificent. I looked down at the city from the twenty-second floor. My peripheral nerves tingled, and I felt a sudden dizziness. I had to step back instantly from the tall, vast windows. The small patio offered a marvelous open city view.

Johnny Carson's ex-wife's unit was decorated with a recessed, octangular beveled mirror on the ceiling in the master bedroom. It displayed an ostentatious wealth. The realtor stated that Carson's ex-wife had paid more than $1 million for her condo in 1988.

During my second year of residency training at West Penn Hospital, Charleston quit his pediatric program in Pensacola. Charleston could not endure seeing little kids suffer. He could not tolerate children's bleeding wounds, especially after any kind of accident. He changed his training program once again, this time focusing on becoming a psychiatrist. He flew to the University of Syracuse in New York. Once more, he did not have any problem securing a position to be trained.

Before he moved to Syracuse, he visited his friend in Alabama on the way to visit me in Pittsburgh. Charleston brought a special gift of a decorative crystal prismatic ball, which had multiple facets; its dispersed beams of rainbows when the sun hit the prisms. It was a nice piece of crystal, but his lack of dedication to medicine made me think twice about our relationship.

Even though he was excited to see me, I was not happy due to his deficiency of perseverance. We had planned to get married, but I was skeptical about his commitment. We mutually decided to end our relationship for that reason. He could be free in New York.

Charleston and I had a good friendship. We went through difficult challenges together. We had cherished memories, but we drifted apart in different directions. It was stressful for both of us. The traumatic emotional stress caused me to need a change environment, and I moved to a different state. I rented out my Tremont condo; left Pittsburgh; and moved to Wheeling, West Virginia.

I had a beautiful hillside town house apartment in Wheeling, where I completed my third-year residency program.

CHAPTER 12

My Decision to Become an Oncologist (Moonlighting)

Wheeling is an industrial city on the Ohio River in northern West Virginia, and it is the seat of Ohio County. Wheeling lies on a level plane, which rises to steep hills alongside the river. Two bridges connect Wheeling Island with the rest of the city. Tourism is the most important industry in Wheeling, which attracts visitors with its parks, historical sites, and local events. West Virginia, part of Virginia until the Civil War and nestled in the Appalachian highlands, has some of the most rugged land in the United States.

Bordered by Ohio, Wheeling had two modern hospitals and served as medical center for the surrounding region. I completed my third year of residency at the Wheeling Medical Center.

I was lonely in West Virginia, and I started moonlighting at an emergency room in Ohio toward the end of my residency training. On July 4, I was working at the ER in the Ohio Medical Center. A beautiful teenager girl came in after her dog had attacked her cheek with its paw. Her skin was torn and bleeding. Her dog had been going after a piece of hamburger meat she was flipping on the grill while helping her mother.

Thank God, I had been trained how to stitch torn skin. I felt awful about what had happened to the center of her face. I hoped it would heal without a scar. This pretty girl loved her dog and did not get mad at the dog. She told me that her dog did not know the difference and had been excited looking at the piece of meat. I was impressed and amazed at her loving kind heart and her maturity at her age.

The next week, I was moonlighting again at the same ER. An extremely debilitated woman came to the ER, complaining of chest discomfort and indigestion. The patient was promptly connected to a heart monitor. All workers at the ER were busy working on other patients' care. I attentively kept an eye on the woman's heart rhythm on the monitor, which suddenly changed to an abnormal beat called PVC (premature ventricular contraction) and then progressed to the irregular rhythm of atrial tachycardia.

Right away, I alerted the director of the ER doctors to the patient's condition. The patient was transferred to the intensive care unit (ICU). At that juncture, the patient had started projectile vomiting, which splashed on me while the nurses transferred the patient onto the gurney. The nurses and I pushed the patient's gurney to the ICU unit.

The patient did not respond to her name and became unconscious. I intubated the patient and ordered the respiratory therapist to set up a ventilator and connect oxygen.

The massive heart attack almost killed her, and I saved her life by observing the patient condition carefully. She regained her consciousness and opened her eyes. I was proud of myself. I had applied the skills I had gained through training and had been able to save the patient's life.

Soon after the patient's condition was stabilized, I found that my clothes were covered with her vomit. I took a quick shower and changed my scrubs. Once again, I was glad that I had an opportunity to be trained under excellent preceptors and at outstanding hospitals.

The Ohio Medical Center staff members appreciated my skills, and the nurses gave me a delightful card and a small gift. They even served me extra food whenever I would eat at the hospital cafeteria, including double stacks of pancakes. It was a wonderful feeling to be loved. I also earned $5,500 for two days of the moonlightings. After completion of my internal medicine training, I wanted to be trained for a subspecialty of hematology and oncology.

I had a flashback to the moment that had first made me want to be an oncologist. I received a phone call from my sister been Seoul. The night before, I had dreamt about one of my front teeth falling out, a sign among

Koreans that marked the death of a close family member. A ghastly sensation overwhelmed me right after I woke up.

Sure enough, my sister's voice on the phone was frantic. "My husband is in critical condition. He's been admitted to the hospital." She could hardly talk, and her voice shook with crying.

My brother-in-law, Kim, Sander, was the son of multimillionaires, and he had graduated from the most prestigious university in Seoul. He loved music and was especially fascinated with opera and chamber music. As a result of his influence and the environment he created, my four-year-old nephew could identify opera songs such as those from *The Marriage of Figaro, The Magic Flute* by Mozart, *Swan Lake*, and *The Nutcracker*. My nephew danced around the room before bedtime prayers. He was cute and smart.

Over the years, my brother-in-law had started an oil business. He went to Kuwait, a small Arab country in southwestern Asia at the north end of the Persian Gulf bordered by Iraq and Saudi Arabia. This desert land was one of the world's leading petroleum producers. Once an extremely poor country, until 1946, Kuwait is now one of the richest and most progressive countries in the world because of its oil. My brother-in-law made money with the sale of oil to foreign nations by the government and had played a role in creating Kuwait's wealth.

It was a well-known fact that exposure to petroleum causes multiple myeloma. Sander gradually developed clinical symptoms of easy bruising, bone pain, depression, mood swings, and extreme fatigability. Eventually, he was diagnosed with multiple myeloma at age forty-two. Multiple myeloma is a malignant cancer that develops by way of abnormal plasma cells. White cells in the bone marrow and plasma cells help the immune system fight off infection. Cancer changes normal cells to abnormal cells, which form tumors in multiple locations throughout the bone marrow, and the condition makes it difficult for the body to fight off infection.

My brother-in-law's family was well educated and wealthy. Sander's sister married a doctor who was an author of a medical textbook and established a large hospital in Seoul. Even his mother went to a famous university in Japan to achieve higher education, even before the Korean War.

His entire family was shocked by his diagnosis and told him to return to Seoul at once. The day after his arrival, his treatments were started by an oncologist who had been trained in America. Regretfully, his treatments were brief, and he developed leukemia as result of the strong chemotherapy. Clearly, the traditional concepts of treatment—and the belief that more drugs would kill cancer cells—were misinformed. On the contrary, modern cutting-edge medicine recognized that high doses of chemo drug treatments had been proven to be the wrong course of action. I believed that precise adjusted chemo drugs, based on the individual condition, brought better outcomes, and enhanced survival rate.

Sander's father owned a part of the university hospital, and my brother-in-law was treated well whenever he was admitted to the hospital with complications and side effects of the treatment.

This time, he had been admitted with serious systemic organ failure. The admitting oncologist informed my sister of his grave situation. He was in critical condition. As I said, her frantic call came after I had had an ominous dream. As soon as I hung up, I planned and flew to Seoul the next morning. My brother-in-law was confused and debilitated, and he was clinically dying. His kidneys had shut down, and he was incapacitated, unable to walk by himself.

He was the nicest Korean man I had ever known. I was so proud that he was my brother-in-law. I stayed with him all night long and let my sister have some rest. My jet lag did not bother me at all, although I had not caught a wink of sleep. That evening, Sander's admitting doctor also informed me that his survival chances were low. I assisted him through the night.

The following morning, he could not breathe, and an on-call doctor attempted to intubate him. I was wondered whether prolonging his life in this nearly lifeless condition would benefit him, given his suffering.

My sister was extremely frightened. All his family members arrived immediately and surrounded his bedside. Shortly after, he fell into unconsciousness and stopped breathing. The on-call doctor's resuscitation was futile. Shocked wailing, pouring tears, and deep sorrow diffused the room like a dark shadow.

My brother-in-law's face was peaceful, despite the anemic, cold, and motionless body without blood circulation. My sister mourned, nearly breaking down, alongside his entire family, whose anguished sobs over their lost filled the room with misery.

I had never experienced such painful, helpless, sorrowful agony.

Everybody struggled with uncontrollable torment with this death—with an outcome that we could not manipulate. Life and death are only controlled by God. Death is an inevitable part of the life process. Life teaches us to accept our creator's purpose.

A grand funeral procession was held for my brother-in-law. A miles-long motorcade and loads of flowers packed inside trucks drove to the cemetery. My sister, Sander's family members, friends, coworkers, and church parishioners followed the motorcades to the burial place. The followers maintained their dignity and praised the Lord our God while singing hymns, and galvanizing pain characterized the funeral procession. No one screamed their grief any longer; peace embraced the mourners, who eventually stood in silent prayer. And then the singing continued until the casket was buried. Acceptance of God's plan set in; life moves on. We walk by faith, not by sight, which will lead us in the right direction.

They memory of my beloved brother-in-law's ailment was imprinted in my brain, and I have got often how adjusting chemo drugs based on individual tolerance could make a difference in so many lives. Bearing in mind my brother-in-law's inappropriate treatments for multiple myeloma, I decided to become an oncologist.

My friend, Lynn, moved to Chicago for her cardiology fellowship training at Northwestern University. I relocated to attend the Hematology-Oncology Fellowship in La Jolla, San Diego, at Scripps Clinic. San Diego, California, lies on a bay that is one of the world's finest natural harbors. The chief naval and aerospace center are in San Diego, and the port also serves fishing fleets and oceangoing ships.

I loved the San Diego Zoo and Sea World. Downtown San Diego extended inland from the San Diego Bay to Balboa Park. There were multilevel shopping malls, such as the restaurants and entertainment complex in Horton Plaza, close to Scripps Clinic.

Noted for the illuminating discovering of the Salk polio vaccine, Scripps was located on Torrey Pines Road in La Jolla, San Diego. I was blessed to be accepted for training on the spot to. The hospital and research center were built on seven acres of land next to the Pacific Ocean, with a breathtaking view all around the hospital. It was situated atop a red soil hill next to the Hyatt Hotel, a golf course, hillside covered in walking trails that afforded cliff-side views of the vast glittering sapphire ocean.

Our fellowship trainees' room had a beautiful Pacific Ocean view through the window. Being able to work in a room with a view of the ocean was more than I had ever expected.

The entrance to Scripps Clinic had of large water fountain, and its elegant display and surrounding flower gardens created a feeling of affluence. The perfect climate attracted tourists, and the city was a popular vacation spot. The average temperature is 55 degrees Fahrenheit in the winter and 70 degrees Fahrenheit in summer. Many of the upscale residential areas and resort areas were located along the ocean, including beaches such as La Jolla, Mission, Pacific, and Delmar. One of San Diego's well-known suburban areas is Coronado, located on a peninsula in San Diego Bay.

After I rented an apartment in La Jolla close to the hospital, I flew back to West Virginia to participate in the graduation, having completed the residency training program at Wheeling Medical Center. I was thirty-six years old. The medical center threw a great party for residents, staff members, and medical preceptors to celebrate our successful accomplishment. My car was transferred by a moving agency, and a moving company moved the contents of my household, which was not much. The apartment was ready for me when I moved to La Jolla, and the transition was smooth.

Scripps Clinic was well known internationally, and I was privileged to be selected to complete my hematology and oncology fellowship there. The clinic boasted numerous renowned physicians who had developed new drugs and innovative treatment protocols.

San Diego properties were expensive. One of my realtor friends showed me an oceanfront house for sale with a market value of $8 million. The house was not big, and the only impressive part of the house was its vast open view of the Pacific Ocean from the front patio. Some of the house's metal decorations had been rusted by the salty breeze.

San Diego was an enchantingly pleasant city to work and live in. La Jolla was a wealthy and well-developed community along the beach that offered many excellent restaurants with picturesque views. Many of the restaurants featured live piano or jazz music. Local San Diego dwellers and tourists alike roamed leisurely around strip malls and cherished beautiful ocean views.

Expensive cars were parked on the street curbs. I saw a Lamborghini, its top down, for the first time. Other fancy cars, such as Porsches, Corvettes, Jaguars, and Ferraris were also parked on the street. Primarily, old people lived in La Jolla Beach, while prosperous young people lived in Del Mar Beach.

In 1991, Pardee Homes, a construction company, held a groundbreaking ceremony for the condominiums it would be building. The builder posted model floor plans, and many people were eager to choose the best location and purchase a condo before anybody else's purchases were confirmed. I chose the top corner lot, which was the most desirable location in Chateau Village, and was selected to purchase the corner lot from among many buyers. I sold my first house and paid for a new condo.

The condo was completed in February 1992. It was fun to design my patio and garden select tiles, carpets, and kitchen appliances. The condo's amenities were excellent, including a tennis court, a swimming pool, and an exercise room. Even though I was privileged to use the facilities, I did not have enough time to play tennis or swim, as I was busy studying and concentrating on my fellowship training.

I loved my quiet condo, especially since there were no mosquitoes, cockroaches, or any other insects to be seen. The upstairs had a bridged runaway surrounded by large windowpanes looking out at gorgeous views and overlooking the downstairs area and a high ceiling, which gave it the optical illusion of being bigger than it was. My condo was surrounded by windows, downstairs and upstairs. There was a hot air balloon rally below my place, and during the daytime, a spectacular assortment of colorful hot air balloons rose into the air, seeming to completely cover my windowpanes. It was an enchanting and magnificent display, and I was fascinated.

One year after my training started, my program director was transferred, and the directorship was taken over by a famous leukemia expert, who had worked at NIH (National Institutes of Health) after he had graduated from UCLA. Some of his classmates had performed prominent bone marrow transplants.

Approximately 40 percent of all research and development in the United States was financed by NIH. My new fellowship director had published 132 articles regarding leukemia treatment and had brilliantly created a turning point treatment to eliminate the targeted leukemia cells using an immunopathology method. This innovative concept protected normal cells from the toxicities introduced by high-dose chemo drugs.

I was only older famale trainee in the Scripps fellowship program, and the new director was curious about me. I was compelled by his ingenious theory and wanted to know how he had discovered the innovative treatments.

"I will teach you everything that I know," he told me.

"Really, do you promise me?" I pressed.

He was a renowned author, and most oncologists recognized his name and the articles he had published in the American Cancer Society publications. I eagerly desired to learn curative treatments from him. Soon after he began working as the fellowship program director, he was promoted to the McDonald Cancer Center as a chairman at Lexington University in Kentucky. My golden opportunity to learn everything from him collapsed, and I was disappointed when he left the Scripps Clinic. My brother-in-law had died from multiple myeloma and leukemia. I was on a quest to discover curatives treatment for leukemia and multiple myeloma.

As time passed, after I had completed my oncology fellowship at Scripps Clinic, I decided to get training in bone marrow transplant at the MD Anderson Cancer Center in Houston, Texas. Initially, I had spoken with the bone marrow transplant chairman at Stanford University in California. One of the Scripps Clinic staff recommended that I would be benefited training at the MD Anderson Cancer Center, and I decided to follow the advice.

My new condo was beautiful, and many people wanted to buy my unit. The location because, five minutes from Delmar Beach, was terrific. I cleaned the condo so that it was spotless and packed my belongings into my small Prelude to adventure to another phase of my journey.

Texas was a large state, and it took me an entire day to cross it. Cowboys, with their ten-gallon hats, have long been a symbol of Texas. Texas weather is different than that of San Diego. It was hot in July. Thank God for my air-conditioning system, which worked hard while I drove from La Jolla to Houston.

None of the medical training was easy. It required tireless hard-working and extreme discipline. I remembered how the residency program had been difficult during on-call duties. Frequently I had gone to the emergency room at the one o'clock or two o'clock in the morning to take care of grotesquely bleeding bodies damaged in car accidents or torn apart by gunshot wounds, dialysis patients experiencing kidney failure, and others suffering heart attacks. In addition, there were many respiratory failure patients, broken bones, narcotics overdoses, and intoxicated alcoholic patients. Some patients underwent surgery for amputation of their limbs.

Even though I had passed the internal medicine medical board, passing the exam for medical oncology was another challenge. Being a medical doctor is worse than being married. It requires a lifetime of dedication.

I missed working at the Scripps Clinic, but I had to move on to advance my training. Scripps Clinic was not only superb, but it was also legendary clinic. Mother Teresa had been admitted to the hospital with pneumonia. The movie star Julia Roberts had slept overnight in the lobby to see Mother Teresa. Many other famous celebrities had been admitted to Scripps Clinic over the years. Most of our preceptor doctors were internationally recognized, and one of the pathologists was known as the father of the cell staging system. Another doctor had discovered the abnormal platelets cells. Some doctors there had developed new drugs, and others had created molecular treatments. I loved Scripps, but I left for advanced transplant training because I wanted to learn additional curative methods.

MD Anderson Cancer Center was a huge hospital on thirty-five acres next to Baylor Medical School in Houston, Texas. The largest city in Texas, Houston has a major industrial center, its downtown full of tall modern skyscrapers. It lies in southeast Texas by the Gulf of Mexico. I had lived in Southern California for a long time, and I had been scared to drive on snowy roads in West Virginia. Dealing with the rolling Hills in Houston was again different from driving in the relatively flat California. Regardless of the geographic location, I was amazed to meet so many leading scientists on the frontiers of their fields and textbook authors and to be introduced to revolutionized modern treatments that opened my eyes to possibilities.

I was trained under the chief of the bone marrow transplant department, a bone marrow textbook author and the president of the Eastern Bone Marrow Transplant Association. Looking at the newly released transplant textbook written by my boss, Dr. Champlin, I felt honored. I have seen his name among those of other experts, one from the City of Hope in California and the other from Nebraska University Medical Center.

MD Anderson Cancer Center was distinguished and well known as a top-ranked cancer center in the world. This was a prime opportunity for me to learn new techniques to cure patients under the most prominent experts.

Patients flew to the center from all over the world, coming from countries such as France, Italy, Spain, and England seeking to be cured.

Bone marrow is a specialized connective tissue that fills the cavity of bones. Marrow is responsible for manufacturing blood cells in the body. It functions as a parental mechanism, and marrow produces cells.

There are two types of bone marrow transplants. The first is called allogeneic transplant, in which the transplanted marrow is not from the same individual but, rather, the donor marrow is collected from somebody other than the patient. The collected donor marrow must be genetically matched to the individual who has cancer. Otherwise, the recipient will develop a graft rejection from the donor marrow. A graft rejection could cause a fatal outcome.

The second type of bone marrow transplant is known as an autologous transplant. This type of transplant utilizes the same individual's blood. The blood goes through a special machine and collects white cells, which fight against cancer cells. The collected white blood cells are reinfused to fight the patient's cancer cells. Autologous transplants do not cause fatal outcomes, but the cure rates are much lower than those of allogeneic transplants. Cancer patients receive an extremely high dose of chemotherapy drugs to destroy all the circulating cancer cells prior to the bone marrow transplants.

If the bone marrow transplant is successful without a graft rejection, then the donor cells will regenerate healthy normal cells in the recipient's body. Tragically, in 1994, 50 percent of patients died during the administration of high-dose chemotherapy drugs from the drugs' toxicities.

My bone marrow transplant rotation was extremely stressful in terms of what I was able to learn. But I was sad and emotionally distraught when my patients died from high doses of chemo drugs during my training at MD Anderson Cancer Center. At the time, there were not many options; either the cancer cells would kill the patients, or there was a slim chance of survival from the bone marrow transplant.

Still, the chemo took its toll. At high doses, chemotherapy drugs caused viral, bacterial, and fungal infections, which contributed to consequential systemic organ failures, requiring mechanical respiratory and/or dialysis support and a variety of tubes connected to the patients' bodies. In the middle of transplant treatments, the patients skin color changed to either gray or green, and complete hair loss was a result of the drugs' toxicities.

Patients suffered tremendously from persistent vomiting and diarrhea, as if they were on a battlefield, constantly avoiding death by mere chance or sheer determination.

Leukemia patients were placed in isolated laminar airflow units. Laminar airflow was used to separate volumes of air or prevent airborne contaminants from entering an area. Visitation was restricted until patients' blood counts were adequate, and nurses entered the room in space suits. The patients were free in that they were not in jail, yet they were imprisoned in isolation rooms, living in confined environments and entrapped within their own bodies. I can only imagine the desolate loneliness.

Doctors worked as caregivers, taking care of sick patients as they went through this horrendous process to strive to regain patients' lives. We doctor also carried the heavy burden of empathic emotional pain and could easily get quickly burned out after working on the transplant floor.

A young patient had a bleeding disorder, and her blood counts had plummeted, requiring frequent blood transfusions. This complicated case had been discussed at the multidisciplinary BMT (bone marrow transplant) meeting with many transplant experts. Unanimous consensus of the experts was that the patient would benefit from BMT; otherwise, her outcome was ominous.

This patient, in her early twenties, had an infant at home. Social workers and BMT staff visited the patient's room and attempted to persuade her to have the essential treatment. She adamantly refused the options of a transplant. For more than a week, the hospital staff unsuccessfully attempted to convince her to undergo BMT treatment.

I visited the patient as a fellowship trainee. We talked about her situation at home, as well as her current physical condition. As we talked, she showed me her baby's picture.

"Your baby is really precious and good-looking," I cooed.

"Thank you," she replied. "I love him very much. He's my reason for living."

I explained the BMT protocol and that there was no alternative, given her present critical condition. She listened carefully and finally decided to have the transplant.

The medical staff and social workers were astounded that the patient had consented to undergo the BMT procedure. I prayed for her successful results and longevity of life.

I was excited to see this patient the next morning, but I could not find her in the room. I thought she had been moved to a special unit.

"Where did she go?" I asked the nurses. "Which room is she in?"

"She died after BMT yesterday," a nurse told me, sadness etched on her face.

A sudden overwhelming anguish penetrated my heart and literally stopped my heartbeat. Tears welled in my eyes when I was informed of her fatal outcome. Did I ever feel the devastating responsibility for her death? Her innocent face and the love of her baby were indelible. An unshakeable dark shadow imprinted in my brain and left me emotionally traumatized.

A doctor's duty and responsibility are to save patients' lives and care for their well-being. Doctors are not robots. We are human, vulnerable to emotional trauma. Practicing physicians and trainees require enduring discipline. Theirs is a crusade to provide treatment under the stormy situation of life and death.

I thought back to a sad story of the chairman of MD Anderson Cancer Center who had previously worked at the UCLA Cancer Center. At the time, his boss and he were recruited to help Russian victims after the Chernobyl plant explosion. A business tycoon from Arm and Hammer had sent his private jet to retrieve doctors to treat the people exposed to nuclear radiation.

As we all remember, the 1986 explosion at the Chernobyl Nuclear Power Plant near Kiev in Ukraine, then part of the Soviet Union, was the worst nuclear accident in history. An explosion and fire ripped apart the reactor and released large amounts of radioactive isotopes. The Chernobyl reactor lacked an enclosure to prevent radioactive isotopes from escaping. Soviet officials reported that thirty-one people died from radiation sickness or burns, and more than two hundred others were seriously injured. Experts expected a significant increase in the number of cancer deaths among those near the reactor.

Doctors from UCLA performed transplants on some patients, while other patients' healthy marrow was collected and preserved before they developed cancer.

The director of UCLA's Medical Center returned to California on the Arm and Hammer's private jet, leaving behind his subordinate on foreign soil all alone to finish the remaining transplants in Russia. I can only imagine how he felt when his boss disappeared on that plan. Dr. Champlin was not safe in Russia by himself and, subsequently, he took a commercial flight back to the UCLA Medical Center.

Dr. Champlin had gone on to become one of the most renowned transplant doctors in the world, and his boss has moved to the Rockefeller Research Center in New York after leaving UCLA. Dr. Champlin had been further promoted since then, becoming not only head of the BMT Department at MD Anderson Cancer Ceter, but also president of the Eastern BMT Association. Indeed, his position and situation had changed with the passing of time.

Apparently good medical training and education supported future success. When I had trained under experts at MD Anderson the teaching doctors had drilled into us trainees that chemo drugs must administered based on individuals' drug tolerance; only that would effectively induce clinical remission. My knowledge grew. And although it was also drilled into us that success did not exist without failure and that our knowledge improved as a result of unexpected poor outcomes, the tragic outcomes and complications patients experienced as a result of treatments impacted me emotionally, causing my stress to soar. My lips blistered, and I developed rashes on my face after three straight months working on the transplant floor.

The treatment of multiple myeloma was particularly important to me, and I was involved with a research team evaluating multiple myeloma-related outcomes by a variety of treatments. One of the BMT doctors and I published the data and the survival rates of multiple myeloma patients at MD Anderson.

The BMT fellowship director often teased me when I stayed at the hospital after midnight. "Fellowship trainee should be off work before the staff, Victoria!" the director would say. "It's time to leave."

I often stayed late, which was not a problem, given that I lived inside the campus dormitory. I also was still young, and had great ambition and motivation to learn with passionate desire. The transplant doctors noticed my drive to find curative therapy, and I perceived this as my mission.

The BMT chairman held a Christmas party at his house, and I was invited to attend, along with several other faculty members. We shared our personal life stories and got to know each other closely. Another time, one of the leukemia experts invited me, along with Dr. Susan O'Brien, Dr. Kantargen, and many BMT members, to gather. We had a fun time, joking with each other as if we were at a family reunion.

One late evening, the director of the fellowship program came to my room, where I was studying. She started bragging about her excellent training under Dr. Donald Thomas, who had received the first BMT Nobel Prize at Fred Hutchinson's Cancer Research Center in Seattle, Washington. My ears perked up, my eyes squinted, and I wrapped my brain around my ext. *I want to meet Dr. Donald Thomas and be trained under him*, I thought. The BMT program director continued to tell me that Dr. Thomas was exceptionally brilliant and that he could diagnose certain diseases just by the smell of the patient's feces. She mentioned that I was overly ambitious and suggested that I would be happy under Doctor Thomas. The fellowship director was single, and she admired the chairman at MD Anderson.

I was enticed. I wanted to train under Dr. Thomas. I requested that Dr. Champlin introduce me to Dr. Applebaum, who was the chairman at Fred Hutchinson.

"Why do you want to go there?" Dr. Champlin asked. "Why don't you stay here?"

"I would like to meet Dr. Thomas, who received the first Nobel Prize for BMT," I explained.

Dr. Champlin promised to introduce me to Dr. Applebaum at the grand BMT symposium in Denver, Colorado. All prominent transplant experts attended the BMT symposium. I was proud that Dr. Champlin was the president of the National BMT Association.

At the meeting, I was introduced to Dr. Applebaum. A network was important to get a position. Dr. Champlin did not understand why I wanted to work at Hutchinson in the middle of the winter. In any event, I received outstanding recommendation letters from the chairman, the program director, and the pioneer of the first gene therapies at MD Anderson.

The gene therapist was down to earth and humble. One day, the president of the United States invited him to the White House. He drove an inexpensive car; his trunk was not even completely closed while White House guard inspected his car before allowing him to enter the gates. The White House guards wondered how this man had become the leading gene therapist. They expected him to have a fancy car. I was inspired by Dr. Disseroth's humility and ingenuity and impressed with his innovative gene therapy, a method that had awakened the American Cancer Society. He was now working as a professor at Yale University.

Right after Dr. Champlin spoke with the chairman at Fred Hutchinson, I was promptly accepted into the BMT fellowship program in Seattle.

CHAPTER 13

Dr. Gates Is Coming

I packed once again and jammed everything I needed into my small Honda Prelude; mainly I brought my books and a few clothes. This time, I drove my car to Seattle, Washington, in a hurry. I started to drive at 6:00 a.m., and I finally arrived in Seattle, at 7:00 p.m. three and a half days later. I ate lunch and dinner in my car while I drove to my new adventure.

When I reached Seattle, I was looking for a huge hospital. I thought that the Fred Hutchinson Cancer Center would be bigger than MD Anderson, since Dr. Thomas had received a Nobel Prize while working there. I circled around Fred Hutchinson many times. My buttocks were bruised, and I was exhausted after sitting and driving nonstop for several days.

An unanticipated windstorm had hit Seattle, and it had ripped off store signs and billboards and blown trash cans around the streets. When I got out of my car to make sure I was at Fred Hutchinson, the strong wind nearly knocked me to the ground, and I held onto my car door tightly. Finally, I found the hospital in front of me—an old and small building. I could not believe this unwelcoming weather and shockingly small entrance, and on top of that, the ground underneath my feet trembled as if there was an earthquake.

I reported to the BMT staff, who gave me a brief tour. The staff showed me the BMT fellows' on-call room, which was literally a small closet-sized space with a bed that had wooden boards under a very thin mattress. I remembered the adage, "Haste makes waste." My biggest flaw was that I always rushing to do something before I analyzed or evaluated the pros and cons of my decision first.

Before I got some rest, the hospital put me on call for thirty-six hours straight. Many BMT training fellows worked primarily at Swedish Hospital, located across from Fred Hutchinson. Its architecture and interior decorations appeared brand new and quite modern compared to that of Fred Hutchinson.

I was deeply disappointed with the training program in Seattle. Even though Washington University medical students were rotating through Swedish Hospital, the training program was completely different than the one at MD Anderson Cancer Center. I made the biggest mistake leaving MD Anderson. Additionally, I discovered that Dr. Thomas was retired. He was no longer working at Fred Hutchinson.

The structure at Fred Hutchinson was not impressive; however, the research center was in a remarkably large building. The hospital provided me with a small dorm behind the center. The dorm was considered an apartment, and the rental fee was deducted from my paycheck. The room had a balcony looking out on the street, a plastic hospital mattress, a plastic pillow, and a bathtub in which the water did not completely drain. The small dimly lit room made me tired. I did not want to live like this any longer. Moving to Seattle was possibly a trap laid by the program director's false advertisement about Dr. Thomas.

My heart was saddened, and I wondered about the program director's recommendation. I also wondered whether her suggestion of Dr. Thomas and Hutchinson was intentional. Suddenly, I felt weary life, as if I were living like a refuge and scrapping the bottom of a barrel.

I needed to cheer up and rejuvenate myself in order not to fall into a depression. I decided to rent a nice apartment in front of the Pacific Ocean on Elliott Avenue in Seattle. Elliot Avenue was close to the popular Pike's Place Market and the Space Needle, a city landmark. There were many art galleries surrounding Pike's Place, which looked out onto the vast blue open ocean. Jubilant people sat on cement steps playing guitars and singing songs in a joyful spirit.

Seattle was a unique city, and many hippies walked the streets with beards, long hair, and large round-shaped shoes. Seattle's vibe was based on love of humanity and peace. Some hippies joined more organized political movements to work for specific social causes. Others turned to spirituality or religion. The majority simply left the hippie stage of their lives behind them while trying to hold onto at least a few of the ideals that once inspired them.

Seattle was the seat of King County. The Olympic Mountains rose west of the city. The city was built on many hills, and some sections were washed into Elliott Bay. There were many coffee shops, and the aroma of roasted coffee wafted through Seattle's Elliott Bay, adding much to the pleasure of drinking it. Seattle was well known for its coffee, which had become an integral part of the business world.

When I moved out of the hospital dorm, the manager of Hutchinson was offended. I might have started off on the wrong foot. Where I lived was not important, but I was disappointed with the BMT program, and Dr. Thomas's retirement made me frustrated and less motivated.

I found an elegant apartment on Elliott Avenue. Close to the oceanfront, it had a large sliding door that opened from the living room to the patio and a breathtaking view. I loved the smell of the salty breeze and the gracefully flapping seagulls that flew over my balcony. The place was delightful, with a large fireplace, adorable seashells on the mantle, and nice furniture. But it did not make me happy. Anxiety about losing my ambition and my future provoked sudden aloneness and unexpected loneliness. The traffic noise identified that the apartment was located on a busy main street for tourists. My well-being was not improved in the fancy flat, and my disbelief at the program director's innuendo about what the move meant overwhelmed me with regret. I should not have left MD Anderson Cancer Center. I could easily return to MD Anderson. I was too tired to move.

My recollection of the past assured me who I was. I clearly remembered when I had dated a multimillionaire but had not cared for material wealth and had realized that money alone could not make me happy. Now, I understood, too, that men cannot live by bread alone. I had long been captivated by my striving to overcome challenges and my unceasing quest for curative treatments—without balancing this journey. It was time to reawaken the long-forgotten supreme power of spiritual connection that I had missed these many days.

I was sitting on the deck of the seaport watching the sun set on the horizon when a young man approached me and started talking to me. "It's a gorgeous sunset, isn't it?" he said.

I did not even look at the young man and answered, "Yes, it is beautiful."

The descending sunset splashed bright colors over the water—painting purple splotches here and there and turning other parts of the rippling waves into red, orange, and blue rainbows. The tide gently caressed the wooden bluff, the swishing a whisper to me that I would be fine, and that God loved me very much.

The strange young man kept talking to me as I was stared at the waves. "Have you heard of Scientology?" he wanted to know. "When I was depressed and hating my job, one of my friends introduced me to this organized church. The church members helped me to be happy again. The place is a couple blocks away. I participated in different levels of religious classes and gained tremendous self-control and confidence to overcome many obstacles. Now, I am successful in my work. The church has numerous free pamphlets, and they will gladly provide you free books."

My spirit was down, and I thought it would not hurt to read affirmations. I learned that Scientology was a religious movement founded by Ron Hubbard, an American writer and visionary thinker. A pioneer, Hubbard combined ideas from Eastern religions and modern psychoanalysis and philosophy to form a practical system for achieving mental health and human improvement.

I followed the young man to the Scientology church. A church member welcomed my visit with kindness and offered me several free brochures and books. I was asked my name and address and told an updated pamphlet would be sent to me soon. I picked up several booklets and returned home.

Ever since that visit, the members of the church sent me flyers and called me regularly. I decided to stop responding to their calls. Later, I heard some rumors about the organization from my friend.

I was not happy at Hutchinson, and the hospital manager suggested that I return to MD Anderson in Texas. The hospital would compensate my airfare expenses. I had driven to Washington and had not flown.

After I carefully reviewed my situation, I decided to go to San Diego to study for the oncology board examination and look for an oncology position. I drove down to San Diego and rented a room from my friend, since my condo had been leased out. San Diego was a charming city. I was so glad to return and walk the sandy beaches with my old friend.

A few months later, Dr. Jackson, the Dean of UTESA, called to tell me that one of the oncologists was looking for a partner in Milwaukee,

Wisconsin. I recognized the doctor's name; he'd been one of the teaching preceptors I'd trained under at St. Francis Hospital in Milwaukee.

Within a month, I flew to Milwaukee and accepted a partnership position with the Oncologist Association, operated by two oncologists for many decades. They were popular and well recognized in community.

I worked with them, practicing oncology and hematology for one year. My partner took extra leisure times since I handled most consultations at the hospitals and treated inpatients as well as outpatients. He enjoyed playing golf often. He was also busy with his daughter's upcoming wedding. The other partner was likewise busy, managing a large motorcycle department in addition to his practice. On the contrary, I worked early in the morning till late at night every day as if I were a medical resident. The medical staff teased me, saying that I worked too much. Many of my colleagues at the hospital, including a neurologist pointed out that I worked like a resident and advised me to slow down.

My partners were gratified by my successful treatment and compassionate care. I took care of every patient as if he or she was family. I was blessed to heal people, and I felt a maternal protection and I diligently looked after their well-being like a mother caring for her children.

Dealing with dying patients required additional humanistic sympathy, benevolent kindness, and understanding families' grief over loved ones. I was referred to see a terminally ill cancer patient. This patient had been admitted by the chief of surgery. I do not know what had happened between the patient and the surgeon, but the patient's daughter was extremely angry with the surgeon and terminated his visit with her father. This was an embarrassing situation at the hospital.

In contrast, the patient was calm when I was evaluating him. I had a brief family meeting with his daughter outside the patient's room after my examination. I carefully explained his condition while sitting next to her. She was mournful and heartbroken, grief etched into her face and she took in the reality of her father's grave condition. I allowed her to vent her painful misery and attentively listened to her concerns in a respectful manner. I completely understood her anguish and anxiety.

During the meeting, my memory drifted to my brother-in-law's terminal condition, and his death pierced my heart with galvanizing pain. Her father was on his deathbed, the outcome of his illness inevitable. Understanding others and listening to their troubles are fundamental cornerstones to cultivating relationships and to enhancing our trust of each other.

The next day, his daughter sent a huge decorative cake and a gigantic flower arrangement in a beautiful vase to my office to express her appreciation. She was a sweet and lovely lady. Apparently, the chief surgeon had not given her the chance to express her sorrow and anxiety about losing her beloved father. Truly, love conquers every problem.

One day, an incredibly angry patient self-referred to see me. She was retaliating against her oncologist. She loudly complained about his manner and treatments. Everyone could hear her bitterness and resentments. I accepted her angry condition and showed my compassion.

Her attitude changed, and she became calm and relaxed soon after she realized that I was paying attention to her concern and that I cared for her. During her hospital care, whenever she heard my footsteps, she got excited and sat up in the hospital bed, telling people, "Dr. Gates is coming."

Love gives us happiness and peace. We are created by God's love. Cancer is a deadly disease and frightens patients. Death produces anxiety, fear, and terrorizing depression. Regaining well-being, hope, joy, faith, and love enhances patients' inner immune system and their bodies' ability to fight their diseases.

Hematologists frequently perform a procedure called a bone marrow biopsy. The biopsy enabled pathologists to examine the bone marrow tissue under a microscope and determine the type of blood disorder or cancer the patient was facing. I was glad that I had undergone BMT training at MD Anderson Cancer Center, because some doctors had a hard time obtaining a good bone marrow specimen from their biopsies. I, on the other hand, had practiced every day as a trainee to obtain bone marrow in Anderson's operating room. This training helped me skillfully alleviate patients' pain during biopsies when I worked as a hematologist.

This is not bragging. Most oncologists took thirty to forty minutes to collect a good sample of marrow, but I was able to obtain a good bone marrow sample within ten minutes. The assisting nurses loved my performance. I was popular at the hospital and among the medical staff. They were willing to do anything for me. The hospital administrator suggested that I could have an entire floor to set up a bone marrow transplant ward.

Most of the time, I worked at three different hospitals. From time to time, I had a consultation at a fourth hospital. St. Francis and Mount Sinai hospitals provided me with a clinic, employees, nurses, and pharmacists who could mix the chemo drugs.

I was extremely busy and popular among the medical staff members. Additionally, I was worked as a teaching preceptor for the internal medicine residency program of Madison Medical School in Milwaukee.

Madison, Milwaukee, and La Crosse had major medical centers near the ports along Lake Michigan and Lake Superior to handle the millions of vacationers attracted to Wisconsin every year. Milwaukee was the largest city in the center of a manufacturing region. Summers were warm and somewhat cooler by Lake Michigan and Lake Superior, though winter was long and extremely cold, with heavy snow.

Wherever I went, whether in or out of hospitals, even at a grocery store, for example, I would be greeted by many patients, who loved to talk with me. With my busy schedule and numerous consultations, I did not have time to talk with the patients for too long. For that reason, I used staircases instead of elevators to save time and not miss my appointments.

I had seven consultations on average per day. I practiced mainly at St. Francis, Mount Sinai, and West General hospitals. Sometimes I gave speeches for physicians and hospital employees at St. Francis and Mount Sinai. I noticed one of the radiation oncologists, Dr. Lemon, appeared to be smart and opinionated and that he preferred to treat patients with combination chemo and radiation treatment. I referred many of my patients to Dr. Lemon.

I usually worked late, staying in my office to dictate my patients' treatment, evaluation, and follow-up care notes. One evening, Dr. Lemon visited my office while I was working at my desk. He appreciated my referrals and wanted to invite me for dinner. I offered him some fresh fruit on my desk; he refused it. He sat in a corner chair and expressed his gratitude, telling me that many of our patients had achieved remarkable outcomes from our combination chemo-radiation therapy.

"I hope you will accept my dinner invitation to celebrate our successful teamwork."

"If you don't mind, I would like to ask my partners whether your invitation is appropriate or not," I told him. "I'll certainly let you know soon. Thank you for dropping by. Have a nice evening, and I'll see you at the hospital."

Dr. Lemon appeared bright, ambitious, and motivated. I did not give him my answer immediately and soon had almost forgotten about his invitation, as I was busy. A few inpatients were receiving combination therapy under Dr. Lemon and me in the hospital. I was giving my last and seventh patient consultation of the day late in the evening. I was hungry but had no time for food. At the time, I saw Dr. Lemon dictating his consultation on the same floor.

"Hello, Dr. Gates!" he called. "Have you eaten dinner? How many consultations have you seen today?"

"This is my seventh consultation, and I have not had a chance to eat yet," I told him.

"Are you hungry? I know a nice Mexican restaurant nearby. Would you like to join me? I'm also finishing my last consultation, and I'm starving."

"That sounds wonderful," I replied. "Let us go for dinner. Please give me five more minutes to finish my progress notes."

CHAPTER 14

Sharks Follow the Smell of Blood (Be Careful, Dr. Gates)

We went out to a cozy Mexican restaurant after we had finished our last consultations of the day, driving there in separate cars. Dr. Lemon had not forgotten his original request and still wanted to invite me for a special dinner to thank me for the referrals. I mentioned that my partners were glad that he had asked me to have dinner with him.

He was recently divorced and single, which I had learned from an oncology associate before going out with Dr. Lemon. The secretary of the Oncologist Association, for a number of reasons, she did not care for Dr. Lemon. She thought he was arrogant and hubristic and looked like a bird.

"Why do you think he looks like a bird?" I asked her.

"He doesn't treat me well," she told me. "He's very condescending. I don't care for him."

For the referral dinner, he accompanied me to an exclusive French restaurant. We were guided to a lovely candlelit table topped with colorful flowers. I reminded myself not to order sweet bread. This time, I had a seafood entrée with a rich sauce. The portion was perfect, and the fish was delicious. A scrumptious dark chocolate cake for dessert made for an overall satisfying dinner.

Initially, I thought we were going to discuss innovative treatment methods to achieve higher curative outcomes. Unexpectedly, he was talking unceasingly about his divorce. He was obviously frustrated over the circumstances of his children's custody arrangements, and he believed that his former wife had been manipulating him in relation to his children's visit. His ex-wife did not want to divorce him and cooperated only reluctantly with anything that may benefit him. She did not want him to be happy, preferring that he be miserable.

His former wife was named Nancy, and her ancestors came from Europe. Nancy's father was Italian, and her mother was Polish. They had two children, a five-year-old girl, and a seven-year-old boy. She evidently had a strong, domineering personality, and he wanted to be free after twelve years of marriage.

He had started dating a physician's assistance (PA) where he was working. This PA, regretfully, was also assertive, and their relationship did not last long. This extramarital affair was another reason his ex-wife hated him.

I was driven by and bewitched with only one thing—the quest for curative treatments. I preferred to focus on this goal, rather than spending my time to going out for dinner or to performances. Dr. Lemon, on the other hand, lived his life to the fullest. While I usually worked hard and saved money, he relished going out for expensive meals and adored watching performances. While he bought season tickets with reserved orchestra seats, I frequently was struggling to keep my head above water.

He perhaps knew how to play the ropes and led his life as he desired, creating his destiny. I directed my life differently. I lived a frugal lifestyle and was very disciplined and determined to be successful. Most of the time, I did not have a spare moment to enjoy my life.

With my hard work, I achieved a wonderful reputation and successful treatment outcomes. My serious and sincere efforts were recognized by the hospital administrator, who genuinely appreciated my work ethic and moral standards.

The secretary of the Oncologist Association regularly purchased office supplies and, along with that, a small list of her groceries. I should not be involved in the small stuff, adhering to the axiom, "Don't sweat the small stuff." My rigid principles, though, was troubled with this deceit over a small amount money from the office supplies budget, causing difficulty in our formerly trusting relationship and making me doubt her integrity.

I further noticed that she was becoming more aggressive and was falsely charging office expenses. I was not the owner of the clinic, but still, I was not fond of her behavior. We live and learn and, hopefully, choose our battles wisely. Sometimes, we win a battle but lose a war.

One year later, I decided to part ways from the Oncologist Association. The hospital administrator still respected me, and he appreciated my reputation and patient care. I was able to rent my own office in the lower level of the hospital from one of the sections of the hospital building.

I went down to see my future office area. Shockingly, the space was not what I had expected. The orange carpet and the protruding old pipes dumbfounded me. The look of the wallpaper and the appearance of the bathroom were equally unpleasant. The hospital administrator suggested that I can contact a private contractor and allowed me to design my own office space.

I requested that the contractor remove all the wallpaper and paint the walls a creamy white, trimmed with gray. I added a built-in bookcase against the wall. I covered the protruding round pipes, turning them into a decorative column; arranged the bathroom to be redone in royal blue and white tiles; and transformed the area into a desirable and more dignified office space. The constructor built a semicircular standing countertop of imitation marble Formica material. Executive cherry wood furniture was purchased through the administrator for the new office. After the renovation, the office had become a modest executive suite.

As a result of this new space, I had three separate offices. Mount Sinai Hospital was newly built, and it had a modernized open-heart surgical unit. I was on the faculty as a preceptor in the internal medicine residency program from Madison. The oncology clinic was on the top floor of the building, surrounded by mammoth windows from floor to ceiling with a wide-open city view. The skyscrapers and city lights were magnificently displayed through the bluish tinted glass on the floor of cancer clinic. Each patient had an individual customized table with a small television and a headset in front of personal leather recliners.

The cancer patients were comfortable when they were receiving chemotherapy in the sophisticated clinic. We had a medication prep room and another room for patience nourishment. Next to the chemo clinic were numerous conference rooms and follow-up care examination rooms.

When I left my old oncology group, many patients wanted to receive their chemo treatments under my care, and they followed me to my own clinic. The name of new clinic was Milwaukee Hematology and Oncology Clinic. Patients brought flowers, plants, and gifts for my new office in the hospital.

A dental clinic was across from my office. Dr. Jackson's office was farther down at the end of the dental clinic. When I decided to leave the group practice, my partners were not happy. They locked my office and kept my personal belongings. They hoped I would change my mind and stay with them.

I had the most referral consultations at the hospital, and patients respected and trusted me. As a result, my old partners practice substantially declined, and they were not happy about the situation. For the time being, the secretary of Oncologist Association stirred up trouble against me. Subsequently, she submitted a suit for $148 to the small claim's court and demanded that I pay back the money she said I owed. I had no idea what that was about. I showed the paperwork to Dr. Jackson, and he advised me to pay the $148 to Oncologist Association, as it was not worth getting stressed over.

My colleagues informed me that my previous partners were resentful and searching for a way to disturb my practice to get even. Despite my old partners' propaganda, my practice flourished, and I had more patients by word of mouth. My clinic was packed with patients, who sat in the waiting room and lined up down the outside hallway.

In the interim, Dr. Lemon had trouble between his female doctor boss and himself. Although he had been working at the largest radiation oncology group with many satellite clinics in different states for a long time, he was still subordinate to his boss. She had worked at this group for many years, and she had also previously been a chairwoman at other hospitals.

Dr. Lemon was emotionally tormented over his children's custody. His ex-wife played games with him to make him miserable. She did not want to divorce him. She misguided him to pick up his kids from her friend's house, only to discover that his children were not there.

He came back with a saddened disposition and an anguished expression. "I could not find my children where she directed me to go, and I ended up wandering around everywhere looking for them and wasted all day without my kids."

All the arguing with his ex made him frustrated. He was moody, and it affected his patient care.

A week later, he anxiously (and briefly) left the hospital to pick up his kids, who were nearby the hospital. He did not ask his group to cover him or get permission from his boss to pick up his kids in a hurry. When he returned to his office, his boss was upset about that incident. Many small issues accumulated, and his relationship with his boss worsened. Eventually, he did not have a choice but had to submit his resignation. The medical field is much like the political world. Dr. Lemon caused self-inflicted damage to his own reputation. He was not a favorite doctor among the staff, and many physicians (with me as the exception) shunned him.

He decided to work for another group on a per diem basis. He flew to California for several weeks at a time for per diem work.

Meanwhile, my business soared. I was terribly busy, which supported the hospital's revenue. The hospital administrator had been contemplating opening a new radiation oncology facility next to the hospital, and the personnel manager asked my opinion regarding the endeavor.

I said I would be willing to contribute funds to build the facility if the administrator was considering Dr. Lemon to be chief of the new radiation oncology department. The hospital administrator and staff members did not give me an answer. They would discuss the issue with the board members.

A huge empty lot on the side of the hospital would be a perfect location for a new facility. I contacted the owner of the lot. Unfortunately, the lot was contaminated with toxic chemicals, and the soil had to be filtered to eliminate all the toxic materials from the ground before a sale. Thus, it was deemed that purchasing the huge empty lot would be a bad investment. A radiation department must be a special structure to prevent leaking of or exposure to radioactive beams or hazardous materials. The option to obtain this land was not workable.

Dr. Lemon still saw patients at the hospital and participated in fundraising dinners. Galas and black-tie parties were held often, and the annual oncology ball was a big event. He wanted to attend the meetings and the parties with me, and I supported his reputation.

Dr. Lemon tended to be critical about other doctors and his colleagues. He was bright and knowledgeable but was insensitive to others. Perhaps he believed his way was the best way to care for patients. His deteriorating personal relationships with his coworkers and his lack of social grace created gossip among staff members, as if he had ignited a wildfire.

His status was gradually downgraded, and his advocates were unwilling to support him due to his criticism and arrogance. He attracted school of sharks, which followed the smell of blood. His lack of humility built a wall around him, and he slowly put himself in a box.

Regardless of the many negative comments against him made by colleagues, I nurtured his weakness, and our relationship progressed. He thought I was a rescuer in his time of neediness, and he appreciated my positive support. He had character flaws. Still, I admired his broad insights and his love of the arts in many different arenas. He had broad knowledge about operas, paintings, histories, sea voyages, and how to live his life to the fullest, which was the opposite of my lifestyle. I wondered why our relationship grew but put it down to the attraction between opposites.

We started dating more often and enjoyed visiting different places, such as museums, theaters, and restaurants. When we went to the zoo, he brought an expensive a camera and a tripod in a fancy bag, as if he were filming a movie. I saw several black swans resting on the grass at the edge of a lake. Wisconsin is in the northern hemisphere, and its swans have white feathers; it was unusual to see southern black swans here. Swans are my favorite birds. I love their graceful gliding. It was a pleasure to watch their long necks stretch to feed on underwater plants and grass along the shore.

I thought that swans would not bite people. I bent and gently stretched out my hand to feed them some dried fruit. He set up his tripod and was ready to take my picture. Suddenly, one of the black swans hissed and extended its long neck trying to bite my hand. My effort to maintain a modeling pose was over, and I almost landed on my buttocks. Simultaneously, my charming smile turned into a fearful expression. I thought swans were graceful, pleasing, and elegant waterbirds; now this one had unexpectedly knocked me to the ground. This experience taught me swans were different than I had imagined. Truly, you cannot judge a book by its cover.

Dr. Lemon was able to adjust his tumultuous problems with the custody of his children and learned how to go with the flow. We had a good time and had fun at the zoo.

A few weeks later, we were invited to a hospital fundraising dinner. Many colleagues and outside dignitaries donated funds for health care improvements. We purchased dinner tickets, game tokens, and gift tickets to bid on auction items.

We joined a card game on the billiards table. While I was arranging the cards, he put his hand on top of mine. I stared at him without saying anything.

"I'm sorry," he said.

Oh, yeah, I thought to myself. *Really?* I sensed that he had intentionally put his hand over mine.

The dinner tables were arranged by groups of physician specialties. The guests next to me were my coworkers, a husband and wife who were nephrologist and infectious disease doctor, respectively. They donated large amounts of funds for the hospital. She had attended overseas medical school and had become a successful and extremely busy infectious disease doctor. Her husband was younger than she was, and they had a lovely daughter. They invited me for their annual Fourth of July celebration at their house.

They had a beautiful hillside house on a man-made lake next to a lush, wooded area. Her husband grilled barbecue, corn on the cob, sweet watermelon, and all sorts of desserts that were very enjoyable. It was a memorable social gathering on a beautiful summer day. Dr. Lemon also had a fun with the group of people.

We attended numerous parties together. At one, I wore an elegant strapless, sequined long evening gown, and he was in a tuxedo with a black tie. For Christmas and New Year's Eve we joined parties at the Hyatt Hotel. We got to know many of the partygoers sitting next to us. The tables were decorated with beautiful flowers, balloons, champagne bottles, and colorful hats. Delicious entrées and sweet desserts were served in cheerful holiday sprits. Splendid and delightful Christmas trees decorated the room, and celebrities joyfully danced on the floor to live music. All these joyful events weaved our indelible happy days together.

Dr. Lemon loved shopping and spending money. He took me to a custom jewelry store and bought me a gorgeous sapphire ring that was delicately designed with diamond baguettes. We relished different ethnic foods and attended many performances, taking in plays, ballets, and chamber music concerts. On weekends, we would go out for brunches and frequently enjoyed high tea. Sipping strained chamomile tea next to a fireplace was my favorite relaxation.

The Hyatt Hotel in Milwaukee was a great place for entertaining. After a play or ballet, we usually went there to order light food and eat on the rotating top floor of the hotel. The night view of downtown was magnificent. Our relationship bloomed like a flower in these exquisite and lovely surroundings.

When his kids visited us, we went to the state fair; visited art galleries, shopping malls, and amusement parks; had picnics; and went biking together. His two kids were extraordinarily good-looking and were smart. They liked pontoon boat outings. Sometimes, we had some conflicts because of their mother, but we nevertheless had great time. I felt that I had a family.

CHAPTER 15

All Is Well

An elderly patient had consulted with me to evaluate his tongue cancer. His previous oncologist had recommended that he undergo surgical removal of part of his tongue. If a surgeon removed his tongue, he would never speak again. The patient was scared and came to see me for a second opinion.

I had been well trained in lymphoma cases at MD Anderson Cancer Center. I would not recommend this patient undergo BMT, but I would treat him with a chemo treatment followed by radiation therapy. Under my care and chemo treatment, the patient achieved a remarkable outcome.

After completing the patient's chemotherapy regimen, I referred him to Dr. Lemon for radiation treatment. The patient achieved successful results and was in clinical remission without any evidence of cancer. Removal of a section of his tongue was no longer required. His speech was clear, and he was ecstatic about his excellent treatment outcome.

The patient, Jerry, and his wife, Nancy, praised my successful treatment. Nancy took pictures of me when I worked at Saint Frances Hospital. She decided to do something special for me, and, just by looking at my picture, she made an oil painting of my face on a large canvas. She created an incredible portrait of me on the canvas and added a unique frame. They brought this large painting to the office and gave it to me as a Christmas gift.

Patient Jerry and Dr. Gates

The most amazing part of the painting was the halo or aura that circled around my head and body, which Nancy had painted a soft orange and yellow color. My portrait showed half of my body, from my head to below my waistline, wearing a physician's white coat and holding a patient's chart.

Nancy was an artist, and she painted me remarkably well. The painting was extremely thoughtful. It revealed their affection and appreciation and their gratitude for Jerry's excellent treatment results.

Saint Frances Hospital held a traditional Cancer Ball at the Hyatt Hotel ballroom during the holiday season. Dr. Lemon and I attended the party. The infections specialist wore a pink hat with a see-through veil, and I wore a long, strapless, tightly fitting evening gown in beige sequins, which was elegantly designed. I received numerous compliments on my beautiful party dress. All the doctors glided on the dancing floor like swans on a lake. The hospital doctors took several pictures of me.

The following day, I was consulting with a seriously ill patient on a ventilator in the intensive care unit (ICU) at Mount Sinai. The ICU was always crowded with sick patients, regardless of day, time, month, or holiday season. The young female patient's condition was rapidly deteriorating. She was in kidney failure, and her blood counts were abnormal; she required dialysis. Her platelets were bottomed out, and she was at a high risk of developing bleeding complications. I ordered platelet transfusions, which slightly helped the patient. The blood bank was next to Mount Sinai Hospital, and the patient received prompt service.

A few days later, the patient suffered a stroke. She became unconscious and unable to move her limbs. I called the blood bank and requested an exchange of platelets through a machine that functions like a dialysis machine. Known as "plateletpheresis," the process used therapeutically would help her blood count.

Unfortunately, her disease progressed further, and blood clots caused gangrene in her big toe. The platelet exchange abetted her abnormal platelets, but it was not good enough to alleviate her critical condition. She was lying on her deathbed, and her illness was beyond the serious condition.

I cancelled all my Christmas gatherings and focused on the patients care and on saving her life. The only option I had was removal of her spleen, which might result in her life ending on an operating table. I discussed the option with the pulmonologist, the nephrologist, and the surgeon, as well as with her family. The ICU head nurse and social workers promptly arranged a meeting the next day. All the team members were in the conference room.

I expected the entire family to have an emotional crisis with this information. Surprisingly, they were quiet and calm and accepted well her inevitable near-death condition. "We pray to God to heal our daughter's critical sickness and guide the surgeon's hand by the Holy Spirit," we were told. "We all know that we do not have any options. Either she will die in the ICU or during the surgery. However, there is a small chance she may recover from the technique used in the procedure you explained to us. If she dies on the table during surgery, that will be God's will."

I was indescribably impressed by their faith, which deeply touched my heart. All the other team members respected her family's decision. I had made sure to clearly explain the high risk and potentially grave outcome. Now I could only pray.

Soon after the surgery, the patient's condition improved. She did not need dialysis treatment, the pulmonologist weaned her off the ventilator, and her blood counts recovered. The only drawback was the amputation of her big toe. Her condition returned to normal. Was this God's miracle? My training as a BMT trainee at MD Anderson Cancer Center had paid off; as a result, I was able to make audacious decisions in extremely difficult, life-and-death situation. Our great team at ICU saved this patient's life.

Christmas and New Years are joyful. During this holiday season, we exchange gifts and share our love. The month and season had been busy and tough and had challenged me. Now, I was no longer exhausted. Rather, I was content and relieved. Our ability to save this patient's life was the best gift from God.

The patient came to my office for her follow-up evaluation a couple of weeks later. She appeared healthy and happy and was planning to get married soon. I was fulfilled by her bright future.

I was thinking of Dr. Lemon and his issues. He was busy and still had problems with the custody of his children. His ex-wife's bitterness had grown. His income had diminished since he had resigned from the group practice. And the burdens of his child support and alimony obligations were piled on top of all of that. He had paid a high price for his poor decisions. What if he had gotten permission from his boss before leaving the hospital to pick up his kid? He would have avoided conflict between them. Hindsight is always twenty-twenty. I think, though, with that move he broke the proverbial camel's back.

If I were his position, I would have crawled into my shell of frustration. He was different. Instead of becoming frustrated, he bought expensive season tickets for chamber music performances. Perhaps that was his coping mechanism for the stress. One evening, he took me to a violin quintet performance. He was so stressed out and fell asleep next to me in the middle of the play. Thank God he did not snore. In a way, I was astounded to witness how he handled his circumstances in silence.

He had not completely given up his practice in Milwaukee, and he wanted to see his patients at my new clinic, since he was out of his group practice. Of course, I didn't mind. He worked at my office for a short time without effective outcomes.

We went out to lunch close to a real estate company in Lake Michigan. Notice a big banner advertising an open house, we had a light lunch and made an appointment to see the lakefront house. The realtor drove us to the subdivision on Lake Wood in Mequon.

The ranch house was located on two acres lot. It had a circular driveway with two lion statues on the pedestals. Large Greek-style flowerpots were set in front of the pedestals. The adorably built shack was attractive against the wooden fence close to the garage. The medium-size flower bed in front of the bay window was overgrown with weeds. Cherry trees, lilac trees, and some evergreens were dotted here and there on the lawn.

The house was not new, but the view of Lake Michigan was breathtaking. It looked like oceanfront property. The backyard was three hundred feet from the bluff. The previous owner used to go fishing. The house had three bedrooms, two baths, a living room, and a dining area, all average size. The magnificent view was stunning and caught my heart. Instantly, I was attracted to that house and could not let go of the property.

Luckily, we were the first people to see the house, and I immediately decided to put down a down payment. I told the realtor to remove the listing and for-sale signs at the front of the house. Shortly after my purchase, several visitors wanted to buy the house. The house was my dream home because of the vast open lake view, which I found no different from a mammoth ocean view without any obstruction. There was nothing but enormous horizon in the back of the house.

Rushing is one of my character flaws, but sometimes it means I get what I want it.

Dr. Lemon was next to me, and he was quiet. The house was not expensive, even though the house on the corner appeared to be a mansion. But it was sitting on a large acreage and the neighbors kept up their properties. The space between the houses had a sufficient distance, maintaining ample privacy.

I loved the lakefront house—even though it took me an hour to get to work. I adored the immensely open view of the blue water and watching the sun set on the horizon. Deer roamed the yard and gracefully nibbled the lilac flowers. Wild ducks pecked seeds on the patio, and some of braver ducks even entered the living room. And I loved it all. Seeing the beauty of nature filled me with an appreciation for God's creation and filled me with an inexplicable peaceful serenity.

The Michigan lake house was soon filled with treasured memories I would long cherish. Spectacular sunsets—the multiple colors radiating from the sun, pink, purple, blue, and orange sunbeams, cascading over the turquoise and bluish green waves that rippled gracefully, their flickering breakers miniature pictures of the heavenly scene—painted my evenings. The seagulls glided over the glistening waves and the splash of rainbow-colored surf. This peaceful view was surreal. It was truly a masterpiece of God's creation, the likes of which I had never seen before even in the movies.

I was the second owner of the house. The first owner had methodically built this house with his skillful engineering background. His wife was a famous ballet director at a performance center in Milwaukee.

Dr. Lemon initially did not want to purchase the house together. Consequently, I purchased the house by myself. A few days later, he changed his mind, and he wanted to share the cost of the house. Subsequently, we purchased it under shared but separate ownership. We mutually agreed to each pay half and to pay off the house. It took several months before we received the title and deed.

His children went to an expensive private school. One day, they were performing at a talent show at school, and he invited me to join him. When we went to the school, his ex-wife was with their children prior to their performance. She probably figured out that I was his girlfriend. She spoke to me, and I replied to her. I found it uncomfortable and awkward seeing his ex-wife at the kids' school, since she was with the kids.

While he was talking to his kids, his ex-wife starting to complain to me about him. She said, "What kind of a husband puts his wife in prison and wants a copy of her mug shot?"

I did not know how to respond to her complaints. I asked her, "Did he put you in jail and they took a mug shot of you?"

"Yes," she said. Her expression implying that she was giving me a warning about his character flaws.

I did not say much to her, but deep inside my conscious bothered me. I could only imagine what had happened to her because of him. Certainly, they had once been in love each other, yet he had put her in social disgrace. This behavior was hard to believe, regardless of what had happened between them now.

The school bell rang, and everyone had to be seated inside the auditorium. The talent show was lovely, the schoolchildren's performance, precious and darling. His daughter, Lauren, was such a pretty girl, and she looked prettier than most kids on television. He brought a camcorder and videotaped the kids' show. He also brought a pair of awfully expensive binoculars to watch the kids' performance. He was trying to impress me with his wealth, which was nothing to me.

A few weeks later, Lauren, and his son, Roger, were selected, along with other children, to perform a dance for the Wisconsin State Fair in

Milwaukee. The fair was held in August and was well known and popular throughout the state.

Lauren wore a flower wreath on her head and looked like a perfect little angel. She had big blue eyes and long brown hair and was a friendly little girl. After their performance had finished, Dr. Lemon picked up the kids, and we all went to the park. Lauren saw a rabbit and chased it into its hole. She dug in the ground to find the rabbit. She was an active, carefree, and innocent little girl who had not yet reached her sixth birthday. She picked a few prairie flowers and made a small flower bouquet. She smiled and gave it to me. His kids were lovely.

His ex-wife did not get along with her mother-in-law, possibly because he had been a mama's boy in the past. He became needy and did not have the strong willpower needed to make good decisions. He had been seen by a psychologist for a while after his divorce was finalized. One day, he took me to his psychology session. I sat next to him and listened to psychologist's advice. In my opinion, this female psychologist made him more confused and more ambivalent. He could not make his own decisions in his state of mind. I believe lacked faith and had no God in his heart. I told him not to see the psychologist anymore.

One evening, he came to my apartment and was more depressed than I had ever seen him. Apparently, he discussed his frustrations with the psychologist. He told me that the psychologist recommended that he take some type of medication to make him feel better.

A few days later, his psychologist paged him when he visited me. At the time, I told him that I would like to speak with her if he did not mind. He allowed me to talk to her. I told her, "In my opinion, Dr. Lemon has a circumstantial temporary depression, which doesn't require him to take pills or depend on medications. I believe it is normal to go through emotional frustration after a divorce, custody conflicts, and job changes. I don't think prescribing medication will solve his problems."

The tone of her voice made it clear she did not appreciate my thoughts, but I had to say what I believed.

He did not take the medications the psychologist recommended. In fact, he was less depressed within a week, and presented me a three-carat diamond ring. He wanted to get engaged before we moved into the Mequon house. I accepted his proposal, and we talked about our wedding plans. I suggested we get married in our garden at the lake house, and he agreed with me. He said that would be wonderful. I contacted several companies about setting up a garden wedding.

We could invite many of coworkers and colleagues, which would be expensive. He did not want to spend too much money on the wedding, since his coworkers and colleagues had not supported him when he'd resigned from his previous group. As a result, he decided he no longer wanted to have a garden wedding. It was not uncommon that his mind changed like the wind. I wished he would have told me about his change of heart before I'd prepared a garden wedding. I was not happy about his lake of commitment to our decision.

The engagement ring was returned, I told him to forget about getting married. He was hurt, and tears welled up in his eyes. He knelt, begging to be forgiven. I understood his emotional instability due to his recent divorce, the frustration with his job situation, and his worry over his kids. I forgave him, and we hugged each other.

Shopping was not my favorite activity, but I needed a decent wedding dress. A second marriage did not require the bride to wear a long gown with a train dragging on the floor. Nor did I need a veil to cover my face. Still, I would need a gown. On the contrary, Dr. Lemon loved spending money and shopping, and he knew where to find a wedding dress I would like. I bought a glamorous lacey white dress with many layers of sheer skirt flowing gracefully just below the knee. It was fancy but not too formal, meaning I could wear it for a special occasion.

I appreciated his assistance in finding a dress. Traditionally, a bridegroom should not see a bride's wedding gown before she walks down the aisle. But we were living in the modern era, and the traditional rituals of weddings ceremony weren't important to us.

The house title and deed were sent to us from the courthouse, and we moved into the Lake Michigan home. He brought a large, elaborate, antique formal dining table with twelve seats, a grand piano, and some decorative household items. My possessions were unpacked, including a sunburst wall mirror, antique coffee table, and Country Roses china sets.

He went out of town to work for a few days, meaning I unpacked most of moving boxes. In addition, I had both the inside and outside of the home painted. The house with the incredibly beautiful Lake Michigan view became cozy.

He wanted us to get married by a justice of the peace at the downtown courthouse. We did not invite any family members. His elder brother was a colonel who worked as a dentist in London, England. His younger brother lived in Houston, Texas, and ran a computer company. His mother lived on the top floor of a condo in Miami Beach with a magnificent view of the water on one side and overlooking the swimming pool on the other side. She was a retired schoolteacher. His had two brothers but no sisters. All three sons had been mama's boys ever since her husband had died. Their mother tended to get involved in her sons' personal business, and she indirectly guided their decisions.

His father had died during his chemotherapy regimen for colon cancer. He had developed the severe side effects from the toxic chemotherapy and hadn't even complete his treatment.

We bought simple gold bands for wedding rings, along with the three-carat diamond engagement ring, which he paid for it. My secretary; his two children; and the guest of honor, his divorce lawyer, attended our ceremony. Nothing was specially arranged. My secretary took some pictures of us. His two children were against their father's remarriage and refused to take a picture.

My secretary took several pictures, and some came out well. She also took a picture when we sat on a bench outside the courtroom. This picture captured a trash can next to the bench where we were sitting on, and I was in my wedding dress. The recorder complimented my dress; otherwise, nothing significant happened during our marriage ceremony. I carried my beeper since he'd decided to

we'd get married by the justice of peace. As usual, my beeper never stopped. When it went off during my marriage, I told the caller to wait for just under an hour, unless it was an emergency. Additionally, I mentioned that I was in the middle of the marriage.

We were supposed to go out to eat and celebrate our wedding that night, but he went to his son's ball game. Obviously, he did not plan his schedule well, and I became skeptical about his integrity, his ability to strategize logically, and his devotion to our marriage. I started wondering whether I was stepping into a quagmire.

CHAPTER 16

The Enchanted Garden (Looking for His Help Was Useless)

I continuously doubted myself. Had I made a mistake marrying Dr. Lemon? Our marriage was more like a contract partnership. We mutually decided to separately maintain our individual funds and assets. I did not brag about my savings because I did not care for material value alone. He thought he had more than I did. In fact, we had an almost equal amount. Or, I had much in terms of individual assets and separate accounts while we were in Milwaukee.

There was not a written prenuptial contract, but we agreed in a professional way to mutual communication and acted accordingly on our agreement. We kept the accounts and funds independently, to the point of paying for groceries and eating out separately. We each had a medical practice and kept separate accounts. Tax returns were initially filed separately, and later we filed as married but separate. The IRS recorded our returns under class C married income tax, although separate individual incomes were reported. We even separately paid the CPA for our IRS summary.

Other documents clearly listed our separate funds and assets—individual savings account, retirement plans, investments, individual properties, and our living wills. He paid his child support and his alimony out of his income.

I generated four times more income than he earned when he worked on a per diem basis. My compassionate care for patients and focus on treatments ensured the outcomes were successful. For example, one of patients had a history of lung cancer. He had previously been treated at the Oncologist Association and followed me when I left my old partnership and opened my own clinic. The patient complained of discomfort in his shoulder blade. When he had had a follow-up evaluation by my previous oncology partner, my old partner had taken a simple chest X-ray for lung cancer, which had come back normal. No further diagnostic tests were done.

When I saw the same patient, who still complained of his left shoulder discomfort, a further restaging evaluation was performed, with a CT scan of his chest that showed a hidden mass next to the middle of his spine. In general, an isolated single mass is surgically moved. In this patient's case, his tumor had begun to invade his spine. It would eventually extend to the spinal cord, which could result in potential paralysis of his legs and, soon, inability to control his bladder and bowels.

I referred this patient to another radiation oncologist to shrink the patient's bulky tumor close to the spinal cord. At the time, Dr. Lemon was out of town for his per diem work. The patient's shoulder pain quickly vanished, and his tumor shrank substantially. His clinical symptoms remarkably improved, and the quality of his daily activities was restored.

We were still in the honeymoon phase of newlyweds, having only just gotten married. But he was not available. He took a per diem radiation oncology position in Marshfield, Wisconsin, and stayed for a couple of months. On weekends, he would visit me for a few days and then return to work in different places. I visited him when he could not visit me.

It usually took two hours to get there and two hours to return home. By the time I got back, my consultations had piled up, and there was a line of patients waiting for me to evaluate them. When there was no part-time job available, he stayed with me at home. During his off days, he picked up his children, and they stayed with us.

Lauren still called me Dr. Gates despite, even though I wished she would call me mom, although she had her own mother. The kids wanted their father's affection and attention as much as I wanted his love as a newlywed. I wanted a romantic and intimate relationship, which was only in my dreams

We had a family reunion during the holidays with his family, including his mother, his younger brother, and his two children. I bought a nice sweater for Lauren and a jacket for Roger. The children did not like my gifts and said they'd rather wear shorts during the bitterly cold Wisconsin winter.

Lauren cried loudly for a long time when I tried to convince her to wear warm clothes. Undoubtedly, both kids had resentments against me because their father's remarriage, and they were too young to understand an adult relationship.

We went to a fancy restaurant with his family. The two kids wore shorts, making me embarrassed as a stepmother—as if I did not care for their attire and did not want to protect them from the shivering cold weather. During this stage, I did not have skills when it came to amicably communicating with little kids. I was always focused on patients' treatments and never had my own children. Nor had I ever been pregnant. I wanted to decrease their resentments about their father's remarriages. This gave me a headache, and I found it harder to handle the situation peacefully than to take care of my patients. I did not know. The only thing to do was say, "So be it." I knew tomorrow would be a new day.

My rapport and genuine relationship with my patients were much easier than dealing with two resentful kids. I loved his kids as much as I loved my patients, yet the kids' affection ricocheted like a loose cannonball. They were only fond of me when I bought what they wanted, and that was not a good way to develop an enduring relationship.

I realize that being a stepmom was a challenging and difficult position. I was aware that I needed a professional lesson. I could not comprehend his kids' confusion and mixed emotions at the time. Patience is the master of all virtues. When they visited me, I prepared the best food and made sincere efforts for the kids to enjoy meals. I bought fresh filet mignons and lobsters, which they loved to eat. Still, I could not make them happy. They complained about it being raw, and they made their own peanut butter and jelly sandwiches. They were fine kids. They just, like me, did not know how to establish a friendly relationship and compromise with each other.

I told him to take his children to resorts to have fun and cultivate wholesome relationships with them without me. This alternative plan worked out. Occasionally, I joined the outgoing to sightseeing vacation spots with his kids and his family. One summer, we went to the Wisconsin Dells and Deer County. We took a few days of vacation to relax and enjoy.

Wisconsin has sparkling lakes, rolling hills, quiet valleys, and a cool pine-scented breeze. A boat outing was fun and helped us to develop a close relationship as a family. I was glad to join his family and be able to share time together. We had a wonderful short trip.

I deeply cared about my patients, and they respected me. One of my patients got arrested for shoplifting at K-mart. He was caught by the store manger slipping a small item into his pocket. The patient came to my clinic and was a distraught after he had violated the law. He was a nice, polite gentleman who had been receiving chemotherapy for leukemia, which occasionally altered the cognitive thought process.

I sent my precise explanation of this phenomenon to the store manager, as well as to the local policeman. His charge was promptly dismissed after my clarification. The biochemical nature of the chemo drugs could cause imbalances, which might have affected his impulses, resulting in abnormal behaviors such as a shoplifting. The patient continuously received his chemotherapy for leukemia and subsequently he achieved clinical remission.

Despite my busy practice, I further extended my endeavors and not only practiced at the hospital but also saw patients at different doctor's clinics as a consultant.

Pancreatic cancer had a notoriously poor prognosis. The average life span after diagnosis was six months to two years. But cancer treatment continuously improved, and innovative treatments were developing rapidly. The traditional theory of cancer treatments— based on the concept of "the more the better," was proven to be wrong. In the field of medicine one size does not fit all. The amount of chemo drugs delivered needed to be adjusted based on patients' tolerance and clinical conditions, and this was crucial to saving patients' lives and providing them quality of daily life. Too often, the toxic drugs killed patients more quickly than the existing underlying cancers would have. Periodically, the recommended amount of chemo drugs, after phase studies, was too toxic for a patient and brought unexpected tragic fatal outcomes.

One of my pancreatic patients had been aggressively treated until he became weak, and side effects of the chemo drugs he was receiving for his incurable cancer increased. During his treatment, he still worked as an officer at the state prison. The patient was quiet, calm, and kind. I could not picture him working as a prison guard in a tough prison environment.

Before he got too sick from the toxic drugs, I connected the mild 5 FU chemo infusion. After so many years of practice, my treatment concept was changed; I focused on giving tolerable amounts of medicine and continuously suppressing cancer cells before the cancer cells could propagate further.

During that time, I encouraged patients to increase their well-being by focusing on hope, faith, peace, and increased willpower to overcome their ailments. I believed that this integrated medicine enhanced the individual's immune system, enabling their bodies to better fight the cancer cells. This treatment method was better than administering high doses of toxic drugs, which wiped out not just cancer cells, but also normal cells, sometimes causing fatal outcomes and killing patients quickly.

What I had witnessed with the passing of my brother-in-law during my BMT training, as well as my father-in-law's fatal outcome because of toxic chemo drugs, had made an indelible mark on my psyche. I had excellent outcomes from my adjusted treatment theory, and many of my patients achieved clinical remissions and were cured. My patients did not suffer side effects from high chemo drugs. They lived longer than expected and enjoyed good quality of life.

My primary doctor thought I was giving mild chemotherapy to generate a higher income benefit. Consequently, the primary doctor advised my patient to refuse his mild 5 FU chemotherapy through a portable pump. Obviously, the primary doctor had not trained in the subspecialty of oncology and did not understand the efficacy of a cancer protocol. As a result, the patient turned down the further therapy.

A few months later, the patient was admitted with a widespread pancreatic cancer, and his physical condition rapidly deteriorated. He was unable to maintain his work, suffered excruciating back pain, and had a protruding abdomen. He was clinical dying. His family members wanted to have a conference with me.

At the meeting, the patient's son was furious with the primary doctor. "My father was clinically doing well on 5 FU portable pump, but his condition deteriorated when he discontinued the treatment. Unfortunately, my father's family doctor convinced him to reject his treatments. Would you please put the 5 FU portable pump back on him?" his son asked.

"It's too late to be treated with 5 FU," I explained gently. "His cancer has spread throughout his body. The best treatment is to make your father comfortable and place him in hospice care. I am so sorry about his grave condition.

"I agree with you," I added. "The family doctor should not have influenced his treatment, as he is not an oncologist. Still, I am sure that the doctor thought the patient did not need 5 FU for a long time."

"Dr. Gates, please forgive us for what happened before my father refused the 5 FU infusion," the patient's son continued.

"You father did well for two years. This was more than I expected. He enjoyed quality activities and enjoyed his work during the treatments. I'll make sure your father's pain will be well controlled."

Wisconsin winters were colder than winters in Chicago. The snow would pile up on the streets, making snowbanks, some nearly six feet high, that did not melt for several months. Dr. Lemon worked hard as a per diem physician, and I was extremely busy. We decided to get away from the cold weather and go to Jamaica, where we could soak in the sun. Jamaica has a pleasant climate and offers beautiful beaches and mountains; springs, streams, and waterfalls; and swiftly flowing rivers that run north and south from the mountains.

We arrived in Ocho Rios and stayed at a resort called Enchanted Garden, which we had booked through travel agents. The garden had originally been a national botanical garden and had later been converted to a resort. The Enchanted Garden had several artificial falls and five different ethnic restaurants inside the resort. The place was next to a lake, and there were two swimming pools, a Jacuzzi, and performing stages close to the pools. Bright exotic flowers decorated the resort.

Momentarily, I was in heaven listening to the chirping birds and the sound of crashing waterfalls and looking at the thatched huts amid lush trees. We lodged close to one of the restaurants, and the pathway to the dining area was covered with bright clustered flowers over arched branches. A small bridge above a pond and a walking through lush green leaves and abundant colorful flowers made for a wonderful welcome to Jamaica.

I adored having a dining table next to an indoor gigantic waterfall. Tiny water droplets caressed my face and the gentle crashing of the water revitalized me. Every night, we enjoyed different ethnic food, sampling

French, Mexican, Moroccan, Japanese, and Italian restaurants. The restaurant served plenty of food and soft beverages but no wine. Lunch was tropical fruits, grilled barbecues, shish kebobs, fish dishes, or sandwiches by the pools. The resort entertained tourists with dancing and music, including an excellent performance with fire torch dancing and a wondrous fire show.

The following day, we went to Dunn River Rock, climbing next to the white sandy beach and blue ocean. Rubber shoes were required, and people wore swimwear because waterfalls along the rock climb splashed all around us. We had too pass through many puddles between the rocks to reach the top.

I had made it a third of the rock climb when I glanced down at the river and got scared. I looked around for my husband to get some help. He was all by himself, way behind me, without any consideration of my climbing. Looking for his help was useless. Surprisingly, a moment later, he was helping an overweight woman and man who were struggling with wobbly gaits. I was worried about whether the heavy couple could make it to the top.

Amid my nervous moment, a little boy without his parents had a hard time climbing up to the next rock. I was afraid to look down. In any event, I climbed up anyway. I found the boy stuck and fearful to advance his climbing. I positioned his hands, and he was able to progress to the next rock. We both climbed up the difficult rocks. At that very moment, I started to doubt Dr. Lemon's commitment to our marriage.

Finally, I made it to the flat, spacious area, which had a huge water puddle, like a swimming pool. People jumped in and splashed each other with water, some trying to swim, some kissing and hugging their significant others, and others videotaping. At last, Dr. Lemon appeared behind me and pushed me in the water, knowing that I could not swim well. It was good cooling area to wash off my fear of heights. The rest of the climb was easier, and we had a fun time after all.

We were refreshed and joined a line dancing and singing group after dinner. On the third day of the trip, we took a bamboo raft for an excursion on the Blue Lagoon. First, the resort bus dropped us off at a tourist bar for drinking and snacking on a large wooden deck above the lagoon. The same heavyset couple who had had a difficult time climbing the rock, was also afraid of water, especially the man. He refused to sit near the edge of the deck close to the water, promptly retracting himself backward, and told us he could not swim. This huge, tall man behaved like a scared baby. The unexpected fearful attitude of a large adult was comical.

On the other hand, many active elderly women jumped into the water and swam like fish. Other men and women danced on the deck under the blasting and cheerful Jamaican music. The weather was perfect, with a clear sky and bright sunlight. The blowing wind lifted one woman's waistline scarves and exposed her bare legs. She did not care about exposing her sexy legs and never stopped dancing. It was a hugely enjoyable moment in Jamaica.

As time went on, it was our turn to jump into the water from the shore. We followed the rower pushing the raft into the deeper water. The heavyset couple was next to our raft. This couple's weight pushed the raft down, and the water seeped into the bamboo float and the vessel started to become submerged. The rower had a tough time propelling the raft, and he worked extremely hard to keep it afloat. This couple could not swim and were not wearing life jackets. Their eyes got bigger and bigger as the raft drifted to the deeper lagoon; at the same time, they were thrilled to be riding on the small bamboo raft together. In the end, they gave the rower a generous tip.

We saw them after the raft excursion, and they told us they had been scared to death, but the raft was the most exciting and memorable part of their trip. They liked us.

Dr. Lemon, on the other hand, swam like a fish. He even took the paddle from the rower and rowed the raft all the way to the destination.

The next morning, we went to Diamonds International at the mall below the Enchanted Garden. It was packed with tourists wanting to purchase jewelry and offered good bargains. For the first time, I bought a pair of diamond earrings and a bracelet that was certified by a jeweler. The price of the jewelry was half that in America. I thought that was a good investment.

The store featured different colors of diamond—greens, blues, and yellows—as well as a variety of shapes, sizes, and design that I had never seen before. I found a distinctive men's green diamond ring, and I could not keep my eyes off it. I bought it for him. To my disappointment, he did not buy any jewelry for me. I was satisfied with my three-carat engagement ring.

We visited the different islands of Jamaica. We went on a picnic to a beautiful private beach. The pristine, greenish-blue sparkling waves riffled the beach's white shore. Some tourist ran after the waves and swam. Others took pictures, and some walked around the sandy beach holding hands. The last day of our trip, we went on a boat outing and had a beach party. We had a blissful trip to Jamaica.

Returning to the Chicago airport, the frozen streets, and the icy windshield of his parked car in the hotel parking lot, I wished to go back to the tropical island. We stayed overnight at a hotel in Chicago and then returned to our Michigan house. I did not think that I could drive safely on the busy, frozen Chicago highway by myself. I appreciated Dr. Lemon's survival skills, which I did not have.

The Mequon Lake house in Milwaukee had experienced a snowstorm, and we returned to no electricity at home. The double-paned winter windows did not help much to keep us warm. We slept wearing ski clothes, hats, and gloves and used sleeping bags in bed.

CHAPTER 17

I Should Not Have Married Dr. Lemon

The highway traffic was dreadful on the way to work. It took more than an hour on a heavy snow day, and it was not safe.

Right after I returned from the trip, a ninety-year-old patient with colon cancer was referred to me. I was not sure whether she would benefit from chemotherapy because of her age and underweight physical condition. Still, the patient's family wanted me to treat her, since she was not at end-stage cancer.

I treated her using 5 FU chemotherapy via a portable device connected to her port-a-cath. The device allowed the patient to take treatment at home for the patient's convenience; that way she would not have to visit my clinic daily. I provided her family detailed instructions and gave them my beeper number so they could page me in an emergency, telling them I was available seven days a week and twenty-four hours a day.

Amazingly, the patient tolerated chemotherapy beautifully, without side effects, and achieved clinical remission. Her tumor marker (a measurement of cancer cells in the blood) returned to normal. After completion of her chemotherapy, the skinny ninety-year-old patient just stared at me and quietly expressed her appreciation, along with her family. I was as happy as they were, and we shared a heartwarming moment.

Before long, another winter had gone by, and spring had turned into summer. It was time to tame growing weeds, as tall as a yardstick, in the flowerbed in front of my bay window. I had a hard time finding a gardener, other than a young man who had been mowing the lawn.

Dr. Lemon stayed at the lake house a few days a week and then left for his next per diem job. This time he went to Modesto, California, for three months. I decided to take care of the wild-looking flowerbed. It was not easy, but I plucked all the weeds, which were deeply rooted. I jumped back many times and fell on my butt when the roots came out of the ground, along with chunks of soil. At the same time, I feared seeing the moving earthworms. At last, the hard work was done, and the garden looked great. Thank God!

The wildflower bed was transformed into a small botanical garden after I planted many colorful spring flowers. The many layers of flowers were beautifully arranged. Dusty Millers were in the outer layer next to French marigolds, tall snapdragons populated the middle, and foxgloves were imbedded into the center. All the gigantic, abundantly decorated Greek-style pots were filled with bright, colorful petunias.

The lake house was embellished with numerous hanging flower plants. Wow! They looked gorgeous and joyful. The red and orange geraniums that occupied the top of the pedestal in front of the circular driveways greeted me upon my arrival home. Now I could enjoy summer with or without him. Flowers made a big difference and gave me cheerful spirits.

I used to bicycle with him. Nowadays, I cycled by myself. I was not lonely, though, and I loved the nature around me. The sunlight's reflection emitted various shades of green leaves and flowers, under a cloudless, cobalt blue sky. Wisconsin summers were wonderful. I loved God's masterpiece. Life was simply how you make it.

I worked hard as usual. I evaluated a female patient who had smoked daily while she had been taking care of her sick husband with lung cancer. She had been devoted to him unconditionally, and sadly, he had died. Her anxiety and frustration were somewhat eliminated while she was smoking. Unfortunately, chain-smoking caused her lung cancer.

She was promptly treated with combination chemotherapy. Initially she was fearful, but she tolerated treatments reasonably well and became relaxed.

Her entire life had been consumed by raising her children and taking care of her sick husband. She was fully aware of the potential poor outcome of her lung cancer. She wanted to do something special after reaching the halfway course of chemotherapy. She desired to take a short trip to Las Vegas, since she had never been there.

Her blood counts and physical condition were remarkable. I permitted her to take the trip with her family. I gave the patient instructions and my cell number. Her family members chipped in from their savings, and they all went to Las Vegas.

My patient, Darlene, was excited and happy. She was thrilled by the huge glittering neon signs, the skyscrapers, and the numerous entertainment places and circus shows. She also loved the different restaurants, ravished by the opportunity to sample from the buffets that offered dishes different from those she had known in her Midwest hometown. She scuttled around like a child in a wonderland, especially in the busy casinos. The attire of the casino service people amused her.

Darlene had allotted herself a small amount of money to play the slot machines. Her first ten dollars was quickly wasted. She hesitated to use another ten dollars. Soon another five dollars was gone, and she was about to give up.

At that very moment, the slot machine hit the jackpot and poured out coins and flashing sirens. It left her exhilarated. She jumped out of the chair and hugged her family, shouting, "Wow! Look at these coins dropping. I cannot believe it. This is so cool! Thanks be to God."

My patient won $750, her experience very similar to Anna's on our trip a long time ago. Darlene had also won enough money to cover her travel expenses.

She took many pictures and brought them to my clinic after her trip. I bet her Las Vegas trip helped her healing and well-being. Life is not in our control. We can only do our best. It is wise to accept our destiny and let go of our deplorable situations. I felt fulfillment when my patients did well clinically and were happy. Darlene had more energy and was cheerful upon her return. She tolerated treatment well and responded to her chemotherapy. Our immune system improves when we are relaxed and at peace.

Dr. Lemon next went to Tennessee for work. At the time, Tennessee had a severe rainstorm. Many inches of rain built a small lake, and water flooded into his car parked behind the hospital parking lot and soaked the floor. He got depressed and was tired working as a per diem physician. He was stressed out.

He had formed several friendships while he was training in Tennessee after graduating from medical school in South Florida. One of his friends informed him that a county medical center was looking for a radiation oncologist.

I felt bad that he had resigned from the group practice in Milwaukee. His boss retired soon after he had left the group. Unfortunately, St. Francis Hospital could not build a radiation oncology department on contaminated ground. Otherwise, he could have had a job and stayed in Milwaukee.

Now he applied for an opening in the radiation oncology department at the Tennessee medical center and accepted the position when it had offered him. He returned from Tennessee and wanted to move to Crossville, a small city with a population of just thirty thousand. Crossville was known to be white community; not a single black person lived. Inbreeding families made up the community, and everybody knew everybody's business. They were self-sufficient people living by their own laws. During the Civil War, the people of Crossville had volunteered to fight for the Confederacy.

Tennessee is one of the states that linked the north and the south of the United States. Life in western and middle Tennessee resembled life in the Deep South. Even during the Civil War, Tennessee royalties were divided between the north and the south. Crossville people did not like northern Americans. Tennessee was the last Confederate state to leave the union. Oak Ridge, begun in 1942, had the world's first nuclear reactor. The device was used to produce material for the first atomic bomb. It was about forty minutes from Crossville to Oak Ridge.

Dr. Lemon planned to move to Tennessee because he could not find a job in Wisconsin at the time. I should not have married Dr. Lemon.

One incredibly cold night in Wisconsin, I was called for an ICU consultation at St. Francis Hospital. The patient was extremely sick. He could not breathe due to his underlying lung cancer. A special procedure that would need to be performed at a bigger hospital was required. This ICU patient was promptly stabilized first, and then I consulted one of pulmonologists at Oak Ridge Hospital. An emergency procedure, including a chest tube placement, was immediately needed. A patient's family meeting was held, and the details of his prognosis were recorded.

By the time I transferred the patient, it was about 3:00 a.m. That night, Milwaukee had a severe snowstorm. I almost had a car accident while returning home. My windshield wipers, though moving at maximum speed, could not keep up with the pouring snow. Passing trucks on the highway dumped snow on my windshield constantly, making me blind at times. The road was terribly dangerous. I got off the highway, drove down an unfamiliar street, and almost lost my direction without any streetlights to show me where I was.

The danger of this long drive in heavy snow made me think of leaving Wisconsin. I told the hospital nurses that I might move to Tennessee. I did not want to leave Wisconsin; however, I had married Dr. Lemon. The choices were either I moved to Tennessee with him or divorced him and stayed in Wisconsin.

When I informed the nurses about the possibility of my relocation, they were sad. "Dr. Victoria Gates, please do not leave this clinic. You don't want to make this oncology clinic a *Titanic*," one of the nurses said, adding, "Besides, we know you don't like insects, and the Deep South has huge bugs."

A patient of mine heard about my upcoming transition to Tennessee. This patient was frightened and called the director of Covenant Health Care, who was managing all the Catholic hospitals, crying over the phone. Notably, Darlene, who had just returned from her Las Vegas trip, was scared, and she sobbed.

A few days later, I received a phone call from the director of Covenant Health Care, Mr. Spear, who was genuinely concerned about my patients. The poor patients under my care wept and panicked about the discontinuation of their treatments. Mr. Spear and I had a lunch meeting on the outskirts of Milwaukee. Directors Spear was worried about my leaving the clinic. The director subtly implied that I might find running a practice in Tennessee difficult, noting the prohibitive costs of an overhead required to run a business in a such small town. He had noticed that many doctors were unsuccessful after they moved to other states. Then he added, "Would you reconsider your situation and stay where you are?"

"Is there any chance you can help Dr. Lemon get a job in Milwaukee?" I asked. "You're managing all the Catholic hospitals under Covenant Healthcare. How about Saint Joseph Hospital? The hospital has a big radiation oncology department, which is in a different network, Aurora Health Care, from the one where Dr. Lemon used to work."

"He has to sell himself," the director told me. "He is not like you."

"Mr. Spear, Dr. Lemon is a bright and excellent doctor. We worked together, and numerous patients achieved superlative and successful outcomes. I have only two choices; either I divorce him to stay in Milwaukee, or I must follow him where he can work. As you know, he could not find a job in Milwaukee—unless you can help him out under the umbrella of your operation."

"If you decide to leave Milwaukee, would you please tell your patients that you are visiting Tennessee and will be back soon? Is there any possibility, can you to tell your patients you will be on a leave of absence for a short time?"

"Certainly, I will do so, sir. If I do not like it there, I may, indeed, come back."

Jerry, one of my patients was receiving his last session of radiation therapy for his tongue cancer. Nancy and Jerry did not care for Dr. Lemon's bedside manner during Jerry's last therapy. They implored me not to leave Milwaukee. But I felt I had no choice. I had to move to Tennessee. Nancy said she would be happy to take care of my lake house. We had become awfully close like family since Jerry achieved outstanding results under my treatment.

Dr. Sessi, one of the most successful family doctors in the area, had a big medical clinic next to Mount Sinai Hospital. Doctor Sassi had a lawyer to protect his clinic, and his office was run by many employees. He had a small-scale radiation department to take X-rays for patients in his clinic, though it was not a radiation oncology. He was interested in buying my house.

My memory drifted back a year ago. He had married a pretty woman who was active in politics. I had mingled with him and his wife at a social event, and they had invited me to a fundraising dinner party for Scott Walker's gubernatorial campaign. This event was held at the house of his administrator, who had been managing his enormous clinic.

The dinner and the social connections among the various people in attendance and the gubernatorial candidate were sensational. The campaign experience revealed a different aspect of life and the motivations of people in medical circles outside the goal of practicing medicine. It gave me a new perspective, and I reanalyzed my life mission. Dr. Sessi's administrator had a gigantic and lavishly built house, with two large wet bars in his living room and full circular staircase leading to the seven upstairs bedrooms.

Dr. Sessi wanted to buy my house without involving a realtor. Even though, I selected a realtor. who appeared to be astute and honest. She controlled the marketing carefully. I promised the realtor I would give her all my hanging flower plants and some household items if she looked after my house until a new owner moved in the lake house.

Nancy and Jerry planted some beautiful flowers close to the bluff next to the lake, wishing for me to come back soon. They set flowers around and prayed for me. Nancy was a serious believer, and one of her sons became a priest.

I packed my house and Dr. Lemon's two kids helped, packing their books and some of their belongings. I was still busy working and did not have time to plan. I simply acted with the flow of the hurried pace I had set. The carpet was spotlessly cleaned, and my moving plan to Tennessee was ready. Some of the chemo drugs left in my clinic and. some of the drugs, I packed into my car in rush. Movers came and transferred my office furniture, including the executive desk and chair and the chemo mixing hood and other equipment.

One of the oncologists at Saint Luke Hospital offered to collect my billing charges that the insurance companies had not reimbursed. He promised to collect the funds from the insurance companies and repay the collections to me. I worked hard and released all my patients' history and documents to this oncologist amid moving.

As of this writing today, I have not received a penny from the collection of my reimbursements from this oncologist. Just because people smile at you does not mean they are your friends.

During that time, a primary care doctor wanted to purchase my practice. I declined because I could not sell my clinic to care primary doctor who didn't specialize in cancer treatments. Appropriately, I referred my patients to another oncologist.

Dr. Lemon did not help me pack the lake house, and he flew to Tennessee by himself. He secured his position at the medical center there. Shortly after that, we went together to find a house in Tennessee. Despite all my efforts to make him happy, shockingly, he appeared to be unhappy with me being attached to him.

Is he scared about this new job? I wondered. *Is he not sure about being married to an Asian American physician in the rural Deep South of hillbilly Crossville?*

His illogical and capricious self-centered behavior made me uncomfortable. His attitude changed, and he became arrogant and narcissistic. Perhaps, newly employed, he had regained his ego. He acted like a pompous jerk. I really did not care for his ambivalent attitude. I did not love him in the way of a romantic fairy tale; it was not the love I imagined should exist between husband and wife anyway. I was, rather, more interested in his broad knowledge and cultured background—what he knew about arts and music—along with his medical skills.

We sat next to each other in silence on the plane. When we exited for our layover, he started accusing me of having committed a fraud and saying he ought to report it to Medicare.

The accusation was incomprehensible. "What did you say just now?" I demanded. I was angry.

He apologized for having accused me. "I am so sorry; I should not have said that."

I had sacrificed a great deal to support him and to make him pleased, and he had turned things around, threatening to report a nonexistent fraud. He almost knocked the wind out me.

It was never too late to change my decisions; however, it was too much to redo. Repacking, canceling the realtor, reopening my clinic in Milwaukee—it all seemed like too much hard work. I got a sudden headache. I was not sure about my future. However, I would not cry over spilled milk. Instead, I would live one day at a time and place one foot in front of the other. Thank God tomorrow would be a new day.

The hospital administrator took us to the Ruby Tuesday restaurant in Crossville when we arrived in Tennessee. The town was small and barren.

I felt that the clock had been set backward and I had returned to the 1950s. Crossville's Main Street was flat as a pancake. There was not a single skyscraper. Here and there were small gas stations; a few office buildings; and, the town's biggest feature, a shopping mall with a Walmart across from Lowe's and next to Staples. There was only one McDonald's, one Wendy's, and a now shutdown Jack in the Box that had gone out of business. It was the smallest town I had ever seen in my entire life.

The hospital administrator took us on a tour of the wards and introduced several staff members. Dr. Lemon requested that the hospital administrator investigate my office infusion charge in Milwaukee. Further, he asked whether I could have my chemotherapy clinic at the hospital to give treatments. Plus, he wished to mix chemo drugs by way of a hospital pharmacist, so I could set up my practice to run just as the practice had at St. Francis and Mount Sinai.

The administrator declined our proposal. The hospital had neither the space nor the resources to accommodate such a setup. Later, this manager got back to Dr. Lemon's request to initiate a fraud investigation against me. He soon learned the infusion charge was clearly permitted by St. Francis Hospital. The administrator at the medical center in Crossville researched and found my billing code charge was appropriate and that no fraud had been committed. Dr. Lemon's accusation against me offended me, especially since he had rudely acted without any communication with me. I began to lose my respect for and trust in him. I started to become skeptical about his integrity and judgment.

There was one empty office, which was owned by a private pharmacist across from the medical center. This office had been occupied by an obstetric gynecologist who had had an extramarital affair and had been caught by his wife. The gynecologist had run out of town in such a hurry he had left some clinical materials behind him. His office had been closed and vacated for two years.

This empty office was located at an ideal spot just across from the medical center. It was a short distance, taking only two minutes to reach the hospital from my office.

During my search for space to locate my clinic, the administrator, Mr. Adams, recommended that I rent one of the remodeling buildings behind the hospital. I did not care for that office space, as it was located behind the hospital and hidden from view. Besides, the office was on a downhill slope, and the space was small. The sections of rooms were not desirably built. Accordingly, I declined to rent from the administrator.

Then Mr. Adams introduced me to the pharmacists, Tony, who owned the building. I considered leasing the unoccupied office space across from the hospital. There was a pediatric clinic on the end at the corner of the lot. My rented office would be conjoined with the office of a urologist, in the same strip mall. One side of the building was the urologist's office, and the other end would be my new clinic space.

Crossville had a famous small playhouse next to a man-made lake and a housing development along the lake. Mr. Adams took me on a tour of the Crossville area. He drove us to another developed subdivision in a small village. On the way, we visited a village near the hospital. There was a burned-down shack, where all that remained were soot-covered poles scattered across a deserted field. A small store selling milk and cigarettes stood on the side of the narrow road. On the other side was a gas station attached to a small convenience store selling discount food store. What was I going to do in this small, insignificant rural town? I felt lost and confused.

Within two or three minutes, Mr. Adams turned the corner. There were a couple man-made lakes, along with many attractive houses. He drove further down to the cul-de-sac, and I saw more elegant houses along the way. Soon, I felt much less depressed and my spirits rised. I released my anxiety with a long sigh. Woo-hoo!

Mr. Adams pointed out the pharmacist's house next to the cul-de-sac. I noticed a mansion was available. The house was built on two-and-a-half-acre lot and privately located on a dead-end street. Building the mansion, the retirement home of a famous developer, had taken five years. The same builder had also developed the entire subdivision next to his house. The homes in the subdivision were owned by professional people—the physician director of the ER, a well-known lawyer, a dentist, a neurologist, and a few surgeons.

Fairfield Glade, where many wealthy retirees resided (mostly for the seven-hole golf course), was about twenty to thirty minutes from Crossville. The Fairfield Glade residents went to Florida during the winter months. The population in that area was around 150,000, much larger than Crossville's population of between 25,000 and 30,000. There were many man-made lakes in Fairfield Glade.

We looked around the lakefront houses, but I did not like any of them. Besides Fairfield Glade was too far from the hospital. It would take thirty to forty-five minutes to get to the hospital.

CHAPTER 18

One Step at a Time

We flew back to Wisconsin and were ready to move to Tennessee. The Crossville pharmacist called me to let me know that the lease agreement for my future oncology clinic was ready to be signed. Tony also informed me that the best house in town had recently been put on the market. He gave me detailed stories regarding the unexpected availability of the house close to the hospital and a brief family history of the owner.

The builder's wife, Frances, was the daughter of the first doctor in Crossville, and the street in front of her parents' house was named for her father, Dr. Larson. Dr. Larson died, and her mother lived alone in a big house close to the daughter's mansion. This mansion had just been completed a year ago. They had put the house on the market because her mother had gotten sick, and she wanted to stay with her mother in her house.

The builder, Mr. Campbell, loved his wife and was willing to give up his gorgeous home. It had taken several years to construct the magnificent mansion. I had noticed the marvelous house when Mr. Adams had driven along the dead-end street next to Tony's home.

The three most stressful events in life are moving, death, and divorce. I had experienced that moving was certainly stressful. I had to deal with packing the household items, selling the Wisconsin home, finding a new place in Tennessee, and preparing for the American Oncology Board examination. On top of that, I had to deal with a capricious and irresponsible husband who lacked commitment. In addition, my unknown future and what it would be like living in the Deep South worried me. I needed God's mercy and wisdom to discern the best course of action given my current circumstance. I reminded myself to take one step at a time.

The three properties I had owned before getting married were rented to generate income, but the rental business added to my stress after I got married. Hence, I sold two houses—the one in Pensacola, Florida, that I had bought before my residency training and the prestigious Tremont condo on Mount Washington in Pittsburgh, Pennsylvania, bought during my residency. My Tremont condo was sold shortly before we relocated our practices in Tennessee to reduce my stress.

Dr. Lemon and I had individual and separate funds, assets, and bank accounts. I did not know his bank or bank account numbers, since we had mutually agreed to maintain our assets independently. My two premarital houses were sold, and the money for both was deposited into the same account at St. Francis Bank in Milwaukee, Wisconsin. The proceeds from the sale of the lake house in Michigan, which we had purchased together right before getting married, were divided in half. I deposited half the money from that sale into the same Saint Frances Bank account and gave the remaining half to Dr. Lemon. I left my bank account in Milwaukee when I moved to Tennessee, since I had known the bank manager for thirteen years and knew I could trust her.

Dr. Lemon did not want to transfer our cars by way of a moving agent. We drove each car ourselves to Tennessee. I did not have a good sense of direction; nor did I have good night vision. I had a hard following his car all night long from Wisconsin to Tennessee. Crossville was located two hours from Nashville and an hour from Knoxville. It was thirty minutes from Cookeville. We had finally reached the Cookeville, and the morning sun in Cumberland County helped our droopy eyelids stay open. We looked for a place to have a cup of coffee and breakfast.

We saw a small pancake house. The café was quiet, and only one customer was sitting at the table talking to the owner of the restaurant. The place offered home-cooked food, and an old lady gave us a friendly greeting with a Southern accent. Instantly I realized that I was in the different environment of a rural community. We refreshed ourselves briefly and finished the drive, pointing our cars toward our destination, Crossville.

There was a Hampton Inn right after the exit to Crossville Highway. We checked in and crashed on the bed. After a short rest, I called the owner of the mansion. I told Mr. Campbell that we were interested in seeing his house that afternoon.

Mr. Campbell was a kind Southern gentleman, and he would be happy to see us. The market price was $750,000 in the middle of a small town. Initially, Dr. Lemon was mad at me, saying we were not rich enough to buy an expensive house. I had sold two houses, which Dr. Lemon did not know about. Before I negotiate the price of the house, I asked him to be quiet. So he kept his silence. I was able to negotiate with the Mr. Campbell and his wife, Francis, and bought the house at a much lower price. Both parties were satisfied with the sale of the house.

The house was located at the end of a cul-de-sac. The place was secluded and provided privacy with Bradford pear trees along the long circular driveway. The land around the house was a in a quiet wooded setting, spread on two and a half acres. There was a half-acre vacant lot next to the house. The front lawn was spacious, with rhododendrons in red, pink, and white that were tall enough to be Christmas trees. The border of the house was lined with white pine trees and numerous dogwoods. Colorful flowers grew between the rhododendrons, and decorative garden lights highlighted their beauty. Peonies, hydrangeas, pansies, and tulips gracefully intertwined in the garden. The red brick pavement was artistically designed. The master bedroom had six huge arched windows looking out onto the splendidly arranged flower garden.

The backside of the house had a private creek, and the sound of the roaring stream revitalized me and soothed my daily stress. White dogwoods and Bradford flowers created a fairyland in spring. The naturally arranged shapes and colors of the flowers and trees accented their breathtaking beauty. Clustered and bundled yellow forsythias and daffodils awakened us from the cold winters. The wall in front of the bedroom was tightly lined with graceful azaleas. This was my dream house!

The entrance door was decorated with beveled crystals, which laced with golden brass on a third of the lattice. The house's foyer boasted formal standing white columns on each side of a semi-spiral staircase with classically carved wooden rails along its supporting bars. The upstairs floor related to the bridge from one room to another room, making the ceiling about the living room thirty feet high. The ceiling above the bridge had an exquisite, recessed stained-glass light fixture. Its light reflected enchantingly around the bridge and semicircular staircase.

The foyer's ground floor was laid with stylish wood, allowing for a spacious formal dining room and an elegantly sparkly mammoth crystal chandelier that had been imported from England.

Two sets of French doors opened to the backyard, one from to the kitchen and the other from the living room. The door from the kitchen led to the covered patio encompassed by red brick pillars. The one from the living room opened onto the large open wooden deck looking over the creek and the rolling stream that made its way through the woods.

The inside of the house resembled a small palace, with white marble-mantled fireplaces and arched windows with semicircular beveled edges.

The kitchen was extremely, and its surrounding windows displayed the spectacular flower garden. A museum quality mosaic rose behind the black cooktop, and an ancient teapot enclosed the backsplash. It was magnificent. Francis was a professional interior decorator, and she had instructed the workers to dismantle the mosaic three times until it became a perfect masterpiece. The floor was a coordinating color, with lightly tinted pink tile that matched the built-in kitchen desk attached to a small china cabinet, the cupboards, the refrigerator door cover, and the drawers. Dazzling custom-made window treatments had been finished by the best designer. Decorated tassels hung from the valances on the top of each window. I was fascinated by this house.

Mr. Campbell looked at me and spoke in a slow Southern drawl. "People come and see my house, and they fall madly in love with the house."

"It's true," I agreed. "This house is fabulous. Honestly, I haven't seen such a well-built and gorgeous house. However, Mr. Campbell, falling in love with your house is one thing. We cannot afford such an elegant house. We are newlyweds and have just come to Tennessee. Is there any possibility that we could pay you $600,000 in cash instead of your asking price of $750,000, which will save you money in the long run? You may lose money trying to keep your house on the market for years.

"Your house is absolutely striking," I added, "but Crossville is a small town with a population of thirty thousand. Eventually, you will sell the house. But how many people can afford to buy your house? Your mother-in-law isn't well, and her condition is serious. What is more important than your family? I believe you should take care of her as soon as possible."

Mr. Campbell and I negotiated back and forth for a while. Dr. Lemon and Francis sat on the recliners next to each other. They were quiet until the final negotiation between Mr. Campbell and me was completed. We compromised, settling on the price $650,000.

Mr. Campbell was a well-known housing developer, and everybody knew him. One of his lawyer friends drew up the house deed for us. Regardless of my marriage to Mr. Lemon, this house would be under separate ownership. As per our mutual agreement, we paid equally. For some reason, he wanted to pay $100,078.52 more, instead of exactly half the down payment. He initially did not explain to me why he wanted to pay about $100,000 more. My thought was that he wanted to compensate me for all my sacrifices. Surprisingly, that was my innocent, wishful assumption.

If Mr. Campbell's house were in San Diego, it would be priced at least $6 million or $7 million.

After we'd purchased the house, I had to take care of my clinic. First, I had to sign the lease contract with the owner, Tony.

Tony opened the space for my future clinic, which had been shut down for two years. It was like a haunted house. The sink was in bright orange sink, the countertops were orange, and several of the examination rooms had orange wall. I took in the dented surface, alongside scattered rust spots on the aluminum door. I nearly passed out looking at the deserted office that was to be my clinic. Orange was not my favorite color. I felt as if I were standing in an orange quagmire that had been splashed everywhere in the clinic.

The movers delivered my extra living room couch to the clinic for use in the patient sitting area. Behind the dented aluminum door was a parking lot. There was a water faucet and sink in that area, which were also bright orange. This emphasized to me that, obviously, the state of Tennessee's color was orange. I must be immersed in the orange color of my new home state.

I was dumbfounded and astonished. I fell speechlessly onto the couch, feeling suffocated in the dusty sick building, which lacked proper ventilation. A sudden dizzy spell overwhelmed me, and I was filled with confusion and despair. I propped my weak legs on the couch, leaned my head against the wall, and closed my eyes. When I slowly opened my eyes, I saw wiggling creatures in different shapes, forms, and sizes. Some of the bugs were fuzzy, and some had antennas.

I jumped out of the building at once, having a panic attack. I needed fresh air before I fainted. I took a deep breath and tried to get ahold of myself. Why had I followed Dr. Lemon to the Deep South? How could it be that I now lived and practiced in Crossville, Tennessee? What was I going to do here? I felt like a fish out of water.

Lord, please give me your mercy, I prayed. *Give me strength and guide me through the Holy Spirit.*

I thought of the Lord's Prayer:

> The Lord is my Shepherd; I shall not want. He maketh me to lie down in green pastures. He leadeth me beside still waters.

> Yea, though I walk through the valley of the shadow of death, I will fear no evil: for thou art with me; thy rod and thy staff they comfort me. Thou preparest a table before me in the presence of mine enemies: thou anointest my head with the oil; my cup runneth over. (Psalm 23:1, 2, 4, and 5)

God, help me. I took another deep breath and buttoned my clothes tightly. Cautiously, I marched into the dusty clinic. I looked around once more. I decided to renovate the office way I desired.

I knocked down a wall and made a lovely chemotherapy room. I added cheerful window treatments made by an expert designer. I installed an indoor water fountain, hung paintings on the walls and decorated with nicely arranged silk trees and silk flowers—after the entire office had been painted creamy white and the orange was gone. I replaced the reception and appointment desk. The built-in medical record cabinet had locks with keys.

Cookies, ice creams, boosts, and other snacks for patients were placed at the corner of the chemotherapy room. The middle door for the chemo room was replaced with a wide, open glass door. Brand new green leather recliners with cushioned seats, end tables, and coffee tables would ensure my patients were as comfortable as they could be. A support group was arranged among my patients, and they established a close network to help each other. The office was remodeled and transformed into an attractive and cozy space.

Now, the clinic looked brighter, and dazzling sunlight shown through the glass door. The gurgling of the water fountain soothed the patients' anxieties. Air was filtered through the newly installed ventilation system that circulated a fresh breeze.

I adored the bright sunlight, which was important for living. All of earth depends on the energy released by the sun as heat. The sunlight in the clinic refreshed us, as if it alone had chased out the dark and gloomy conditions I'd first encountered. Now, in contrast, the chemo room conveyed an alluring, sweet aura. The changes transcended the space, creating a hopeful, joyful, peaceful, and healthy atmosphere.

The following day, the movers delivered our household furniture. Moving boxes were piled on the kitchen floor. Looking at the boxes made me tired; unpacking and rearranging would be a lot of work.

I hired several young students through the realtor. The students unpacked all the boxes, and that helped me a great deal. Dr. Lemon opened only a few boxes. I ended up putting everything away and decorated the big house by myself, since he'd already started working at the hospital.

He cherished his expensive antique dining table from his previous marriage. He was excited to find the place that would suit it. We decided to set it under the gigantic chandelier, which had a perfect center view of the bay window.

In a room above the three-car garage, the builder had built enormous bookshelves, with two doors that opened and closed, which occupied one entire wall. A large, recessed area was the perfect place for a huge television below the book cabinet. The area was flawless—a perfect place for our library, to watch movies, and to entertain.

I purchased two adorable, sculptured water fountains. I'd placed one in my chemo room, and the other, of the same style, was for the house. It fit delicately into the recessed area of the semicircular staircase. Many clustered silk flowers dangled over the fountain. The morning sunbeams hit the crystal on the front lattice scattering bursts of rainbows across the fairy tale fountain and its silk flowers and trees. I loved flowers and wanted to make more silk flowers for the clinic and the house.

Dr. Lemon liked to take trips, both short and long distances. He was willing to drive to Knoxville, which was a much bigger city than Crossville. We found a huge home décor department store. This place had a zillion interior decorations and a variety of silk flowers, silk trees, and vases; you name it, the store had it all.

My excitement propelled me from one section to the next and between aisles. The store carried more than I needed. I moved quickly and hurried to get the shopping done as quickly as possible. Dr. Lemon became bored, uninterested in purchasing flowers, and soon he got steaming mad at me. He tossed a bundle of silk flowers in the shopping cart and walked out of the store.

I paid for all the items and went out looking for him. He was sitting inside his car listening to his music. When he saw me, he got out of the car and helped me put the items inside his trunk. He did not like flower shopping, but he loved eating out at an Italian restaurant, Carrabba's. We enjoy the fried calamari dipped in lemony salsa as an appetizer and had a seafood and pasta dish. His mood improved after the excellent food.

He purchased a king-size bed and a top-of-the line mattress, along with a down feather comforter and layover cover. Francis sold us two of her lithographic paintings; a beautiful female sculpture; and a double-sized love recliner, which had custom-designed fabric. Dr. Lemon paid in full and did not collect half of the purchase from me at the time.

I thought it was his generous contribution to the house decorations; unquestionably he clearly stated that what he paid for solely belonged to him as his private possessions.

I finished the house decoration and settled into the 6,500-square foot house for only two of us. The house arrangements were finished within one week.

The completion of my clinic did not take long either. Some patients were already scheduled to see me within two weeks of my arrival in Crossville. I was young enough to handle the transitional work quickly. He was three years younger than I was. Yet he only hung two pictures on my clinic wall.

CHAPTER 19

What Medicare Fraud? This Is Where the Story Unfolds

Dr. Lemon wanted me to extend my oncology practice, utilizing the main group of the primary doctors' building to increase my earnings. Then the group wanted me to lease space next to a small radiology floor with one X-yay machine. The primary doctors generated some income from X-ray evaluation of their patients. It was not a good idea to practice next to a radiation hazard department. I decided to settle with the one clinic that I had leased and decorated nicely for my patients.

Through the grapevine, I heard that I was being investigated for Medicare fraud, but the matter had been resolved. "What Medicare fraud?" I murmured to myself. I recalled that Dr. Lemon had accused me at the airport. Later, he had given my office's infusion code charge number to the hospital administrator and suggested an investigation into possible fraud. Mr. Adams told Dr. Lemon that my charge was allowed and was appropriate and that no fraud had been committed. Somebody might have eavesdropped when Dr. Lemon was asking Mr. Adams about my charge code. His question of that code number might have snowballed to a concern among the group of primary doctors.

When I look back, I realize that we moved to Tennessee in a hurry. We arrived in Tennessee on June 30, 1999, and I opened the clinic on July 12, 1999.

Thanks to word-of-mouth recommendations, many patients came to my clinic as soon as I had opened. Immediately, I got busy with consultations.

My first patient was Connie, the wife of a retired medical oncologist at Cincinnati Medical School in Ohio. Connie worked in the laboratory department at the university. She was diagnosed with ovarian cancer, which had been treated at the university hospital. Later, she and her husband had decided to move to Fairfield Glade for the mild weather in Tennessee and to play golf together.

I preferred to have my clinic and to provide patients chemotherapy in the hospital. But the hospital administrator had declined my request due to financial limitation. Finding qualified employees, including nurses, billing clerks, business manager, receptionist, and housekeepers, was not easy at the beginning of my new practice. I prepared all necessary paperwork myself, including charts for my patients.

A local oncology competitor, Henry, was born and raised in Crossville. He grew up in this small town and had many relatives and knew everybody. Henry's wife was a chemo-certified register nurse, and she prepared chemo drugs for Dr. Henry.

One of the church parishioners, Karen, had a managerial background and helped at the starting point of my business. Likewise, I had worked in a variety of positions; I had been a doctor, a nurse, a pharmacist, a receptionist, a manager, and a billing clerk. I used to mix several chemo drugs in the pharmacy department at St. Francis Hospital. I knew how to properly prepare chemo drugs under specialized equipment known as a hood. I had brought some chemo drugs and the chemo mixing hood from Milwaukee and used it in Tennessee.

Crossville was a small rural area, and most people had worked at factories or in business offices, not in a medical clinic. Qualified registered nurses, especially chemo-certified nurses were not available at the time of my practice in Crossville. Besides, the Tennessee Board of Nursing prohibited LPN nurses from mixing chemo drugs.

A well-recognized oncologist from Knoxville was looking for a part-time physician to assist him at his clinic. He invited me for lunch. He, his wife, Dr. Lemon, and I had lunch together in Knoxville. His clinic appeared to be arranged decently and his practice, opened for years now, well established. It would be nice to work with him, though it took more than an hour and a half to get to work from my place. The lunch invitation was appreciated, but I declined his offer.

The method of purchasing chemo drugs from supply companies was explained by the chief oncologist at Thompson Cancer Center in Oak Ridge. When I worked in Milwaukee, I had a computer software system that was assisted by a company and facilitated billing charges to insurance companies, including Medicare. I knew how to enter my own billing codes on the computer, but I was too busy to handle billing. Unfortunately, I could not find a trained billing clerk in the small town of Crossville.

During that time, a nice local woman came to my office and declared she knew how to use computer software. Having been desperately seeking a billing technician without any success for some time, I hired her on the spot. She worked extremely hard, but she was slow, lacked skills, and made numerous errors. I reminded her to copy the billing charges on the backup disk, which she entered each day, but she could not satisfactorily comprehend my billing system. Despite her good work ethic and sweet attitude, regrettably, she did not have sufficient knowledge to handle my clinic's billing. My practice became overwhelmingly busy, and Dr. Lemon and I sadly decided to let her go.

Another candidate visited my office, telling me she had worked as a billing clerk at a doctor's office. This employee had some computer knowledge from having handled a primary doctor's billing system, though she did not know about cancer billing codes. In any event, she was better than the former employee, and she got the job.

My office manager, Karen, worked diligently submitting the charges and bills to the insurance companies. She carefully monitored what had been paid or what had not been paid and kept apprised of the status of reimbursement. If she discovered any unpaid charges from insurance companies for more than three months, she resubmitted the bills to the companies without evaluating why the companies had rejected the bill and not paid. For example, she should have billed a chemo drug code, instead of a diagnostic billing code. The complicated billing system was handled by untrained professionals, which, years later, would trigger the opening of an investigation into health care fraud.

Karen, my manager, became frustrated and could not handle the extremely busy practice. She quit and found another managerial position at a business office. Subsequently, I needed to hire more employees—not only a new manager but also billing clerks.

The new billing manager was calm and read the billing carefully. Then she tried to analyze the system. The husband of one of the billing clerks was a computer technician, and he had set up the computer network at my office.

I hired a receptionist who mainly answered phone calls and scheduled follow-up appointments. She was attractive and worked efficiently.

Dr. Lemon worked as a hospital employee, yet he could charge his own fees for service, utilizing the radiation oncology machine at the hospital. Hence, Dr. Lemon used my billing software for his billing charges. In addition, I used the system to pay all my employees' salaries.

One thing good about Dr. Lemon was that he had computer skills and could quickly figure out a computer system.

We took our billing charges home. He reviewed his billing charges, I double-checked mine, and I dictated to complete my patients' progress notes before I went to sleep. Dr. Lemon and I constantly trained the billing clerks on the annually upgraded billing software. After we participated health care billing code seminars in Nashville, we visited a medical oncology billing company that produced upgraded software annually in Boon, North Carolina.

My billing manager, Belinda, was instructed on how to use QuickBook. She learned promptly and was able to pay my employees' salaries from my account, not from Dr. Lemon's account.

Dr. Lemon enjoyed putting his hands into different pots and excitedly did so. He loved to involve himself in other people's business. He came to my office and suggested that I have my receptionist, Barbara, double-check all my billing charges.

"I do not think that's fair and will potentially offend my billing manager," I told him. "Beside we have billing clerks, and they are doing reasonably well. Plus, I did not hire Barbara as a billing clerk. She is a receptionist."

"Barbara is not busy answering the phone. Let her double-check my billings," he insisted.

I did not like Dr. Lemon interfering in my business. Still, he was my husband and the man of the house. I considered his advice.

Barbara had built-up resentments due to her husband's numerous extramarital affairs. She had witnessed with her own eyes her husband's physical engagement with another woman. She had some physical symptoms of not doing well, possibly related to the difficulties in her marriage. Recently, she complained about her baby's mistreatment by a doctor at a hospital in Nashville. Surely, she was not happy, and everything bothered her. A relationship based on physical attraction without a kind and loving heart would not receive blessings. She became awfully bitter.

Dr. Lemon's recommendation bothered me and gave me uneasy feelings. At last, though, I agreed with him. I let Barbara review my billings after the billing clerks had entered the charges on the computer. My intuitive judgment and discernment of Barbara was accurate. Certainly, I had agreed to allow a Trojan horse to enter my clinic.

Two months after I agreed to let Barbara double-checked my billing charges, she said that I had double-billed Medicare. Karen, my first manager, had resubmitted the charges when she had not received the reimbursement for more than three months. She should have evaluated and checked into why the insurance company had not reimbursed my charges. She was extremely busy, and simply, she did not know any better. So, she resubmitted the bills.

Medicare has been a government-operated health care business since after World War II and has a very sophisticated system and organization. I believe Medicare is the most superb and meticulous insurance company in existence. Medicare would not have paid twice for my private billing charges.

Soon after Barbara mistakenly discovered my "double billing charges," she assumed that I had intentionally double billed to gain financial benefit. She then quickly reported the matter to TBI (Tennessee Bureau of Investigation).

This report—a result of her incomprehension—hit the fan. Once the government agents started an investigation into a private medical practice, it was worse than falling into quicksand.

Barbara worked in an exercise club before she had worked as a receptionist at my office. She did not have any background in billing or nursing. Barbara's assumptive complains to TBI were incorrect and completely lacked material evidence. The TBI agents verified that Barbara had mistakenly reported to the investigation office. This matter was clarified. However, once someone us reported to the bureau, a red flag is raised. Zealous agents at the bureau would not let go of any case without a further investigation—as if an eagle snitched on a little bird under their claw.

It was a case of the blind leading the blind. Barbara was showing TBI what she had discovered without any skills or knowledge. Her understanding of the specialized cancer treatments coding was not much worse than that of the bureau agents, who most likely did not have a background in the medical field.

Despite the unexpected commotion, my business grew rapidly. I needed more qualified employees, such as a chemo-certified registered nurses, LPN nurses, and a phlebotomist. I ran around like a chicken with its head cut off.

Barbara could not satisfy what she had alleged against me. My guess was Barbara's severe resentment and her low self-esteem drove her to gain power to control me. Until proven otherwise, comparison is the thief of joy. Looking at my large-carat diamond ring, seeing that I was married to a handsome young doctor, myself a busy doctor, who generated a large income compared to her nine dollar per hour paycheck, she had easily fallen into the trap of stirring up her own psychological misery as a weapon against me. Apparently, Barbara did not trust her husband, herself, or me. Misery, indeed, loves company.

Barbara was an attractive woman, and she had a precious baby. However, she had gone through an inconceivably difficult situation, much of it self-inflicted, and she drank her own poison. We can overcome anything if God is in our heart. Our life journey is unfair and difficult. We must see the half-full glass, instead of the half-empty glass and face life with a positive attitude.

My LPN, Haley, worked hard, and she interacted with the patients well. I was satisfied with her job performance. Most of my employees were young and associated closely with each other as a peer group. Everybody knew everybody's business and entertained each other with gossip. In this small community, LPNs were not allowed to mix or adjust the chemo drugs, although they were permitted to infuse patients with chemo drugs and inject the medication.

My daily routine at work started at 7:00 a.m. and went till 5:00 p.m. Then I went for consultations and rounds to evaluate the condition of inpatients at the hospital. Dr. Lemon finished up his workday earlier than

I did while were in Tennessee. He would often call me for dinner at home. Usually I had to finish my leftover work after dinner and worked until close to midnight, while Dr. Lemon would be doing something or other on his computer. Around midnight, we tried to get some sleep and got up before 6:00 a.m. Some nights, my beeper went off constantly, and I had to take emergency consultations or admissions after midnight.

I mixed the chemotherapy drugs early in the morning before my work started for urgent chemotherapy patients, conducted follow-up evaluations, and had consultations with newly diagnosed cancer patients.

Most regular chemotherapy drugs were prepared with one of the nurses' present. I was physically exhausted most days, and I was continuously searching for a qualified chemotherapy-certified registered nurse; there were none. The previous hospital pharmacist who currently worked at a private pharmacy declined my request to mix the chemotherapy drugs I was using.

Procrit was a popular drug used to increase red cell blood counts after chemotherapy treatments. It was like vitamin B12 and not a chemo drug. Most chemo patients developed common side effects from Procrit, including bone pain, muscle pain, extreme weakness, respiratory tract infection, diarrhea, edema, fever, skin rash, cough, difficulty breathing, nausea, and vomiting.

Like most liquid drugs, each small bottle of Procrit contained 16.8 percent more of the drug than the listed amount. So pharmaceutically manufactured Procrit contained 1.168 cc in each individual container. If patients required 1 cc of Procrit, there would be 0.168 cc leftover in the bottle.

The required treatment of 1 cc of Procrit itself induced significant side effects. Therefore, giving extra, overfilled doses greater than 1 cc of Procrit would accentuate further severe side effects. This would knowingly injure patients, worsening their physical conditions on top of their already fragile condition after chemotherapy. Consequently, I told Haley to save 0.16 cc of Procrit out of each 1.16 cc, as each Procrit bottle had an extra 0.16 cc.

It is common knowledge that all physicians swear to uphold the Hippocratic oath, which states, "First, do no harm."

The educational courses and training for licensed practical nurses last for a much shorter duration than do those of registered nurses. None of my

LPNs had previously worked with cancer patients. Accordingly, my LPNs were not aware of the extra amount that came in each Procrit bottle.

Many of my patients had indigent state insurance. The company went bankrupt and did not reimburse Procrit. My logical thought was that I could save the extra 0.16 cc after providing a correct dose of 1 cc for patients. Afterward having used eight bottles of Procrit, I could combine the remainders of each to make an extra 1 cc of Procrit for indigent patients. The remaining 0.16 cc could be easily withdrawn by using the smallest of needles.

Additionally, I explained to all my LPNs that they were to save the empty bottles, which each contained 0.16 cc Procrit. Numerous "empty" upside-down bottles were thus stored for future use in the refrigerator. According to the pharmaceutical company that sells it, Procrit can be stored for two weeks.

My memory drifted to what Director Spear had stated in Milwaukee— about how he had known doctors who'd relocated to another state and whose businesses had failed when they did not carefully manage the overhead expenses. I was extremely frugal and saved everything, not wasting anything.

I did not care for living in Tennessee, though I genuinely and compassionately cared for my patients. My patients respected and loved me as much as I loved and respected them.

In general, people tend to complain about others and to entertain friends and family with negative "breaking news," instead of appreciating people's altruistic contributions to people or society. I did not believe that most of the population had good will, by reason of their living tough lives.

Barbara's drama entertained her peer groups and my LPNs. She struck a match and ignited a flame that became a wildfire of exciting breaking news. The TBI investigation into my having double billed Medicare was fruitless. But having been rolled, the snowball was, as snowballs do, becoming bigger and bigger. With or without material evidence of its validity, a piece of gossip was something the small rural community loved to spread.

Barbara added insult to injury, telling people that she had heard Dr. Gates instruct her LPN, Haley, to give 0.9 cc, 0.8 c, and 0.7 cc of Procrit to her patients. Barbara was not a nurse. Nor did she have a background related to medical treatments. Her inconsistent statements based on overheard comments were spread, and soon incorrect "news" was spreading.

I clearly instructed Haley to save 0.16 cc from each 1.16 cc bottle of Procrit after administering 1 cc to a patient. This was shown as exculpatory evidence on the Tennessee Bureau of Investigation's videotape in which the refrigerator in my medical clinic was filmed. It featured the small bottles of Procrit, placed upside down to facilitate the collection of the last bit of liquid, which, having accumulated on the cap, would be sucked out with an exceedingly small needle.

To be safe, my billing manager called the Center for Medicare and Medicaid services regarding utilizing overfilled amounts of Procrit. She received an answer from Medicare stating that there was no violation in billing overfilled amounts Procrit by performing maximum utilization. There was no fraud.

Medicare had no policy regarding not charged, overfilled drugs until 2004. TBI questioned my charge regarding extra, overfilled amounts of 0.16 cc in January 2002, investigating it as fraud.

CHAPTER 20

My Pizza Party (I Love Them All)

I usually started work early in the morning before 7:00 a.m., rounding on inpatients at the hospital and then returning to my clinic. The proximity of my clinic to the hospital was convenient. Patients who had come for follow-up appointments would be waiting in my clinic lobby before I made it back to my office. Most days, I would not take lunch until 3:00 p.m. due to busy daily schedule.

I would sip homemade tea between patient evaluations. Sometimes, I did not have spare moments to use the bathroom. I instructed my employees not to interrupt me while I was concentrating or evaluating my newly consulted patients. Nevertheless, Barbara constantly knocked on the patients' room doors and disturbed my work.

One day, when I was extremely busy, I asked Barbara to bring my follow-up patient's blood count reports. She handed me sheets with the lab results. Thank God, I always attentively checked my patient's name. She had brought the wrong patient's blood count results. At this point, I was not sure whether Barbara was intentionally conducting unethical and dangerous behavior in plot against me. If I had trusted and assumed that she had brought the correct blood count results without double-checking, I would have easily mistreated and injured this patient.

Normally, I clearly remembered my patients' abnormal blood counts until patients were correctly treated. Any issues caused potential harm to patients, which was what upset me most. Just like a mother would not tolerate when her babies got hurt without reason, I was annoyed by Barbara's negligence. No matter whether good or bad, right or wrong, I should learn not to get excited or angry. Anger is nothing but our emotional expression without a solution.

Believe me, this time I was upset. Barbara then reported to the TBI agents that I conducted the clinic like a commander in an army.

A person cannot be successful without people. Agreeable interpersonal relationships are critically important when it comes to achieving goals. Overall, neighborhood folks in this small rural Crossville were kind and friendly. Particularly, my patients were genuinely special.

Dr. Lemon and I were blessed to be living in a beautiful house, and my busy practice was blessed as well. As a show of gratitude and to reach out to make friendships, I figured an enjoyable dinner party with the local primary care doctors and hospital staff members would establish amicable friendships among those of us who were working together. Thus, elaborate dinner gatherings were held, hosting different groups of doctors at our elegant home.

For the first time, I was glad that Dr. Lemon had brought the distinguished antique dining table set with its twelve ostentatious dinner chairs. An attractive tablecloth, along with the runway and candles and lovely flower arrangements; brand-new fine China dishes and gilded gold utensils; wine buckets and first-rate scrumptious entrées, along with heavenly desserts made for magnificent dinners. We all relished the food and companionship and nurtured each other. I did my best to please our guests, serving them as kings and queens and hoping to become their close friends.

Strangely, one of the female primary care doctors commented after dinner, "You're not living in a house; this is a mansion." Her tone of voice sounded offended.

Neither my unexpectedly flourishing medical practice nor my reaching out for friendship by inviting the doctors to my comfortable house was intended to offend. The last thing I wanted to do was make anybody be a green-eyed monster. Jealousy is dangerous; it is a product of emotional insecurity, fear, and envy over lack of possessions. Dr. Lemon and I had successfully found our house without any expectations, as if we had hit a jackpot.

I understood some of the primary care doctors' feelings.

A couple of the doctors wished to see the entire house, and we took them on a tour. The master bedroom was close to the formal dining area. Sunlight

Moonlight Melody

burst through numerous large arched windowpanes covered with pleated, sheer champagne blinds that ballooned from golden French brackets, their ends gracefully puddled on the floor like wedding gown trains.

From the center of the ceiling in the master bedroom hung a huge circular presidential chandelier with matching sconces on each inside wall next to the dresser. The whirlpool bath was adjacent to the master bedroom. It had two charming columns on top of the pool in front of an enchanting stained-glass window. Designed Peacock pillows decorated each corner, along with unique sculptures.

The showcase powder room boasted huge wall mirrors and a double sink with gilded gold faucets across from a massive glass-encased shower room, with double showerheads and a built-in sitting area. The gigantic walk-in closet, larger than an average master bedroom, was located next to the master bathroom. It also had custom-made wall dressers and drawers, shoe racks on each side of the wall, and large built-in wall shelves. Our stationary bike, a StairMaster, a desk, and many more items sat in the expansive walk-in closet, and there was still plenty of space. Dr. Lemon used to practice his clarinet, playing Mozart's sonatas in that room.

We did not use outside shoes in the house and provided seventeen pair of house slippers next to the entrance during the dinner party. There was a royal white ottoman for sitting, where one could change his or her shoes.

Looking back, I understood why some of the doctors were jealous of our living conditions. Perhaps I did too much for them.

A sarcoma patient was referred for a consultation. Sarcoma is a rare kind of cancerous growth in connective tissues. Soft tissue sarcoma affects tissue connecting, supporting, or surrounding any of the body's system. This patient had a tumor on his right shoulder. This type of cancer was usually treated by not only removing the mass, but also amputating the limb.

I was ready to consult an orthopedic surgeon, but I decided to have a second opinion of the tissue biopsy at the bigger hospital in Nashville. The second opinion from Nashville was diagnosed as lymphoma instead of sarcoma. God bless my patient. I was extremely glad I had sent out his biopsy specimen for a second opinion and avoided amputation of his right shoulder. The patient did well and responded to combination chemotherapy under my care. He was healthy and able to use both of his arms without any problems. Eventually, he did not need to receive chemotherapy and achieved clinical remission.

Correct diagnosis is extremely important before treating a patient successfully. Practicing in a small town was quite different than when I had worked at Anderson Cancer Center in Houston. Occasionally, I got in trouble because of my assertive opinions on behalf of my patients. Had I not learned that silence is gold? Sometimes it is, yes; other times, no. I accepted my mistakes and reminded myself that we all live and learn.

I was too busy to make deposit slips. Again, I was not guarded. Barbara made my bank deposits. I paid a large sum of money to supply companies to purchase medications. Accordingly, I received generous reimbursements from insurance companies. This allowed Barbara to find out much about my business account, which was a big mistake. I should not have exposed myself by giving access to my financial information to anybody but me.

A surgeon, Dr. Fox, referred an ovarian cancer patient who had been a nurse for twenty-five years at the medical center, and her husband taught chemistry to most doctors in Crossville. They were a wonderful couple. This sweet patient, Helen Holladay, had end-stage ovarian cancer with widespread massive blood clots. She was told she had less than three months. I was eager to prolong her life and provided the textbook recommended chemotherapy. After several cycles of chemotherapy, she lost all her hair and experienced substantial weight loss, going from 130 pounds to 90 pounds. She was admitted to the hospital with dehydration and low blood counts. Rumors spread among hospital nurses that I had burned her with highly toxic chemo drugs. This was recorded on the TBI report. She begged me to let her go and wanted me to stop her chemotherapy.

"Please hang tight and give me a chance. Let me see what I can do for you," I told Helen.

All my patients respected me, and they followed my instruction. Her massive blood clot problem was treated gingerly yet persistently while supplementing maximum nutrition and plenty of hydration. I adjusted chemotherapy dosages based on her clinical condition.

She gradually regained her strength, and her overall condition improved.

Unfortunately, she developed another cancer alongside her ovarian cancer. I referred her to a surgeon to remove the new tumor in her uterus. The surgeon refused the surgery.

Consequently, I transferred Helen Holladay to the bigger hospital, Thompson Cancer Center, in Oak Ridge, Tennessee.

She was recovering from the surgery, and chemotherapy was resumed carefully. I continuously adjusted her dosages based on her clinical and physical status. Supplemental treatments were provided when I added different chemo drugs for the second tumor. Repeated tests for blood clots were remarkably improved on Doppler studies.

She gradually improved and regained her weight, back up to 135 pounds from 90 pounds. She enjoyed trying different blond wigs from my free wig closet. Nobody realized that she had lost her hair. She was very neat, and her hair was always perfect. Some rural folks complained that I had not really given her chemotherapy, because she had never lost her hair.

Helen's tumor markers returned to normal, and the restaging CT scan of her abdomen revealed no evidence of recurrent cancer.

Years later, I noticed slightly elevated levels and an abnormal liver function test on her lab report. I referred her to Thompson Cancer Center for a second opinion. The oncology department at Thompson was not worried about her slightly elevated liver enzyme. Rather, the oncologist there was skeptical about my concern for this patient.

Two month later, I repeated her tumor staging CT scan, which showed a small mass, a lesion on her liver of about two centimeters. I sent her back to Oak Ridge Hospital. Her tumor was removed by laser surgery, which used a highly focused, powerful beam of light to cut through tissue inside body. I fulfilled my duty and responsibility to closely follow up with my cancer patients. Ovarian cancer is a chronic disease, and careful monitoring for a long period of time is necessary. The patient achieved a second clinical remission.

Having had successful treatment, Helen was a happy and active member of the community. She began to paint, participated in art contests, and won first prize in one. Her oil painting was exhibited, and she brought the picture for me. She was ecstatic, and I was proud of her well-being and happy to see her cherishing life. She did not need any further chemotherapy. She maintained her clinical remission for more than ten years until I lost contact with her. (See her testimony in the appendix.)

Another of my patients, Connie, was the wife of a retired oncologist from Cincinnati University. She survived for more than ten years with ovarian cancer. During my care, she tolerated her chemo treatment well and kept up her daily activities. She enjoyed playing golf with her husband.

Still another, Richard Demar, was born and raised in Crossville and knew my competitor well. By word of mouth, he came to my clinic with widespread cancer of his kidneys, bones, lungs, and axillary lymph nodes with unknown origination of primary cancer. His life expectancy was less than four months. The patient was treated every three weeks with chemotherapy, and he was able to run his construction business. After six months of chemotherapy, he had miraculously achieved clinical remission. Repeating a PET scan showed no visible tumor for eight to nine years. He was middle-aged and had private insurance. (See his testimony in the appendix. His living wife would also confirm the story of his treatment.)

High school principal Sara Drake, at forty years old, was diagnosed with a terribly aggressive form of breast cancer. Her cancer genetic markers showed the worst prognosis, such as a negative estrogen receptor, that she was HER2-Nu-positive, and her relatively young age. Intelligent and kind, Sara desperately wanted to live at least one year to attend to her daughter's wedding in Hawaii.

One dreary night, Sara dropped by my office after my office was closed. The night rain had wet her glasses. She wanted to talk with me regarding her life-and-death situation. Staring seriously at me through her wet glasses, she asked, "Are you going to prolong my life so that I'll be able to see my daughter's wedding?"

"I promise I will do my best," I told her.

She had life-threatening breast cancer, yet her cancer had not spread to other parts of the body. For that reason, I treated her with curative intent, following a full dose of the recommended chemo drugs without adjustment for the stage. During her chemotherapy, I flew to New York to participate in a breast cancer symposium. I discussed Sara's breast cancer treatment with the speaker, an expert oncologist from Memorial Sloan Kettering Cancer Center in New York. The expert agreed with my chemotherapy treatment plan.

Sara's chemotherapy was exceedingly strong, and I was treating her with curative intent. Her skin was sloughing off from her feet. Although she was not sick enough to be admitted to a hospital, she experienced nausea and vomiting. Whirlpool physical therapy for her shedding skin continued. Rumors swept the small town once again; Dr. Gates had given highly toxic chemo drugs and injured her patient. Sara's friends thought she would die soon. She was well known and popular in Fairfield Glade. Literally the entire community prayed for Sara's expeditious healing.

I vividly recall that Barbara initiated the negatively inflamed gossip spread among the rural folks, colluding with her peer group of nurses in the twilight zone that was Crossville.

I adored Sara, who was smart, warmhearted, and had altruistic leadership skills. Finally, her chemo treatments were completed; it was necessary for the whirlpool physical therapy to be continued for a while. Her feet effectively recovered as well as she achieved clinical remission. We both delighted and thanked God for her successful treatment and clinical remission. I admired her powerful willpower; she had endured a rough regimen of chemotherapy. She had a great time and cherished the memories she made at her daughter's wedding in Hawaii.

When Sara returned from Hawaii, I monitored her heart condition very closely because one of the breast cancer chemo drugs could potentially cause her heart problems. She never complained of chest pain, even though she had a family history of cardiac disease. For assurance, I sent her to a cardiologist in Nashville for evaluation of her heart condition. Three blockages in her blood vessel were found, without any symptoms. Sara underwent open-heart surgery. She recovered completely without any complications.

Sara appreciated me profusely for her successful treatment outcomes.

"Your victorious healing from cancer was God's supreme blessing," I told her. "He used me as an instrument. You sought and believed in him, and you received."

Years later, she was thriving. She had been actively involved in helping

VICTORIA GATES, MD

people at church and in the community ever since she achieved the clinical remission under God's grace. In 2013, her first grandson, the child of her daughter who had married in Hawaii, had turned nine years old, and her second granddaughter was seven. She preciously treasured her grandkids, who now, as of this writing are, of course, much older.

Sara's lovely grandkids in 2013

Sara's grandkids made her happy and kept her life busy. Sara was cured and had no detectable breast cancer for over ten years. She did not care for Crossville after I left the town. Sara had been followed up for evaluation by an oncologist in Oak Ridge. (See her testimony and pictures in the appendix.)

I had another patient, Cown Starr, who came with his lovely wife to my clinic. Cown was an athletic tennis player who had newly diagnosed testicular cancer. As the head of Southern household, he was extremely fearful about the potential castration and losing his masculinity. His son was a lawyer, and the patient was a proud man.

Before treatment was started, his wife, Shirley, made a beautiful dogwood flower pin and put it on my physician's coat. "My husband is in your hands until he completes his treatments," she told me. "We love you and trust your skills."

Shirley was a fine artist. As a woman in her seventies, she drew many wonderful paintings. What a hidden talent she had!

Cown was afraid and shaky about his newly diagnosed cancer. While he was receiving chemo treatments, he literally paged me day and night every ten minutes until his treatment were completed. Eventually, his chemo and radiation therapy were successfully completed. He did not need to have a castration; nor did he lose masculinity. Mr. Starr achieved clinical remission. He enjoyed playing tennis again and was much happier, the nervousness no longer threatening his well-being. (See the *Chronicle* newspaper article in the appendix.)

Every six months to a year, I threw a weekend pizza party for my patients. None of my patients was depressed or deprived during treatments. In contrast, they were pleasant amid their chemo drug treatments. They looked after and cared for each other through their network and organization. Everybody knew everyone else's condition, keeping apprised of one another's' statuses even better than I were aware they did. They were always excited about my pizza party, not because of the pizza but because the love among them was like a warm embrace that held them together and buoyed them, and the party was a perfect way to celebrate that connection.

All my patients were invited, and they could bring their spouses, boyfriends, girlfriends, and neighbors to the party. It was my pleasure to provide plenty of food including turkey rolls, pies, cakes, and other deserts, along with the drinks. I would order fifty boxes of pizza and other food for all my patients and share with my employees. At each pizza party, I rewarded something special to my patients who had completed their chemotherapy.

This time, the winner was Cown Starr, along with the other patients who had successfully finished the chemotherapy regimen. They received a certificate of completion and a graduation prize.

A *Crossville Chronicle* reporter took Cown's picture holding his certificate and a graduation bag, and the photo was printed in the newspaper.

As always, all of us had a marvelous time. The patients and their loved ones surely loved my pizza parties.

A few doctors and health care providers in general have no idea how much fear and anxiety are involved in being informed of a terminal cancer diagnosis. They will never know what patients undergo emotionally, mentally, psychologically, and socially while they are in chemo treatments. We can only imagine what they are going through as they deal with the threatening ailments that are a part of the regimen. The patients look pale and haggard, their heads are bald, they experience persistent nausea and vomiting, and their daily activities are disturbed or halted—all of this completely changing their lives.

Attending my pizza parties revived their social grace. They proudly wore stylish wigs, put on makeup, groomed their appearance, and came to the party with elated moods. I think their peace and joy enhanced their natural immune system's ability to fight against cancer cells, alongside the treatments.

One of my lymphoma patient's wives complained that her husband could not eat for days. He came to the pizza party and ate several pieces of pizza. This is proof of how our mental status, though invisible, is mighty powerful. I noticed some patients were eager to finish their chemotherapy so they could receive graduation certificates and win their prizes. Love conquers everything.

A colon cancer patient said to other patients who were receiving chemo treatments, "Today is my last chemotherapy. What am I going to do every Wednesday? I will miss coming to Dr. Gates's clinic."

"That's true. I will miss Dr. Gates's clinic too," another patient answered. "My chemotherapy also will be done soon."

My chemo clinic was not fancy. Nor was the building new or prestigious. But the small chemotherapy room was filled with love, joy, peace, and hope. Certainly, we learned to love each other.

CHAPTER 21

Pure Americanism (I Should Have Packed My Stuff and Left Town)

Dr. Lemon had a hammock that he placed on a portable stationary metal pole in the covered patio at home. Our backyard was surrounded with the lush trees, flowers, and shrubs, as well as butterflies, birds, squirrels, raccoons, and mosquitoes along the creek. I loved that—everything except for the mosquitoes. The southern mosquitoes were bigger than the ones I'd encountered Wisconsin, and they loved to bite any exposed skin.

I convinced Dr. Lemon to install a ceiling fan with a remote control since the ceiling was solid. Then I suggested that we cover the patio with a dark mosquito screen, which would be held in place by the red brick pillars and iron rods between them. The constructor built a new aluminum frame, where mosquito net would fit from top to bottom. He also made a mosquito screen door at the side of the patio. Along with the hammock, a swing decorated in a flower pattern, patio chairs, and a glass table occupied the patio. The mosquito screen-covered patio was my favorite place to enjoy fresh air and listen to the roaring sound of water from the creek.

The large open deck next to the covered patio had a full set of outdoor furniture, including a parasol in the center of the glass table and waterproof lounge chairs and cushions. One day, we had lain in the hammock looking at the surrounding colorful autumn leaves and the cloudless sky, listening to the birds chirping. I felt inner peace and was overcome with an enchanting sense of harmony.

Lord, thank you for your blessing and for making my life full. I made it through medical school and difficult trainings, passed the internal medicine and American oncology board examinations. My practice has been successful through your grace. What else could I ask for more? I said to myself.

Like the waves of the ocean, life never stands still. My reputation was credible and respected. My practice grew, and I generated a good income. I was elected chief of the oncology department.

Dr. Lemon wanted to take a week cruise since I had passed the oncologist specialty board. We took a Mediterranean cruise and went to Rome, Italy; Athens, Greece; and Istanbul, Turkey.

Rome was my beloved city. Supreme artistic skills were on display. Unconceivable ideas and ingenious creations were all around, and I was deeply impressed. The spirit-filled spectacular Saint Peter's Basilica had priceless art collections. I greatly appreciated the treasured paintings and marble statues displayed in the Vatican Palace. The breathtaking masterpieces by Leonardo da Vinci, Michelangelo, and Raphael were unforgettable. It took hours to line up to enter the Sistine Chapel, but seeing the amazing paintings was worth the wait.

I had not known that Saint Peter's Basilica stands over the tomb believed to contain Saint Peter's body. The building's most outstanding architectural feature was its magnificent dome, designed by Michelangelo. The church was given an impressive setting by Gian Lorenzo Bernini, one of its architects. One side had a window close to the ceiling, through which sunlight penetrated, emitting a soft beam aimed over the dove that was hung in the middle of the altar. The sanctified space gave me heavenly peace. I was fascinated by the incredible divine grace of the surroundings. The statues, architecture, and paintings were inexplicable supernatural arts.

The city of Rome lies along the Tiber River. There were many famous fountains. We went to the Roman Forum, the center of the Roman government. The Pantheon was a temple dedicated to Roman Gods. The Colosseum was a huge amphitheater. The catacombs were used as Christian burial places.

My favorite Italian island was Capri. At the entrance of the Gulf of Naples, Capri has a breathtakingly marvelous cliff view. Its famous blue grotto is a wave-cut cave that is filled with a sapphire blue color when the sun shines through the water.

We used ski lifts to see a view of the cliffs. On the way I could hear the roosters crowing to announce the crack of dawn from the distant village below. The faint sound gave me a feeling of profound serenity.

Capri was the home of the lovely maidens called sirens, whose music enchanted Ulysses and his sailors.

Athens was different. We learned that ancient Athens was the leading cultural center of the Greek world. The Parthenon was an ancient Greek temple in Athens. Visiting the Greek Orthodox Church on the top of the hill where the disciple John hid in an underground cave in that church was an astonishing experience. Riding a donkey at Patmos Beach was exotic and fun. The water of the Greek beaches was a rich emerald green—like a massive gemstone spread across a vast ocean. The visible small fish swimming in the shallow water displayed the dazzling nature.

Crete was the largest of the Greek islands. A hurricane hit several cruise ships. Thirty-six tourists were killed, and a cruise ship captain had a heart attack and died. Our cruise ship captain promptly announced the tragic breaking news and cancelled the visit to Crete Island. Thank God, our cruise ship was not damaged by the hurricane. It was a good time to get out of the water.

Walking around the Greek street markets, I found a lovely white Artemis goddess statue. Artemis was a huntress and was depicted with a bow, arrows, and a deer at her side. The store did not have a shipping service, and I had to carry it myself. The statue was large, about the size of a two-year-old baby, it was wrapped in packing paper. Dr. Lemon stared at me, without helping. Later, he ended up taking the statue for himself.

Our last stop on the itinerary of the cruise was Istanbul, Turkey's largest city. Istanbul was once called Constantinople and was the capital of Rome. This period was followed by the Byzantine Empire, which was the capital of the Ottoman Empire from 1453 to 1922. The display of Ottoman China dishes and a sixty-carat diamond on a turban showed the power of the Ottoman Empire.

The magnificent orthodox Christian cathedral called Hagia Sophia is known as Saint Sophia and was impressively sophisticated. Dr. Lemon wanted me to purchase a Persian floor carpet. I was glad that I did not buy it. Passing through Turkey's airport under several militiamen with rifles was rough.

I missed my patients, whose care was being covered by the Knoxville oncologist, without any problems while I was gone.

Dr. Lemon invited his secretary for lunch at our house after we return from cruise. She was nice and friendly and spoke with a Southern accent. But then I overheard a disturbing exchange.

"Dr. Lemon, our community does not have any blacks," she stated. "If black people come into town, my papa brings a shotgun and chases them out of town."

"Do you know my wife is not white?" he asked.

"We think she is white," his secretary replied.

I was dumbfounded. I should have packed my stuff and gotten out of town ASAP!

A self-referred patient with an ovarian cancer came to my office. She claimed that she had just moved to Crossville and that her doctor had not performed a cancer staging evaluation. She denied both sexual activity and pregnancy. Her previous medical record, except for the biopsy report, which showed ovarian cancer, was not available. Afterward meeting with her, I ordered a CT scan of her chest and abdomen and requested the previous progress notes from her doctor.

When it came time for the next appointment, the patient did not show up. My receptionist attempted to contact her at her home, but no one answered the phone. Neither could we reach her at her place of work. My receptionist then documented the no-show, and we had no further appointments scheduled for her.

A few days later, Dr. Stacy plotted against me and started throwing doubt about me. She spread a rumor and complained that I had ordered a CT scan without giving my patient a pregnancy test. This was the same doctor who had commented that I was living in a mansion at the dinner party at my house. In fact, the patient never showed up to my clinic; nor did she have a CT scan evaluation. Later, I realized this was a setup to derail my position.

Dr. Stacy had been looking for trouble ever since she had had dinner at our house.

One of the LPNs told me her terrible true story that had happened in this village. "Dr. Gates, approximately thirteen years ago, I was a little girl and witnessed with my own eyes a horrible murder that occurred in Crossville. A mass of local people lynch mobbed a young black man they had chased into a corner. They brutally stabbed him twenty times without any cause. The people hung his dead body from a tree. The regional newspaper reported the breaking news—that the community had found the dead body, saying that a black man had committed suicide by hanging himself. This was a blatant lie, and people in Crossville knew the truth. But, no one confessed, and silence covered this tragic story."

A sweet young lady with a history of breast cancer was referred to me by a primary care doctor in 1994. A few years later, in 1999, the patient was diagnosed with ovarian cancer. It was then recommended that this patient, Helen Newby, have chemotherapy for the ovarian cancer. Helen became my patient soon after I opened my clinic in Crossville. Her friends and family recommended that she be evaluated by an oncologist at a bigger hospital, since she had two types of cancer.

Helen was very faithful, and she loved Jesus. She fervently prayed that she would be shown the right choice—should she see Dr. Gates, or should she go to her competitor? She told her friends that God's answer was that she should see Dr. Gates. She explained that she thanked God for Dr. Gates and that she absolutely loved Dr. Gates and found her clinic a comfortable and friendly environment. Everyone in her office worked together as a team.

She tolerated the chemo treatment reasonably well, except for a fungal infection. During the treatment, she was twice admitted to the hospital.

She eventually achieved clinical remission successfully. Helen was able to work at Walmart. Her initial tumor marker, CA-125, which was awfully high, returned to normal after her chemotherapy. No treatment was required for two and half years.

At her follow-up evaluation at that point, I noticed that her CA-125 was gradually increasing above the normal level with a small visible mass in her lower abdomen on the CT scan. Chemotherapy was resumed carefully, and we once again achieved a normal level of CA-125. There was no longer detectable cancer on the repeated CT scan.

As with Helen Hollady, ovarian cancer patients required chronic care and needed to be constantly monitored. (See their testimonies in the *Chronicle* newspaper article included in the appendix.)

While Barbara, my LPNs, and my competitor and his friends and family continued to plot against me, my patients and I had great relationships, and we cared for each other. I did not worry myself over the criticism or the malicious scams and plots against me. I was too busy to worry about nonsense. Rather, I focused on my patients' care and was interested only in their successful outcomes.

One of my patients had been treated for acute leukemia in 2001 at the Mayo Clinic. The patient, Kenneth Holtz, had a poor prognosis. The doctor explained to him that his survival and life expectance was less than two months. Therefore, his doctor did not provide chemotherapy for his leukemia. The patient was then placed on hospice care in Crossville.

It was exceedingly uncommon for hospice care patients to come to see a doctor seeking treatments. By word of mouth, Kenneth came to my clinic. He was severely depressed, had lost substantial weight, and could not stand by himself without his wife's support.

He staggered and leaned on my office desk. "Would you help me and treat me? I cannot believe that I am dying. I can't eat, and I can't sleep."

"The Mayo Clinic is a reputable hospital, and I believe the doctor accurately informed you," I told him gently. "I am not a God to cure you without a miracle drug treatment. However, since you have not received any treatments, I would consider treating you extremely carefully.

"First and foremost," I explained, "you are weak because you have not eaten, and your blood counts are bottomed out."

I provided him with supportive blood products and encouraged him to eat and rest. I gave him a wellness tape and cassette for him to listen and be relaxed. I was a cheerleader for him to regain his willpower. I stroked his forehead and sat next him, listening to him talk about his condition.

Kenneth's blood counts were gradually improved. He looked better every day and started to eat and recover his strength and weight. He and his wife, Betty, loved to see me, and occasionally he even laughed.

His pastor was visiting him one Monday afternoon when I was doing my rounds. "I tried exceedingly hard to reduce his depression," the pastor told me. "I could not make him feel better. I cannot believe he is smiling and even laughing now."

Traditionally, oncologists treated cancer patients with chemotherapy first. If the chemotherapy was not effective, then doctors treated the patients with a biological therapy as a last resort.

Initially, Kenneth's blood counts were bottomed out, and I provided blood supplement, nutrition, and fluid for hydration. Emphatically, I encouraged him to regain his physical, emotional, and mental strength with a possible biofeedback. The patient finally overcame his depression and desired to live.

My treatment plan was explained to him. First, I would treat him with a total of four cycles of biological therapy instead of chemotherapy. At the beginning, I gave him little less than the recommended dose, followed by a slightly increased dosage in the second treatment, close to the recommended dose. Kenneth did well, and he no longer required a frequent blood transfusion. He then received the full dosage of the biological therapy for his third and fourth cycles. He completed this treatment without severe toxicities or side effects.

This biological therapy was required infrequently and was not commonly used. The leftover amounts of medication from the first and second rounds of the therapy had nothing to do with financial gain. Rather, I had adjusted the doses to prevent him from getting sick and to avoid endangering his life. Even though the people around me did not understand cancer treatments, they thought that I was cheating my patients out of drugs for my own financial benefit.

The truth was, if I had given Kenneth the full recommended amount in his condition on the first dose, the drug toxicity could have easily killed him. Kenneth tolerated his treatment well, and his blood count improved remarkably.

Local folks also accused me of not actually giving my patients chemo drugs when the patients were clinically doing well—when they were active and maintained their daily quality of life. If patients were receiving drugs, they reasoned, they should have been extremely sick and confined to their beds. Unquestionably, they claimed, I had given my patients full doses of drugs, given that my patients were mobile and alive—all of which proves that lay people do not understand the purpose of chemo treatments.

After Kenneth successfully completed his biological therapy, I started his first cycle of combination chemotherapy conscientiously and gingerly, slightly modifying the dose from the textbook recommendations based on his clinical condition and blood counts. He responded to his treatment splendidly, and the second dose was slightly increased. After that, the third and fourth dosages were the full recommended amounts. His treatments were successfully completed without him experiencing severe toxicity, sickness, nausea, or vomiting and without him being admitted to a hospital. There was no evidence of infection, organ damage, or systemic failure. Kenneth's blood counts returned to normal. He could eat, walk, and play golf in good spirits.

Before I had started his biological therapy, I had called the most renowned leukemia expert at the MD Anderson Cancer Center. "Dr. Gates, your patient has end-stage leukemia with malignant blast cell counts of 84 percent. He is on his deathbed. I think the Mayo Clinic's decision to place the patient in hospice care was appropriate," I was advised.

Looking at my patient now, I saw that Kenneth looked excellent, and his spirit was revitalized. Kenneth thought I had a supernatural skill to cure him and thanked me repeatedly.

"You had faith in God and a trusted in him, and God blessed you to be healed through me. Please, help others who need you," I told him.

Kenneth, just like Sara Drake had, became active as a wonderful church member, along with my other patients, including Paul, Jim, Rachel, Helen, and many more. They had been helping others daily.

Several years later, Kenneth's platelet counts started to gradually be falling without any evidence of infection or recurrent leukemia. I researched his rare condition attentively and then decided to remove his spleen. After the splenectomy, his platelet counts returned to normal.

He has been leukemia free for more than ten years and has enjoyed traveling with his wife. (See his testimony and letters in the appendix.)

One of his letters, sent to me on January 11, 2007, at which time my clinic was closed, read:

Dear Dr. Gates:

Betty Jo and I were so happy to receive your address. It is rare for a day to go by that we do not think about you and wonder how you are doing. You have been such an important part in our lives that we are enjoying today. I am taking no medications, and the blood tests every four months indicate no problems. At the last visit with Dr. Nichols, he said that I was the healthiest person he had examined that day! Your professional skill, along with the Lord, has given Betty Jo and I over four years since the remission we are so thankful for. We are busy with church activities and see Paul Cardwell, Sara Drake, and Jim Buxton often. To help stay healthy, we go to the fitness center five days a week. My golf game and Betty Jo's bridge helps fill in the rest of the time available. May the Lord be with you and bring you the peace and comfort you deserve.

Ken and Betty Jo Holz

One of my patients Lawrence, who had colon cancer, was treated with combination chemotherapy, and achieved clinical remission. But his remission was brief. The recurrent cancer was detected through increased tumor markers. He was referred to a surgeon for a colonoscopy. It was then discovered that he had rectal cancer instead of recurrent colon cancer. Radiation treatment was added for rectal cancer after the completion of the chemotherapy.

The patient tolerated chemo and radiation therapy well, and he enjoyed playing golf regularly during the treatment. He achieved clinical remission that lasted for over ten years.

Lawrence was humorous, calm, and quiet. He never got sick during treatment under my care. He was a sweet Southern gentleman, and we joked with each other a lot.

An attractive model at the country club in Fairfield Glade was referred to me with breast cancer. The patient, Ida, had heard about my reputation, and she wanted to be treated under my care. Her biopsy was performed by a surgeon, and it was confirmed to be breast cancer. A total mastectomy had been recommended. Ida was afraid to undergo a total mastectomy, given that she worked as a model. She was fearful and tearful. In my opinion, she did not need to have a total mastectomy. A lumpectomy would be sufficient because she had an early stage of breast cancer. I sent her to another surgeon for a second opinion, and the doctor recommended a lumpectomy. The patient was hopeful and was less nervous.

When she returned to see her original surgeon for follow-up care, he strongly recommended the mastectomy. "There is no partial pregnancy. You cannot remove part of cancer. You must remove it all," the surgeon told her.

Recent oncology data confirmed that the outcome of a lumpectomy followed by chemo radiation therapy compared to that of a mastectomy with the same follow-up course was the same in terms of survival rate and life span. After the patient had a lumpectomy, she was treated with chemo radiation therapy. The treatments were successfully completed without significant side effects. She was then cured, without any evidence of recurrent breast cancer for more than fifteen years. She still lives in Fairfield Glade. She wished I were in Crossville when her husband was in the ICU years after I left. (See her testimony in the appendix.)

My recommendation for lumpectomy against the surgeon's opinion might have caused irritation and retaliation. During this time, my competitor, his friends, his manager, rural folks, and my nurses seriously colluded to find any issues to cause me trouble.

As part of the history of Tennessee, the Ku Klux Klan originated in Chattanooga, just an hour a half from Crossville, and Chattanooga was a key city in the Civil War. The Ku Klux Klan is a secret society dedicated to the supremacy of white people in the United States. In the South during the time of reconstruction, the KKK terrorized many Southern blacks and carpetbaggers who had replaced white Southerners in positions of power. The Klan gained renewed strength in the 1920s and again in 1960s. It has been stated that the KKK aims to preserve "pure Americanism." Its members have attacked Jews and Roman Catholics as well. Often, the members want their target to move out of a particular vicinity.

On a Friday afternoon in 2004, I read a Crossville newspaper story about a young Tennessean setting off a pipe bomb at a Mexican household, killing the Latinos inside for no reason other than the desire to chase the Mexicans out of town. This happened even though, in 2004, we were not living under the Confederacy.

Jamestown Clinic needing an oncologist, and I covered that clinic once a week. I got along well with a friendly receptionist. One week, I had not seen her. I wondered what had happened to her. The following week, I called her to find out why she was not there. She told me that her father had been killed that afternoon. I was shocked. I asked her, "Why was your father murdered?"

She explained that her mother had been picking some lettuce to make lunch while her father was working inside his garage. A young man walked in her house and shot her father killing him instantly. Neither she nor her mother knew who the young man was. This murder case was not mentioned on the newspaper. Nor did police investigate her father's murder. The receptionist was white and not black. Yet people lived in fear in this lawless rural community. Jamestown was close to Crossville, just twenty minutes away.

One year later, I heard another bit of tragic news. A white gay couple had gone to a tavern for a drink. The people in the tavern killed one of the gay men because he was queer. No investigation was done; nor was anyone charged.

Along with the influence of the Celtic culture, the people situated in the Cumberland Mountains had a strong confederate mentality, thinking and acting differently than the rest of the country.

I was extremely busy, and my mind was focused on my patients' care. I paid no attention to their plots and schemes. I trusted God and myself, and I devoted myself to my work and responsibilities.

CHAPTER 22

I Think You Love Your Patients More Than You Love Me

Another Fairfield Glade patient, Jean, came to my clinic with near end-stage colon cancer, along with strikingly high tumor markers. Her high tumor markers indicated a poor prognosis. I was concerned about her outcome. In contrast, her overall physical condition appeared to be reasonably good. Camptosar, a chemo drug for colon cancer treatment, had just been approved by the FDA and released to the markets by pharmaceutical companies.

Jean was the first patient I treated with the newly released Camptosar, which I combined with other chemotherapy drugs. Her tumor markers responded to the new drug and were nicely decreased to almost normal level.

Most lakefront house owners in Fairfield Glade had boats. An annual boat outing was popular among the boat owners. Inhabitants tied all the boats together and had a potluck party inside each boat. People walked from one boat to another boat and sampled different food and socialized with each other. We were invited to the boat outing events annually. I saw my patient at one such event. Jean looked excellent, and she was highly active in the boat party.

For unknown reasons, Jean's private insurance, Blue Cross Blue Shield, did not reimburse her Camptosar chemo drug charges. The drug was new and expensive. The purchasing cost was too great without reimbursement. I explained what had happened. I decided to treat her at the hospital. The same drug and the same amounts of Camptosar were given to Jean at the hospital. She tolerated the Camptosar treatment well.

However, she did not like receiving her chemotherapy by herself at the hospital and declined further treatment. Her family members convinced her to receive an experimental drug with curatives intent. Consequently, she was transferred to a bigger hospital in Nashville. Unfortunately, Jean died during her experimental drug treatment at the big hospital in Nashville. The tragic story broke my heart.

Conspiracies began to mount among the LPNs, who had insufficient knowledge of cancer treatments and whose backgrounds and education had not prepared them to deal with the specialization. As noted earlier, none of my LPNs had any concept that the FDA required overfill amounts of Procrit. Nor did they know the exact amounts in the liquid chemo drug bottles. I had explained the situation to the nurses—that the overfill amounts were a mandated requirement under the biological license application through the Food and Drug Administration—without success.

The three LPNs concocted allegations against me that I had deceived patients by using the tiny leftover liquid Procrit kept in the refrigerator. Because of their incomprehension, they claimed that I should have given the patient the whole bottle.

The main ringleader among them was Casey, who misled others about my integrity and patient care. Casey had worked for several years in the operating room at the medical center. She had had some problems at the hospital. After not having a job for more than a year, she came to me to apply for an LPN position. I accepted her, lacking the foresight that she was another Trojan horse who would attempt to sabotage my career.

Casey was not only involved in the conspiracy against me, but she had also been communicating with TBI and feeding them falsified information. She wanted to work for my competitor. For example, even though Kenneth had been miraculously cured from his end-stage leukemia, Casey accused me of maliciously shortchanging his biological medication and chemo drugs.

Billy, one of the most debilitated patients I had treated, became another subject of her consternation. Billy had come to me with prostate cancer that had spread widely throughout his body. He required continuous home oxygen therapy due to his end-stage chronic obstructive lung disease. He also had severe diabetic problems. I attentively treated him with extreme caution and provided substantially reduced medication prior to chemotherapy. For example, I would give him the smallest dose of Benadryl, which cost less than a dollar, along with a tiny dose of Decadron, less than half the amount I would give other healthier patients.

LPNs were not permitted to give patients injectable chemo drugs. Still, Casey observed that I had given him small amounts of Decadron and Benadryl prior to chemotherapy. The following week, Casey prepared the premedication, using a full dose of both Decadron and Benadryl, which were not chemo drugs.

She injected the full dosages of premedication behind my back without asking me. The full dose of Benadryl decreased Billy's blood pressure instantly as soon as Casey had injected the incorrect amount. Furthermore, soon after she had administered the Decadron through his IV, Billy's blood sugar increased, rocketing sky high, and he passed out immediately. Casey thought she was preventing me from cheating. And by administering these dosages, she almost killed my patient.

Paramedics arrived at my office, and the patient was admitted to the hospital. Thankfully, due to the knowledge of what had happened to Billy, he recovered quickly.

I can only imagine what local people would have thought if Billy had not recovered. Rumor would have flooded the town that one of Dr. Gates's patients had died at her chemotherapy room. Thank God I knew what had happened to Billy. He reawakened right away. Billy's chemo drugs had already been mixed, and the IV tube was already connected. So, Medicare allowed the doctor to bill the chemo drug. Having been mixed, the drug could not be use for another cancer patient. Dr. Lemon and I had learned this at the billing seminar in Nashville. Yet, this matter was sensationally blown up—talked about as a criminal act in which I had incorrectly billed the drug charge.

"Why did Dr. Gates give the patient half a dose of Decadron which cost only fifty cents?" the TBI agent asked Casey.

"Dr. Gates cut corners, even cutting the cheap medications, such as Benadryl and Decadron, in half," she replied.

Casey's egotistical, false accusations made me look like the culprit. The truth was that Casey had nearly killed Billy by not following my precise orders, based on the patient's unique clinical condition. Now I understand why old people say, "An empty bottle makes more noise than a full bottle." A little knowledge can be dangerous.

For the most part, the TBI agents did not have medical backgrounds. Nor had they been trained in cancer treatment. The agents' skepticism about my premedication dosages proved that they understood neither the patient's medical history and clinical condition nor the drugs' side effects. Billy had private insurance, and Medicare should not have involved a commercial insurance company.

One nearly blind patient, Robin, was treated with end-stage lung cancer. He had Universal insurance, and the company went bankrupt halfway through finishing his treatment course. The patient had such a beautiful personality. He was extremely polite and humble. Even though, I did not receive reimbursements for my charges, I continued treating him and completed his chemo treatment course as I had planned.

I admired his positive attitude. Despite not having much, he was sweet, peaceful, and happy. He thanked God daily that he was alive. I adored his faith.

Lo and behold, his outcome was remarkable. Robin miraculously achieved clinical remission from his end-stage lung cancer. Repeated tumor restaging evaluations of CT scan showed no detectable lung cancer. Yes, I was a licensed cancer doctor, yet some patients were unexpectedly cured. God is real!

I often wondered about the excellent outcome. Had it been influenced by the patient's positive spirit, peace, faith, and will to live? It might have fortified his immune system, enabling it to better fight his disease, even cancer. My joy filled me with contentment whenever I saw my patients' victorious outcomes after my treatments.

Another uncommon case was that of Alfred, who had end-stage lung cancer that had spread throughout his lungs, along with a second prostate cancer, which also involved his pelvis and was producing massive blood clot problems. In the beginning, the patient could not move with his miserable pain and was confined to his bed. I treated Alfred with palliative care.

There were two types of cancer treatments. The first was curative treatment, which focused on curing the cancer and was administered if the cancer had been diagnosed in its early stage. Palliative care was supportive care, its focus to make patients comfortable when a curative treatment was no longer appropriate.

Palliative care could be considered like placing a patient in hospice care or sending him or her home to be with family. My main goal for Alfred's treatment was prolonging his life and making him as comfortable as possible. I did not adjust Alfred's medication, and he received exceedingly small doses of chemo drugs. He tolerated the chemo drugs well, and his daily activities improved. He was also gingerly treated with anticoagulants for his massive blood clots. His life expectancy was extremely limited; he had less than two months. He lived longer and enjoyed good quality of life.

The patient had worked as a school bus driver, and he loved his job. The students sent him a get-well card, along with twenty dollars collected from their piggy banks. Alfred was deeply touched by the precious card. He missed his students, and their outpouring of warmth and concern propelled his desire to drive the school bus with them one more time. My patient taught me a lesson. Love conquers any obstacles and adversities. We must only open our eyes to see a virtuous, divine pathway, even when facing death. I was willing to do anything for my patients, especially for Alfred.

Undeniably, the patient did well and was able to go fishing and to enjoy going out to have a meal with his family. Thus, I submitted my request by letter to the school principal that Alfred be allowed to ride the school bus with his beloved students one last time. He was thrilled when permission was granted, and he cherished riding with the students.

A female patient in her twenties, Sheila, was diagnosed with Hodgkin lymphoma, Stage III, and was transferred from Cookeville Regional Hospital to my clinic. The patient had received one cycle of chemo treatment and refused further care at Cookeville. She complained about her swollen arm and the pain caused by the infiltrated chemo drug. The hospital was located close to the Tennessee Bureau of Investigation offices, just thirty minutes from Crossville.

After I had evaluated Sheila, a surgeon inserted a port-a-cath for easy IV access, and her chemotherapy continued without any problems. The patient tolerated treatment for Hodgkin's lymphoma well. Sheila was able to work at the grocery store and enjoyed her active lifestyle during her treatments under my care.

Prior to completion of the six total cycles of chemotherapy that I had planned, after she had received her fifth cycle, restaging evaluation of a CT scan of the chest and abdomen were performed. The patient's bulky tumors had melted away, and there was no visible lymphoma on the CT scan report. Unexpectedly, her port-a-cath site was red and slightly infected after the fifth cycle of chemotherapy. Sheila was admitted for a new port-a-cath placement by a surgeon.

During her admission, the hospital nurses convinced Sheila to see my competitor or to go to a bigger hospital in Chattanooga. Sheila was then transferred by her request to Park City Hospital in Chattanooga.

Her new oncologist treated my patient with an old regimen known as "MOPP" combination chemotherapy. I did not think Sheila needed a strong chemotherapy regimen, with no evidence of tumor on her recent CT scan. And she had done great under my care. She had finished the fifth cycle of chemo drugs and had only one cycle left to go. I wanted to give her the last six cycle to complete her course. Before she received the last cycle, she left my clinic and went to Chattanooga.

A couple of months later, I heard that Sheila had gotten awfully sick after receiving the MOPP regimen. She ended up being admitted into the intensive care unit and did not fully recover from the chemo drug-induced toxicities. She was unable to work any longer and asked me to sign her disability benefit from Medicare. I could not sign the form, because I had not seen her for many months.

The last time I had seen her was right after she had received the fifth cycle of ABVD chemotherapy course I had prescribed. At the time, the patient did not have any complications, troubles, side effects, or physical discomfort. Wanting to see another doctor, Sheila had left my practice and gone to Park City in Chattanooga. Now, she was sick, she could not work, and her prognosis seemed grave. I did not understand why she had left.

While I was rounding at the hospital, one of the hospital nurses entertained me with an episode that had happened at her house. She said, "After lunch, I came out of my house and saw a huge snake in my front yard. I ran into the house to get my shotgun, and I killed the snake. I chopped it into pieces and deep-fried it. Boy! It was totally off the chain, much better than Kentucky fried chicken. Dr. Gates, have you ever tasted fried snake?"

"I have not tasted snake," I told her. "I am afraid of snakes, and I would have passed out if I had seen the snake."

Her story sounded weird. My eyes got bigger, I and murmured to myself. "Is this Crossville, Cumberland County, culture? Where am I?" I felt that my clock had been set backward and I had somehow ended up in the 1920s.

My buzzing ear made me delirious. I felt like I was on a different planet. I rushed out of the nurses' station. My long sigh released the creepy anxiety.

I recalled when, back in California, one of the surgeons had gotten engaged to a beautiful woman. The pair had purchased a house the top of the hill. One weekend, upon starting to plant plants in their yard, she'd found a snake and had run for her life into her room and shut the sliding door. The surgeon had run after her and tried to get in, but his fiancée was afraid of the snake and would not open the door for him. He repeatedly begged her to let him in, without success, and ended up using the side door.

In California reacting to a snake with fear was the norm. This was Crossville, though, and the nurse had not only killed the snake but had also fried it and eaten it. Obviously, these were cases of different people acting differently in different places.

Another patient, Jack, had colon cancer that was spread to his bones and lungs. He was a skinny, middle-aged man and a chain-smoker, and he tolerated chemotherapy well. He worked at K-Mart during his chemotherapy under my care. He was friendly, talked with all my patients, and enjoyed the free snacks available in my office.

Jack had Universal Health Care insurance, along with Robin, who I previously mentioned. As I said, the company went bankrupt. Jack had received an expensive drug called Camptosar, which was not reimbursed.

My billing manager reminded me that his insurance company was bankrupt, but I continued to treat him. Casey, not knowing his insurance had gone bankrupt, tried to convince him to see my competitor. Jack declined. I discontinued the Camptosar and maintained 5FU chemotherapy through a portable device. My patient was then sent to Vanderbilt Medical Center for a second opinion. The oncologist agreed with my treatment. After Jack returned to Crossville, he went to Thompson Cancer Center to see an oncologist. The receptionist did not accept him due to his lack of insurance.

During Jack's treatment, I had never seen any of his family members. Jack never come back after his visit to Oak Ridge. He would have received free chemotherapy under my care. I did not mind giving him free drugs because some patients were humble, polite, kind, and happy, even though they did not have much. I was amazed by their positive attitude and they way they accepted their destiny. These poor folks literally did not have a pot to pee in; yet they were self-sufficient and happy. Jack never came back after his visit to a bigger hospital, and I missed him.

Another patient, Howard, had a history of heavy drinking. He also smoked nonstop. And his prostate cancer had spread to his lungs and bones. Prior to his treatment at my clinic, the patient had been arrested for driving under the influence, and he was locked up after his arrest.

I decided to send a letter to the police department about the patient being under tremendous stress over his potential death in the extremely near future. He had just been diagnosed with end-stage metastatic prostate cancer that had spread throughout his body. One could only imagine what his mind and emotions were going through. His life expectancy was substantially limited due to his hopeless terminal ailment. No one wished for him to die in a prison cell.

His charge was dropped, and he underwent chemotherapy without significant side effects, except for his blood counts, which bottomed out, causing him to experience transient debilitation.

Occasionally, he had been admitted to the hospital for appropriate supplements. He impressively stopped drinking and cut down on his cigarette consumption. He became happier, more sociable, and attended one of my pizza parties.

Dr. Lemon remarked one day, jealousy in his tone, "If you ever love anybody like you love your patients, you will never have relationship problems. I think you love your patients more than you love me."

He then changed the subject, asking if I wanted to participate in a cutting-edge cancer treatment seminar in London, England. "It will be only for a few days, less than a week," he said. "I know you don't like to take a vacation because you don't want to leave your patients without good coverage. But I wish you would join me and meet my older brother in London."

CHAPTER 23

Everybody Knows Everybody's Business

Dr. Lemon already had been complaining about my workaholic devotion and me not taking vacation with him. "You are making too much money," he said. "This is a small town. Everybody knows everybody's business, including your bank accounts. There are no secrets here. Why don't you pay for my health coverage and expenses, including my credit card bills? The government will know all about your large amounts of funds in the bank. Thus, we should record it on my spreadsheet accurately, how much you paid for my expenses. I promise you that I will pay you back without a dime short," he said.

I thought that this strategy was uncommon between a married couple. This was beyond a partnership contract to be married to Dr. Lemon. Nevertheless, it was nice to discuss the patients' treatment plans with him, since he was knowledgeable on the subject.

Our relationship improved somewhat. He respected me after I had passed the subspecialty American Medical Oncology Board exams and started producing a substantial income.

He usually spent his time at his desk in the master bedroom listening to music, watching TV, and playing with whatever brand-new electronic device he had—scanning with a color printer or learning the intricacies of a digital camera. He would email his kids and his family and called his mother in Miami, Florida, frequently.

Most of the time, I worked at the built-in kitchen desk with a small candle lit, listening to music, often chamber music, or nature sound compilations such as birds chirping or crashing waves, and finishing my progressive dictation.

We shared the household expenses. We kept our accounts and funds separate, to the point of each of us paying separately for groceries and eating out. Each of us had a separate medical practice and kept our accounting separately. Our income taxes were filed separately most years, and during the years when we filed joint returns, we filed under Class C, filing separate schedules for each of our practices.

He took a vacation with his two kids every two months. Sometimes his mother joined the trip. He would reserve the best hotels and went to many famous resorts. He visited places like Vancouver, Canada; Hilton Head; and Cape Code and, wherever he went, took in the historical sights. He bought many gifts for his kids and his mother. He recorded that I had been paying for it all, along with a promise to pay me back for these expenditures.

My income was four times greater than his. I was appalled when he demanded that I pay back the overpayment he had made when we'd purchased our Tennessee house in the amount of $100,078.52. He asked me to pay him back the exact amount including the $0.52. I paid him back the exact dollars. I earned enough; money was not an issue at the time.

I generated more than I could use. In fact, I was too busy and had no time to spend any of the money that I had earned. I was very frugal and purchased inexpensive shoes and clothes and a lower-priced vehicle. We lived quite different lifestyles in a variety of ways

I agreed to go on this trip, though. I had not been to England, and I was excited to join his seminar and meet his brother.

We stayed at International Western Hotel next to Hyde Park, close to downtown Piccadilly Street. Hyde Park is one of five large parks near downtown London. A large, lively city, London is also a historic place.

The meeting was sponsored by the director of the radiation oncology department at MD Anderson Cancer Center. We both knew the director and his wife, who was an oncologist. After the meeting, we toured England with other physicians who had participated in the seminar.

Westminster is the oldest part of the West End, and it includes the House of Parliament. The church to the left of the parliament building is Westminster Abbey, one of London's oldest and best-known churches.

It dates from the 1000s and has hosted coronations, royal weddings, and other important ceremonies. I saw Princess Diana get married to Prince Charleston in Westminster Abbey on television. St. Paul's Cathedral and Westminster Abbey are the most famous churches in London. Dr. Lemon went up to the roof of St. Paul's Cathedral. I did not like heights and could not go up more than half of the way.

I met Dr. Lemon's brother, his brother's wife, and their daughter. We all went to the Hard Rock Café close to the hotel and had a simple lunch. His brother congratulated me on having passed my oncology boards. His brother was a dentist and took us to the Tower of London, which houses the Royal Jewel Office. Here the crown, scepters, and other royal treasures of the England ravens, known as the regalia, were closely guarded.

Many famous people were imprisoned in the damp, dark cell of the Tower of London, deep within its great, thick walls.

I loved the water fountain in the front of the Buckingham Palace more than Windsor Castle.

We saw many performances, and the Royal Opera House known as Covent Garden was most impressive. My favorite places were the Wallace Collection and Madame Tussauds wax museum. On Tuesday, the wax museum was closed for our group of doctors' private dinner party. I took many pictures with 007 James Bond's waxed figure and with Princess Diana in her wedding gown.

Suddenly, Dr. Lemon was very affectionate, continuously kissing me on my forehead and hands in front of the director. The director commented to us quietly, "Good thing you're married."

Dr. Lemon's moods would swing occasionally, and his emotions were conditional based on the situation. I thought he was in a good mood this time because I had passed the American board and was generating a good income from my successful practice.

Normally, I did not like shopping, but this time, I loved buying from the art collections on the street market on Portobello Road. Dr. Lemon bought an ancient royal wine case with small wine glasses inside. It was made of a shiny turtle shell with decorative golden beads lined along the elegantly designed artistic case.

There was a white alabaster sculpture I could not keep my eyes. It was of an alluring French lady who wore a wreath of Laurel leaves and was holding a lyre in her hand, her delicate fingers curled around its frame. She was lovely and graceful. I adored this magnificently carved sculpture. It was an exquisite masterpiece.

Dr. Lemon, noticing I had my eyes glued to the statue and was not moving, bought it for my birthday gift. This French lady, wearing a long, thin royal dress had been in someone's attic for more than a hundred years. It was covered with dust, even though the antique dealer cleaned it up nicely. I was glad that the dealer had restored the sculpture, which became my beloved statue.

We bought several additional items separately. They were hard to carry, so we went to the luggage store and purchased a large duffel bag and carefully placed the items inside the bag.

April In London was cold, and I got sick. At Heathrow Airport, Dr. Lemon reported to the ticket counter agent that I was ill. The agent gave us first-class seats, and we returned comfortably to Tennessee.

One of the amazing parts of the trip was that Dr. Lemon had known where to get matinee tickets for orchestra seats, performances, and shows. He easily led us from one theater to another. He was capable of use the subway system in London or wherever we went, even in different countries. We saw at least five different performances, and he did not have any problems with directions. Surely, that would not be my case. I got lost easily.

My short trip to England was a good break from my busy work schedule and provided a much-needed release from tension and stress and concern for my terminally ill patients. I loved the Serenity Prayer. We must learn to accept all things that we cannot change. Unquestionably, death is not in our control, and it is an inevitable process of our life.

A new patient, Hubert, had private insurance, and came to me with lung cancer that had spread to his skull, spine, and legs. He initially was unable to walk at all and was confined to a wheelchair. The tumor on his skull completely disappeared after chemo treatment under my care. He was not sick. Nor did he have to be admitted to the hospital.

The patient's condition gradually improved, and he was able to walk with a cane, no longer needing a wheelchair. He enjoyed boat outings, dinner outings, and gathering with his family. The patient and his family greatly appreciated my treatment and his successful outcome. They brought me a ceramic cherub decorated with red roses between the wings. I placed this figurine in the chemotherapy room for all my patients to enjoy.

Paul owned a heating and air-conditioning company. He came to my clinic with end-stage colon cancer, which had widespread throughout his body, along with massive blood clots. He was quiet and down to earth and accepted his condition well without any resentments. His life expectancy was a year. But he lived more than five years, with his physical condition reasonably well maintained.

Paul relished his limited lifespan and shared love with family and friends. His family respected and graciously appreciated my treatments, my compassion for him, and my ability to prolong his life.

In contrast, the rural folks and my LPNs continuously plotted against me. Casey even incorrectly recorded patients' chemo drug amounts on the patients' flow sheets. LPNs are different from registered nurses. Some did not have a particularly good understanding of chemo drugs; they simply copied what had previously been recorded on the chart. This did not reflect the situation accurately. When a patient got sick, I would adjust his or her dosage based on the current clinical condition.

One of my patients, Rainy, had Medicare, and had been referred to me with widespread colon cancer in his abdomen. Casey intentionally falsified the notes on the chemo drugs. Though they had not been administered to the patients, she wrongfully recorded that they had been. I found her falsification and crossed it out with two lines and recorded it as an error. Of course, I did not bill for his treatment.

Rainy did remarkably well for a long time. He was quiet, polite, and lovely. He smiled all the time and was the happiest patient.

An article I read reinforced and confirmed my beliefs about accountability in my practice, which helped me. According to the article (on page 145 in a section about accountability and responsibility in the regulation of business), "It is impossible to tell whether errors increased significantly in 1995 and, if so, whether the increasing complexity of medicine and the commitment to cost-cutting of managed care were to blame." What was clear was that errors seemed to be everywhere, as if the system was out of control.

The year began with the news that Betsy Lehman, a thirty-nine-year-old health columnist for *The Boston Globe* had died, not of breast cancer but of a fourfold miscalculation in the amount of Cytoxan chemo drug she was being given during her time at Dana-Farber Cancer Center battling her breast cancer. The total dose to be given over four days had been, instead, administered in one day. The error had not been corrected by the doctors, nurses, or pharmacists involved. The high dose killed the famous patient.

At about the same time, a vascular surgeon at University Community Hospital in Tampa, Florida, was accused of amputating the wrong leg. This was followed by other reports that the wrong side of a brain had been operated on at the Memorial Sloan Kettering Cancer Center in New York.

In an echo the Dana-Farber error, a patient at the University of Chicago hospital died of a huge overdose of chemotherapy medication. This also happened because the wrong dose had been written down and the error was not was noticed until the drug had been administered—yet another example of not the chemo drug being the actual culprit but, rather, a nurse's mistake was to blame.

At 10:00 p.m., the baby began to vomit while drinking a bottle, the first sign of drug overdose. Digoxin works by changing the flux of irons in the heart, altering the cell membranes. Too much allows the heart to flood with calcium, so it cannot contract. There is an antidote called Digibind, and the nurse, her fears confirmed, called for it immediately. But even immediately was too late.

"They killed my son," the boy's father, Jose Martinez sobbed on the local television news.

I had to manage my treatments and protect my patients' safety and their well-being personally and carefully. I could not take a chance allowing LPNs, with their insufficient knowledge of the process, to manage the administration of chemo drugs. I discovered many errors on the patients record and advised the nurses not to white out errors. Whiting out anything on a patient chart was a violation of the law. Rather, they were to cross an error out with two lines. Nevertheless, Haley consistently whited out her mistakes. Worse, she had falsified the patient record that I'd found. I forwarded this information to my attorney, Richard, but he did not pay any attention to this information.

A wonderful patient Dolores had a newly diagnosed, advanced stage III ovarian cancer. She came to the clinic accompanied by her husband. Her husband always sat with her while she was receiving her chemotherapy. The patient initially had substantially high tumor markers, which came down effectively after each of her chemo treatments. She tolerated the treatments remarkably well, without significant side effects from the toxic agents. Her clinical condition improved, and she was happy and active.

Dolores had a history of constipation and diverticulosis. This is a lining of sacs in the bowel, like tiny balloons stretched out on the bowel's mucus membrane, which can rupture due to pressure. Halfway through her chemo treatment cycle, she complained of severe abdominal pain, which was promptly diagnosed as a ruptured diverticulosis.

Dolores underwent surgery, performed by an excellent surgeon. But while the surgery was successful, the residual ovarian tumor in the abdominal wall caused wound-healing problems, which was not uncommon. She was admitted to the ICU but was not referred to me. I could have given her aggressive nutritional supplement via an IV, but the primary care doctor admitted her. The doctor's thinking was that no chemo treatment was required at the time. Of course, I would not have given her chemotherapy, but I could have helped her wound-healing ability and helped her regain her strength. I was trained in BMT and knew how to handle a critical patient's condition. I took care of patients with multiorgan failure. But there was no way I could see her without a consultation, and I had not heard from her. Apparently, she had a problem with an open surgical wound and did not recover from it. I was emotionally tormented whenever my patients suffered from their ailments and I could not help them.

That weekend, we wanted to visit Dollywood to get in some relaxation. Dollywood, in Pigeon Forge, was not far from Crossville; it only took a few hours to get there. It was a great entertainment place, offering live music, performances at different theaters, water rides, and many other attractions highlighting a fun life and the folklore of the smoky mountains.

Dr. Lemon was clumsy while hiking on the trails leading to a waterfall. I had to keep reminding him to keep away from the edge. Gatlinburg and Sevierville had many strip malls and were popular places to buy artificial jewels and unique souvenirs to or just roam leisurely through the different chocolate and candy stores. There were many nice restaurants and pancake houses.

The city built a large aquarium with colorful fish and an artificial seascape of a coral seabed and rocks. It was amazing to see sharks and schools of fish of all shapes and sizes swimming near the glass ceiling as we stood on the rotating floor listening to enchanting, heavenly music. I even touched the back of a stingray, which was velvety soft.

Dr. Lemon liked to participate timeshare groups for condos and loved invitations for free meals. He eventually ended up purchasing two separate units in the Smoky Mountains close to Pigeon Forge. We each paid an equal down payment under a separate ownership agreement. Later he convinced me to pay to upgrade the deluxe condo, which I alone ended up financing. Regardless, the Smoky Mountains were splendid, peaceful, and serene.

The moment I entered my office upon my return, patients were lined up waiting for me. Shirley, a registered nurse with Stage III breast cancer who had private insurance, had been depressed and had developed insomnia since her diagnosis. For the first time, I described an antidepressant briefly. But once Shirley started her chemotherapy course in my clinic and began to socialize with my patient, her depression lifted, and she stopped taking the antidepressant medication within two weeks.

I was in a choir group at the church, and Shirley and I attended the same church. She liked my singing voice and always complimented it.

She tolerated chemotherapy well, and she looked marvelous with a wig from the free wig closet in my office. She was cured for ten years, with no evidence of breast cancer.

Another Universal Care insurance patient, Charleston, with metastatic lung cancer spread throughout his body was receiving palliative care. I treated him even though his insurance company had gone bankrupt.

Palliative care patients do not require heavy doses of chemo drugs, as most suffered illness at stages that would be difficult to cured. My logic was that I would adjust the chemo drugs they required to prevent severe side effects. I gave the leftover drugs to the Universal Care patients who were unable to reimburse my charges. What was I supposed to do when my patients needed chemo treatments that the insurance company would not cover? I gave them their treatments without worrying about whether I would be reimbursed.

Charleston enjoyed his life much longer than had been anticipated. He even helped his wife with household chores during his treatments. I always concentrated on helping my patients the best suitable way and leading them to efficient outcomes—correct evaluations and discernment, along with right decisions.

———*/*/*/———

Normally, stomach cancer is not sensitive to chemo drugs. One day, a woman named Parten came to see me with end-stage stomach cancer. She was an older female patient, quiet but with a stern personality. She had lost her husband to stomach cancer two years prior to being diagnosed with the same cancer. Parten did not complain much or talk during her chemo treatments. She did very well and achieved clinical remission for seven years, with no detectable evidence of stomach cancer.

What you eat is important, and food is medicine. The Japanese had a high rate of stomach cancer due to eating charcoal fish or burned meat prepared with a porous black carbon. Chinese people had frequent throat cancer, caused by the habitual drinking of hot tea or hot soup. Indians often develop mouth cancer from chewing betel nuts. Indeed, what you eat makes you what you are and can contribute to the disease process, along with exposure to environmental and chemical pollutions.

For example, a perfectly healthy young person can easily catch a cold when they are stressed or emotionally distraught, which decreases their immune system's capacity. I believe all my patients did far better than anticipated because they were happy and without fear while they were under my care. It is proven that mental health and confidence are just as important as physical health.

One of my patients, Huber, had severe COPD and advanced lung cancer and required continuous home oxygen therapy. His was expected to live only six months. He lived for well over three years, while gradually improving his overall condition. He had also had Universal Care and did not have insurance coverage when he saw me. I did not mind treating him with palliative care.

After close to four years, his daughter decided to enjoy him at home without any treatments. The patient and his family members sincerely appreciated my care for their beloved father.

Arthur and Calvin came almost at the same time to receive chemotherapy. Both had the same last name. They acted like brothers and teased each other during the treatments.

Arthur, who had private insurance, was diagnosed many thousands of folds above the normal tumor markers of colon cancer. His cancer had spread throughout his body, and his abdomen was filled with blood, which is called bloody ascites. This was confirmed by a special procedure. Arthur prepared for his life to be cut short and sold his beloved red truck, his house, and moved into a small condo with his wife. Unexpectedly, he just relaxed and tolerated his chemotherapy efficiently, and the treatment knocked down his tumor marker quickly. He did not get sick, and the chemotherapy went very well.

His attitude changed, and he decided not to worry about tomorrow and let tomorrow take care of itself. He played golf with his wife, and they enjoyed each other. Arthur and his wife loved my pizza parties, and chemotherapy did not diminish his appetite at all. I was so happy seeing them behaving "normal" and not as a chemo patient and the wife of a sick man.

Later, Casey convinced Arthur to refuse my care and treatment with her assumptive allegations. Unfortunately, he believed the good-looking American LPN. Most Fairfield Glade patients enjoyed playing golf in all seasons except for the winter months. During the winter, they stayed in

Florida until the weather got warmer. Arthur went to Florida, and once a month, he returned to my clinic for his chemotherapy treatments. After Casey plotted against me, though, he thought it would be easier for him to stay the entire winter months in Florida. When his chemo cycle day came, my patient went to the Florida Cancer Center and received his chemo treatment there, instead of returning to my clinic.

During Arthur's first cycle of chemotherapy in Florida, he got extremely sick, and after his second cycle of chemotherapy, he lost thirty pounds and could hardly walk by himself. Apparently, the cancer center gave him three to four times more of the medication than he received at my clinic.

He came back to Crossville and called me. "Dr. Gates, would you please forgive me? I did not come back for my treatment after Casey informed me that Florida Cancer Center would treat me better. I lost thirty pounds and could not eat for several weeks. I have no strength. Please forgive me and accept me as your patient again."

"Arthur, I missed you and wondered what had happened to you," I told him. "I'll evaluate you immediately."

"My primary doctor admitted me to the ICU just now," he said. "I want to see you at the hospital."

The primary doctor did not inform me what was going on, and I did not hear from him again.

A few weeks later, my billing manager tearfully informed that he had not made it out of the ICU.

Calvin was sad when he heard about Arthur. Calvin had end-stage lung cancer that had spread to his aorta, the body's main blood vessel. He was a heavy smoker, and he could not breathe even on continuous home oxygen therapy.

Calvin worked at a government office and had private insurance, carried by Blue Cross Blue Shield. A Knoxville pulmonologist diagnosed Calvin with end-stage lung cancer and gave six months to live. At the time, not many Knoxville oncologists were willing to treat Calvin because he was extremely debilitated and unable to walk by himself. Even under physical therapy, his gait was unstable.

He was treated very carefully and, gradually, his gait improved. After his third cycle of chemotherapy, his tumor size decreased by more than half. Eventually, his tumor disappeared after completion of his last chemotherapy.

I referred this patient to Dr. Lemon for a course of radiation therapy to achieve a durable remission.

During the radiation therapy, he could not breathe. The radiation had induced pulmonary fibrosis, which I treated immediately with a small dose of steroids, and he improved quickly.

Casey persuaded Calvin to see my competitor. Calvin did not want to see him until he had completed his chemotherapy under my care. He brought a large chocolate cake for everybody to celebrate his last chemo treatment. He was most happy about his successful chemo treatments. A subsequent CT scan of the chest showed no detectable cancer anywhere in his body. Calvin could walk without a walker, and he no longer needed continuous home oxygen therapy. His overall condition miraculously improved.

Thereafter, Calvin went to my competitor's care—thanks to Casey's persuasion. Calvin achieved a durable clinical remission for more than seven years after my treatments.

CHAPTER 24

Busier Than a Fast-Food Restaurant (Trojan Horse)

The Knoxville pulmonologist (lung doctor) saw Calvin. He could not believe how miraculously he had achieved clinical remission. Calvin's pulmonologist called me, suggesting that I publish my successful lung cancer treatment. It sounded wonderful, but with my busy schedule, I had no time to write an article. Accordingly, I declined his request to publish the details of Calvin's successful treatment outcome.

Many LPNs said that my clinic was busier than a fast-food restaurant. Dr. Lemon would occasionally drop by my office commenting, "Your clinic is always so busy, and it makes me suffocated."

I usually did not have time to eat lunch, and he ate by himself.

A Hollywood film producer's mother was referred to me with a leaking bowel, fistula, and potential colon cancer. She was admitted to the ICU because her waste product had leaked somewhere in her body, which severely weakened her. My patient developed a bladder infection, and she had no energy.

I consulted a urologist and instantly discovered that part of the patient's bowel connected to the bladder wall, and the fecal material had leaked into her bladder. I treated her very aggressively, including plenty of nutritional supplements and hydration through IV and TPN, and her overall condition improved while she was in the ICU.

The next step of my plan was to repair her fistula. Before I carried on with my evaluation and plan, my competitor's nurses, and friends, along with my LPN and former receptionist alleged that I was giving the patient TPN to make money. How could I make money providing TPN to the patient in the ICU? The TPN was mixed at the pharmacy in the hospital, and the hospital billed the charges, which had nothing to do with me. This was another one of their smoke screens, constantly fogged with nonsense. I signed off on this patient's care and referred her to another doctor.

Without TPN, the patient became debilitated again. Crossville doctors were not familiar with ordering TPN, a nutritional supplement, at the time. The patient did not do well, and her daughter sent me an apology letter, requesting that I see her mother again after she found out that TPN was an essential element for restoring her mother's condition. This patient's daughter was a licensed physician's assistance, PA, working at George Washington University hospital.

When the media spreads false rumors, people tend to believe the negative side of the stories, rather than trying to find out accurate facts. We are clearly living in a mundane society. Time was crucial! Unfortunately, the patient's physical condition had rapidly deteriorated without nutritional support. Again, we live and learn. I could not see the patient after I had signed off.

The patient's son was well known as a *CSI Miami* producer in Hollywood, and he received an Emmy. A few days later, I heard his mother had died before undergoing the surgical repair she required. Her son stayed with his father to grieve together.

Soon after his mother died, the film producer brought a collected cupful of blood from his rectum. I was not his primary doctor, but I was an American board-certified internist and oncologist. I admitted him to the hospital immediately. I ordered a bleeding scan on his admission and discovered the location of his bleeding site. At once, I consulted one of the surgeons. However, the surgeon refused to perform the surgical repair.

His PA sister was nervous, and she wanted to take him to George Washington University Hospital where she was working. I called a gastroenterology surgeon at the University Hospital and suggested he prepare for urgent surgery as soon as the patient arrived. All the paperwork was done, and the surgeon was standing by awaiting his arrival. His sister drove in the middle of the night, and he underwent surgery.

Two months later, he brought a flower bouquet and an appreciation card to me. Ever since I saved his life, his family never forgot my care.

Time went on. A year later, the father of the film producer complained about his gradually increasing shortness of breath. His father, Joe, had an extensive cardiac workup and chest X-ray without diagnostic findings by his primary doctor.

Joe came to my clinic. He wanted me to do something for him. I ordered a CT scan of his chest, which showed a small dime-size mass. It was promptly diagnosed as early-stage lung cancer. The tumor was small, it was removed, and he did not need any treatment. He was cured. Now, the whole family praised my name in Fairfield Glade.

When we reach the highest pole, the wind will be blowing stronger. The rural folks, my competitor's friends and relatives threw more darts at me.

In the interim, Dr. Lemon insisted that I go see my parents before they got too old. "Why don't we invite your family to Hawaii?" he suggested. "Hawaii is close to Korea and not far from Tennessee."

"I have a few sick patients, and I can't just leave them without coverage," I protested.

"Why don't you ask your competitor to cover for you?" he suggested.

My competitor was still dealing with substance abuse problems, and he was in and out of a rehab center. One of the doctors who covered the competitor's practice from time to time, Dr. Derick, had not worked for five years. He was a kayaking champion who lived with his girlfriend.

"You cannot leave your clinic without a physician at your office," Dr. Lemon said. "It will be just for three weekdays plus the weekend."

I had met Dr. Derek once before, and I did not care for his character. I was extremely uncomfortable about him covering my practice. Dr. Lemon always interfered with my business. I reluctantly agreed with his suggestion. Dr. Derek would cover me, and he would be paid $5,000 just to see my follow-up evaluations and any new consultations.

Recall how Dr. Lemon had wanted me to have my receptionist double-check my billing records. That was a huge mistake. Although I frequently found myself wishing that I had not married Dr. Lemon and had remained single, most of the time, I agreed with him to avoid dissonance and conflict between us.

We went to Hawaii to see my parents while Dr. Derek was covering my patients. We met my parents, my sister, and her fiancé, who owned pharmaceutical companies in South Korea. Dr. Lemon was silent next to me and not excited; nor did he greet my family. We stayed at a timeshare condo next to the Hilton Hotel.

We had two-bedroom condo units, one for my sister and her fiancé and the other for Dr. Lemon and me. My parents used another accommodation. Dr. Lemon liked collecting clocks and wristwatches. My sister had brought a special custom-made wooden clock for him. He looked at it with no emotion and did not even thank my sister. My parents brought a wristwatch for him, and he barely thanked them. Expectedly, he commented that my parents' luggage was almost empty. He did not have to mention this detail, which unimportant and not his business. Dr. Lemon did not give any gifts to my family.

In contrast, I thought my parents were incredibly wise. What did he expect from my parents, who came from Seoul, Korea, and had never been to America? All they knew was that America was a much more advanced and wealthier country than Korea. My sister's fiancé, Kim, had more funds and assets than Dr. Lemon. His arrogant attitude made him believe that he was superior to anyone in my family. Dr. Lemon had also been aware that I came from Seoul and that I was not Rockefeller's daughter when he had married to me.

I was so happy to see my family once again. I had not seen them for more than ten years. My sister and I made a variety of Korean breakfast for my parents and Kim. Dr. Lemon had never been fond of Asian food.

Hawaii's mild climate and the beautiful scenery made the state a favorite year-round playground, known well around the world. Maui was my favorite island, even when Dr. Lemon and I had come to Hawaii before. Maui was formed from many canyons cut into the volcanic mountains.

The highest point of this island is known a Haleakala, which is the largest dormant volcanic crater in the world. Dr. Lemon loved to see the crater, and we all drove to see it. This was my least favorite place to go. Getting there took more than two hours on winding road—and all so Dr. Lemon could get to the top of the mountain. The crater had a different temperature than the rest of the island, and it was very cold. I did not care for watching the volcanic crater.

Kim drove back to the condo, and we had dinner on the way back. Most of the meals were paid for by Kim, and I paid occasionally. Dr. Lemon did not pay for anything.

Kim and my sister played golf next to the ocean. Kim was wealthy, and they were willing to pay $450 for a one-hour golf game. Dr. Lemon and I rode in my sister's golf cart together. Kim and my sister enthusiastically played golf' they had played in many other countries, including Canada. Dr. Lemon and I played tennis, but we were not golfers. While they were excitedly enjoying their golf game, Dr. Lemon and I ended up getting a bucket of golf balls on the driving range and practiced beginning golf.

Kim was a golf pro and tried to teach us how to play. Kim and my sister bought expensive golf shirts, hats, and matching gloves in Hawaii. Dr. Lemon and I, on the other hand, though we were specialized doctors could not afford to buy extremely expensive golf clothes, and we rented ours.

The next afternoon, the weather was beautiful. We decided to hike Akaka Falls, a long slender waterfall on Kolekole stream near Hilo on the island of Hawaii. The falls plunge over a 442-foot cliff into a wooded gorge with intertwined bright and exotic colorful flowers and ferns. I could feel mist droplets when we went close to the waterfall. This marvelous view of nature and serenity could not be compared with any amount of wealth. It was simply too beautiful.

Dr. Lemon loved ice cream, and he took us to the best ice cream shop, which was close to the falls, after we had hiked. It was amazing how he could figure out every detail about a place and not get lost but often could not find his own car in a small parking lot. That was kind of strange.

We had dinner close to the hotel resort. We relaxed and lay on the beach lounge chairs looking at the gorgeous, vast blue ocean, which was a heavenly view.

My parents were relaxed and fell asleep peacefully. Dr. Lemon, my sister, Kim, and I went to the rocks next to the white sandy beach after the tide had recessed. There were many colorful fish caught between the rocks. My sister loved to watch them and captured some in her hat and released them into the ocean. She appeared to cherish her moments of amusement.

One day, we were roaming leisurely around the Hilton Hotel on a small hill and looked down at the magnificent view. I felt that I was most blessed. My sister and Kim played golf whenever they had a chance. They also loved shopping. I thought the cost of living in Hawaii was awfully expensive.

Hilton Hotel's buffet displayed plenty of seafood, and my family very much enjoyed it. The view and the crashing waves against the wall of the restaurant was something I had never seen. We took many pictures with my family, and those were extremely gratifying memories.

I had no idea what was waiting for me at my clinic. Hiring Dr. Derek was no different than allowing a Trojan horse to enter my clinic and start a war. It was the root of destruction and the impending sabotage of my successful practice.

When I returned to my clinic, all my patients were extremely glad to see me. Many told me things Dr. Derek had told them. He had advised each patient to see my competitor and leave my clinic. My patients were dumbfounded and absolutely troubled by his recommendation. Several patients were terribly upset about his deception, while he was being paid to cover my clinic.

Initially, all my patients stayed with me except for Calvin. He left after he had completed his chemotherapy under my care to see my competitor. One of my patients, who had breast cancer and was doing remarkably well, became highly active in the Fairfield Glade community. She decided to be treated in Florida. Obviously, the patient had been convinced by Dr. Derek's deception while I was not there. This patient went to Florida. Within two months, she died after her second chemo treatment in Florida.

Sara, who had achieved clinical remission from breast cancer, highly praised my treatments. She was extremely angry with Derek when she heard that one of my breast cancer patients had changed her course of treatments, gone to Florida, and died. My patients had been looking after each other and cared for one another through the channel of their network.

While I was visiting my parents, I had a new consultation at the hospital with a reputable local attorney who had advanced lung cancer. The patient had been treated at the University of Southern California Hospital. This lawyer had heard of my reputation and decided to return to his hometown to receive his care in Crossville. He was transferred to the medical center in town and requested to see me during the time I was away with my parents.

Dr. Derek took the consultation and handled the follow-up care. He went to see my patient at the hospital and told my patient and his family to see my competitor. Both the lawyer and his son got so angry with Dr.

Derek that they immediately threw him out of the hospital room. One of my patient's sons informed me about what had happened at the hospital when I came back to my office.

Possibly, Casey was attracted to the unmarried Dr. Derek. She might have entertained him with her drama, telling him that Dr. Gates saved small amounts of Procrit in the refrigerator for later use. Her drama perked his ears and stirred the pot. Another piece of evidence was that he intentionally did not write any pertinent information while he was evaluating my patients, or their CT scan reports. On the contrary, he recorded two lines of the information, stating, "Dr. Gates did not give enough chemo drugs. Recommended that patient to move to another doctor."

Subsequently, Medicare sent me a letter regarding recent follow-up progress notes that were insufficient and affected Medicare diagnostic code charges. Medicare directly asked me whether I had a medical school student at my clinic and stated that the prognosis notes were not presented in a logical format. This letter was about Dr. Derek.

One of my patients, with end-stage multiple myeloma, achieved an extraordinarily successful outcome under my treatments. Prior to his treatment, he had been confined to his bed and unable to move due to severe bone pain. He gradually improved and went from using a wheelchair to a cane for walking. Later, he did not need any support and walked by himself. His condition improved remarkably, and then he went back to work at Walmart as a supervisor.

One day, he brought his mother's precious decorative dish, which she had given to him before she'd died in England. I hesitated to take it, but he wanted to express his appreciation to me, so I accepted it and displayed the beautiful dish at my clinic.

Even though my multiple myeloma patient recovered thanks to the chemo treatments, Dr. Derek reported to Medicare that I should be investigated. He alleged that I was treating this patient incorrectly. Simultaneously, Casey reported to TBI that I was cutting corners and administering drugs illegally to make money off my patients' Procrit injections. I had no idea what was going on behind my back. I was terribly busy, and I was focused on my patients' care.

Victoria Gates, MD

I finally found a chemo-certified nurse who could assist and work for me. She came from the big city of Knoxville, and I trusted her training and knowledge. She made modifications to chemo drugs and helped with my busy schedule.

Meanwhile, a Jewish oncologist, Dr. Tard, moved to Crossville and opened his practice. He was not yet busy, and he wanted to work with me as a partner. I did not know him well enough to hire him as a partner. So, I declined his proposal. It was too soon to allow another Trojan horse in my clinic.

Dr. Tard also joined in the throwing of dirt on me, saying I had not given full doses of Procrit without accurate or material facts to prove his statement. He went to work relaying the negative propaganda against me.

In defiance of the blowing dust, I had many new referral patients from primary doctors, as well as many self-referred patients who had come thanks to word of mouth and learning of my reputation for successful treatment. I was known as the best chemotherapy oncologist in town, even though the LPNs and my competitor's friends continuously plotted against me.

Irene had end-stage recurrent cancer. She was treated for her recurrent cancer under my care and achieved clinical remission without any evidence of visible tumors. After care, her tumor disappeared, and she had normalized CA-125 tumor markers for a year. A year later, the CA-125 started increased again, indicating a second recurrence of ovarian cancer, which was still responding to my chemo treatments. Unfortunately, her blood counts were bottomed out, and she required platelet transfusion. After the supplement of blood products, the patient regained strength and quality of daily activities for a while, until she was set to do another cycle of a chemo treatment.

Irene was an older woman, and after a long discussion with she and her husband, we decided to place her in hospice care. Irene had done very well under my therapy and had lived many times longer than the national stage survival rates with twice-recurrent ovarian cancer predicated. Irene was happy while she was on treatments, and her family appreciated greatly my care for their loved one.

Several prostate cancer patients and other survivors had their blood counts decreased after chemo treatments. Decreased red blood cell counts were supported by a Procrit injection. Decreased white cell counts were supported by Neupogen or Leukine shots, though there was no medication for low platelet counts, which required platelet transfusion. If the patients' overall condition was excellent and they tolerated chemotherapy, I supported them to the maximum.

However, the blood bank complained of a shortage of platelets and prohibited me from ordering platelets on more than one occasion. There was an additional case where my patient, Eddie, had been receiving chemo treatments at my clinic and was doing well, with an excellent quality of life.

One night at 2:00 a.m., Eddie was admitted the emergency room. I rushed to the hospital. I reviewed the result of his blood tests, and his platelet counts were bottomed out. Accordingly, I ordered a platelet transfusion, but the blood bank refused to release the blood product for Eddie that night. The patient's wife was a nurse, and she was furious. I then immediately ordered a head scan, which showed a cerebral hemorrhage. I demanded that he be provided a platelet transfusion at once.

Shockingly, the hospital still refused. Therefore, I ordered IV medication to stop his bleeding, but the efficacy of the drug did not last long. Later that morning, Eddie died.

I believe no one could control a patient's desire to live. Medical ethics prohibited the discontinuation of feeding tube, even for patients who were comatose or unable to move their bodies. My philosophy was, if patients wanted to live and if patients were clinically doing well, you treated them with maximum supportive care, including platelet transfusions.

Dirt hit the fan, and rumors spread like wildfire in town. Some people tried to ruin my clinic and derail my position. Meanwhile, more patients self-referred to my clinic for their treatments. Everyone in this small rural community knew each other. Surely, my patients talked with other patients and brought more patients to my clinic. Despite the grapevine rumors, my practice soared.

On November 11, 2001, Ms. Merry Berry (Sanford) of the Tennessee Health Related Board (THRB), a registered nurse, came unannounced for an on-site visit in the middle of my business hours. She identified herself to me. Subsequently, she informed me that she was at my clinic to investigate my chemo mixing room, including the prefilled Procrit syringes in my refrigerator. I guided Ms. Merry Berry to my medication room. I left the investigator for a while until her evaluation was completed. After the investigation was finished, she interviewed LPN Casey. Then the investigator gave me a summary of her conclusion.

All the prefilled syringes of Procrit dosages were accurate, and there was no fraud related to either it or other medications. Apparently, my employees, including Casey, had contacted the THRB with their allegations, without knowledge of medicine or facts.

Casey was not satisfied with the THRB investigation's conclusion. Casey told my billing manager I might have changed my preparation procedure. In fact, nothing was changed at my clinic. There were still many Procrit bottles upside down with small amounts of leftover medication in the refrigerator during the inspection. And the THRB investigation found no evidence of fraud related to my clinic and practice.

CHAPTER 25

My Throat will be burning

On January 9, 2002, after the THRB inspection in November 2001, I went to the hospital to perform three patients' bone marrow biopsy procedures. My new receptionist, Maggie, paged me right after I had finished the first bone marrow biopsy and before I'd started the second biopsy.

"Three agents from Tennessee Bureau of Investigation are in the clinic lobby, and they told me to tell you to come down to your clinic immediately," Maggie told me.

I canceled the two unfinished bone marrow biopsies and returned to my clinic at once. Three agents, two male and one female, requested to speak with me in my office. I guided them into my office. I was at my desk, and the three agents sat in front of the desk. Before any conversation began, all three agents showed some sort of large, laminated documentation. Two male agents revealed visible handguns above their belts. I did not notice a handgun on the female agent. The agents wanted to search my clinic. I could not believe what was happening, though I saw their visible pistols. The agents requested to see my patients' charts and planned to scan the information.

Medicare policy states that bureau of investigations is required to notify the physician's office at least forty-eight hours before they request an inspection of the clinic premises unless it is an urgent situation. All my patients were doing far better than anticipated, and no patience was ever hurt or injured by my treatments. What was this unannounced visit about?!

The agents raided my clinic during my business hours without my presence. I was performing bone marrow biopsies at the hospital when they arrived. The three agents videotaped my medication room and inspected individual drugs and needle puncture sites of Procrit bottles and prepared chemo drugs, including the prefilled Procrit syringes that were prepared for two weeks in advance in the refrigerator. The female agent was a registered nurse (RN) who worked for TBI. All the dosages were accurate, and the prefilled syringes were correctly stored in the refrigerator. The videotape ran while the RN narrated every aspect of the detailed inspection of my chemo mixing room. No evidence of fraud or inappropriate procedures was found during the inspection.

I was unaware that the agents would invade my private office without my permission. They performed an Illegal search without a search warrant. The LPN who had stirred up this investigation did not have comprehension of procedures in treating patients with chemo drugs. Her knowledge of Procrit was insufficient because she did not have any concept of the FDA-permitted extra doses in each bottle. Casey granted the TBI agents' permission to videotape my clinic, which she had no authority to do without my permission, as she was not the owner of the clinic.

The three agents initially showed laminated badges, not search warrants, and they did not notify me of their on-site visit. Nor did they receive my permission to videotape my clinic. It seemed that they had broken into my private premises and violated HIPPA laws.

The agents wanted to scan my patients' charts without my agreement and commanded that I provide a space for them to scan all the charts, including those of privately insured patients. With visible pistols and, eventually eight law enforcement agents involved, they acted as if they had search warrants, assertively demanding things and ordering, under duress, that my manager provides the patient charts. I guided them to the transcription room and told them not to disturb my patients while they were receiving chemotherapy. I requested that they bring the scanners through the lobby to the designated area, not through the treatment room.

One of the agents took off his jacket. His handgun was always visible. The agent parked his car, marked with its TBI emblem, in front of the large glass door of treatment room. The community right away noticed what was going on. Regardless of my request, the five agents brought scanners and other equipment through the chemo room and frightened my patients. The patients' eyes got bigger than saucers, and they were scared by the officers' presence, while they were receiving chemotherapy, their half-naked torsos exposed. The agents simply dictated their commands and disregarded my requests regarding patients' privacy, rudely intruding and invading my patients' privacy.

In the middle of evaluating my follow-up patients, the two male agents, Corbett, and Turner, wanted to interview me. The follow-up patients were rescheduled for the following days. I went to my office with TBI Agent Corbett, who was from Cookeville, and Agent Turner from HHS. They never identified themselves. Their handguns were still visible on their belts. I was interviewed under duress. Furthermore, I was not given my Miranda rights by the interviewing agents.

During their interview with me, I told them that I saved the leftover dosages of Procrit and used them for indigent patients who did not have insurance coverage. Medicare allowed physicians to charge for the maximum utilization of the extra amounts of drugs at the time. There was no restriction from Medicare. Nor did Medicare have a policy regarding the extra dosages in the drug bottles in 1999; no such policy existed until after 2002. Besides, I was not interviewed under oath. Nor did I give a sworn statement to the agents. I told them the truth and nothing but the truth.

The agents scanned the Medicare patients' charts, as well as privately insured patients' charts. Clearly, the agents violated HIPPA laws and invaded my patients' privacy. Additionally, the agents stayed until 7:00 p.m., after my business hours. My clinic closed at 5:00 p.m.

The next day, my receptionist informed me that my competitor's manager wanted to speak with LPN Casey. I was busy and behind on my patients' care. I must have pushed an incorrect button. Casey's conversation with the caller was recorded.

"The Tennessee Bureau of Investigation searched Dr. Gates's office, and her clinic will be closed soon. Would you like to come and work for us?" my competitor's manager said.

The phone call made it sound like somebody had planted an evil seed and set up my practice to be sabotaged.

I indirectly asked Casey whether she liked working at my clinic.

"I like your patients, and I will not leave here," Casey said.

I believed her.

Surprisingly, when I came to work the following morning, I found two keys and Casey's resignation on my desk. She had even forged her time sheet to gain more hours of work. Consequently, I would have to be nurse, doctor, manager, and do multitudes of other tasks. Thank God I had a chemo-certified nurse who was helping me mix the chemo drugs.

The new receptionist and the transcriptionist were well trained, and they were working hard. The two billing clerks were more efficient. I hired two more LPNs after Casey left. My clinic was running smoothly.

The dust had not settled yet in the community, ever since TBI's on-site visit—despite that the agents' inspection had uncovered no fraud. People like to entertain themselves and each other with "breaking news."

Shortly thereafter I finished my rounds at the hospital as usual and returned to my clinic.

Maggie told me, "Dr. Gates, a lady called and said, 'Dr. Gates needs to get out of her office immediately. If she does not get out of town, we'll come to her clinic and kill her."

All my employees were shocked. Maggie had put the call on speakerphone, and all the office employees had heard the threat of homicide. One of the younger billing clerks dialed "*69" and found out the phone call was from a health care nurse, one of my competitor's friends.

Meanwhile, during the few days Dr. Derek had covered my patients while I was visiting my parents, he had reported to Medicare a bunch of concocted nonsense about my multiple myeloma patients. Dr. Lemon found a high-profile criminal attorney named Richard in Knoxville after the THRB had visited my clinic.

Around that time, the hospital held a meeting for medical staff, and they invited an outside attorney as a guest speaker. The message was that, when the hospital had a legal issue with one of the patients' admissions record, along with medical record problems, before the hospital could get sucked into a whirlpool, the hospital offered a half-million dollars to settle the case without the government involvement.

At that time, I did not get the message clearly. I did not pay attention to the potential legal issues or bureaucracy of the federal system. I did not worry about the rumors because I had not done anything illegal.

The medical center administrator knew through grapevine that I had had an assumptive allegation. The hospital lawyer could not comprehend what had happened to my practice, and he repeatedly said to Knoxville attorney, "Dr. Gates is an excellent physician and known as the best chemotherapy oncologist in town. She had miraculously cured many of her patients. Some mistake must have happened here; it's impossible to think Dr. Gates has legal problems."

All my employees wanted to call the police after Maggie received the threatening phone call. I thought it was not bad idea since I had been donating funds to support the local police department. I did not know much about the legal system. So, I called the newly hired high-profile Attorney, Richard.

"Do not call the police," he advised. "I will take care of this issue."

According to Richard, he hired a private detective for further investigation. However, the private detective did not contact me at all.

"Why did the private detective not talk with my employees regarding this matter?" I asked.

"Well, he did not want to," was the reply.

This made me wonder if Richard had really hired a detective at all. This answer did not make sense to me.

The next morning when I came to my clinic, I found a chopped square wooden block nailed next to my chemotherapy room door. Someone was retaliating against my successful practice in this small Confederate town. The nail was gigantic, as if somebody were casting a spell on my clinic. It made me think of witchcraft or black magic. I felt I was living in medieval times.

My gardener pulled the nail out of the wall and removed the huge wooden block.

First it was a threatening phone call. Now someone had decided to a nail block next to the chemotherapy entrance door. There had to be many green-eyed monsters in town.

So be it! I tried to dampen all the negative thoughts and focus on my patients' care.

Mr. Green came to my clinic with a scattered and protruding facial tumor. He received treatment for three months under my care. He had been tolerating his chemotherapy very well without any side effects. And he was active and enjoyed playing golf with his wife. Mr. Green returned for his follow-up session after three cycles of chemotherapy. Amazingly, his tumor had completely disappeared. When I looked at his face, I was delighted. The disappearance of his tumor chased away all the sadness that had started to loom around the clinic. We both were elated.

He also informed me that, when he had returned to Vanderbilt Hospital, his doctor had told him he could not believe the treatments had been so successful. "Mr. Green, I felt distinctive tumors on your face with my fingertips, which are no longer palpable," he said.

Later, I received Mr. Green's progress note, stating his diagnosis from his oncologist. Mr. Green and his entire family were ecstatic and relieved with the results and his excellent prognosis.

Amid extremely busy patient care and numerous new consultations, my secretary informed me that one of my previous patient's wives insisted on seeing me. I told Maggie to guide her to my office, and I would see her soon.

In my office, she began to discuss her husband's treatments. "My husband's cancer spread all over his body, and he was terribly sick and extremely weak. You treated him twice and stopped the treatment because he did not tolerate his chemotherapy well. He was then placed in hospice care." She paused. "I wish you would not have given up on him so soon."

His wife looked haggard and distressed. Her eyes welled with tears. She held her throat saying, "My throat is burning, burning, burning." She repeated this complaint as she moved her hands up and down along her throat.

I did not know what to think of this distressed woman. I felt deeply sorry for her. I comforted her for a while and then excused myself to see waiting patients. Maggie put her arms around the woman's shoulder and took her to the clinic lobby, and then Maggie told her goodbye.

I used to drink nearly a pot of coffee a day. That consumption tapered off completely after I passed the oncology board. I began drinking decaffeinated tea. I had been bringing a small stainless-steel thermos to my office and sipped tea between patient evaluations. That day was no different. Thirty minutes before I closed my clinic, Dr. Lemon dropped by my office for a few minutes and then left without saying anything.

I was still busy seeing a patient. Some tea remained in the cup of the thermos and my leftover lunch remained unfinished in the Tupperware. I came to my office to look for Dr. Lemon, who had already left. I drank my tea, ate one bite of my lunch, and went to see the final patient. When I come back to my office, I got a sudden hot flash from my throat to my face, and my heart began to beat rapidly. I could also feel tremors in my hands.

The billing manager had just emptied my office trash can. I brought the trash back. I felt that I should go through the trash bag and check for any evidence of poisoned items in the contents of the trash.

I told my employees to close the office, and I rushed to a gas station on the way home. I picked up a carton of milk and told the cashier to keep the change. I drank nearly half a gallon of milk in a hurry. Milk is known to counteract the onset of poison.

I came home and smelled a strong leaking gas odor when I opened the garage door. I got a feeling of impending doom and danger. I quickly got out of the garage and started to worry about Dr. Lemon. My heart was beating faster, and I felt sick. I paged and called Dr. Lemon numerous times; however, he would not answer my call.

I rushed to the nearest primary care doctors' walk-in clinic to seek help. The secretary of the clinic made me wait for a while. By then, my stomach and intestine were causing me uncontrollable discomfort. While I was waiting for a primary care doctor, I noticed a vending machine across from the clinic. I bought five of the largest sized water bottles and started to drink them to dilute whatever I had ingested.

It was getting late, after 5:00 p.m. I called my friend Rachel in Fairfield Glade. She answered my call right away. I told her I was at the primary care doctors' parking lot because I had gotten suddenly sick and had experienced nausea, vomiting, and diarrhea. Later, the primary care doctor wanted to go home, and he recommended that I see the hospital emergency doctor. At the time, I could not trust anyone, not even the ER doctors, or any doctors in the town for that matter.

Soon, violent nausea and vomiting began. I asked the secretary at the walk-in clinic to allow me to use the clinic restroom. I started throwing up and had massive diarrhea.

Rachel could not believe what was happening to me. I told her to take me to a hospital outside Crossville. I was still concerned about Dr. Lemon, who had never answered my calls. When Rachel called him, though, he answered at once.

I was genuinely concerned about Dr. Lemon not responding my calls. I initially thought he could have been suffering just like me, because this small Confederate town was different from Wisconsin.

We could not wait for Dr. Lemon to arrive in the primary care doctors' parking lot. Rachel drove seven minutes toward the freeway, but before we could go any farther, I had to use the bathroom. We stopped at a restaurant before getting on the freeway. I rushed to the bathroom and started to throw up and continuously had massive diarrhea.

Meanwhile, Rachel communicated with Dr. Lemon. Rachel told him I was awfully sick and to meet us at the restaurant parking lot. He finally arrived at the restaurant. He did not seem at all concerned about my acute vomiting and diarrhea. I did not want to go to Cookeville, I requested, rather, that we go to Harriman Hospital, which was closer than Cookeville Hospital. He declined my requests and drove to Cookeville Hospital.

Rachel told him, "Victoria is extremely sick, and I witnessed her massive vomiting and diarrhea."

Dr. Lemon did not say anything. Nor did he have any response to my illness. He maintained his silence. He continued driving just like a cold turkey. He appeared to be without emotion or sympathy.

When we arrived at Cookeville Hospital emergency room, I explained to the ER nurse that I may have been poisoned and needed a blood test done urgently. I was not comfortable at Cookeville Hospital because the TBI office was close to Cookeville Hospital. The ER staff refused to do the blood test and simply checked my urine, which was extremely diluted to the large amounts of water I had consumed. I wondered why Dr. Lemon was so quiet when the ER refused to give me a blood test, knowing I still had symptoms.

I remembered when my sister informed me that a wise elder had advised her that I would become intensely sick in 2002 and to be overly cautious with my health.

Strangely, I was admitted to the emergency room, yet the ER nurse did not ask anything about my symptoms, even though I was still experiencing a lot of vomiting and diarrhea. I purposefully drank a ton of water to rinse out the ingested toxin that had caused gastrointestinal attack. After this, my symptoms were somewhat under control. When I returned home, I drank more water.

Dr. Lemon was next to me on the bed and continuously observed me in silence. I took a bathroom trip and noticed there were many chemicals, including ammonia bottles on the shelves in the laundry room closet. I did not know what those chemicals were for, and I hid them behind the laundry detergents.

CHAPTER 26

Bigger Snowballs (Do Not Eat Your Meal)

My practice never slowed down, and I worked exceedingly hard without sufficient nurses for a month before I hired two LPNs. After the TBI's on-site visit of my office, the local people made up stories and entertained themselves. One of my patients, Helen Newby went to a beauty salon on Tuesday. The people were talking about Dr. Gates.

"I saw Dr. Gates handcuffed by federal agents, and they took her to jail, along with a large bag last Saturday," one Crossville woman said.

Helen listened for a while before saying to the other customers, "Really? I am Dr. Gates's patient, and I saw her the following Monday. The government must have released her from the jail on Sunday."

All my employees laughed. They also were expecting soap opera dramas on the next ticking twilight.

People constantly watched and followed everywhere I went. One day, I went to Walmart to pick up a few office supplies. One older skinny man stared at me for long time as he sat on the chair across the cashier's counter. I paid for the purchased items and got out of the store. The same man followed me, carrying a stick. I sensed a bad vibe and was aware of the old man. As soon as I left the Walmart door, he was approaching close behind me.

Thank God, I saw one of my patients parked close to the entrance putting her purchased items in her trunk. I called her name loudly. "Joann!"

She turned around and was incredibly happy to see me. Promptly she ran toward me and hugged me. "Good to see you, Dr. Gates. You are at Walmart. How nice to see you here outside your office?"

The skinny old man put down his stick and was stunned when my enthusiastic patient ran and hugged me. His eyes got huge and, seeming disappointed, he walked away through the parking lot. I said goodbye to Joann. I was bewildered. Was I living on the same planet? Had I somehow gone back to the Dark Ages?

Once the TBI had raided my office, the rural folks were excited. It was as if making up stories about me was something to distract from their boring daily lives in the small community.

Around this time, a retired vice president from a successful company purchased the half-acre empty lot next to my property. The new owner started to build a $1 million French house next to mine.

I racked my brain to figure out why the same white minivans that had followed me when I'd grabbed the carton of milk from the gas station were now following me, along with several local people, when I went to Walmart. They were trying to scare me. It was like I was being stalked by a lynch mob. I was not scared, but I felt I was living in medieval times. And I wondered who was in the two white vans that now seemed to follow me everywhere.

After the incident at the Walmart, when I had been saved by God and Joann, Dr. Lemon called and asked me to have an early meal with Rachel and Carter in Cookeville, since my clinic was closed on Saturdays. Rachel and Carter had invited us to watch *The Count of Monte Cristo* and then go eat together in Cookeville.

They knew I usually attended Saturday Mass and were willing to attend my church service with me. All four of us went to the matinee in Cookeville. I saw many old cars following us in the small town. I felt threatened and the atmosphere seemed ominous and dangerous.

Dr. Lemon drove Carter's car, and Rachel and I sat in the back seat. I was tired, and I leaned my head against the seat and dozed on and off. I heard Rachel and Dr. Lemon talking to each other. It sounded like the TBI had called both and had possibly threatened them; they were saying that the agents were combative and hostile.

The movie was wonderful, though I sensed an unusual hostility in the theater while we were waiting to enter and find our assigned seats. People were whispering in negative tones and shooting me unpleasant glances as they passed by me.

After the movie, we went to Red Lobster. The lobby was unusually packed, and everyone there stared at me as soon as we entered the restaurant. Looking at the expressions on their faces gave me an eerie feeling, and I had the sense of being menaced. I told Dr. Lemon I wanted to go to another restaurant, Charley's, which was across the street from Red Lobster.

All this commotion occurred right after the TBI had invaded my clinic. We left Red Lobster and went to Charley's. It was a short distance away, and I did not see many people in the lobby. We were sat in the middle of the restaurant. Before we ordered our lunch, I asked Rachel to go to the restroom with me. When Rachel and I went to the restroom, a young waitress followed us. The waitress did not use the restroom. Nor was she washing her hands. Rather, she appeared to be eavesdropping. When we left the washroom, the waitress came out right after us. I told Rachel in the hallway that I did not want to eat my lunch. I would rather have a small piece of her rib. She had a baffled expression on her face.

Rachel and Carter ordered ribs. Dr. Lemon ordered a tuna sandwich, and I wanted a bowl of potato soup. Everyone's food came within ten minutes.

"May I have a piece of your baby back ribs? I asked Rachel.

For some reason, Rachel pretended not to understand what I was trying to ask her. At the time, the Holy Spirit repeatedly told me, "Do not eat your meal."

I told her that I did not want to eat my food. Rachel appeared to be confused. I had one piece of Rachel's ribs.

When the waitress brought my potato soup, the edge of the bowl was wet with a clear liquid. I knew what they had done to my soup. If the waitress had simply been clumsy, the creamy liquid of the soup would have been on the edge of the bowl; rather there were scattered clear spots along the edge of the bowl. Besides, the waitress brought my soap more than forty minutes later.

Dr. Lemon nudged my arm and motioned for me to eat a portion of the tuna sandwich he had ordered. I was not hungry at all. Rather, I felt extremely uncomfortable and terribly disgusted in public.

I then heard little girl crying behind our table. "Mommy, Mommy, I do not want to see her dying here," the child said. "She will pass out on the floor. Let us go Mommy. Charley's gives me the creeps."

Ordinarily, I do not pay attention to others' conversation, but that day I vividly recalled my sister's astonishing warning. A wise elder had advised that I would receiving shocking news and would be terribly sick in 2002. That statement repeatedly haunted my mind. I became extremely vigilant, and the Holy Spirit spoke to me. I knew my competitor's friends, folks in small town had poisoned my food in the past, and this event would be the third time. Now, a child was crying out behind my table.

I asked the waitress to pack my soup, saying I would like to take it home. The waitress was shocked. She seemed momentarily lost as to what to say. Then she said, "We do not have a container for soup."

"Can you use a large drinking cup?" I asked. "I'm not hungry now, but this soup looks delicious. I would like to have it for dinner."

"I will ask my manager and will back soon," she replied.

A few minutes later, she poured the potato soup into a large soda cup.

At the same time, two young men in business suits sat in front of our table. They watched the waitress packing the soup. They were flabbergasted to witness the unexpected scene and unconsciously spoke aloud. "Oh, no! She will turn in the poison soup," one of the men said.

I carried the soup toward the exit door. An older Crossville man who had a potbelly dropped the pay phone he was using, and his jaw opened widely, as if he had seen a ghost. His fearful eyes followed us.

After I had drunk poisoned hot water and had gotten sick at the fast-food restaurant, I'd decided not to trust anybody and to carefully monitor my food and drink.

I was suspicious that people were trying to poison me, a suspicion that was proven by a private detective's conversation.

One afternoon, I saw in the grocery store a decent and well-groomed middle-aged couple pretended to shop next to me. They were obviously undercover agents.

"A waitress, a friend of Dr. Henry's was working at a fast-food restaurant, and she put highly concentrated bleach in Dr. Gates's hot drink. Is she going to be okay?" the lady detective said.

The man listened to the woman's question, but he did not answer.

Looking back, I recalled that I had gotten sick after drinking the hot water from the fast-food restaurant on Main Street and had thrown up in the hospital bathroom. The hot drink was my second experience ingesting poison; the first episode was at my office.

Luckily, I could not drink a drop of alcohol, as it made me sick. Due to alcohol dehydrogenase enzyme deficiency, drinking alcohol would cause me to develop anaphylactic shock. If I ingested any toxic component, my system would reject it from my body through evolving symptoms. My thoughts drifted back to the restaurant, Charley's in Cookeville. After the meal, we had gone to a Saturday church service together. Soon after we had entered the church, the crowd had followed us, audibly whispering to each other. I heard them saying that I had brought the poison soup from the restaurant.

Undoubtedly, the whole town had communicated with each other by cell phones. I sat in the first church pew. One of the parishioners asked the next person who might have known about my case.

"Is Dr. Gates going to be safe? What will happen to her in the future?"

"If she's charged, it will be very serious," the woman sat next to her said.

"It was scary to see so many people following her today."

I worshiped God and sang the hymns loudly without any fear. I noticed that a bunch of birds were on the rooftop of the church and were chirping loudly as they sang along with me. The people recognized the unusual sounds of birds chirping for a long time. The priest, as well as many parishioners, stared at the roof during the service. I was at complete peace with the Holy Spirit.

I brought the poisoned soup from the restaurant and hid it in a safe place. I needed to put the soup in separate containers to send them out to be tested. This time, Walmart was quiet when I dropped by to purchase several small TupperWare containers. No one followed me; nor did anyone even look at me.

That evening, Dr. Lemon was at the desk and busy using his computer in the master bedroom. I quietly sneaked out of the bedroom and allocated the soup into samples in different containers inside the extensive walk-in pantry. The containers were filled with the poisoned soup on the shelf when suddenly, Dr. Lemon flung open the pantry door and yelled at me, "What the hell are you doing?"

He swept the containers from the shelf with his arm and knocked them onto the floor. He then picked them all up and tossed them into the trash can. He left the pantry without saying anything. Only a small amount of the poisoned soap remained in containers on the corner of the pantry. Dr. Lemon had missed these samples. I never confronted him about his erratic behavior in the pantry that evening.

Love was blind. A woman's heart could be weakened by the deceptive sweet lip service of a man. I hid the remaining containers with the soup in the freezer in the garage, out of his sight.

The next morning, I called Rachel and asked her to send the soup containers to a poison center. I told her I would give her more than $1,000 to have Vanderbilt Hospital examine the soup. Rachel was willing to do this for me.

Two days later, Rachel called, saying that Vanderbilt had refused to test the soup. My mentor, Dr. Jackson, suggested keeping the soup samples in the freezer until the time was right. He warned that I must not say anything about the poisoned soup, because people might think I was schizophrenic.

In the interim, my competitor's manager and LPN Casey were sent to Las Vegas. The trip expenses were paid by my competitor. Casey appeared to be entertaining the TBI with her drama. Unfortunately, Casey's new job did not last long, given her tainted principles. Her deplorable behavioral only lasted for two months, and then she was fired. My competitor's manager was indicted for embezzlement and arrested.

Casey's fake charm opened another door, and soon she was working as an LPN for one of the primary doctors in Crossville. Dr. Pierre knew about Casey's dishonest and misleading personality—how she backstabbed others to gain power and compensate her self-confidence. Sadly, Crossville was a small community, its population only 25,000 to 30,000, and there were not many qualified LPNs or RNs available. This was the only reason I had not let Casey go, despite all her horrible behavior and the actions she took behind my back while employed at my clinic.

At the beginning of her employment, I discovered her many errors—the manipulation of numbers, the deception, and falsified notes on my patients' charts. I tolerated it for a long time due to the nursing shortage, until she broke the camel's back. Soon after she was fired by my competitor, Casey was indicted for selling stolen narcotics on the street. She also forged the patients' names and exchanged stolen vitamin B12 shots from Dr. Pierre's officer at her Suntan Spa.

The local news reported that Casey had stolen a large quantity of controlled substances from her employer, Dr. Pierre. Only Dr. Pierre and Casey had access to the narcotics box key. Later, Casey moved to Alabama and began working for another primary doctor.

When I received employee interview statements from TBI, the three LPNs babbled their nonsense, saying that I had instructed them to give a 0.7 cc, 0.8 cc, and 0.9 cc of Procrit to patients instead of 1 cc. No other employees said anything about fraud except the three LPNs. The concocted allegations were far from the truth.

Even Richard, my attorney, said, "The three LPN interviews sounded crazy."

The TBI agents continued its investigation. Now agents were visiting my patients' houses. Two agents, their handguns visible, visited my patient Olson's house.

Olson's wife opened the door, and the TBI agents said they wanted interview her husband. The patient had had colon cancer, which was now cured.

Mrs. Olson told the TBI agents, "I will not speak to you about anything before I speak with Dr. Gates." Regardless of the handguns, she angrily shut the door and told them this was an invasion of their privacy.

Mrs. Olson called me immediately. She was extremely furious about the intrusion and said that she had kicked them out of her house.

Later, I received more phone calls from patients and their family members. They also told me about vexing experiences with TBI agents did. And they too had closed their doors, refusing to talk with the agents. They all called me to inform me about the TBI agents' intrusion on their homes, saying the agents were not welcome and that they were awfully upset.

Making no headway by that strategy, the agents sent letters, telling my patients to file complaints about Dr. Gates; then they would collect compensation funds for patients. All my patients were irritated and angry over the letters, which they crumbled and tossed into trash cans.

Moreover, one of my patients called to say, "The agents made me so angry. One refusal was not enough. They sent me letters three times. Each time I received the letters, my blood pressure went up, and the whole thing gave me severe headaches. Dr. Gates, honestly, I hate them, and I tossed those letters. I tore the last letter up and almost wanted to burn it. Why don't they leave you alone?"

TBI agent Corbett contacted Calvin and convinced him to begin a civil suit against me, suing for $11 million. Calvin had end-stage lung cancer, had been unable to walk, and had required continuous home oxygen. He had been told he had only six months to live. Yet he had achieved remission for seven years, could walk without support, and had discontinued oxygen. Calvin completed his chemotherapy under my care. Then he left my clinic and went to my competitor after Casey convinced him to make the change. I had saved his life. Now he was trying to sue me under the influence of TBI agents. I could only imagine!

CHAPTER 27

"She's Here, and She's a Big Fish" (Richard, the Money-Grabbing Attorney)

Dr. Lemon fervently tried to persuade me to protect my funds and assets from the government and a potential civil lawsuit from Calvin. I made and had too much money. I should give my money to him, including adding his name to the deed for my property in San Diego—to protect my assets. He unceasingly talked about how I needed to shield my funds, as many doctors went bankrupt and lost their life savings because of falsely alleged malpractice suits.

One night, I unexpectedly discovered, by way of his computer spreadsheets, that I had been paying all of Dr. Lemon's expenses. He convinced me that I generated way more income than the average oncologist. He promised that he would return every dime of my money when the government issues were resolved. I trusted him blindly.

When I looked at his spreadsheet, I saw many discrepancies recorded. At first, I thought he had simply made mistakes. But when I examined it the second time, I saw the miscalculations were consistent and by no means honest mistakes. He had been cheating when it came to what I paid for his expenses.

He repeatedly explained his "concerns" with his well-honed sweet talk. "I am giving you this advice by virtue of my love and affection for you," he would tell me. "The best thing that ever happened to my life was getting married to you. I will support you no matter what happens to you. We will grow old together until the roots of our hair turn white. If anything happens to you, I will take care of you. We are getting along so much better nowadays, and our love grows deeper every year. Our marriage brings me joy and happiness. I want you to know that you are my best friend, my wife, and my partner. When I was needy, you nurtured me and restored my life. You are my savior!"

I fell for all of it. What was I thinking?

At the time, it sounded like he really loved me. Thus, I decided to add his name onto the deed for my property in San Diego as a joint ownership—but under one condition. If he divorced me, the house would be returned to me, and it would be listed solely under my name.

Even if I were deceived by his promises, I really did not worry too much, since I would be married to him until one died. What difference did it make how we spent my money during our marriage?

Had I never thought we might divorce? Innocence is nothing but ignorance. Obviously, I ignored many warning signs of his dishonesty, unreliability, and lack of integrity. It is true; hindsight is always twenty-twenty.

The quitclaim deed was not typed. Rather, it was a handwritten document drawn up by Dr. Lemon and notarized at his bank. My original document was not drawn up.

I still had several million dollars of funds in Milwaukee. I had been with St. Francis Bank for years before marrying him, and I kept there all my separate funds from the group oncology clinic, as well as my private practice. Additionally, I added there the profits from the sales of my California house; my house in Pensacola, Florida; the Tremont condo in Pittsburgh, and my half of the lakefront house in Michigan. All those funds at St. Francis Bank were separate and solely under my only name. I had many CDs between 1994 and 2003 at the same bank in Wisconsin. The interest rates were good at the time, as high as 7.5 percent to 8 percent. My funds quickly compounded with the high interest gain.

One Sunday afternoon, Rachel called and asked if I wanted to go out for dinner at Gondola, a fast-food restaurant.

Gondola, I said myself before answering. *Oh no!* "That sounds good," I said. "I will let Dr. Lemon know and we'll all go together. By the way, did you like your baby back ribs at Charley's?"

"The food was okay, but I had severe diarrhea that evening," Rachel replied.

I did not say anything to Rachel. But I knew that the concentrated bleach might have splashed and contaminated her utensil, causing her diarrhea. When the waitress brought my potato soup bowl, it had been close to her utensil. The thin clear liquid on the bowl's lip might also have dropped onto Rachel's utensil.

We went to the fast-food restaurant Rachel had suggested, joined by her husband, Carter. I asked the waitress if we could be sat in the back room, as I wanted to sit in a quiet area.

This time, I prepared my own containers inside a bag and covered them with colorful tissue and ribbons, so that it appeared I was carrying a beautiful birthday gift. I do not recall what the others ordered, but I ordered chicken soup and hot water, since the restaurant did not have decaffeinated tea, and I did not drink soda.

The same old, red-haired waitress delightfully guided us to the back room of the restaurant and subsequently brought us dinner. I pretended to eat my dinner without putting any food inside my mouth. Once we had finished our meal, I extracted two empty bottles from the bag and poured the chicken soup and the hot water into the containers.

The typical Crossville waitress saw what I was doing when she brought the bill. The restaurant's cook and the owner's faces turned red. They were agitated, distressed, and nervous. I heard them reprimanding the waitress and her replying, "I said not to do it." They were terribly upset. I could hear their uncontrolled and irritated voices.

After that evening, I could not trust anyone. My nurse Susan and my patient Helen Newby begged me to go see a movie, *Passion of the Christ*, in Cookeville after my clinic was closed. I told them to have a good time. They would not leave without me, persistently urging me to join despite my decline and not taking no for an answer. Helen and Susan loved Jesus. I finally joined them for dinner and a movie. The two of them were my favorite people, and we enjoyed riding in Helen's new van.

A few minutes after the movie started, my stomach turned, and I could not tolerate watching the movie. I wretched when Jesus was brutally beaten. I told Helen that I could not take it and went out and sat in her car in the parking lot. When the movie was over, we went to Red Lobster—the same place I had gone when people in the lobby had stared at me with unkind expressions. I asked Helen to share her food with me and said I would pay for everything. The waitress brought an extra plate, and I had a small portion of Helen's seafood. Despite my vigilance and monitoring and though I had been overly cautious about eating out, that night, I was covered with hives.

The following day, a couple of my patients brought bouquets of fresh spring flowers. But I could not enjoy the flowers and could not keep anything near me. The itching was terrible, and I went to a dermatologist close to the hospital. For some reason, the dermatologist was afraid to see me. Something had happened obviously. I did not know what. I asked Dr. Lemon to prescribe a small dose of Benadryl pills, which helped my rash.

I was displeased and refused to go out to eat. Even choosing produce items in a grocery store made me suspicious.

Still, despite dealing with all these absurdities, my business was busier than ever before.

It was not long before another difficult situation cropped up—this time in the form of a money-grabbing, high-profile attorney in Knoxville. We went to his office. He did not explain anything about legal system. Nonetheless, he said, "If you're convicted, you'll be locked up for ten years for Medicare fraud."

In the middle of our meeting, Richard's secretary called him to answer a call in his private office. Dr. Lemon and I were next door and were both anxious, dealing with an unknown future. I was pacing the hallway and was passing by the door to his private office when I heard him say to whoever had called, "She's here, and she's a big fish."

Back in his office, Richard again did not say much, other than that he would handle the pretrial for my case. I had never had legal problems. Nor had I violated any laws. I felt like a fish out of water.

After the appointment, I was not hungry. I could not pretend my tribulations weren't weighing on my, and a feeling of disappointment had started to sink in. Dr. Lemon always loved to go out to eat, and his favorite Italian restaurant was Carrabba's. We went. He had pasta, and I ordered a barbecue chicken pizza. While he was eating the pasta, I sensed the restaurant cooks, and the employees knew who I was. They had, perhaps, watched the television news report about my clinic. We were sitting in front of the cooks' counter, along with many other diners. Once people recognize me, there was a negative vibe in the room. I refused to eat any food.

We brought the barbecue chicken pizza home. I wanted to throw it out and to tell Dr. Lemon not to eat it. I did not say anything though. He would most likely think I had become paranoid.

The next day, Dr. Lemmon ate a small piece of chicken pizza, and he got deadly sick. Good thing he ate only a small portion of the pizza. I tossed the remaining pizza right away.

Many of my patients advised me to get out of town and informed me that the government will railroad on me. Meanwhile, several new brain tumor patients were referred to me and were doing well under chemotherapy. But with all the upheaval and annoyance, at times, it was exceedingly hard to concentrate on my patients' life-and-death care.

The first pretrial was held in Nashville. I arrived at the courthouse thirty minutes before my hearing. Almost half a day was wasted as I attended the pretrial. Before the first pretrial, Richard wanted to interview all my patients. Subsequently, my employees and I arranged my patients' appointments with him. One of his employees was a former FBI agent, who visited some of my patients for interviews. Meanwhile, Richard interviewed most of my patients at my clinic.

All my patients supported my treatment and praised my care. The results of the interview were successful and positive. Richard did not receive a single negative comment from my patients.

He charged me an enormous service fee for these interviews. Surprisingly, he did not mention the interviews with my patients at the pretrial. The only thing I received from him was the invoice. He claimed that he spent hours, days, weeks, and even months collecting information from my patients. I just lost money; that was all.

Dr. Lemon's audible hearing was substantially diminished, and he appeared to be ignoring friends and family, including me—all because he could not hear well. We found the best ENT doctor in Nashville for the surgery his condition required. Lo and behold, the ENT doctor knew me, though I had never encountered him in the past. He complimented my successful practice. He complained about being a professor and working for a university hospital, which did not financially satisfy him. His income had been greatly filtered by the school. I was overwhelmed about how far my reputation, both good and bad, preceded me.

Tornadoes occasionally hit Crossville, and one year we had serious tornado damage. One of the hospital nurse's houses was demolished. Moreover, lightning struck one of the doctor's houses, and it burned to the ground. This doctor decided to move out of Crossville after he lost his house in the tornado.

Our gardener alerted us promptly that a pine tree was in front of our master bedroom and had hit the roof just above the head of our bed. The pine tree was humongous; it could have instantly killed us both. We were blessed and just had minor roof damage, which was repaired quickly.

Unmindful of the negative media, more patients sought treatment under my care. As time went on, the hospital wanted to build office spaces for doctors next to the hospital. I suggested to the administrator at the medical center that they utilize the empty lot in front of the hospital, which they did. The president of the hospital offered me the first choice of locations on the model plan. Nevertheless, I declined because of the uncertain future with the TBI investigation.

The historical high school on the top of the hill across from the hospital was a landmark in the community. It had been emptied for many years. Audaciously, I was interested in renovating the historical building, whose outside designed in a gothic style had been wasted for years. The mayor and the city council granted me a permit to remodel the building with my own funds, and in exchange for restoring the unoccupied building, I could occupy it rent-free for thirty years to life. Mainly, I was interested in opening a large cancer center and a hospice care facility, along with a vocational school to educate the youth in Crossville. I went there with the constructors and the realtor.

Dr. Lemon was mad at me. "Why do you want to work yourself to death instead of enjoying your life?" he asked me.

I never had a dull moment, which had to be my destiny. One of the television stations came to the hospital, broadcasting that Dr. Gates worked in the facility and attempting some negative PR against both me and the hospital.

As result, the hospital administrator held a staff meeting and asked about what had happened at my clinic. I explained to the administrator and the staff members that there were no errors at the hospital. I did not provide any of my own Procrit or chemo drugs to any inpatient or outpatient of the hospital. False allegations from the TBI investigation that was simply I had shortened Procrit dosages and the dosages of two other chemo drugs without any material facts.

Despite my explanation, the hospital decided to restrict my admission privileges to protect the hospital's reputation. Unless I'd made an error at the hospital or the hospital had found mistakes on my part, there was no reason to restrict my privileges. I did not have a single error at the hospital. I understood that the hospital did not want to get involved in the center of media attention or with political influence. I should have packed out of this town a long time ago—long before I stepped into the quagmire or fell in quicksand.

In contrast to all they negativity, my patients remained loyal to me, despite my admissions privileges being restricted. The hospital often explained to my patients that they needed another doctor to admit them to the hospital. I took care of my patients at my clinic, and if they needed to be admitted, I referred them to one of the admitting doctors. All my patients returned after they were discharged from the hospital.

One of my patients, Adam, who suffered from chronic lower platelet counts had been treated at my clinic for quite some time. His low platelet counts were not responding to the mediciation. and I referred him to a subspecialized hematologist, an expert in blood platelet disorders for a second opinion at Knoxville University Hospital.

The hematologist recommended a splenectomy without use of Decadron after the surgery. Adam was admitted to the hospital for a splenectomy under surgeon and oncologist Dr. Tard.

The splenectomy was successful. I had asked the surgeon to call me anytime of the day if there were any complications, and he reported the patient's condition to me daily at 6:00 a.m. each morning. A couple of days after the surgery, he told me the patient's red cell counts were down. It was most likely that the patient was bleeding from the surgical site. Promptly, I recommended a bleeding scan. My presumption was correct, and the surgeon repaired the bleeding spot. I reminded the surgeon that Decadron must not be given to this patient, which was adamantly discussed with the platelet expert during the second opinion at Knoxville University Hospital.

Dr. Tard was my patient's admitting doctor that day. The surgeon told him not to give Adam Decadron. Against the surgeon's advice, he administered Decadron. Soon after Adam received the Decadron, he died in the hospital.

What disturbed me the most was that the whole situation could have been avoided, and my patient would be alive today. I could only imagine a mushroom of smoke in the air, as if somebody had dropped a hydrogen bomb.

During the interval, as I battled with the hospital, Richard, my defense attorney, was still preparing for another pretrial. A deposition was scheduled for Calvin's civil lawsuit against me, which he had filed despite the fact I'd saved his life. Richard and my civil attorney, London, were in attendance.

Calvin's attorney began the questioning regarding medical information. Despite that this attorney did not have knowledge of or a background in medicine, he asked very sophisticated medical questions as if he were an expert. I answered all the questions correctly, and that was the end of the deposition. Richard participated in my civil action and charged me $30,000 for doing nothing except sitting next to my Civil Attorney London.

A few weeks later, Richard called me into his office. He wanted to hire a nurse consultant to evaluate Calvin's treatment related to Taxol drug and antiemetics. According to the nurse's evaluation, he found that I had overcharged for Taxol but had undercharged for antiemetic medications. Statistically, this proved that the nurse's evaluation was not accurate. Nor were we dealing with reliable source. However, his findings were used against me inaccurately in the hearing, based on the information from one single patient. This time, Richard charged me an additional $40,000 to help the opposition dig my grave.

CHAPTER 28

Innocence Equals Ignorance (Victoria Gates v. America)

In 2003, I was elected president of the Tennessee Medical Society of Cumberland County. The PR liaison from Vanderbilt Hospital often came to Cumberland Hospital. She suggested placing my blown-up picture inside Vanderbilt Hospital. I declined the offer, and the picture was taken back from her. She was visibly upset. That was my first mistake in establishing my relationship with Vanderbilt Hospital. I did not realize who I was dealing with. I was a tiny fish compared to Vanderbilt Hospital. I should have known who I was and where I was.

Soon after the photo incident, I met Dr. Davis, the director of Vanderbilt Cancer Center, who had been elected president of ASCO (American Society of Clinical Oncology). He talked about the expansion of the cancer center. One of the benefactors donated a large sum of money for the construction of the cancer center. It was to be renamed Ingram Cancer Center in Nashville. We discussed the experimental treatment and research at Vanderbilt. Dr. Lemon and I visited different departments at the hospital.

After that visit, Dr. Davis referred one of his patients from Vanderbilt to my clinic. The patient was a famous pianist with recurrent breast cancer. Dr. Davis recommended that I not adjust one drug when I was treating her. I started out with his recommended dosages.

Regrettably, two weeks later, the patient developed severe vomiting and became awfully weak. She could barely stand up straight. For this reason, I reduced and adjusted her treatment dosages based on her clinical symptoms.

The patient recovered remarkably and tolerated treatment well. She was able to travel and enjoy her life with her husband. Her drug was inexpensive, and the leftover dosages were wasted. My reduced and adjusted dosages were not reported to Dr. Davis because I did not want to disrespect his recommended dosages. The main point was that I adjusted the dosage to help the patient's overall condition and to ensure that the treatment defeated the cancer without making her sick. The pianist's restaging CT scan revealed no visible cancer.

The entire community was delighted that the famous pianist had done well under my care. Yet, a false drama swept the town, and people disregarded facts and evidence. In my opinion, the rural folks were determined to get me and to show their egotistical power.

We wanted to invite Dr. Davis for dinner to informally discuss innovative, cutting-edge treatments in Nashville. He accepted our invitation. The day came for our social dinner with him. One of my patients became extremely ill, and I had to admit the patient. I called Dr. Davis and cancelled our dinner meeting. That was my second mistake. He was a powerful, famous, and busy doctor. I was honored to have dinner together, but I canceled it for my patient. Blame it all on my poor interpersonal skills—or lack thereof.

The second tornado hit Crossville again, and this time, wind knocked down several of my pine trees. A landscape crew came and removed several fallen trees. I contracted for the service, and surprisingly, they eliminated more trees that I'd asked for—for unknown reasons. They chopped down and burned smaller trees while carrying out others that had fallen. It seemed as if they were looking for something, and they left me to clear the area where a dense forest had once been.

Wearing Dr. Lemon's old tennis shoes, I went down to see the remaining ashes of the burned wood. He came behind me to survey the area.

Upon returning to the house, he asked me not to use his shoes. I had expected that he would say thanks for taking care of the fallen trees and for paying for the work. Out of the blue, he had dealt me a negative comment. At that moment, I saw him as a faker. He probably did not love me at all. Dr. Lemon was impersonating someone who loved me for his own benefit. At any rate, his love was drifting away under the TBI's current investigation of my clinic. The TBI agents were still going through my life with a fine-tooth comb.

Something deep inside me told me that Dr. Lemon was helping the TBI in its investigation of my clinic. After Calvin's potential lawsuit, he had persuaded me to hide Taxol chemo drugs under the bed at home. I did not understand the purpose of his suggestion. I hid a couple bottles of medications under the bed to avoid any conflict with him but moved them later. I did not realize that he'd checked underneath the bed for the medications and had been disappointed to be unable to prove the rumors and false allegations true to the TBI. He never made his childish request again, realizing he was the fool. Until proven otherwise, I will forever believe that Dr. Lemon was helping the TBI agent and attempting to set me up.

I grew up in California. To me, this small rural community was amazing; everybody knew everybody's business in detail. Patient after patient would tell me they had heard whispers that Dr. Lemon was the perpetrator in my case and possibly part of the conspiracy to poison me. The other conspirators who had tried to poison me were becoming worried that they were going to get caught.

I asked Dr. Lemon, "Why are my patients telling me that you are the perpetrator?"

He did not say a word and avoided eye contact, as if he did not hear what I had asked him.

At this time, Richard requested another $200,000 for representing me. The service fee increased each time he talked to me—climbing from $30,000 to $40,000 and then $75,000 and then soaring to $150,000 and, after that, $200,000. Yet he had provided no real help, not even with the homicidal threat call from my competer's friend to my office. It was a joke. I got growing tiredness of my money-grubbing attorney, who also hid the truth and caused my case to linger when possible. I felt he was using me as an ATM.

I called and told him I did not want him to represent me any longer. He immediately drove through the rain from Knoxville to my office in his wet suit. He pleaded and telling me he cared about my case and worried about my reputation. I was a great doctor, and he did not care about the money. "If I had cancer, you would be my doctor," he said. He promised he was carefully working on my behalf and all that mattered was clearing my name. He said this with tears in his eyes and in a soft voice, just like my husband. He was a good actor, a pretender, and I even end up handing over $200,000 in a cashier's check. I was very naive about the whole legal process and had no idea that I was a sitting duck.

I realize now that innocence equals ignorance—at least it did in my case.

Amid all this chaos, my sister and her family, including her daughter, son-in-law, and grandchild came to visit me. They arrived in San Diego. Dr. Lemon did not want to come with me, and I met them there. My niece's husband had many friends in San Diego. We went out all together and had a great time at Sea World, eating out and visiting my San Diego condo.

While we were shopping, my sister saw a couple of exquisite gold watches. She bought them for our wedding gift—one for me and another for Dr. Lemon. We flew back to Tennessee. Dr. Lemon picked us up, and we returned home in Crossville.

I prepared the rooms for my family with care in an elegant fashion. I thought of everything—flower arrangement, fruit baskets, and even his or her perfumes. It would have been perfect if Dr. Lemon had not taken his perfume to his own cabinet.

The following day, Dr. Lemon drove to Opryland, Benihana, and out shopping in Nashville. He wore his new gold watch, and we had a fabulous time together as family. Upon returning to the house, my niece requested that we should have a family meeting. She explained that her husband wanted their second child to be born at our house, since my niece was almost nine months pregnant.

Dr. Lemon began to express that this was a stressful time for me, and he preferred to decline my family's request. After Dr. Lemon expressed his position, my wise niece decided that both of her children would be born and raised in Korea. I allowed Dr. Lemon to give an answer to avoid any conflicts. I believed that was one of the biggest mistakes of my life—besides, having married him. I unfavorably failed my own family plan and put all the eggs in one basket. I only focused on my patients' care and my quest to discover curative treatments, and I dedicated entire my life for medicine.

My family stayed about a week, and then they returned to Seoul.

I went to Nashville for another pretrial hearing. Richard; his associate, Ross; and an attorney from the America Medical Association came with us. Richard presented the argument that, during the process of the TBI raiding my clinic, my rights had been violated more than once. I had not been informed forty-eight hours in advance. My Miranda had not been read to me; nor was I handed a copy of them. Furthermore, all the interviews by the agents were taken under duress, as the agents were carrying visible handguns. Richard demonstrated that, when the videotaping during the on-site visit occurred, I was not even at my office. The agents videotaped without any permission. And they did not have a search warrant. Additionally, the videotape indicated no fraud, as narrated by both the TBI agents and the RN on staff.

The prosecutor had no leg to stand on. Apparently, the prosecutor must have informed the state attorney general about an AMA attorney being present at the pretrial on my behalf. The attorney general submitted an amicus brief to the judge, stating that the AMA attorney should back off. The judge read the brief out loud, mentioning that this attorney general had argued that this pretrial was not not about the United States physicians versus the United States of America. This pretrial was Victoria Gates versus the United States of America. Dr. Victoria Gates was an American board-certified internist and oncologist; accordingly, she was a United States physician.

The prosecutor denied that the agents had violated my constitutional rights when they had searched my clinic on January 9, 2002. While presenting the case against me, the prosecutor accidentally made the statement, "When the agent searched, the doctor was in the clinic." She instantly changed her words saying quickly, "Excuse me, I meant to say it was a tour, not a search." She misled the court to cover up the agents' violation and reduce the impact of their actions.

This time, my attorney presented my case well, but it was not over yet.

In the interim, I needed Dr. Lemon's support. I wanted to please and surprise him by transferring one of my certificates of deposits (CDs) into his name without his knowledge. He loved money more than God. My

Milwaukee bank manager strongly opposed my plan, but I went against her advice. I was still married to him, and I thought this was the right thing to do.

This decision caused me to fall into a bottomless pit and kiss the death. It was worse then opening Pandora's box. I never touched any of his personal items, whereas he dug through my affairs and searched my personal items when I was not at home. I hid that CD, along with all other CD information in a large handbag and placed the bag under the mattress in our guest bedroom upstairs. We never combined our funds and assets. Dr. Lemon did not know my premarital assets, and he had no information regarding the existing Milwaukee bank accounts.

The guest room upstairs was hardly ever used. Thus, I felt it was a safe place to store this information. I found out later that was a huge mistake on my part. It was as if I had created a hole in the dam.

Richard informed me that I needed to provide all my bank history to him. A financial analysis had to be reviewed for my case, and he charged me $35,000 to do so. After the review of my bank records, he charged me an additional $250,000.

By this time, I had already paid Richard way over half $1 million in legal fees. This was brought to the attention of TBI Agent Corbett, who then began to investigate Richard. The investigation alleged that Richard was unlawfully overcharging me as his client. Richard called me one evening at home and asked me to sign a waiver, saying that he had not overcharged me for his services. He was my lawyer and working for me on my case. I agreed to sign the waiver.

My clinic was doing well, even though I had hospital admission restrictions. As time went by, another governmental issue cropped up. The insurance reimbursements were not being paid properly. Medicare stopped paying me altogether. Blue Cross Blue Shield was paying only half, and both companies were regulated by the government. Although this disturbed the clinic's cash flow, I was still getting patient referrals daily, and I was busy.

Richard was ready to go for another pretrial and presented to the court that TBI had violated the Interstate Commerce Act by attempting to prosecute me through the state of Tennessee. Medicare is a federal government program, accordingly, regulated under the Interstate Commerce Act.

The Federal Judge dismissed my case without prejudice in June 2004.

Subsequently, Richard promptly charged me another $250,000 in cash for his work.

I thought that I had kissed my trials and tribulations goodbye and speculated that my legal case was over. I would later find out I was wrong.

In the meantime, I was racking my brain. How was I going to fix the cash flow issues at the clinic? Some doctors at the time did not want to deal with Medicare and were working on a cash only basis or accepting only private insurance. I thought about doing what other doctors were doing. I had lost so much money between my attorney and my insurance reimbursements.

Despite all the obstacles, I decided to continue working as I had been, regardless of consequences. Somehow it was never about the money for me; it was always about my patients' care. I loved them like my babies, and they loved me genuinely. That was all that mattered.

Love conquers all problems, I believed.

Helen Newby, who had had breast cancer and second recurrent ovarian cancer and was still in clinical remission, decided to get married. Sarah, her husband, and I went to her wedding. We brought some gifts. She decorated and prepared food before her reception, and it was simply nice. We sat there waiting for the ceremony to begin, but as time passed, we were invited to eat first. After we ate, we returned to see her wedding ceremony inside the church.

Suddenly, the pastor appeared and announced to the guests that the wedding ceremony had been cancelled. We exited the church and gathered in the parking lot. Then Helen appeared and came to speak to us about the cancellation of her wedding. She explained that the man she was about to marry was already married to someone else. She had received a phone call from her fiancé's wife detailing the information.

I was so amazed by how well Helen was taking this blow. She even said that she planned to write a book about this experience. She was disappointed but had faith in God and courage to get through this disastrous moment without shame or sadness. We walk by faith, not by sight!

Victoria Gates, MD

A local farmer came to my clinic with newly diagnosed, widespread metastatic prostate cancer. Frequently, the farmer brought boxes of produce from his farm to my clinic. The patient brought potatoes, green beans, and corns, which he shucked himself, showing me how fresh, healthy, and sweet the ears were. I remember how big and rough his hands looked as he peeled back the sheave on the corn. He was a down-to-earth, caring man, as sweet as his corn.

The farmer did well for a long time, receiving a combination of chemo and radiation treatments. The radiation treatments were done in Knoxville. After some time, the radiation oncologist informed us that the patient's prostate cancer was beyond effective radiation treatment. The patient developed severe pain and was admitted to the hospital for pain control and tumor staging evaluation.

I called for a family meeting to discuss his terminal care plan. I visited the patient's room. His eyes were bright, and he was happy to see me. I told him that I had to hold off the treatment and place him in hospice care for his pain control until he became stronger. Swiftly, his face and eyes changed, and he became serious and sad with disappointment. After our discussion, he closed his eyes. I thought he was tired and I quietly left his room.

Family members called to inform me that, after I left, he never woke up. He had died that evening.

When I worked at Jamestown Clinic, I had a referral consultation with a chronic blood disorder patient. This young woman tired easily, and all her blood cell lines—white cells, red cells, and platelet counts alike—bottomed out. A bone marrow biopsy was performed immediately, and she was diagnosed with acute leukemia. I treated her carefully, and her condition gradually improved until she achieved clinical remission.

She had been living with an older man for several years, and they were very much in love. They decided to get married since she was in remission, even though they were not financially able to afford a wedding. I decided to offer my clinic as a setting for her wedding. She was thrilled.

We transformed the clinic into a chapel—with flower arrangements, ribbons, and a beautiful altar. The local newspaper came to photograph the event, and the marriage was reported in the newspaper for all to see.

One day, Jerry—my former tongue cancer patient from Milwaukee—called me with gradually increasing fatigue, cold intolerance, and weight gain. Since his successful chemo-radiation treatment, he had achieved in clinical remission for more than ten years. He had been incredibly sad when I'd announced I was leaving for Tennessee.

Jerry had undergone numerous tests ordered by his primary doctor, but not had revealed the etiology of his clinical symptoms. He became extremely nervous and paranoid about the potential for recurrent tongue cancer. I calmed him down and suggested that he ask his primary doctor to check his thyroid function. It was not uncommon for patients to develop lower thyroid function, known as hypothyroidism after radiation treatment.

He was instantly diagnosed with hypothyroidism, treated accordingly, and all his symptoms disappeared. He praised my skill, judgment, and prompt evaluation. Jerry wanted to come down to Tennessee for his follow-up evaluation. I advised him that was not necessary. He could call me anytime.

As noted earlier, my legal case was dismissed in June 2004. Unexpectedly, Richard informed me that the federal government had superseded my case. I appeared before a magistrate in the federal courthouse. The news was all around town; it seemed everyone else knew before I was informed.

I was still treating Helen at my clinic, this time for third time recurrent ovarian cancer. She was frustrated with her private insurance carrier, BCBS, as it was only reimbursing me for half of her treatments. These insurance problems piled on top of the wedding disaster compounded her grief.

Helen felt she needed to change her environment and told me she was planning to see Dr. Derek. The unmarried Dr. Derek had finally convinced her that his treatment was superior to mine.

Dr. Derek told Newby that I was cutting the chemo medication short and remarked that I had committed fraud. Afterward, Dr. Derek decided to treat her with an unadjusted full dose of chemo treatment at the hospital. She was then admitted to the hospital for her treatment. After a single unadjusted full dose of chemo drug treatment, Helen died during the treatment at the hospital under Dr. Derek's care.

The following day, Helen's sister called me from Florida to tell me that her whole family appreciated all that I had done for Helen. Her sister expressed gratitude that she had achieved both breast cancer and ovarian cancer in remissions under my care and had enjoyed a longer life than she would have otherwise.

CHAPTER 29

Closing My Clinic My Money Too and No One to Trust

I wanted to speak to my attorney about my case being superseded in federal court. I had no idea what that meant. I called Richard's office, but he was not available. The associate who answered the phone explained that he had been admitted to the hospital. The matter was confidential, and please do not tell anybody.

My secretary rescheduled the afternoon follow-up patients, and I drove to see him as quickly as possible, bringing a huge gift basket and floral arrangement for him. His visitation was restricted. Even though I was not family of Richard, the nurses at Oak Ridge Hospital knew I was a doctor, and I was able to see him.

His ailment concerned me, and I asked Richard what had happened. He looked at me with a smile, telling me his appendix had ruptured. But there was no evidence of surgery. I know a ruptured appendix could cause deadly illness. There was no way he would be able to sit up on his bed and smile at me if his appendix had ruptured. I sensed he was not disclosing his condition for some unknown reason. My impression was that he might have been diagnosed with cancer. However, he appeared to be keeping it secret.

"Having worked on your case, now I understand the terminology of white and red blood cells and platelet counts," Richard told me.

"That's good," I replied.

I surmised he was not telling me the truth. My entire life had been devoted to medicine. This man had not undergone an appendectomy

Victoria Gates, MD

because of a ruptured appendix. My conclusion was confirmed when he was discharged the next day. I did not appreciate his dishonesty, and I disliked people who lied.

Dr. Lemon and I began discussing the possibility of leaving Tennessee. He was already having problems with the hospital administrator, who did not want to renew his contract. He began looking for a job in other states and attending different radiation oncology seminars. Finally, he found a radiation oncology position in Tulsa, Oklahoma. At a seminar, he interviewed with the head of the department at Saint John's Hospital. After he returned from the seminar, he called the department head, who was a female doctor, and she informed him that he had been hired. His transition out of Tennessee had begun.

Soon after our relocation plan started taking shape, I received a phone call from my sister in Korean. My mother had just been diagnosed with breast cancer. I flew there immediately. As soon as I arrived, I started the process of scheduling her surgery and postoperative treatment. Favorably, my mother's cancer was detected in an early stage, and her prognosis seemed excellent.

During my mother's postoperative care, I received a call from Dr. Lemon, telling me I needed to return home at once. He did not say why, but it sounded unpleasant. I left the Korea within a week.

When I arrived back in Tennessee, Dr. Lemon informed me to go see Richard. My attorney informed me that I had been indicted by a grand jury for a false statement based on the LPN's allegations regarding Procrit dosages. The indictment stated that I had instructed LPN nurses to give partial doses of Procrit to patients but to record the dosages as full. The charge was that I had denied this accusation during a TBI interview on January 9, 2002, when TBI raided my clinic. That was my false statement charge—brought three and a half years after the TBI on-site visit.

The truth was, I never told the nurses to record partial doses as full doses. I told them to save the extra amounts of 0.68 cc of Procrit bottle. Even if it was authentically proved that I had so instructed the nurses, why was I not indicted right after the on-site visit on January 9, 2002? Why did the government to take three and a half years to indict me in March 2005?

The prosecutor and TBI agent confirmed that I had overcharged for Procrit amounts by saving the extra, overfill of 0.68 cc. The agent alleged that you could not possibly withdraw the liquid from the neck of the bottle. The US attorney added the already dismissed Taxol and Camptosar drug miscalculations on top of the Procrit discrepancies and alleged additionally that that I had lied to the agents, thus making a false statement.

Richard's motion to the court asserted that prosecutorial vindictiveness tainted the allegation.

Around that time, in August 2001, Robert Ray Courtney, a former American pharmacist, was arrested in Kansas City, Missouri. He pleaded guilty of having intentionally diluted 98,000 prescription drugs, including Taxol and Gemza, which were given to 4,200 patients. The patients died soon after being treated with the diluted chemo drugs, and their deaths led to the investigation. Courtney was convicted on February 25, 2002. The breaking news disseminated throughout the United States. This case was completely opposite my case. My speculation was that the government most likely assumed my case was the same as Courtney's case.

The only difference between my case and Courtney's case was that I cured my patients, whereas he killed numerous patients. He diluted chemo drugs for his financial gain. I adjusted chemo drug dosages to save patients' lives from hopeless terminal cancer.

Richard had to meet with the prosecutor and said he needed an additional $250,000 to proceed with my case. I discerned that something was awfully wrong. I contacted my mentor, suggesting that I wanted to change my lawyer and get a second opinion. I felt, after I had spent all that money, I should not be indicted for an assumptive allegation. Richard had already visited Dr. Jackson in Wisconsin on two occasions. He managed to convince Dr. Jackson that he could win my case and that I would not spend a day in jail.

Naturally, when I complained to Dr. Jackson, listing the reasons I wanted to switch lawyers, he told me to stay the course. Richard was the president of a national defense firm and had the power and expertise to win my case.

My intuition said otherwise. I was feeling terrible vibes surrounding the case, and I felt that somehow there was an obscuring of truth and facts. I felt helpless and frustrated with my lack of knowledge of the justice system and the operation of the federal government.

Richard did not have much concept about medicine or cancer treatments, to say the least. He could not spell hemoglobin, even after I had repeated the spelling several times. How could Richard convince a judge or prosecutor regarding a misunderstanding of cancer treatments if he lacked the knowledge to grasp the misunderstanding?

I began to consider voluntarily closing my clinic. My whole staff tried to persuade me to keep the clinic open, pointing out that, after the TBI raid, my practice had been busier than ever. They were confident, regardless of the circumstances, that I would recover, and the clinic would continue to be successful.

In the end, though, I was tired of these unceasing legal problems, which were interfering with my concentration while I was treating critically ill patients. I felt as if I were under investigation by the Nazi-era gestapo.

My specialty was dealing with life-and-death situation. It required my entire devotion, concentration, and close attention to patients' clinical signs and symptoms. I contemplated for a month. Then I decided to close my clinic. I explained my decision to my employees. And most of my patients were referred to different oncologists outside of Crossville. I practically gave away everything in the clinic. My patients were devastated, mournful, and heartbroken.

A woman from Fairfield Glade was experiencing gradually increasing shortness of breath, night coughs, and sweats but otherwise appeared to be healthy. I ordered a simple chest X-ray, which showed a dime-size mass on the upper lobe of her right lung. A CT scan was promptly done, followed by a needle biopsy, which confirmed lung cancer. My patient underwent a surgical resection of the tumor without any further treatment after the surgery. The tumor was diagnosed promptly when it was in an early stage and the mass was small. She was cured. When I told the patient, I would be closing my clinic, she could not stop crying.

I felt horrible saying goodbye to my beloved patients.

My office was closed, and Dr. Lemon was preparing to move Tulsa, Oklahoma, to start his new position. I had brought my office computer home since my clinic was closed. My billing manager came to my house to finish the remaining billing charges.

Later, Dr. Lemon told me that Richard needed to take the billing computer and have it analyzed. I wanted to go see Richard and ask what was going on, but Dr. Lemon insisted on delivering the computer himself. This was my legal case, but he was insistent on taking care of it without me, which made me suspicious of his motives.

Dr. Lemon finally moved and settled in Tulsa. He rented a furnished apartment close to the hospital. Not even a month later, he called me, crying and frantic, saying that his whole apartment was flooded. Apparently, while he was taking a shower, the showerhead had come loose, and the water had inundated his apartment due to broken pipe. His entire wardrobe, shoes, and business suits and all his personal belongings were soaking wet. Crying, he said he wanted to come back home.

I told him to stay there and that I would be there shortly. I flew to Oklahoma to support him right after his phone call. When I arrived, I called the apartment manager to switch the unit. All his clothes were sent to a dry cleaner, and I proceeded to dry out his remaining things myself, while Dr. Lemon was at work.

During that visit to Oklahoma, I did not have my car. Nonetheless, I was interested in possibly purchasing a house nearby, so I walked a couple of blocks from his apartment. I saw a newly developing gated town house community. I liked what I saw and purchased two town houses side by side.

I designed the town houses myself and added many amenities. I purchased all the light fixtures and an outdoor remote control for the ceiling fans on the patio, selected all the carpets, and chose tiles for the kitchen bathroom and outside patio floor. It was a lot of work in a short time prior to my trial.

Our Tennessee house furniture would barely fit in the two town houses, and the smaller town house could accommodate family members when they came to stay with us. The town houses were small, even though they both had three bedrooms. I did not buy a large ostentatious house at this point, given the uncertainty of my future.

Dr. Lemon had been interested in another house, which was a little further from the hospital. But while the house was bigger and had a decent view, it was not well constructed and had many unusable waste spaces, which, I thought, would make for poor resale value. I pointed this out to Dr. Lemon, and he was happy with the two town houses.

I rushed to transfer my Tennessee household before going to trial. The entire Tennessee house was packed in twenty-four hours—all by myself and without a blink of sleep—which might have been a way of releasing my anxiety and fear of the unknown. In the morning, I noticed both feet were covered with scattered bruises. I had worked like a slave trying to eliminate my frustration and, somehow, smooth out my twisted destiny.

I had a carpet cleaner steam the carpets throughout the house. All the trash and unwanted items were removed from the house. The house was immaculately clean. It looked like a brand-new mansion. I left chandeliers in the master bedroom and dining area, along with many other household items and decorations so that the house would be attractive during the sale process. I also gave away some of my household items to my neighbors.

The Tennessee house was elegant and exquisitely beautiful. It was more than my dream house. I loved it very much! It dawned on me that, without my choosing, I had to kiss it goodbye and let it go. I did not want to sell my house. I hoped to come back one day and retire here. I called Dr. Lemon and asked him to sell his half of the house to me. I would pay him much more than he had paid down when we'd initially purchased it. I really wanted to keep the house under my name only, in case of divorce. He refused to sell his portion of the house to me.

I had been paid all the expenses for my clinic with the money I had generated, except for one time when he had voluntarily paid the sum of the chemotherapy expenses. I paid him back whatever he asked for. Additionally, I had paid more than two-thirds of the down payment for the two town houses and had spent $40,000 cash decorating them. I started to be skeptical of his integrity and wondered about his motivation for marrying me. I worked all the time like a slave at the clinic as well as at home. He did not help me much.

I did not practice medicine in Tulsa, anticipating my trial in Nashville, and decided to study real estate. I met Martha, a psychologist. We studied the real estate course at my Tulsa house. Martha's husband was a dentist. Mark cleaned my teeth. Martha and Mark, along with their children had come from Canada many decades ago. They seriously believed in God and were devoted to church activities. I trusted them like my own family, and I shared my honest thoughts.

I told Martha everything about my legal case, including daily trivial events. We had dinner at my house, and Dr. Lemon appeared to enjoy the company. Martha and Mark were devoted Christians, and we attended each other's church. Martha gave us her testimony. One day in Canada, she had had nothing to feed her nine children. As they sat at the table together with empty plates, Martha and Mark started to pray.

While they were sitting there, their youngest daughter asked Martha, "Mommy, Mommy, where is the food? I am very hungry."

Martha answered her daughter, "It is on the way."

As soon as she finished speaking, the doorbell rang. Martha's sister had just come from the grocery store. Her sister had bought two extra bags of groceries, since most of the food items were half priced that day. Clearly, God answers our prayer.

Martha's children were grown now. All of them were successful professionals—a lawyer, a doctor, dentists, and a CPA. However, Martha's youngest son had been arrested for DUI and had been in prison a couple of times.

Martha and I completed the real estate course successfully. On my final exam, I scored 100 percent, and the program teacher complimented me, saying no one had ever scored 100 percent in the past. He wanted me to work for him. He did not know I was waiting for a trial.

Dr. Lemon wanted to store most of his personal belongings in the smaller town house. I was busy working and organizing his personal items when I unexpectedly discovered my income tax returns among his legal papers in his personal cabinet box. It was clear that he had made copies of my income tax returns and all my individual certificate deposits. I also discovered documents pertaining to his lawsuit against my bank in Milwaukee, claiming that he had a right to access all my accounts because we were married. I could not believe what I had stumbled onto that day. I was absolutely dumbfounded. I felt like the wind had been cruelly knocked me out. I felt my heart stop beating.

We drove to Tennessee to meet Richard to prepare for my trial in Nashville. Richard stayed in a luxury hotel that I paid for across from the federal courthouse. Dr. Lemon and I stayed in a less expensive hotel. We met Richard at his hotel room to discuss the trial plan. He did not look healthy and appeared to be extremely tired. I assumed that he was exhausted and overburdened with work, including my complicated case. He went over the details and pertinent information with me. Then suddenly, his eyes rolled back, and he fell asleep in the middle of the conversation. I observed similar episodes a couple of times. Later, I learned he had been diagnosed with terminal cancer.

I made several trips back and forth to Tennessee by myself. Dr. Lemon accompanied me only twice. When he drove to Tennessee, his behavior was erratic, and he seemed angry with me, almost hitting my arm on the highway once. While we were driving, I could not shake off my chain of thoughts. He had gone through not only my personal papers but also my private items without my permission or knowledge.

One weekend afternoon, I caught him digging in my personal bag, and he discovered $10,000, which I had saved for a long time. He held my money and was crying like a baby saying, "This is my money too." He would not let go of my money and held it tightly. He was crying and wanted the money.

I racked my brain. Something was wrong with him. It did not make sense. I let him have the money now because he would not let go of it and kept repeatedly saying, "This is my money too."

After I discovered copy of my CD and the lawsuit he'd filed against my bank—over accounts I'd had many years before Dr. Lemon and I married, I realized that he was after my money. This must have been going on behind my back for quite some time.

My sister advised me numerous times to divorce him before I went to trial. I was grasping at straw to survive and felt as if I were drowning. When we hit rock bottom, we easily fall for deception. In my desperation, I hoped that Dr. Lemon's deceitful sweet talk was genuine love, but I was only kidding myself. For some reason, I still depended on him. This was wishful thinking—that he could help me in the future. He continuously misled me in my state of confusion and despair over the situation at hand.

Dr. Lemon delivered more of his luscious lip service, telling me, "I cannot live without you. If you go to jail, I want to go with you."

I did not know who to trust. It seemed like everyone wanted my money, including the government, my attorney, and my husband. At this point, I could not trust one single person except for my patients. Thus, I started to hide money in cash.

I rented out a storage unit and kept it separate from him. Initially he wanted to share a storage unit together, but I preferred to keep everything separate as we always had. This was an unfamiliar experience, and Martha offered to help me. She gave me a book called *How to Hide Assets*.

Martha said she could help me hide or save my separate money for my future. She wanted me to invest in a property. She promised she would return the investment funds after my divorce was over. I gave her $185,000.

In the end, her daughter who was a lawyer advised her not to get involved with me because I was going to trial. Martha returned my money and then became concerned about her affiliation with me. She wanted to consult a lawyer for her protection and asked me to pay for the consultation with the lawyer. We went together for her visit. For unknown reasons, Martha wanted to see the lawyer by herself in private. She did not inform me of anything she discussed with him, even though I had paid $480 for her visit.

I wanted to return her book, *How to Hide Assets*, which I had not even opened. However, she insisted I keep the book.

I told her, "I don't want to keep it."

"Keep it at your house in case you need it," she insisted.

I had a lot of junk at my home. But I kept the book to avoid argument, thought I never read a single page of it.

Before I went to the trial, Richard asked me another $250,000. I was shocked when he not only demanded his fee but also screamed at me not to transfer my money to Dr. Lemon. By this time, Richard had collected way over $1 million from me.

CHAPTER 30

Where Did You Go to Law School? Nothing but a Stage Show

The first trial day, Dr. Lemon came with me. He was somewhat supportive of me morally and emotionally. The prosecutor had brought several of my former employees to the courtroom. The three LPNs who had colluded against me, Haley, Casey, and Mary, were there, along with my former receptionist, Barbara—all as the government's hostile witnesses.

Richard had invited two registered nurses and Doctor Pierre.

As the first witness, Haley assumptively testified, without sufficient knowledge, about the Procrit dosage discrepancy. From the witness stand, Haley drew a picture of an inaccurately sized Procrit syringe on a flip chart. I would not be in this trial if Haley had not convinced the grand jury to indict me with her false evidence.

In the middle of the court proceedings, an unidentified gentleman associated with the prosecutor kept going in and out of the courtroom using his cell phone. Cell phones were prohibited in the courtroom. The man had to be working for the government. Otherwise, he would not have passed the entrance of the federal building with his cell phone on him.

He went in and out of the courtroom and talked to the three LPNs. Notably, all three were discussing something outside the room, which also was considered a violation of law. It appeared to be the gentlemen had recruited the four hostile witnesses to testify against me. In addition to the rule banning cell phones, a witness was not allowed to congregate

MOONLIGHT MELODY

with another witness outside the courtroom. Two federal regulations were violated, but they seemed to be getting away with both.

Dr. Lemon detected the gentlemen and told Richard what was going on. The judge was also aware of the cell phone violation, and the man was quickly barred from the courtroom.

Richard stood up and presented my casing, stating first that LPN Haley was incorrect. After Haley's assumptive allegation was proven untruthful, the judge promptly recessed the court.

Conspiracy might have happened prior to the recession behind the courtroom. Undoubtedly, a few minutes later, the judge returned to the courtroom and announced that the court was adjourned until the next day.

LPN Casey was supposed to testify that day, right after Haley's testimony. In the end, the prosecutor rescheduled Casey's testimony for the next morning.

A retired FBI agent working for Richard found out that the prosecutor contacted Casey, and they communicated with each other, which was again a violation of federal law. The prosecutor should not advise the governmental witness what or how to testify against the defendant. Conspiracy was again a violation. The phone was not tapped, but the prosecutor and Casey plotted against me the night before her testimony. Casey was supposed to testify the morning after Haley gave incorrect testimony and depicted the size of the syringes incorrectly. The following day, Casey testified on the witness stand that she knew Dr. Gates hardly ever administered 1 cc syringe size of Procrit to her patients. As a result of Haley's false accusation, LPN Casey confidently claimed that I used 2 cc syringes to give Procrit.

Richard overruled her statement, because 2 cc syringes are not manufactured and are nonexistent. Richard continuously cross-examined Casey regarding the 16.8 percent overfill amount of Procrit.

Casey did not admit the truth but changed her story and adamantly said to Richard, "Dr. Gates should have given patients an entire bottle of Procrit, but she saved a small amount. Therefore, she committed Medicare fraud. There was no overfilled extra amount in the Procrit bottles."

Once again, Casey's false allegations were incorrect. She proved that she did not have any knowledge of overfilled amounts of Procrit. She exposed herself in open court.

After Casey's testimony, it was close to lunchtime, and the judge blatantly invited Casey to have lunch together before the court adjourned. The judge should not be biased. I did not think socializing with a hostile witness amid a trial was appropriate.

The entire court proceedings and the rules of law baffled me. I kept thinking, *who am I?* Was I blind and deaf? Did I exist in the courtroom? It appeared to me that everyone around me violated rule after rule and got away with it.

The last LPN, Mary, had a history of substance abuse that she admitted. Mary also accepted that she did not have any knowledge of chemo drugs and had never worked in cancer patient care. She collaborated that I had given patients Procrit dosages in the amounts of 0.7 cc, 0.8 cc, and 0.9 CC. Mary got confused.

Altogether, the LPNs' concocted tales, false allegations, and hearsay testimony did not make any sense. But the jury, lacking medical background, knowledge, or experience, might have been convinced. Mary, even as a nurse, was not aware of overfill amounts of Procrit and admitted she did not have knowledge of the subject.

The next testimony came from my former receptionist, Barbra, who claimed she had overheard me instruct Haley on Procrit dosages. Barbara also admitted that she was not a nurse. She had never touched or handled Procrit bottle or syringes and had no knowledge of medicine whatsoever. She believed that my prolonging of patients' lives and providing chemotherapy should be in God's control.

Both my part-time and full-time registered nurse testified that I had never instructed them to give partial doses of Procrit or chemo drugs. These RNs were qualified, certified, knowledgeable nurses, and both stated that I had always given accurate doses to my patients.

The prosecutor stated that the agency had been investigating during the postindictment period, which meant after indictment. According to the agency, I had corrected my practice behavior after my first indictment on January 9, 2002; this the prosecutor presented after the two RNs had testified.

The agent showed the jury an exhibit to the jury that depicted the 16.8 percent Procrit discrepancies, contrasting the prosecutor's statement. Richard's son, Wayne, who was one of my attorneys, countered that the Procrit exhibit spoke for itself, delineating exactly what I had been saying, that the discrepancies were overfill amounts, not shortages or fraud. The prosecutor's exhibit precisely proved that, both before and after the indictment investigation, the same amount, 16.8 percent (overfill amounts) remained. The evidence showed that there was no fraud.

At this moment, the prosecutor urgently objected to the material fact and asked that the Procrit exhibit be removed. The judge ordered the exculpatory evidence of the Procrit exhibit be expunged from the record.

Richard called the next witness, Dr. Pierre, to the stand. He talked about Casey's character and what he had experienced when she had worked as an LPN for his office briefly. During that time, five hundred bottles of controlled substances had gone missing. As a matter of fact, only Dr. Pierre and Casey had keys to the narcotics box. Dr. Pierre was upset and ready to say more about Casey's malicious character. Unexpectedly, Richard stopped the doctor and asked him to answer simply, "Yes," or, "No," to the prosecutor's questions by the judge's request.

Richard spoke of Casey's criminal acts while she was working for Dr. Pierre. She had stolen five hundred bottles of substances, forged patients' names, and sold the drugs on the street. In addition, she had stolen vitamin B12 and exchanged the vitamins for spa passes, according to local news reports. Richard's associate, the former FBI agent, had discovered Casey's criminal acts.

It was a conundrum. Why had Richard restricted Dr. Pierre's testimony? Richard did not give him an opportunity to testify about his experience with Casey. Occasionally, when he did not reveal evidence, I wondered whether Richard was working for me or for the government or both. It was possible he was working to ensure that my case lingered on (and thus generated more money for him). Who knew?

I had paid $45,000 to an expert for jury selection prior to the trial. The jurors selected from the pool turned out not to be any better than a blind random selection without an expert would have been. The jurors included a security guard, a truck driver, a pizza delivery person, a retired homemaker, and a prison guard. Only one of the jurors, a schoolteacher, appeared to understand my case reasonably well, but she was eliminated by the judge. I noticed that most jurors were sleepy and had no medical background; it seemed difficult for them to comprehend the Procrit dosages, an understanding even LPNs lacked.

One of the jurors, a university professor, was alert and paying attention to every word that was said in court. The professor nodded when she understood clearly and was interested in the testimonies. The professor and I happened to look at each other, and we shared frequent eye contact. The day of the trial was adjourned, and her husband drove her home. On the way home, someone hit her car from behind. She went to the emergency room and had stitches in the roof of her mouth. The ER doctor told her she could continue her jury duty, and she was willing to return to jury duty. Against her will, the judge and the prosecutor decided to let the professor juror go.

I felt the professor juror was my one chance for a hung jury, and so did Richard. Undoubtedly, the intelligent juror was prohibited from attending her jury duty. Richard sensed the court might have been tainted and manipulated. Yet he did not do anything about it.

Richard submitted an authentic Amgen report that the Procrit overfill amount was 16.8 percent between 1999 and 2002 when I began to practice in Tennessee (and when I was indicted in 2002). Afterward, the prosecutor inconsistently stated that a doctor could not withdraw the last overfill amount of Procrit from the bottle's neck.

Agent Turner took the witness stand and changed his calculation, saying the overfill amount was 7.8 percent instead of 16.8 percent. He claimed that it was not possible to withdraw the extra overfill amount from the bottle's neck. Agent Turner's Procrit calculations were materially false and misleading. My attorney counteracted with an example that there were extra amounts of soda in a bottle after you drank it. The leftover soda could be withdrawn if the bottle were tilted upside down for long enough. He explained that I kept Procrit bottles upside down and was able to extract the extra overfill amounts with the smallest needle, which was flexible and thin and allowed me to remove the last droplets from the bottle's neck.

Richard submitted foolproof evidence of correctly prefilled Procrit syringes prepared two weeks in advance, which were clearly depicted on the agent's videotape on January 9, 2002. The prosecutor promptly requested a copy of the videotape, which he had shown at the pretrial. Knowing what was on the tape, the prosecutor muted the sound before submitting the tape. Richard did not object to the videotape being muted.

Again, I was a puzzled. Why would Richard allow them to use the tape without the sound? How would the jury interpret the video of the

MOONLIGHT MELODY

upside-down Procrit bottles and prefilled Procrit syringes and mixed chemo drugs in the refrigerator? Without the sound, how could the jury understand that the RN in the video was narrating that everything was correct and that no fraud was evident? The prosecutor misled the jury.

Richard questioned Turner. "Did you see all the prefilled Procrit syringes that were filled with correct and full doses, along with matching labels?"

"I never saw the Procrit bottles," Turner replied.

"Were you there during the taping of this video?" Richard asked.

"No, I was not there," Agent Turner answered.

Richard quickly asked, "Did you narrate the video while holding the ziplock bag that contained many prefilled Procrit syringes?"

The agent, who was a registered nurse, answered, "No, I did not hold the bag."

Richard counteracted with, "Is that your watch on the video?"

The registered nurse looked embarrassed and hesitantly replied, "Yes, that is my watch."

Clearly, the agents had perjured themselves under oath. Richard did not object to their perjury.

Although he asked that the agents provide the documents pertaining to the raid on my clinic on January 9, 2002, the agents did not produce the documents until they were subpoenaed over three years later. Richard had concerns about the authenticity of the document.

Next, Dr. Rotan testified against me. The governments requested the charts of seventy-five patients who had received either Taxol or Camptosar, or Procrit. Procrit is like vitamin B12. The government paid a witness, Dr. Rotan, who selected twenty-six patients with poor prognoses. Then he further narrowed down and handpicked six of the twenty-six who were terminally ill.

Three of the six achieved clinical remission, and the remaining three did far better than anticipated. Still, Dr. Rotan—who reviewed the twenty-six charts in forty-five minutes, which he testified to under oath—testified that his review revealed malpractice. Normally, an oncologist would review a single patient's consultation at least an hour to understand the intricacies of the situation. In addition, the handpicked six were represented without the patient's blood counts results. Nor did he check the amount of the drug given on the patients' flow sheet.

Nevertheless, Dr. Rotan testified that to not administer a full dose of Procrit constituted malpractice. Additionally, he incorrectly asserted that a partial dose of Procrit would cause cancer recurrence and fatal outcome.

Several years later, the FDA published information about Procrit clearly opposing Dr. Rotan's opinion. Physicians and caregivers were warned not to give high doses of Procrit or Camptosar, which caused fatal outcomes and recurrent cancer. The FDA report was completely opposite of Dr. Rotan's accusation against me in court.

Richard cross-examined Dr. Rotan's asking about his inaccurate statements and pointing out that he had overlooked many of my patients' charts and had skipped the pertinent information on those he reviewed. His handwritten report to the prosecutor was simply false and inaccurate, yet he maliciously accused me in open court.

My defense attorney requested that the judge submit Dr. Rotan's false report as evidence. The biased judge overruled Richard's requested to submit it, considering he was a medical expert, and the judge was not mandated to submit his report. I thought whole procedure was tainted and corrupt and will continue to believe so until proven otherwise. Everyone perjured him or herself under oath and got away with it.

Dr. Rotan was an assistant professor, who was promoted to professor at Vanderbilt after my trial, and Casey's theft charges were dismissed after she testified against me.

Next up in the court procedure was Richard's attempts to verify the exculpatory evidence. Merry Berry, a registered nurse from the Tennessee Health Related Board (THRB) paid an unannounced on-site visit to my clinic in November 2001 prior to the TBI raid. Merry Berry's name was changed to Sanford after she got married. Mrs. Sanford investigated my clinic, and her postinvestigation concluded there was "no fraud" related to the Procrit, Taxol, or Camptosar. She gave me the report documenting these conclusions. Richard wanted Mrs. Sanford to testify about her investigation and postinvestigation conclusions.

Strangely, the government barred her from coming to the courtroom due to her being in her last month of pregnancy. As a result of her condition, the prosecutor, Richard, and I were scheduled to see her at her home early in the morning. Initially, the prosecutor planned to videotape her testimony and to reveal the evidence. After the prosecutor learned the conclusion of the investigation, she changed her mind.

The following morning at 5:00 a.m., I was ready. We needed to leave at 6:00 a.m. The prosecutor again changed and canceled our visit to THRB RN's home. Additionally, no videotape was made. The truth and evidence were buried under the power of the government.

That night I reviewed twenty-six patients' charts at the hotel and pointed out the LPNs' errors to Richard.

He told me, "Be careful what you found about the nurses' errors. If you show the errors to the court, you will be convicted."

I trusted Richard's expertise. I was naive and a novice of the federal system. I did not know much about judicial decisions. Granting all this, the utter lack of sensibility surrounding all that was happening was exhausting. I racked my brain trying to understand it all. In my opinion, Richard appeared to be acting as a puppet for the prosecutor and the government.

Richard concealed material facts and exculpatory evidence, he allowed the video to be muted, and he had done nothing to prevent or question the hearsay portions of the LPNs' testimonies. Furthermore, he had let stand the false information provided both by them and by Dr. Rotan's falsely concocted report. The agents had committed perjury under oath. And now Mrs. Sanford's flawless report—foolproof evidence that no fraud had been committed—was being left out. And to top it all off, Richard had initially wanted Dr. Lemon to testify on my behalf, but that had been cancelled for some unknown reason.

I began to be skeptical about Richard's integrity and was not satisfied with his representation. He was careless, forgetful, and confused. And his representation was deceitful. He recognized that I was silently angry with him, and he frequently stared at me. He then quickly informed me that his associate lawyer had taken digital pictures of the prefilled Procrit syringes, which showed unquestionable evidence of full and accurate dosages. These pictures were taken from the TBI videotape.

The digital pictures depicted that the inside plungers matched with outside landmark line of the syringes as precisely accurate and were full dosages of Procrit. There was no fraud.

When I took the stand, I wanted to mention the digital pictures of the prefilled Procrit syringes. Richard's expression made me keep quiet. He put his index finger to his lips when I looked at him. I did not understand, and that Richard would conceal evidence made no sense. While the prosecutor was questioning me, Dr. Lemon noticed that Dr. Rotan was sitting behind the prosecutor. Dr. Rotan continuously passing his notes to the prosecutor in the middle of the trial. After his testimony was finished, he should have exited the courtroom. Additionally, he was passing notes to the prosecutor, which was prohibited. All the court's procedures were violated by the plaintiffs. Dr. Lemon alerted Richard, and the judge barred Dr. Rotan from the courtroom.

Another FBI agent was hired to go over my drug discrepancies. The former FBI agent assured me that I would be acquitted, as there were no material facts; nor did the government have complete source documents. The FBI knew the rule of law. No reasonable jurors would find me guilty beyond a reasonable doubt. A gateway claim of actual innocence required the reviewing court to consider all the evidence, both new and the old. The incriminating exculpatory evidence should not have been denied regarding its admissibility.

Based on the record, the court had to make a probabilistic determination about what was reasonable, and the judge had to properly instruct jurors what they should do. My case was overlooked, and the material facts were concealed with assumptive, untrue allegations. The prosecutorial abuse and misconduct and the discriminatory ruling made for a heaviness that was palpable in the courtroom. Intentionally suppressing evidence of material facts to punish innocent people is unconstitutional in the United States. Whatever my defense team revealed it did so precisely, unquestionably, and clearly by the rule of the law. Nevertheless, none of the defense evidence was considered by the court.

Next, Richard recruited two medical experts on my behalf and charged me $450 per hour for each individual expert's review of my patients' charts. Richard also demanded I pay an additional $75,000 for one of the expert's traveling costs (he flew by private jet to the court).

Toward the end of the trial days (and before my medical experts' testimony), Richard informed me that I most likely would be convicted. He also told me that the government was considering giving me a four- to seven-year sentence before the jury verdict was handed to the judge. Richard might have colluded with the government. How did he know before the verdict what the outcome would be? If he knew that I would be convicted, why did he spend many years participating in numerous pretrial hearings and trials? I had originally refused to have a trial, but he had insisted. I had doubted he would win the trial after the matter had, for so many years, remained unresolved. Why had Richard concealed obviously clear exculpatory evidence?

One of my defense medical experts, from Pittsburgh University Cancer Center, simply stated asked a question. If I had given smaller amounts of medication for financial gain, how come many of my patients had achieved excellent treatment outcomes? There was no proven fraud, he concluded. He explained that I might have adjusted chemo drugs based on my patients' clinical conditions and that what doctors were trained to and was my duty as a doctor.

Indescribably, the prosecutor and Dr. Rotan admitted that almost all my patients did very well under my care and had survival rates exceedingly higher than the national staging report indicated. What were the criminal problems? Why had the government been punishing me for so long? Perhaps, they did so because they had the power to do so!

Another of my medical experts, this one from Carolina had worked with Dr. Rotan at Vanderbilt Hospital in the past. The expert was extremely angry at Dr. Rotan's false allegation against me and his attempts to put an innocent person in prison. The expert passionately defended my case, pointing out that my patients' treatments had remarkably high success rates. He had a large cancer center of his own in Carolina, and he was an expert in ovarian cancer. He seemed astonished by the absurdity of the proceedings, and he talked about how my patients consistently survived for unbelievably long times under my care. He held up a thick and voluminous stack of charts and yelled at the court, "Dr. Gates has outstanding treatment outcomes, yet you want to put her in jail and destroy her life. Shame on you!"

Richard tried to calm him down.

In the closing argument, he requested that the court dismiss the three charges for discrepancies related to Procrit, Taxol, and Camptosar. The judge overruled Richard's request, and the charges were unchanged.

Richard's son Wayne compared my cancer patients' survival rate to statistics based on national survival rates stage by stage. He presented on a bar graph, showing that my patients had achieved successful treatment outcomes, undeniably surpassing the national survival rate statistics.

Simultaneously, the judge became outraged, as if he had been personally attacked.

"Do not vouch for Dr. Gates," he yelled at Wayne, following this up with an inflammatory question. "Which law school did you attend?"

The judge made Wayne withdraw the bar graph exhibit.

Richard continued his closing argument, and again he presented the material facts of my remarkable treatment results.

Instantly, the judge was once again on the attacked, saying Richard's personal bias was coming into play. "Do not vouch for Dr. Gates," he menaced. "You too, where did you go to law school?"

Richard was embarrassed, and his face turned red; he hesitated to display the material facts. The closing argument was the most sensitive point prior to the jury reaching a verdict.

I perceived that the judge was obviously prejudiced and biased. His outbursts against both of my defense lawyers during the closing arguments impeded their ability to effectively represent the exculpatory evidence during the most critical and vital point in the trial. As a result of the judge's explosion and personal attack against my defense attorneys, they were unable to introduce a graph that demonstrated the superiority of my treatment outcomes. There was no fraud, no patient injury, no unethical misconduct, and no negligent malpractice.

These were strongly discriminatory disparities of the judicial system. Undoubtedly, the criminal judge's shouting at the defense attorney would have impacted the jury the negative outcome of the case. The jury surely would think that the offender had committed a crime and the defense attorneys were trying to cover it up. In contrast, the prosecutor concealed authentic evidence, misled the court, and engaged in vindictive misconduct to enhance her power and fame until proven otherwise.

Prior to my verdict, Richard implored the judge give me a lenient sentence. How did Richard know whether I would have a guilty verdict or not?

I truly thought my trial was nothing, but a stage shows and that everyone involved had known the results and how long I would be sentenced before the verdict even came in.

My impression was that my case was very well set up and that I had been framed before the trial had even commenced. After the closing arguments were completed, as soon as the court released everyone for lunch break, one of the jurors announced with a loud voice, "It is time for a pizza party."

It had cost me $45,000 to hire an expert to select jurors who did not have sound mind set. One of the jurors was more interested in having a pizza party than in weighing the facts of my case—knowing that my life was potentially at stake.

When the jury returned to the courtroom after lunch, Richard, his associate, and I heard another of the juror's shout, "It's showtime!" before the chief juror handed their verdict to the judge.

I was pronounced guilty on all four charges. The first charge was for having given a false statement, and the next three were related to the Procrit, Taxol, and Camptosar discrepancies.

The judge asked the senior prosecutor about the length of my sentence.

The prosecutor's recommendation came quickly, "Four to seven years."

I wondered how Richard had known the exact length of my sentence before the experts' testimony and prior to the verdict.

In anticipation of the court's adjournment, the prosecutor asked me to give "allocution" before I was sentenced.

I went to the stand and told the court, "I thank God that I was blessed to heal many of my patients and with the desire to work as a doctor for as long as I can remember. Anyhow, if God has purposefully planned another mission for me, I am more than happy to follow his divine pathway."

As soon as I ended my allocution speech, the senior prosecutor literally jumped up and down, his face flashing with anger. He almost screamed, "Listen to her. She doesn't have any remorse."

I thought myself, *I am not afraid of any man. I fear only God.* Even if he had had a gun pointing at my head, I would not be afraid of an unrighteous man. My conscious was clear

I had memorized the Serenity Prayer, and I said it to myself silently now. *God, give me the serenity to accept the things that I cannot change, the courage to change the things that I can, and the wisdom to know the difference.*

I had many regrets, and Richard was one of them. All things considered;

Victoria Gates, MD

Richard was ineffective counsel in my opinion. At the end of the trial, after I had received the guilty verdict ironically, Richard turned toward me, carefully took my hand, and a placed a kiss on my hand. I was purely disgusted!

CHAPTER 31

A Sitting Duck (Dr. Lemon was a Perpetrator)

The final trial was over. I drove home all alone that night and informed Dr. Lemon about the verdict. He already knew the result before I told him. The highway had a few dim lights and winding roads due to construction. Driving by myself on the long narrow streets, I felt as if I were passing through a shaky earthquake. For the first time, I felt lonely after nearly ten years of marriage to Dr. Lemon.

When I called him, he answered the phone with a sleepy voice and did not say much.

"My brother will call you," he said and then he hung up.

A few minutes later, his younger brother called. "How do you feel?" he asked. "What are you going to do?"

"I will have the best time with Dr. Lemon that I can before I'm locked up," I answered.

He did not say much, except to advise me to drive carefully and to return home safely.

My mind drifted and conjured beautiful images of our cherished Baltic cruise after I had closed my clinic. Taking the Baltic cruise was like having the last supper with Dr. Lemon. We decided to take a cruise and landed in Copenhagen within three days. We flew to Denmark five days before we joined a cruise ship.

The first thing I observed was that Danish people were slender and many of the Copenhagen natives used bicycles to get everywhere. There were many bicycle racks throughout the downtown. The city would have less air pollution because not many people used automobiles.

We had a pleasant lunch at Nyhavn Canal in a well-maintained old building and a fashionable cafe. Copenhagen was the capital and largest city of Denmark, as well as the country's cultural, economic, and political center. Colorful shops and restaurants were clustered in an area of Copenhagen

I enjoyed seeing the sculpture that adorned the tomb of Queen Margaret, who united Denmark, Norway, and Sweden in the Kalmar Union in 1397. Twenty years of peace and economic growth were sustained under Queen Margaret's skillful leadership. I was proud Queen Margaret was a female.

The following day, we continued our tour, going to Christiansborg Palace, the home of the Danish Parliament. My favorite attraction in Copenhagen was Tivoli Garden. When we visited, there was a special fireworks display, in addition to the garden's attractive, exotic, and lighted grounds.

I delighted in the story written by Hans Christian Andersen about a famous mermaid sculpture in the front of the beach. Submerged historical statues were still visible as we rode the ferryboat tour. There was an impressively beautiful opera house of modern architecture on the water.

Staying five days in Copenhagen made for a pleasing trip. Eventually we joined the Baltic cruise ship near Russia. We went to the Kremlin, a fortress in central Moscow that contains the central offices of government of Russia. It was vastly different from America.

We visited the spectacular and magnificent Winter Palace, in which many walls were decorated with shiny embers. The Winter Palace was beautiful. We learned about Catherine the Great, an empress of Russia in the late eighteenth century who encouraged the cultural influences of Western Europe in Russia. Catherine the Great, who was German, grew up under an abusive mother. She moved to Russia at a young age and later married the Russian Peter the Great, who never loved Catherine. After Peter's accidental death, Catherine became an empress, and she ruled Russia for nearly forty years.

Dr. Lemon spent money and purchased a special dinner and a private ballet performance at a Russian nobleman's mansion. Prior to the party, we learned about Grigori Rasputin, a Russian monk who gained great influence over both Czar Nicholas II and his wife Czarina Alexandra.

The history of Rasputin was incredible. He was able to stop the bleeding of Nicholas's son. The czar granted permission to poison and shot Rasputin, but he did not die. He could not swim, and the supporters put him in a sack and threw him into the Neva River, where he drowned.

Saint Basil's Cathedral in Moscow had a bright and a colorful onion-shaped dome that made it one of the most widely recognized buildings in Russia. It was now a historical museum.

Empress Catherine's flower garden was gorgeous. The luxurious Summer Palace in Saint Petersburg was splendid. In the 1700s, the palace grounds were beautified by 126 water fountains, a strikingly impressive art piece and genius creation.

I was thrilled to see the place where Nobel Prizes were awarded each year at the City Hall in Stockholm. Sweden maintained its neutrality through post World War I and II.

We enjoyed seafood and fresh fish in Norway. Scandinavia undoubtedly had an interesting history of Vikings. The fierce Viking warriors terrorized many seaside and riverside towns in Europe. The ancestors of the Vikings were Germanic people, who once lived in northwestern Europe and Scandinavia, which includes Denmark, Norway, and Sweden.

Finland was famous for its scenic views. Helsinki was the heart of Finland and its capital. And the gleaming lights of downtown brighten the eighteen hours of night during the winter months. I loved the picturesque Finland's lake and ocean views, and there were many remarkable museums that we visited.

The Baltic cruise was unforgettable and a cherished memory. I enjoyed the visit tremendously.

As I reached the Tulsa town houses, having left the federal court with a guilty verdict, my watch struck 2:00 a.m. The sudden pleasant images of my cruise turned into puffs of smoke and evaporated. I felt as if I were in Cinderella's carriage and that it had suddenly turned into the pumpkin of bleak reality.

I opened the bedroom door. Dr. Lemon was sleeping, and I lay next to my motionless, emotionless, cold husband. After a while, I finally fell asleep for a couple of hours.

When I woke up, he was gone for work. Initially, he wanted to visit his mother with me in Florida during the Christmas weekend. He changed his mind like weather, and he went alone. My chain of thought was on the guilty verdict, going to prison, my potential divorce, and the unknown future. I did not know who to trust and was blind to the federal system. And it all provoked my anxiety.

These volatile unexpected changes caught me unawares and confused, as if I were suddenly in the middle of a sandstorm with winds blowing in every direction. I did not even know the difference between federal and state prison.

Martha advised me to prepare hygiene supplies for six months. Hastily, I packed six months of cosmetic products for facial care, continuing education books for medical oncology, sweatshirts and sweatpants, and many daily useable items into my black leather bag. I prepared all this without any knowledge that federal prison was different from a state prison. Martha's son had gone to state prison, and she probably thought the systems were the same.

When I returned to my town house from Martha's house, Dr. Lemon packed his belongings and moved to our smaller town house next to door. He was gone with the wind. My trial had lasted for one week and had ended on December 15, 2005. A legal separation was filed by Dr. Lemon on December 16, 2005. He had lived in Tulsa for less than six months. Thus, he waited for two months to register an official divorce. Oklahoma divorce law required a person to live in Tulsa for at least six months before filing for divorce.

I kept the bigger town house since I had paid two-thirds on both houses, as well as both houses' property taxes, and had spent $40,000 for the house decorations. The next day, he called me and asked me to help him set up his place. I cleaned and rearranged his belongings in the smaller house next to mine. I nurtured, comforted, and cared for him unconditionally, hoping he could support me when I needed it. That was only my imagination of Dr. Lemon.

Most likely, his mother had advised him to stay away from me and divorce me, as he was a specialist, working on a referral-basis. Being married to a convicted wife could destroy his medical practice quickly. When it rains, it pours.

The manager of my town house gave me information about a sincere lawyer who could protected my separate funds and premarital assets and possibly reinvest my money in case of divorce. At the same time, Rachel advised me to divorce Dr. Lemon, simply signing a premade standard divorce packet, which cost only $200. Rachel was my close friend, and she knew us very well, including that we had never joined our financial affairs. She had recently moved to Delaware to be close to her family since her husband Carter had heart problems. My sister also recommended numerous times that I divorce him before I was incarcerated.

Dr. Lemon deceived me with his lip service, telling me that he would visit me every week and that he would take care of my assets and funds while I was incarcerated. If I had my own family in America, it would have been much easier. I was goal oriented and had failed to maintain my own family plan. I had fervently wanted to be a compassionate doctor, and I had become an excellent doctor. I had helped many dying patients achieve successful outcomes under my care. Who said life was fair? I could not accomplish or attain everything I had planned. Things happened unexpectedly, which was part of my destiny. I believed in God and he had a purpose for my life.

I could not proceed with the divorce at the time because of two issues. First, I became needy and wanted Dr. Lemon to help me. Second, the divorce might trigger the government to seize a large sum of my life savings. I had seen that a judge could be biased and could make his or her own rules and laws in a courtroom. Judges would do whatever they could get away with, despite disparities, by way of their discretion and power.

Several days after the trial, Richard answered my call while he was at the airport heading to Pittsburgh University Cancer Center. For the first time, Richard admitted and confessed to me that he was facing terminal cancer, which had spread throughout his body to his brain, lungs, and intestines.

I recalled that I had asked several times about his health in the past. For a long time, Richard had not looked healthy, but he had denied his physical illness, emotional instability, and distraught mental condition. Occasionally, he could not catch his breath during the trial.

My logical thinking process had told me that Richard would not win. He could not prove the material facts and could not make the jury understand, despite foolproof evidence. Richard had assertively informed me there was no other way. I had to go to trial; there was no settlement or plea deal. I found that Richard and Dr. Lemon had colluded with each other and robbed me blindly. Before my sentencing hearing, I fired him. I could not blame anybody but myself. This fault was my lack of discernment, and my poor decisions had tossed me into the wind tunnel I found myself in.

Richard's battle with cancer prior to the trial contributed to his ineffective counsel my case. At times, he was confused and incoherent while he represented my case in court. His personal feelings and proximity to the situation caused him to treat the case as a personal vendetta, as he identified with my patients. I was a sitting duck.

The most horrifying and shocking truth was that Richard told Dr. Lemon he did not want to handle my trial due to his terminal condition. At once, Dr. Lemon had flown to Knoxville from Oklahoma and convinced him that I needed my trial. Dr. Lemon had known Richard had terminal cancer and was walking into a federal trial he would never win. I did not know anything about this—it was all kept secret behind my back. Nor did I have any knowledge of the federal legal system.

I hired my divorce attorney, Sam, who was recommended by the town house manager. Sam appeared to be successful, and the community recognized him. He owned a law firm with three associates, a self-storage unit, and was preparing to open an MRI scan center across from his law firm. As a matter of fact, I had met him before the trial and prior to my divorce. I did not hide anything from him or deceive Dr. Lemon. I told Dr. Lemon honestly about Sam and I recommended Dr. Lemon to invest in his MRI scan department.

Before Dr. Lemon had filed for his divorce, I had introduced my Tulsa friends to him, so he could have friends when I was gone. Reverend Kim, another dentist, Martha and Mark, and Pastor Brown were my close friends. We had dinner with different friends at a time.

He initially wanted to have a storage room together. Then he changed his mind and said he would rent his own storage place.

To prepare for my incarceration, I had planned to move my separate funds and assets to be reinvested. I believed that Dr. Lemon was a perpetrator. The love of money was the root of all evil. Lemon had willfully premeditated and deceived me regarding financial matters numerous times during our marriage. He was a doctor and generated a decent income and had plenty of his own savings, but he seemed to have all of mine too.

CHAPTER 32

He Was a Culprit So Be It!

Strange things began to happen at the town house. Each time I put my trash outside to be collected, it disappeared before the pickup. Other neighbors' trash would still be there in front of their garage. My intuition told me that Dr. Lemon had something to do with it. I felt I was still living in a twilight zone.

One day, my curiosity took over, and I decided to take his trash from the smaller town house. Inside the bag, I shockingly discovered a handwritten note showing that he planned to leave me penniless. Another handwritten note showed that he had called my prosecutor about my funds in Wisconsin. Then he had written to the prosecutor, saying he would contact her again. Additionally, Dr. Lemon had made innuendoes that I had not treated his two children well when they visited our Tennessee home. In fact, he had taken trips during the kids visit and hadn't stayed our house. I saved this note as evidence to reveal his premeditated motives.

I had an extra key to his town house. I went to his town house to see what he was up to. My eyes could not believe when I saw—a huge glamour portrait of Dr. Lemon smiling and showing off the gold watch my sister had given him. Dr. Lemon had been using this glamour shot for his profile picture on a dating service.

Astonishingly, I also noticed that he had purchaser large exercise balls, a big jug of protein powder, speedos, and exercise tights. Apparently, he was working out for his new dating life. In his drawer, I found several phone numbers for potential female dates from the dating services and learned that he had paid $1,000 for gourmet cooking. Obviously, he was trying to impress his dates.

We never joined our bank accounts; yet he had copies of all my financial documents, even current information on the Tulsa bank account, which was solely under my name. He had a different bank for himself. I could see clearly see his premeditated plan to get every penny from me. He was waiting for me to be incarcerated. I could only imagine. I had never thought he would display such a beyond atrocious and malicious character. I remembered how he'd visited my town house, telling me, "I don't need a mother. Find your own friends!" Then he left.

I did not expect him to be celibate. However, all of this seemed premature, heartless, and cruel. He could have waited at least until I was sentenced to do his pleasure-seeking nonsense. Ironically, I still had feelings for Dr. Lemon, despite his unscrupulousness and ill will; I was like an abused woman who could not leave her spouse and longed to be loved.

The walls of our town house were very thin. Being just next door, I could hear his phone ring several times a night. He spent hours in conversation. I could hear him laughing and teasing loudly. Living next to him was not a good idea. Some nights, I grabbed my stethoscope, and I could hear the conversation by placing the stethoscope against the wall. I never confronted him about his absurd behavior.

I did not understand his future and reached out to his mother. I called her to express my feelings, hoping she could talk with her son about his hasty actions and madness right before I would be incarcerated. Before I even began to make my request, his mother asked me not to call her anymore and hung up. It was worse than if she had slapped my face. Thank God! The Holy Spirit protected me, and I would not give them consent to hurt me.

Shortly after his mother hung up on me, I received a call from his older brother telling me not to contact their family again.

Wow, they are being very coldhearted, I told myself.

Birds of a feather flock together. A friend in need is a friend indeed. I never felt so alone despite many people being around me. It did not matter to me. I knew my family loved me dearly, and I knew that I was always loved by God.

Early in the morning, at 5:00 a.m., I went to Kim's church and met Martha there for joint prayer.

I suspected that Dr. Lemon had premeditated for many years—even before the TBI agents raided my clinic on January 9, 2002—to have me incarcerated. He was carrying my sole Bank of America account in Tulsa in his car trunk. He must have realized that I had found out he had stolen my financial records.

His character was seemingly flawed, and he appeared to be completely blinded by money. Like a leopard cannot change its spots, he could not change his basic character once it had been formed. Once again, I flashed back to when he had knocked my head and yelled at me at the airport in Wisconsin before we flew out to Tennessee, saying that I had committed Medicare fraud in Wisconsin. Furthermore, I recalled that he had attempted to derail me when he'd given my billing code to the hospital administration for additional investigation. At the time, Dr. Lemon had not been able to do much, as the administrator had told him that the billing code was appropriate.

Taking care of my patients was my life mission. Dr. Lemon had tricked me into see my parents urgently in Hawaii. I had fallen for his second plot to deceptively lead me into a corner. My intuition was right when I had not wanted to hire my competitor to cover my clinic. Undeniably, he had successfully carried out his plan, letting Dr. Derek enter my clinic as a Trojan horse. Events were well thought out by Dr. Lemon, it seemed.

After the TBI came for the on-site visit to my office, Dr. Lemon did something to my tea at my office. After I drank my tea while attending to my final patient of the day, I had suddenly gotten extremely sick, and he had never answered my numerous phone calls. Whereas, when Rachel called him, he had answered her at once.

There was much evidence that led me to believe he was the culprit:

1. Lemon quickly destroyed any evidence when I had allocated the presumably poisoned soup from the restaurant in Cookeville to different containers. He threw them off the shelf in the pantry without explanation.
2. My patients said that Dr. Lemon was a perpetrator. My patients knew everything that went on in town. They were the original rural folks who had long made up the town's population, the fabric that held the town together.

3. He and Richard colluded together. When Richard told him he had terminal cancer, Dr. Lemon flew to Knoxville and convinced Richard to represent me at trial. No one explained what happened between them behind my back. I did not know, but they knew I could not win the federal trial.
4. My husband never supported me before, during, or after the trial.
5. Dr. Lemon took my financial records and copied them without my knowledge or permission.
6. His severed my relationship, as if he used a chainsaw, between my family and friends.
7. Now he was seeking pleasure on dating sites.

Was I blindly yearning for love that had not existed? Was I desperate to get any help under my difficult situation? The dream of a happily married couple was nothing but a fairy tale romance. I was chasing a beautiful rainbow that was just a dream—untouchable and, like a rainbow, made only of tiny water droplets, which reflected my reality.

The palpable presence of the real political world made my hair stand up on the back of my neck, chilled my spine, and paralyzed my heart. What kind of a nefarious hypocrite was Dr. Lemon? As I entered his town house, I listened to a phone conversation between him and a new partner about his sexual pleasure. He was in his bedroom using his home phone, and I stood frozen, listening to his conversation in the kitchen. I saw his cell phone charging on the kitchen countertop. I saw his new woman's name and her home telephone number on his cell phone.

Forgiveness is the key to happiness, but the Bible did not calm me down. Nor did my daily 5:00 a.m. church service. I was furious. I could not control myself after what I had heard. My anger became my master now.

Dr. Lemon kept his premarital furniture at my town house—the furniture he most treasured, as he loved to show off his material items. I decided to redecorate it. I should not have done it. Nevertheless, I took my car keys and scratched his hutch and coffee table and bleached the cushions of his wing chairs and damaged the ruffles of the chair. It was as if madness was a contagious disease. His madness was sexual pleasure and money. My madness was betrayal. His furniture was more than twenty years old, and the resale value would have been approximately $5,000. Yet he claimed I had caused damage worth more than the furniture itself. He was awarded $90,000 from my separate account by the divorce judge.

What I did was wrong and the biggest mistake that I had ever made. It was a poor decision. Trying to get even was not the way to win. Before we got married, he tossed his daughter's lovely white cat in front of a stranger's house when we moved to the lake house in Mequon, Wisconsin. The shiny green eyes of the cat staring at us through the headlights in the night, penetrated my heart deeply, and I was overcome with sadness. I should have known better that time; I should have seen then what kind of character he had.

I met Dr. Lemon's girlfriend at her house. I called her and identified who I was. She told me she did not know he was still married to me. His girlfriend knew my situation, and I told her to take good care of him while I was gone. She informed me that Dr. Lemon was not her type of man, and she had many boyfriends besides him. Plus, she was ready to leave for Dallas, Texas. She was kind enough to let me know that she had advised Dr. Lemon to leave my separate funds and assets alone, if he could make his own income working as a doctor.

Her neighbors informed me they had thought Dr. Lemon was her fiancé, by reason of his visiting every night. I did not say a word to her neighbor. Dr. Lemon's credit card revealed that he had been spending a large sum of money entertaining many dates.

I should have divorced him before I left. I did not understand myself. Why did I hang on to him? Why couldn't I kiss him goodbye, knowing he was not a good person?

It was hard to believe that I was going to jail soon. If this were an inevitable destiny, I would accept it and move on and go through it. I would not cry over spilled milk.

One weekend afternoon when I bicycled around my town house, I saw Dr. Lemon and his mother inside the car. They were passing by, and his mother was looking at me.

"Hi, Mom!" I said to her.

Intentionally, she avoided me, despite my acknowledgement of them. She stiffened her wig and showed off her dangling earrings at age seventy-seven. I noticed Dr. Lemon had curled his hair with heavy jell. His grooming was not attractive; rather, he looked like a scared cat.

CHAPTER 33

Ready to Go through the Fire (Detestable and Nefarious Misogyny)

Martha and Mark invited me for a religious event with Kenneth and Gloria Copeland in Missouri, and we stayed at their timeshare. It was a new experience for me, coming from a Roman Catholic background, to see fervent activities and passionate praising of God from the audience.

I wanted to talk to Mr. Kenneth Copeland, but he had left the stage. I asked the usher if he was going to return. The usher told me, "No."

Unusually, I decided to send a handwritten message on a greeting card that I would like to see him on stage. I gave the message to the usher to deliver to Mr. Copeland, who, as an evangelical celebrity, was normally not available to the public, except on stage. Once he left the stage, he hardly ever returned.

Surprisingly, Kenneth Copeland appeared on stage again. The usher guided me to the stage, along with many other people. I stared into this evangelical man's green eyes while he prayed for me. His eyes conveyed a strong spirit and were filled with extraordinary sparkles. They were different than other eyes, and I felt he was anointed.

I became close to Martha and told her everything about my plan. I stored expensive gemstones, cash, my CDs, my tax returns, all other evidence related to my investment funds with my divorce attorney, Sam, in a storage unit.

Cold-blooded Dr. Lemon began to harass me with a deposition regarding the divorce. Sam was my initial divorce attorney. Dr. Lemon hired the most

Moonlight Melody

detestable divorce attorney, Edgton, who was a third-generation attorney in his lineage. Apparently, he had some political gain from his family.

The first deposition was held at Sam's office. I wished Dr. Lemon would support me and have some sympathy regarding my difficult situation. This naive thought was nothing but unwise discernment that opened the door for hungry lions to devour me.

The greedy pair, Dr. Lemon, and his attorney, furiously growled at me during the first deposition. I was shell-shocked and could not even talk under the mixed emotions of betrayal and disappointment over his deception. Sam commented that Dr. Lemon and his attorney looked like a pair of weasels. A substantial amount of my funds was invested with Sam. I also lent him money with a reasonable interest rate. I had plenty of premarital funds. Sam, in turn, lent my money to a doctor friend who he trusted who had opened a new business, with a fair market interest rate. They promised me they would pay my income tax report from the interest gain to the IRS after my incarceration.

Additionally, I invested in Sam's new MRI center since Dr. Lemon would not consider helping me. I strongly sensed Lemon would not stop until he had completely siphoned away all my life savings. Lemon also wrote his plan on the scratchpad, "I will make her penniless." I had found that note from his garbage bag.

I did not do well at the deposition due to my emotional turmoil. Initially, Dr. Lemon wanted both the town houses for divorce settlement. Sam declined his proposal. I did not know, and that was the biggest mistake I ever made. Sam was no longer my divorce attorney, due to a conflict of interest involving personal business and investment of my funds. Even though the investment shared between Sam and I before Dr. Lemon had filed divorce.

I saw Dr. Lemon leaving for his girlfriend's house at 5:00 while I was going to church.

I had a difficult time finding a good attorney, since I had been in Tulsa for only two months. I looked through the yellow pages, and I chose the biggest advertisement for a divorce lawyer. I hired this attorney at first sight without conducting any background check.

We both signed a promissory document. However, due to my looming incarceration, I paid $5,000 in full to Chris, my new attorney, and he would take care of the proceedings without me. The attorney's fee was capped on our mutually agreed contract.

I told my former Defense Attorney Richard, that I had hired a new attorney Thomas for my sentencining hearing.

"Who is Ms. Thomas?" Richard asked. "I've never heard her name."

After a while, he went to have a bone marrow transplant in Pittsburgh. Soon after his treatment, he died, two days after my sentencing hearing.

This new Attorney, Ms. Thomas, charged me $35,000 for a one-day sentencing hearing. Prior to my sentencing hearing, she wanted to discuss my case and I drove hours to provide her with all the material facts. Her office was in the middle of a residential district; she had her office space in an old house. Ms. Thomas charged me an additional $5,000 after she received my records without any discussion. I went to her office from Tulsa to Nashville twice for nothing.

I deeply regretted that I had left Milwaukee with Dr. Lemon. I was exhausted emotionally and physically, driving back and forth for nothing but to be drained of more money.

In anticipation of the sentencing hearing, Ms. Thomas called me and recommended that I see a Vanderbilt psychiatrist to lessen the terms of my sentence. She wanted me to send her a cashier's check for $7,000. The amount did not worry me so much as the unknown Vanderbilt doctor, who might have colluded with Dr. Rotan. They could easily fabricate my assessment, painting me as an incompetent person or someone with mental disorder. If that happened, the government and Dr. Lemon would seize all my possession and put me in a psychiatric unit. Who knew what they would inject me with against my will? I would better off staying in prison longer, rather than losing my brain and mind. Having experienced what, they had done to me already, I could not trust anyone.

I felt frustrated with my lack of knowledge about the federal system and uneasy about dealing with so many distrustful people, all of whom wanted my money. I knew I was not crazy, even though I could be permanently diagnosed with a mental disorder to receive a lesser sentence.

Unceasing torment immobilized me. I felt as if I were trapped by a web spinner or had fallen into a quicksand. Seeing and witnessing Dr. Lemon's passionate love affair next door was suffocating me. I asked Ms. Thomas to call the judge and have him put me in a prison for whatever the sentence may be. I was ready to go through the fire. Ms. Thomas informed me that I would be in a detention center that lacked clean conditions. Then I received the sentencing hearing date, April 24, 2006.

I planned to go to the federal courthouse by myself. However, Reverend Kim, Episcopalian Pastor Brown, and Martha wanted to attend my sentencing hearing. Pastor Brown's wife had been incarcerated at Carswell Federal Prison Camp over alleged issues related to a fundraising campaign. His wife was very pretty, intelligent, and a pro-social activist. She was a smoker and had lung problems. Pastor Brown requested to share his wife's sentence and volunteered to go to a state prison to reduce his wife's sentence. Pastor Brown gave me insight about the Carswell Camp, which was not far from Tulsa. Kim, Pastor Brown, and I drove for six hours from Tulsa to see Carswell Camp.

A few months after his wife was released from the camp, she died of lung problems. Pastor Brown was a genuinely righteous man. He allowed me to use a storage space in his church when Richard wanted to get rid of my files after I had fired him. I had never had any type of legal problems before. All my important documents and evidence of my investments, CDs, and bank accounts were filed in the binder and kept inside my desk drawer at my town house. The storage unit under my name was transferred to Pastor Brown because of my impending incarceration. He could then pay the monthly rent with my money. I left a substantial amount of saved money, along with the $7,000 I had decided not to use to see a psychiatrist at Vanderbilt in my ski jacket in the storage unit.

I hid keys for the storage unit under the ceramic tile in the water tank closet at my town house. Before Dr. Lemon moved out to the house next door, he searched my financial records and looked for saved cash like a crazy maniac. We had moved to Tulsa from Tennessee, and we had several microwaves and unpacked boxes in the garage. He dug in every corner, even looking inside the microwaves. He might have been searching for my CDs or and, in the process, broke one of the microwave's plates. He did not even bother to pick up the pieces, leaving them on the garage floor.

I left a retainer of a $200,000 check from my separate funds with Sam to find a criminal lawyer to handle my appeal once I was incarcerated. One day before my sentencing hearing, Dr. Lemon and his lawyer requested that I have a second deposition. Once again, they cantankerously attacked me and demanded that I return the $200,000 check. I told him I did not have it and that it was my own money and had nothing to do with Dr. Lemon. As soon as I said that Dr. Lemon's attorney wanted to search my car and purse without a search warrant.

"Hell no," I told his attorney.

Then the hubristic Edgton wanted to lock me up in jail, alleging that I had been in contempt of his authority and disobeyed his direct order. He abused his power and behaved in a confused manner. Contempt charges applied in a court when an offender disobeyed a judge and could not be brought by an arrogant local lawyer. Edgton was not a judge; nor was I in a courtroom. I was in his dilapidated office building. Enraged, he threatened to call a judge at the Tulsa courthouse.

I told him, "Go ahead."

Edgton called the judge, and the judge refused to validate his contempt charge against me.

Then he quickly confronted me about my signature, saying that I had signed over one of my CDs to Dr. Lemon.

"Yes," I told him. "I did sign it over to Dr. Lemon. And yes, that is my signature over his name. I wanted him to have some of my money before the government cleaned up my life savings."

I was more upset about Dr. Lemon finding sexual pleasure with another woman more than I was with Edgton's bad temper and quarrelsome behavior regarding my separate funds and assets during the second deposition. They deposed me just one day before my incarceration. I thought Dr. Lemon was a cruel and cold-hearted man—one who I had loved unconditionally. He and his divorce attorney mistreated and kicking me hard while I was down the spiral. He knew I would be sentenced the following day. Nevertheless, he and his lawyer severely tormented me once again.

Dr. Lemon was attempting to emotionally assassinate me and try to cause me to have a nervous breakdown. I left the deposition with my new attorney, who bought me a cup of coffee and commented that the pair had displayed detestable and nefarious misogyny. I believed him; they both had very dark spirits. Their unjust attempts to unlawfully gain from my life savings would not be their last victory.

Reverend Kim and Pastor Brown drove a rented minivan to get my legal documents from Richard's office. Martha volunteered to drive my car to the federal courthouse. I packed six months of hygiene supplies, skin care products, and other items in my leather bag that I placed in my car trunk. I also prepared a picnic—food, fruit, and drinks—into an icebox for the trip to the courthouse. Inside my car, I had my garage door opener and a cell phone. We stopped at the public park in Little Rock, Arkansas, where we had a picnic and shared our stories of faith, God, and destiny.

I reserved three hotel rooms close to the courthouse. Kim and Pastor Brown stayed in separate rooms at the hotel, and I shared a room with two beds with Martha. We relaxed and went to bed.

That night I had a terrible dream. A house burned to the ground and fell to the field below, a heap of ashes and debris. A person had a large boil on her thigh. I held a cup of water in my hand; there were several moving tentacles, like the arms of an octopus, stretching out of the cup. I woke up with a horrible feeling.

CHAPTER 34

Too late, Like Water under a Bridge (You Do not Look Like a Prisoner)

Reverend Kim and Pastor Brown came to my hotel room and prayed for me before I was sentenced. Both wore dark suits with white shirts, appearing like priests. While they were praying, I felt as if I were in the middle of a funeral procession. Pastor Brown brought a religious necklace and placed it around my neck; it was later taken away by an agent of the court.

Out of the blue, I learned that the prosecutor recruited my deceased patients' family members to appear at the sentencing hearing. One of the patients was Alfred, who had had widespread cancer. I had treated him with palliative care. He had done far better than anticipated and had ridden his school bus one more time before being admitted to hospice care. Alfred was a school bus driver, and he had loved his job. At the time, his family members had appreciated my care greatly. Astonishingly, his daughter testified against me, saying she wanted to be compensated and to use the funds to adopt a baby from China. (See my transcript in the appendix.)

Next came the family of Jean. She had end-stage colon cancer with an extremely high tumor marker, which had responded beautifully under my care, and the markers had gradually gone down, returning close to normal. As mentioned earlier, I treated her at the hospital instead of at my clinic since Blue Cross Blue Shield did not reimburse for Camptosar. Jean did not want to be treated at the hospital, and she got upset. Her family wanted her to have an experimental drug with a curative intent in Nashville. Unfortunately,

Jean died during her experimental drug treatment, yet her family falsely accused me.

The third patient was Dolores, who had had a very advanced end-stage ovarian cancer with substantially increased tumor markers. Those markers had victoriously come down after each of her chemotherapy treatments under my care. Dolores had tolerated chemotherapy remarkably well, without any side effects from the toxic agents. Sadly, she had ruptured diverticulosis. And though the rupture was successfully repaired, she developed a complicated wound infection after her surgery, which caused her poor outcome. This had nothing to do with my treatment. I had not seen her daughter while my patient was receiving chemotherapy at my clinic. The only family member who had accompanied her had been her husband. Her daughter came to the sentence hearing, though, and bitterly complained about me. My patient's daughter continued said her mother had done extremely well without any pain and was active because I had not given her chemotherapy.

The fourth patient whose family members were there was Jack, who also had end-stage colon cancer. His cancer had spread to his bone and lungs. Jack was a chain-smoker. He tolerated chemotherapy well and still worked at the Kmart during his chemotherapy. He had Universal Care insurance, which went bankrupt while he was receiving an expensive chemo drug as known as Camptosar. Despite my billing manager reminding him numerous times that his insurance company had gone bankrupt and was not reimbursing his drug costs, I completed his chemotherapy. Jack was then placed on continuous maintenance treatment of 5FU via portable pump.

Though my LPN Casey influenced him to see my competitor, he refused but instead went to Thompson Cancer Center. He was not able to see a doctor there without proper insurance. I was more than happy to treat Jack without any charge. However, Jack never came back to my clinic.

This was the same scenario as with Jean's daughter. I had never seen Jack's daughter during his chemo treatment. And now she had come to my sentencing hearing and was dramatizing Jack's poor outcome and begging the judge to give me the maximum sentence.

I wanted to explain precisely regarding the four patients. Ms. Thomas advised me not to talk much. I briefly stated the facts of Jack's condition and treatment. I also let his daughter know that I had been treating Jack without charge. The sentence was set, and the hearing was over.

The following day, Jack's daughter sent a letter to the judge, expressing her regret and apology for having requested that I be given the maximum sentence. Nevertheless, her letter did not help my long sentence, which was impacted by her drama at the hearing. The term of the sentence had already been announced. It was too late, like water under a bridge.

One size glove does not fit all. Every patient had different clinical conditions and symptoms, which required adjustment of the chemo drugs. Adjustment was not cheating and based on a skilled doctors' expertise. The eye-opening, evolutionary integrated cancer treatment recently introduced focuses on enhancing an individual's own immune system to fight cancer cells. The traditional concept was the more the better when its chemo drugs. But this understanding was changing; oncologists were giving adjusted doses, accordingly, based on individuals' chemo tolerance, which resulted in better treatment outcomes.

All my patients did far better than anticipated. Many achieved clinical remission. And I had a higher curing rate than the national average. I recognized the integrated medicine concept before the public had come to accept it. Lack of understanding of cancer treatment by laypeople ultimately cost me a high price—which I paid with a disproportionately lengthy incarceration.

The judge sentenced me to serve 188 months. Initially, I thought he had said 188 days. I had not wanted to have a trial, but Richard had convinced me that he would win. He had also told that, if he failed to win the trial, I would serve approximately eighteen months at a federal camp. A sentence of 188 months was quite different than one of 18 months. I just sat there—utterly numb.

"Are you planning to appeal?" the judge asked me.

"I don't have any more money," I replied.

"The court will appoint you an attorney for your appeal," the judge quickly responded.

"Okay," I said simply.

My restitution was set at $432,238, in addition to two years of supervised release.

Even if Medicare fraud were absolutely confirmed beyond a reasonable doubt, the punishment could not be over ten years in the absence of patient injury. I had cured many of patients. Almost all my patients had done far better than anticipated and lived longer than the national survival data report. I believed this injustice—my discriminatory lengthy sentence—was most likely the result of a tainted judicial system and vindictive prosecutorial misconduct. And I will continue to believe that until proven otherwise.

My sentence was unconstitutionally, enhanced with assumptive accusations and presumptive, redundant, and repetitive issues.

The enhancement of Dr. Gates's sentence

1. Sophisticated skills—two levels up
2. Dr. Gates was involved in conscious or reckless risk of death with serious bodily injury—2 levels up
3. The defendant, Dr. Gates, should have known that a victim of the offense was a vulnerable victim—2 levels up
4. Dr. Gates abused a position of trust and used a special skill—2 levels up
5. Dr. Gates willfully attempted to obstruct—2 levels up
6. False statement 18 USC section 1347—2 levels up
7. Dr. Gates's sentence judgment of the total restitution is $432,238. Medicare and TennCare owe Dr. Gates nearly $80,000. In contrast, the government collected improper restitution. Additionally, the government added assumptive loss without calculation, with $1,295,653.36 claimed as intended loss. The court improperly collected $863,415.30—16 levels up
8. Dr. Gates involved ten or more victims, without evidence of injury or damage—2 levels up

Total offense levels—34 levels

The rule of law stated that, if there was no violation resulting in serious bodily injury, such a person should not be imprisoned more than ten years. I was falsely charged and convicted of health care fraud. I had not killed or injured anybody.

The highest honored public authority should be obligated to govern with impartiality. Prosecution should be made in the public interest. A legitimate reason for societies to establish criminal justice system and prosecution services is to serve the "public interest" and the common good. Prosecution motivated by personal profit or other self-interests is oppressive. Therefore, in a criminal prosecution, the purpose should not be to "win" a case, but that justice shall be done.

At the sentencing hearing, Ms. Thomas wore a large hooped and shackled necklace. Looking at her weird necklace gave me chills, and it suggested my time had come. It was time for me to go through the fire:

> O Lord, my heart is not haughty, nor mine eyes lofty; neither do I exercise myself in great matters, or in things too high for me. Surely, I have behaved and quieted myself, as a child that is weaned of his mother; my soul is even as a weaned child. (Psalm 131:1–2 KJV)

An agent in the court removed my religious necklace, my earrings, and my funds except for $50. I was not allowed any books. Nor could I bring the leather bag with me.

> The Lord is my Shepherd; I shall not want. He makes me to lie down in green pastures: he leadeth me beside the still waters. He restoreth my soul: he leadeth me in the paths of righteousness for his name's sake. Yea, though I walk through the Valley of the shadow of death, I will fear no evil: for thou art with me; thy rod and thy staff they comfort me. (Psalm 23:1–4 KJV)

I was peaceful and did not worry about my future. The bailiff approached me, and I stretched both my hands toward him. He told me to put arms behind my waist and handcuffed me.

The bailiff stared at me and repeatedly commented, "You do not belong here. What happened to you? You don't look like a prisoner."

We took elevator through to the holding tank. A young white female was sitting in front of me and complaining she was hungry and craving a smoke. I gave her my hamburger and French fries. I talked with her for a while. She felt that someone cared for her, and her nervousness-induced craving to smoke disappeared. While I was her friend for that short time in the holding tank, she calmed down and told me, "You look so peaceful."

One of the bailiffs appeared again. I was transferred to a county holding cell. I had never seen so many human tragedies and miseries as I saw here. There was a toilet that was slightly bigger than a science room closet. Chipped paint and dirt covered the floor. Disgusting stains marked the plastic mattresses on the floor, which were coveted among the many locked-up offenders who did not have mattresses to sleep on.

I was in a dress suit and sheer stocking and low-heeled shoes—the usual attire for hospital work. My clothes were odd, like a fish out of water, in that cell. I sat on the floor. A beautiful young white female lay on the mattress. She appeared to be intoxicated with alcohol. She had a perfect body shape. This holding cell was worse than a wild animal cage. My mind drifted away from the holding cell, and I recalled movie scene—the oppressed Jews crammed tightly together in a filthy room in a concentration camp enduring Nazi persecution. Well, at least, I was not in a gas chamber. A few females were passed out, and some were nervous. One of the young offenders was craving cigarettes badly. When I talked to this young offender, two other girls joined, and we started talking about how our willpower controls our body. Food and cigarette consumptions were habitual, and we could change our desire to something else. I told them that, one day, I would like to write a book.

Then all three ladies asked me, "May we have your book?"

"You will see my book in the future," I told them.

There was a tiny window on the top of the door, which was taped with a piece of paper. The holding cell guard kept peeping through the window and staring at me. Then they repeatedly said, "She is extremely strong."

I completely ignored the guard's comments. I was curious myself and subconsciously desired to explore and experience how people can live and react to unexpected tragedies under horrible circumstances. Here I was, sitting on the floor in an unimaginable and abominable, dirty, small cell with confused youngsters. I decided to lead myself one step at a time.

I trusted Martha, Pastor Brown, and the Reverend Kim. Martha promised to renew my California license, my driver's license, and apply for a black tag on my car. She would drive my car occasionally to keep the engine running. Shockingly, after Martha returned to get my car in my town house, she gave my garage door opener, car, and house keys to Dr. Lemon. I had left behind a ton of freezer food and all my furniture and personal belongings, believing I would return in six months.

Now, the gate was flung open to Dr. Lemon, and he took everything of mine. One day, my divorce attorney saw Dr. Lemon cooking inside my town house. Chris warned Dr. Lemon to immediately get out of my town house. According to Martha, when she reached my town house and opened the garage door, Dr. Lemon came into the garage and took everything, which was difficult to understand. My car was then parked outside of my garage.

Several hours later, I was transferred from the holding cell to a new facility, David State Prison. Early in the morning, I was moved from there to CCA, a detention center in Mason, Tennessee. This place was like a scary jail that I had seen only in the movies. White metal barred doors controlled by electronic rolling gates were like gigantic mousetraps. Each time the door shut with a loud clanking sound; it almost electrocuted my brain.

The place was noisy and filthy and appeared to be a real modern slave dungeon. I had never seen such a terrifying place. It was surreal!

When Martha Stewart was a convicted as a felon, she could no longer tolerate her trial and she asked the judge to put her in jail. She was a billionaire. The judge placed her at Alderson Federal Prison Camp in West Virginia for six months, and she had six months of home confinement, a total of a one-year sentence for a false statement.

I had said the same thing to my judge, but he had thrown me in a rat hole. The judge had given me five years over what was allowed for the charge of false statement. My false statement was not even false.

George Papadopoulos lied to the FBI. He was charged for a false statement and got only fourteen days in prison. I could only imagine how rampant the disparities of the judicial system were—how often racism and gender discrimination, deeply rooted in the United States, played a role. Literally, I had to pinch myself to check if I was in a nightmare.

My roommate in the two-man cell at the CCA was a black woman. I was certain she suffered from mental disorders because she had been combing her hair all day and all night long. When I asked her to stop combing her hair, she became upset and threw my mattress outside the room. Then she got in trouble with the guard.

I began to regret the begging the judge to put me jail in a hurry to avoid an encounter with Dr. Lemon. Coming to prison earlier was like jumping from the frying pan into the fire.

I reached my attorney and asked her to get me out of here as soon as possible before I lost my mind. While I was at the CCA, I received a letter from Ms. Thomas regarding a summons of civil action against me. Ms. Thomas had forgotten to give it to me after the sentencing hearing was over. The summons from the prosecutor had been left on the defense table where Ms. Thomas found it. She was forwarding it, and I was to respond to it within ten days.

I asked her to help me to respond to this summons. She declined, saying she was not a civil lawyer and that I had to handle it myself.

Lord, have mercy!

How was I supposed to do this with no envelope, stamp, pen, or paper and no knowledge of how to respond to a civil action? Where there is a will, there is a way. I managed to borrow a pen, stamp, and paper and replied with the best of my acknowledgement. Then I mailed the letter.

I thought of the wise words of Mother Teresa:

> People are often unreasonable, illogical self-centered.
>
> Forgive them anyway. If you are kind, people may accuse you of selfish, ulterior motives.
>
> Be kind anyway. If you are successful, you will win some false friends and some true enemies.
>
> Succeed anyway. If you are honest and frank, people may cheat you. Be honest and frank anyway.
>
> What you spend years building, someone may destroy overnight. Build anyway.
>
> If you find serenity and happiness, they may be jealous. Be happy anyway.
>
> The good you do today, people will often forget tomorrow. Do good anyway.

Give the world the best you have, and it may just never be enough. Give the best you have any way.

You see, in the final analysis, it is all between you and God. It was never between you and them anyway.

CHAPTER 35

Rock Bottom

What do you expect? You are in prison.
Within a week, I was transferred to Oklahoma Transit Center, where I stayed a few days before leaving for Tallahassee, Florida. Moving around from place to place made me think I was on a free federal prison tour. This was quite different from the Baltic cruise.

Tallahassee FCI was better than CCA or Oklahoma Transit Center. The many different units circled a large garden. I was assigned to one of the dorms, which had a large space like a gym with numerous cubicles. Each cubicle had two sets of bunk beds that housed four people per cubicle. We each had a small locker. The first thing I though to myself was, *you've hit rock bottom*.

This was worse than I had imagined a ghetto lifestyle. Looking up, I observed exposed scaffolding and bare pipes collecting heavy dust around them on the ceiling. It seemed like I was in a bomb shelter.

Two days after I arrived in Tallahassee, there was a gunfight between an FBI agent and a Tallahassee prison officer. They exchanged gunfire, and both the FBI agent and officer were killed at the FCI. According to the breaking news, the FBI agent had investigated unscrupulous sexual misconduct by the prison officers with inmates. Many inmates were raped by the officers, and some inmates lured the officers and became involved in sexual activities at Tallahassee FCI.

A few officers provide inmates with cigarettes, chewing gums, drugs, cigarette lights, and more pleasing items, tucked under their favorite inmates' pillows. These select inmates were frequently called by officers after count time. Several times a day, the FCI officers routinely took head counts to make sure no one had escaped; this was called count time.

Some inmates were forced to perform oral sex on the officers, while other inmates and officers were mutually attracted to each other. They had sex inside officers' car or wherever they could find space to carry out such sexual conduct. A few inmates got pregnant by officers.

The entire FCI was locked down for more than a week after the gunfight erupted. TVs were disconnected, and no one could go out. We had bags of baloney sandwiches, three meals a day for ten days. The locked-down inmates were tearfully calling their family members and complaining about their miseries and anxieties. Over a week later, the prison resumed normal operation.

A few days after the shocking events, I was called to the main office to sign a summons. Dr. Lemon had sued my Milwaukee, Wisconsin, bank. He was demanding to transfer all my separate funds and premarital assets to the Tulsa Divorce Court.

Dr. Lemon had been waiting for me to be incarcerated so that he could "clean up"; he planned to get control of all my life savings. He falsely accused me of eliminating my due process right.

Crowds of inmates packed in the cafeteria during mealtimes and working in the kitchen was not easy for anybody. Inmates' food was served on plastic trays, which were heavily stained, and the appearance spoke for itself. The same trays had been used for many years. Some inmates complained about the old plastic trays that produced toxic chemicals contaminating the food. I decided to have a special diet of common fair tray, which used disposable materials. Typically, the common fair trays were for Jewish people.

One of the kitchen officers was an institutionalized slave driver and abused his authority when it came to interacting with most of the inmates. One day, an old inmate took two corn dogs from the cafeteria, which was considered contraband, and was caught by this officer. He ran after her and knocked her down on the ground. She injured her knee when she fell and complained about her pain, but the officer did not pay attention to her pain. Instead, he put her in a special housing unit, which was an isolated jail in prison. I did not respect the officer who cruelly punished the woman over two corn dogs.

My path grew rough and dark. The storm clouds quickly rolled in. The waves began to rock my ship. I found I had no hold to turn to. The ship that I had built was made of foolish pride. It fell apart and left me bare, with nowhere else to hide. I had no strength or faith to face the trials that lay a head, and so I simply spoke his name and bowed my weary head. (God's grace.)

A few weeks later, I received a teleconference call from the US attorney at the Nashville courthouse regarding the civil action against me from the prosecutor's summons. I answered the attorney's questions honestly. Thereafter, Judge Echoles dismissed the governmental civil action against me.

As time went on, I received many letters from patients. When I transferred to Tallahassee, two of my patients drove to the FCI and tried to see me. My patients obviously did not know the prison system. Visitors were required to obtain special permission by the prison. Both patients drove to Florida from Tennessee separately. One even tried to give me a message through the prison guard. Of course, they would not deliver the message. They both returned to Tennessee in disappointment and sent me letters. One was from Paul and his wife, and the other was from Joe.

Joe wanted to send me chocolates and asked me which I preferred—white or dark chocolate. He did not know he could not send any outside items. I had precious and priceless relationship with my patients that could not be bought by any currency.

Thanks to God, they were doing well!

Inmates were always required to carry federal IDs. Sometimes my ID card had fallen out of my pocket. So, I made crochet cardholder with a loop of string and wore it around my neck. One afternoon, as I left the cafeteria, a tall slender young officer stopped me and questioned me about the pink crochet cardholder.

I told him, "I do not want to forget to carry it at all times and wearing it in this cardholder makes it easy for me."

He said, "You cannot wear your ID in a crochet cardholder."

I quickly removed the federal ID from the pink crochet cardholder and gave it to him, as it was considered contraband. He did not take the cardholder and informed me that he only wanted to help me be informed. He did ask me what I did for living in the outside world.

"I was a cancer doctor, an oncologist," I told him.

Unexpectedly, this office wanted to know whether I was interested in teaching inmates. I was excited and quickly answered him, yes, yes, yes! Getting out of the kitchen job was more than a blessing, especially since I did not like the officer who acted like a slave driver.

All the inmates were attracted to this one tall and slender officer at first sight. They wanted to know and get close to him. He was handsome, had a PhD in education, was kind, and was extremely smart.

This officer, Dr. Stile became the head of the education department. I did not realize that he was that handsome. However, after so many inmates were talking about him, I looked closely at him and saw that he was attractive. Notably, after he offered me a job in the educational department, he looked even handsomer than before.

There was a large, wasted space next to the educational department. The huge room was piled with a bunch of debris, dangling loose wires, broken chairs and windows, dirt, and dust. When we pass through that room, we instantly covered our mouths and noses.

Dr. Stile ingeniously transformed the wasted space into a state-of-the-art modern computer lab. He designed surrounding glass windows, which created a bright and wide-open space. The octagonal shaped tables maximized the space, enabling them to hold several computers. There were many tables in the computer lab, used for a variety of educational purposes, from GED studies to linguistic arts, you name it. He also introduced a language program using Rosetta Stone, a college program, a music collection program, a yoga exercise program, and many more courses that enabled inmates to learn and cultivate their improvement. I respected his humility.

We were encouraged to utilize the resources available to us for the betterment of our future. The students in the GED classes held the highest passing rates. Inmates were given the opportunity to take college courses and programs.

I taught CLEP (college level) biology. Among the inmate teachers, we competed to be the best instructors, influenced by our respect for Dr. Stile.

Officer Stile taught us many different computer skills including PowerPoint. Surely, he expanded our horizons.

My divorce was ongoing without me. Chris had taken $5,000 before he had made any motion for trial. Initially he had promised to finish my divorce proceedings. He pleaded to the judge to remove him from my divorce case. Then he took a vacation and was gone with my $5,000. I was left alone without a divorce lawyer for a while.

At the beginning, I did not have any money and was unable to buy anything, even shampoo. The court in Nashville had allowed me to keep only $50 in Nashville, and CCA had never transferred it to Tallahassee.

Dr. Lemon's Attorney, Edgton, froze all my funds before we got divorced. I earned a small amount of money from the educational department in prison, which helped to pay for my phone calls.

My third attorney, Greg's partner, was able to obtain $1,000 from the Tulsa courthouse for my living expenses. Soon after I had received the $1,000, Edgton, Lemon's divorce attorney, took $1000 from my account to compensate my expenses and moved them into his account. Greg's partner was nice and sincere, but he did not like to work with Greg and left for San Jose. Thereafter, Greg got involved in my divorce case.

My fourth divorce lawyer smelled the money. He flew to Tallahassee without my request. At first, I hoped that he would do a good job after we met and got to know each other. I kidded myself, given that most attorneys are licensed thieves.

Prior to my incarceration, I had sent $2,000,000 of my separate money to a close friend, Mary, in Tennessee. I gave small portions in cashier's checks to my family members, hoping they would return it when I needed it. The money was divided into sums of $9,000—less than $10,000 to avoid banking violations around sending large sums.

I was not sure whether I would be able to send money to my family overseas, without much knowledge of the legal governance around sending funds that way. I had earned these assets before I had become a doctor. They were my premarital funds, and I paid taxes every year. I know the government can throw any mud on the wall; anything stuck when they used fabrications to create charges.

Mary held my cashier's checks, awaiting future decision.

I had a close relationship with Nancy, the wife of Jerry, the tongue cancer patient, who had been cured in Milwaukee. She advised me to tell everything to my divorce attorney and give him my cashier's check. It was a case of the blind leading the blind. The $2,000,0000 cashier's check was mailed to Greg by Mary while I was incarcerated. Evidently, my attorney colluded with the Dr. Lemon's attorney. The entire sum was decimated and split among them.

When I asked for my fund and assets, Greg, told me, "What do you expect? You're in prison."

I had a smart CPA throughout the time I was working in Tennessee. He informed me that I would receive an IRS tax return in the amount of $178,000 because I'd spent more than $1,000,000 for my defense attorney to protect my own medical oncology practice, which was considered an indirect business expense. I appreciated his intelligent management. He helped me to open a bank account outside Tennessee during my incarceration. Everybody loved my money, though, grabbing it like it was free. His fee increased each time I talked to him. And when he charged me $450 per hour, I was unable to pay him. We could no longer work together. Innocence is nothing but ignorance.

My friend Mary talked about everything honestly to Greg and to me. I told him I was waiting for the $178,000 tax return. Greg not only seized the $2,000,000 but also claimed the $178,000 was community funds because I had earned that during the marriage. Obviously, he was strongly associated with Edgton.

Indeed, silence is gold.

I had premarital bank accounts for nearly fifteen years, and the bank manager knew all my funds were solely under my name in Milwaukee. There were many reputable attorneys in Milwaukee, but no one was willing to take my case. I was simply in prison. A popular law firm, Reilly's, sent me a response letter from Wisconsin. My high expectations and hope quickly vanished as soon as I opened the letter. Reilly stated that he was busy, and he could not take a new client. I did not believe that any attorneys refused to make money. Most likely, he had refused to take my case because my letter had come from prison.

I called Greg and asked him to contact Reilly. Soon after Greg had called Reilly's, an associate, Shirley, eagerly proposed that she would work with Greg. I did not respect the philosophy of Reilly's law firm; their choice of who to represent was biased, based on the prospective client's financial status. Somebody might have transferred my premarital funds to the courthouse in Milwaukee, Wisconsin. I had many attorneys, but no one could explain to me what was going on with my funds. I was in the dark and had no idea what was going on.

Straightaway, Shirley zealously involved herself in the funds related to my divorce in Wisconsin. She instantly called me at Tallahassee FCI. She wanted to file a civil action against Dr. Lemon. At that point, I could not trust any lawyers. My first impression was that her suggestion was based on one thing—her desire to drain my lifesavings the same as the other lawyers I had been involved with.

"I don't have money," I told her simply.

"You have plenty of money in Wisconsin," she replied.

I declared that I did not need her. I refused Shirley's services because when I had initially contacted her law firm, they had refused to help me. Now that they had found out that I had abundant funds in Milwaukee, they were voraciously work for me. My lack of legal knowledge led to making poor decisions one after the other. And repeatedly, I was hitting bad luck. I should have kept her. On the other hand, I did not know who to trust. I could not trust any lawyers. I was the one who punctured my own gold sack and drained all the gold due to poor decisions and lack of enlightenment. Later, Shirley charged me $10,000 for her one-time phone call to Tallahassee FCI. I felt I was worse than a sitting duck.

Meanwhile, Dr. Lemon's attorney tricked me out of controlling my funds in Wisconsin and forced me to transfer them the divorce court in Tulsa. Edgton graduated from Vanderbilt Law School, and he certainly knew lawyers in Nashville.

Synchronously, Dr. Lemon reached out to the federal prosecutor in Tennessee and informed her that I had had large amounts of funds transferred from my bank to the courthouse in Milwaukee. Promptly, the federal criminal judge who'd overseen my case ordered my funds in Milwaukee transferred to my divorce account in Tulsa, Oklahoma and revived the civil case that had once been dismissed by Judge Echoles, many years later.

The prosecutor got away with many violations because of prosecutorial power, my integrity, and the fact that I was completely stricken and powerless in prison. I suffered several mistreatments at the hands of the legal system, among them:

1. Each state has its own sovereignty. The funds that I had earned in Milwaukee weren't connected to any fraud. The money I had in the Milwaukee bank account had not been earned in Tennessee. Nor was it marital funds. It was inappropriately transferred and treated as such.
2. My criminal judge should not have involved himself in a private civil divorce case.
3. The Tennessee civil statutory time limitation was a year. The renewed civil action had been dismissed by Judge Echoles in 2006 and was now being revived many years later.

By the rule of law, a federal judge does not have any jurisdiction in a civil divorce case. I consider the judge's ruling pertaining to my divorce a tainted court order and will until it is proven otherwise.

Dr. Lemon's began pretrial proceedings at the Tulsa courthouse. Edgton summoned my CPA, Steve, to testify against me. Steve had handled the filing of both my and Dr. Lemon's annual income taxes for many years in Tennessee. He explained that Dr. Lemon and I had separate funds and filed a joint income tax return under Class C, which means separate individual income taxes. We never joined our individual assets.

He testified honestly, but it did not matter in the eyes of the corrupt divorce court. The CPA flew to Tulsa from Tennessee and then charged me $1,000 from my bank account for the appearance.

In the aftermath, Edgton summoned all my friends, including Martha, Reverend Kim, Pastor Brown, Dr. Heinz, and Sam, trying to find out if I had left any other money that he and Dr. Lemon did not know about.

Afterward, Greg, my attorney at the time, informed me that the first divorce trial date had been set. I told him that I would like to participate via teleconference. Greg assured me he would speak with the prison counselor to arrange the date and time.

The day of the trial came, and I received a call from Greg. I had a constitutional right to participate in my own divorce trial. However, the attorneys on both sides colluded with the divorce judge. The first divorce judge withdrew from my divorce case. The second judge appeared to be acting as a puppet for Edgton.

On the scheduled date for my divorce trial, the FCI counselor called me. I was waiting for Greg's phone call in the conference room. His phone call was delayed from the scheduled time. Finally, when I received Greg's call, he explained that I could not hear my divorce trial because the telephone was out of order, and the phone company tried unsuccessfully to fix the phone line in the courtroom.

As a result, Greg advised me that I should wait and participate in the second day of my divorce trial. The next day, I again waited at the counselor's office, but the call did not come through until extremely late. Finally, Greg called and told me that the courtroom telephone still did not work.

Downstream, the truth was revealed by two honorable female justices at the state supreme court. They discovered that the Tulsa divorce judge violated my due process by prohibiting me from listening to the proceedings of my own divorce trial.

The divorce judge stated that I was a prisoner and was "not required to participate in my divorce trial." (See the supreme court justice statements and my divorce transcript in the appendix.)

The divorce judge's biased discretion was unconstitutional and an undeniable discriminatory decision. This is a violation of a basic principle in the American legal system that mandates fairness in the government's dealing with people.

Justice for all—or for none!

You hypocrites first take the plank out of your own eyes, and then you will see clearly to remove that speck from your brother's.

Due process is a fundamental law, guaranteed in the Fifth and the Fourteenth Amendments to the Constitution of the United States. These amendments forbid federal, state, and local governments from depriving a person of life, liberty, or property without the due process of law.

Greg blatantly lied to me under oath amid a trial, which was proved by the state supreme court justice. Incontrovertibly, all my own attorneys, as well as Dr. Lemon's attorneys perjured themselves under oath and got away with it without any consequences—later proven to be a corruption of bureaucracy. My divorce transcript was not provided for nearly ten years.

At times, Greg would send me a piece of the trial transcript hearing as I requested.

Edgton claimed that $1 million should be awarded to Dr. Lemon because I had wasted marital funds by hiring Richard and defending my business.

After I was incarcerated, Dr. Lemon broke into my storage unit and town house, both of which he was restrained from entering by court order. By doing so, he discovered information about my separate financial assets and funds and, thus, led the trial court to believe that my unilateral actions regarding my own separate assets were fraudulent. He destroyed all my files, my personal collections, and my evidential documents and stole all my certified gemstones, replacing them with fake stones, including my engagement diamond. Astonishingly, I actually paid the storage unit rental fee for a year before we realized the unit had been cleaned out by Dr. Lemon—without court permission to do so.

Edgton knew all about it, but he did not report what was going on to my attorney. Nor did anyone report the violation to the court or to a judge. This was worse than illegal rooting. I believed that was a criminal act of theft, but no one did anything about it. Not even the divorce attorney I had paid to protect me and my assets did anything about it, despite knowing about Dr. Lemon's criminal acts—that he'd perjured himself under oath, destroyed evidence, made materially false statements, and stolen items from me. Yet my attorney was happy to bill me $250,000 for services not rendered.

Dr. Lemon and I had independent medical practices. We had always kept the practice's accounting isolated. I had paid all my legal fees with moneys that were under my name alone and related solely to my business.

Greg was ineffective. His meek counteroffer was to offer Dr. Lemon $500,000 instead of $1 million that he had asked for—still a portion of what I'd paid Richard for my defense with my own money.

The puppet judge granted Edgton everything he asked for. Greedy Dr. Lemon was never satisfied and further claimed the San Diego property I had purchased ten years prior to our marriage as his asset. Later, he wanted both town houses, as well as the Smoky Mountains time-shares and all my separate bank funds. He acted like a bottomless pit. He wanted everything for himself, since I was in prison proven and had been proven to be a "bad person."

Additionally, Dr. Lemon cleaned me out when it came to the household items, I had left in my town house. He took all my valuables, including antiques, collections, albums, and even new clothes, storing only junk he did not want, along with my patients' charts. He absolutely carried out the premeditated plan I had found written on his scratch pad—to make me penniless. Dr. Lemon additionally claimed that he had stored my junk and asked for compensation, which the judge awarded him.

While I was married to Dr. Lemon, I owned seven houses. He manipulated the judge and his attorney and was able to unlawfully seize everything. Concurrently, Edgton increased his service fee, which I and not Dr. Lemon was held responsible for and which was taken away from my divorce account at the Tulsa courthouse. Edgton's charges grew—from $40,000 to $438,000. And in the end, he took $768,000, along with some convoluted charges derived to hide his illegal service fees—all for services I had never contracted for. One day the vice chief judge of the Tulsa divorce courthouse stated that the usual divorce cost fees were around $34,000 in Tulsa, Oklahoma. Edgton's increased his fees sky-high.

To add insult to injury, he accused me of having professionally committed a crime because the book Martha had given me, *How to Hide Assets*, was found among my belongs. His claim against me—that I had, with premeditation, hidden marital funds, claiming them as mine alone—was a mirror image reflection, projecting his shame onto me. The truth was what he and Dr. Lemon claimed as marital funds were solely mine. And I did not want nor to claim one penny of Dr. Lemon's money.

Edgton punished me and labeled me as having unclean hands for unilaterally transacting business with my own separate monies. Dr. Lemon and his attorney claimed my $7 million belonged to them. At the same time, almost none of Dr. Lemon's assets were characterized as marital. He claimed everything was his, both what was mine and what was his.

Dr. Lemon and Edgton seized my life savings. And having alleged that I had committed fraud, they were true hypocrites. My divorce was memorialized on August 11, 2009, after I was not allowed to participate in the actual trial process.

I confronted Greg about his poor representation in my divorce proceedings. He repeatedly told me, "What do you expect? You are in prison."

Then he took a cruise.

Victoria Gates, MD

We all go through dark nights of the soul—times when we wonder if God has abandoned us. As with David, our aching can give way to joy when we approach God honestly, plead for help, and reaffirm our trust in a God whose love for us will never waver or change.

CHAPTER 36

The School of Suffering (Lessons We Could Learn in No Other Classroom)

It was remarkably refreshing to teach biology and to be involved in academics. It brought reminiscences of my cherished school days, when I was full of dreams and living a carefree lifestyle. Most of the inmates were not studious; however, they loved to eat, horseplay, and argue with each other.

When I started to explain the basics of all life—that all life comes from a cell—the class was not interested. So, I changed the cell to a pizza. I asked the students, "Who wants to have a pizza this afternoon? Would you raise your hands?"

Everybody raised her hand.

I said, "Wow! Everybody would love to have pizza. Let us go over how to make a pizza. First, we would prepare the round pizza dough and put a large pepperoni with a round black pepper on top of the pepperoni."

I asked the students, "Do you want mozzarella on the pizza?"

And then, "How about put a few walnuts?"

"Let us sprinkle it with some parmesan cheese.

"Can you picture this pizza?"

All the students were looking at my picture and nodded their heads.

"Now we know what the basic units of the cells that make up our body," I continued. "A cell is like a pizza. Human cells have a nucleus, like a pepperoni, and a nucleolus, like a round black pepper on the pepperoni. Mitochondria are shaped similarly to a walnut. The Golgi complex is like the mozzarella spread around the pepperoni. And Ribosomes are like the parmesan cheese."

Then I went over each function of a living cell. The students loved it, and they remembered all the structures of a cell.

Dr. Stile appreciated my teaching methods. Many of the inmates told him that they had hated biology in school. In contrast, they enjoyed learning biology with me. They also said that the best thing that had ever happened to them was understanding their body functions. He treated all the inmates as students and explained to us that our incarceration was our sabbatical—providing time to learn and a retreat for our spirits.

Most the officers in the prison were trained to discipline juveniles and adult inmates inappropriately. Juveniles were put in a jumpsuit, and the officers shouted at or punished them harshly, which would not help society. For that reason, recidivism was higher than 80 percent—meaning released prisoners returned to prison again and again.

Unlike other officers, Dr. Stile guided all the inmates in a positive and constructive, way emphasizing that, "The school of suffering teaches us lessons that we could learn in no other classroom."

The depth of a lesson arises from long suffering, which awakens us to the true meaning of life's journey and a deeper understanding of human pain.

He included yoga classes in the curriculum and placed a beautiful greenhouse next to the GED computer lab. Human beings suffer because they wrongly believe that their soul is bound to their body and mind. The practice of yoga relaxed and rejuvenated my mind and body. I was mesmerized by the exotic and esoteric yoga music and the graceful movement that aligned my body, mind, and soul. Dr. Stile did yoga very well himself, and occasionally he invited yoga experts for us practice together. The flowers around the small pond that Dr. Stile designed were lovely. Seeing nature through the wide-open glass also soothed my pain during my yoga lessons.

Learning was my pleasure, and I learned many aspects of life under Dr. Stile. I greatly respected him, and my overall conditions somewhat improved after yoga.

When Dr. Stile was later significantly promoted to Washington, DC, I simultaneously was transferred to Waseca in Minnesota.

I had a minor heart attack and developed an abnormal cardiac rhythm, and my oxygen levels rapidly decreased soon after I had reached the new facility. A paramedic took me to the regional emergency room. Lying on the ER stretcher as a prisoner was highly odd and surreal. While I was waiting for a doctor, I had a flashback. I remembered myself walking around wearing a physician's white coat seeing patients.

I received fluid, nitroglycerin, and oxygen therapy, and my overall condition improved slightly after several hours.

I began using my free time to investigate my divorce case and criminal case in the prison library. My CPA, Steve, found another divorce attorney through the internet since Greg had left. This new attorney, Rhonda was adamantly represented the wrong done in the unfair divorce proceedings and awarding of all my assets to Dr. Lemon.

For some reason, Rhonda hesitated to submit a motion for appeal after she had received the initial $35,000. First, she confronted Edgton about his unethical misconduct in a letter, which was not reported on my divorce transcript. Thereafter, she charged me an additional $40,000 to go forward with a divorce appeal. Meanwhile, I submitted my own evidence as pro se along with Rhonda since I know my divorce case well.

Each time I dashed Edgton's conscience with my true foolproof evidence, he would get vexed and increase his fees—taking them from my account, instead of billing Dr. Lemon. I did not have any funds except for the IRS return from my income tax that the CPA had deposited into a bank account.

At the beginning, Rhonda answered my phone calls. It was not long, though, before I could not reach her, even after she'd received the additional $40,000 for my appeal. After numerous phone calls, I finally got a hold of her and expressed my uneasiness and upset. The prison phone system was different than using my cell phone. Inmates lined up to use the phone and waited for thirty minutes between calls. She said that her child had gotten sick and she had taken her child to the hospital.

If that were true, then she could have emailed me. I thought that was just an excuse. My dubiousness and skepticism were growing, and it became increasingly difficult to trust any lawyers. One of my friends found the most famous female divorce attorney in Oklahoma City. I was anxious to retrieve all my premarital funds from Dr. Lemon. I asked Rhonda to work with this new divorce attorney, Lana. Rhonda said that she did not mind working with her.

I wanted to file a civil action against Edgton. Lana said that she would sue Edgton, and she would also bring her partner, who was a criminal lawyer. I planned to hire her on a contingency fee, even though she wanted me to pay her at least $10,000 up front. The small amount of my IRS income tax return had been shrinking rapidly. In any event, I paid her $10,000 based on our mutual agreement that she would file a civil suit against Edgton. I paid $450 for the court file and to deliver the summons to Edgton. Before she received the money, she promised me she would handle the civil action. Her mind quickly changed after she had received the $10,000, at which point she informed me she could not sue one of her colleagues.

I thought she was joking. Afterward, I sent a letter to Lana, requesting that she return my $10,000. She responded to my letter by billing me an additional $1,000 fee for reading my letter. She said that she had driven to Tulsa to meet Rhonda and transfer my divorce transcript to a CD and had used all my $10,000 deposit.

This time I could not suppress my anger and told Rhonda to do something about it. Instead of resolving the matter, Rhonda unexpectedly took the $40,000 and withdrew my appeal and then quit. I paid $450 for the court's filing fee and received the receipt, but no sheriff delivered a summons to Edgton.

I paid my CPA to find another divorce attorney. He found a young man who was the nephew of my current divorce judge. He charged me $5,000 to review my divorce case and said he would help me retrieve my lost money and correct the judge's inappropriate awarding of everything to Dr. Lemon. He promptly answered my calls a few times, saying he hoped to tell his uncle what had exactly transpired. Nonetheless, this attorney was no different from the others. After he had received the $5,000, once again nothing happened. This new attorney likewise withdrew from my divorce case, citing a conflict of interest, since the judge was his uncle.

I was certain that a few attorneys were decent and altruistic. Unfortunately, I had not yet found them. Birds of a feather flocked together. All my attorneys were horrible tricksters and deceivers. God have mercy; it was too much to take at times.

To be or not to be—that was my question. It was difficult. Either I went forward, or I gave up. But knowing that Dr. Lemon had taken $4.5 million dollars of my assets and funds, I could not just give up, let go of it, and stay still.

Undeniably, I had no luck; it was as if I were sinking deeper and deeper into quicksand. I could not believe that my egregious divorce, which had appeared to be never-ending, had wound up with a puppet divorce judge awarding nearly 100 percent of my premarital and separate funds to Dr. Lemon.

I did my best, but my best was not good enough to accomplish anything without knowledge of Oklahoma divorce law or any authority in prison. If I had stayed in Tennessee and had not moved to Tulsa, I would have saved my premarital funds. It was in small-town Crossville, where everyone knew everyone else's personal history and individual business, that Dr. Lemon became aware of my assets.

Several officers in Waseca teased me, saying I was like a light fixture at the legal library, because I worked nonstop without any breaks. Most of the inmates sympathized with my unfortunate situation and tried to help me. One inmate gave me information about a legal research firm in Kansas City, Kansas. She said Mr. Stanford there understood inmates' frustrations because he was an ex-convict. I called him, and he zealously wanted to do anything I needed it. I hoped he would support and understand my difficult situation.

Dr. Lemon claimed my premarital property in San Diego was his and took $650,000 cash from my divorce account in Tulsa, claiming the property's value as higher than the market price. I did not have the cash, but the rental house in San Diego was still there. Managing the rental property in prison was difficult. I struggled to deal with the unknown tenants and a cheating and manipulating property manager and found the whole thing disheartening.

At that time, Mr. Stanford volunteered to be my power of attorney, and he charged me $5,000. I agreed under one condition—he could not sell or cash the rental payment deposit. He informed me that he had found an excellent female divorce lawyer who had been a judge in Kansas. Later, I found out that she had only worked with the judge but had not herself been a circuit judge.

This lawyer, Judy, told Mr. Sanford that too much of my money was lost, and she could reverse my discriminatory divorce case. She would fight tooth and nail for me. Concurrently, she requested $75,000 up front without a penny short. At the bank, I had only $75,000 left from the IRS tax return. I tried to negotiate with her, but she had ironclad determination. Her assertiveness, in a way, gave me a confidence she would win. I was optimistic about my divorce outcome.

In Waseca, everyone knew about my unceasing legal battle that played out day and night. I was like Captain Ahab fighting with Moby Dick, the monstrous white whale. I did not lose my leg, but my life savings was slipping away. My divorce reminded me of Ernest Hemingway's novel *The Old Man and Sea*. My hard work, life savings, and professional career were eaten a little at a time by heinous political power, and I was left bare—no meat on my bones. My obsessive quest to find a curative treatment for cancer and my desire to be a compassionate doctor had been buried under the embers.

When I worked at the chapel, my boss, the chaplain, suggested that I not spend any more money on lawyers. "Lawyers are criminals. Save some money for yourself. You may need it when you are released."

I never liked gambling, and I was not a good gambler. Nonetheless, I decided to roll the dice and paid the $75,000. At the beginning, Judy's associate worked on my divorce case, and then he quit the firm. Then another partner represented me in my appeal hearing. Peculiarly, the same judge ruled on my defendant motion at an appellate court. Strangely, the hearing was not in an appellate court. My appeal hearing should have been heard in an appellate court by a different judge.

Judy's partner stated that he had worked on divorce cases for thirty years; he had never seen such an egregious case as my divorce. Regardless, no one did anything to retrieve my funds; hence, the blatant, unlawful misconduct among the lawyers continued.

I desperately wanted to know about other Oklahoma divorce cases. Searching for the right books sitting in a prison was impossible. I met a twenty-five-year-old inmate named Nikki who was working at the library. She said that one of her friends owned a bookstore. Her friend was an expert t finding books and could immediately mail five different books about Oklahoma divorce cases. Nikki had a limp, and one of her legs was skinny and short. She talked innocently and was kind to others. Would I ever learn not to judge a book by its cover? I never imagined this pathetic little girl would cheat me.

I seriously wanted to buy books that contained information on many divorce cases and gain insight and knowledge by studying other cases. Nikki contacted the bookstore friend, who wanted a cashier's check in the amount of $2,500 to ship the books via overnight mail. I thought law books would be just as expensive as medical books.

A hasty decision under oppressive desperation made me blind, and I stepped on a booby trap. My cashier's check was gone, and the books never came. Nikki was a con artist. She scammed many inmates, and she ended up in the special housing unit, which is jail in prison, until she was released.

I had many divorce attorneys. Nevertheless, not one of them did any better than the other—at anything except siphoning my life savings, that is. I continuously submitted on my own a pro se appeal brief to the appellate court in Oklahoma City, followed by a writ of certiorari to the state supreme court.

After I submitted the writ, the nine state justices voted on my divorce case. The Oklahoma Supreme Court had seven male justices and two female justices. Two female justices distinctly stated that my divorce case was unconstitutional because the divorce judge had violated my due process. The judge had willfully, intentionally, and knowingly prohibited me from participating in my own divorce trial.

Undoubtedly, America still had gender discrimination that was palpable, along with a silent racism that sabotaged many good people. Had the seven male justices been females, I would have won my writ of certiorari.

I strongly believe that the judge in my divorce case in Tulsa was biased and that his misconduct was egregious misconduct. He abused his public authority and unconstitutionally awarded 100 percent of my separate and premarital funds to Dr. Lemon under tainted and political influence. The ruling in the Tulsa divorce court was completely in favor of Dr. Lemon, who was the true perpetrator.

A grievance letter regarding Edgton was submitted to the bar association. However, the president of the Oklahoma Bar Association was a close friend of Edgton's. The bar association responded to me by letter, stating they would not investigate nor discipline Edgton.

After less than a year in Waseca, I was furloughed to Bryan Federal

Victoria Gates, MD

Prison Camp in the middle of winter. Waseca was nice to me, providing me a colorful Nautica winter jacket, a long scarf, $100 for meals, and travel expenses. I had a nice meal with some blueberry cheesecake in Dallas during the bus's layover. The $100 was more than enough for the one-day bus trip. Inmates were not allowed to have any money. I left unopened snacks and change at the Bryan bus station. An inmate who worked as a driver picked me up at the bus station to the camp. Both Waseca and Bryan Camp had been college campuses before being converted to federal prisons.

Waseca had a beautiful flower garden, and I had enjoyed looking out through the chapel window while I was working at the chapel. The colorful garden reminded of a fairy summer night dream.

Bryan Camp had Spanish-style buildings and indoor and outdoor exercise rooms. It had a gazebo where inmates could sit and relax next to picnic tables and benches close to a track. There were several large trees, and the cherry blossoms were gorgeous during the spring season. As a prisoner, I found the place decent, with pillars supporting the building. The walkways had stepping-stones that gave the camp a less intimidating atmosphere than one might expect of a prison.

Brian Camp was considered the best academically orientated facility in the United States. The horticulture program was outstanding, and the Blinn College program was excellent. The instructors were college professors from outside colleges.

On the other hand, the medical clinic was substandard, in my opinion.

I applied for a GED tutor position as soon as I arrived to avoid kitchen work. Mr. Porter, the GED teacher, hired me on the spot. He had worked for twenty-five years in the educational department at Bryan Camp. He was amazingly kind, unconditionally helped inmates, and as a genuinely good-natured person. I enjoyed working with Mr. Porter as much as I had loved working with Dr. Stile.

I realized once again that GED students were not often motivated to learn. Nor were they eager to obtain their diplomas. First, I encouraged their confidence and a positive outlook.

When I explained about the nine planets that travel around the sun, I used an acronym to help them remember better. My very eager mother just the sent us nine pizzas:

- My—Mercury
- Very—Venus
- Eager—Earth
- Mother—Mars
- Just—Jupiter
- Sent—Saturn
- Us—Uranus
- Nine—Neptune
- Pizzas—Pluto

Now, the students were excited about the nine pizzas. And within a short time, they remembered the nine planets correctly. After they learned about the existing planets, I continued with the inner planets and outer planets, as well as how each planet rotates as it revolves around the sun.

I taught the fifty states over and over, using the song, "Yankee Doodle," since "Yankee Doodle" was popular in the United States. "Yankee Doodle came to town, riding on a pony. Maine, Vermont, New Hampshire, New York, Massachusetts, Connecticut …" This word association made it easy to remember the state using the rhythm of the song.

I demonstrated DNA with twist ties, colored yarn, and beads. The DNA molecule is shaped like a twisted rope ladder—or, as it is called, a double helix.

I explained the food chain and ecosystem using the prison system as a level of succession—from inmates to wardens. Grass is produced, and rabbits eat the grass, and wolves eat rabbits, and so on and so forth.

The students enjoyed my class. They were eager and motivated to learn, and 99 percent of them passed their GEDs in a short time.

I received many letters from my patients, and they were doing remarkably well. Many of my patients were cured, and they were devoted to church activities. Their church pastor gave a sermon on Sunday about a miracle that had happened to four parishioners. They were cured, he said, through Dr. Gates's treatments. This Sunday sermon was videotaped.

A letter from one of my nurses, Susan Brink, was one of the first letters I had received after being incarcerated. It still comforted me. The letter appeared to have been sent to the judge who presided over my criminal case. It read:

> To whom it may concern:
> I am writing on behalf of Dr. Victoria Gates.
>
> My name is Susan Brink. I have known Dr. Gates for several years, having first met her at church. We both sang in the church choir at St. Alphonsus Catholic Church here in Crossville. My first and lasting impression of her is as a devout Christian. Victoria is a very spiritual person who prays daily and loves deeply. Whereas most people use the phrase "speak of the devil "when someone comes up, Victoria always says "speak of the angel." She loves angels and has a collection of them, which she displayed in her office. She also referred to her patients as angels and treated them as such. It is not in her nature to cause hurt or pain.
>
> When she asked me to come to work for her in her office, I agreed without hesitation. I am a certified nurse technician and all-around girl and have worked in the nursing field on and off for over twenty years. I had never worked in an oncology office before and was a little nervous as to what to expect working with terminal patients. It could have been a cold and depressing experience for all involved, but our office was very warm and comfortable. Patients were never left in the waiting room for more than five minutes at a time. They were brought back as quickly as possible. Many patients just came on back to the exam rooms or even stopped to just to talk to the staff because they knew they were always welcome. Dr. Gates loves her patients, and she was always available to them. If one of the patients called and needed to talk to her, they could. She would always take their calls and would personally

call each patient when they missed an appointment to see if they were sick or if something were wrong.

I am not saying that Dr. Victoria Gates was perfect. Which of us is? But I have never seen a doctor who loved her patients like she did. And yes, she had a few differences with some of her employees. I just attributed those to our cultural differences. She expected total obedience from her employees, sometimes to the extreme, but the bottom line is it was her office, and she was responsible for the lives of her patients. She took this very seriously.

Frugal? Yes. Victoria is frugal. Whether it is because of her background of working so hard get to where she is to become a doctor specializing in internal medicine I do not know. What I do know is that we saved everything. We saved and used every drop of medicine in the bottles. At first it was annoying, but these medicines cost hundreds and thousands of dollars, and every drop counts. Because there are a few extra drops in each vial, over 1 ml, we could gather up all the extra. And out of 12 vials of injectables, we could get enough for 13 injections. How is this wrong?

I worked with Dr. Gates for over a year and a half, during which time I assisted her. Dr. Gates mixed the chemo medicine herself. We did not have any chemo nurses who were trained in this field, and she wanted to be sure it was measured and mixed properly. She *never* mixed the medication by herself. Either I or one of the other staff was always a present when the medicines were mixed. She measured the dosages exactly as instructed on the package. Occasionally, when a patient became too ill with the recommended dosage, she would temporally cut back a little on chemo medicines or increase fluids as the patients needed. They still received their treatment but at a less toxic dosage for a visit or two. To the best of my knowledge, all doctors adjust the dosage of medicine for their patients. Once the patients stabilized, she readjusted their dosages. It was because of her theory "chemotherapy doesn't work if it kills the patient" that our patients lived longer with a better quality of life than was expected. Rick D—— [HIPPA prohibits my including full names] was expected to die within six months to a year. It has now been approximately five years and he is no longer suffering from cancer. Doris E——, whose cancer should have killed her ages ago, lived long enough to meet her goal, which was the to attend the marriage of two grandchildren, months longer than her condition usually allowed. Especially Victor G, who was so carefully treated that, when he was forced to see a new doctor (as our office was closing down), he became angry when new doctor told him he had no sign of illness. So why was he being treated? We had to show him the patient's old lab work to prove the illness to him.

Dr. Gates is an excellent physician. Her abilities and expertise were reflected in the lives of our patients. She treated them not just medically but with the loving tenderness a mother would show to her children. And why not? They were her children. She had put off having children for caring for her patients and being the best doctor, they could have. She would lovingly stroke them and speak words of encouragement. She loved them, and they loved her. After all, they placed their lives in her hands. Does this sound like the monster that she was made out to be? This is a woman who could not even sit through the movie *The Passion of Christ* because she could not bear seeing her Christ, or anyone else, being so mercilessly beaten. I found her crying in the lady's room. Her response was that, if she had been there, she could have helped him, even though she knew this was all Christ's choosing for the betterment of the rest of us.

Even now, with all that has happened in her professional and personal life, still her thoughts are only of who she can help and not on worries for her own future. She feels that God just has another plan for her now.

I hope my experiences with Dr. Gates help you to see the kind of person she is. Please, I ask that you take this into consideration when sentencing time arrives. If she is guilty of anything, it surely is caring so much. We lost a great asset to our community.

Respectfully,
Susan Brink

CHAPTER 37

I Had to Save My Own Life

My computer skills were not good, and I took a Blinn College program. I got all As, except in typing. My school curriculum back home did not have typing classes. I got a B and still could not type well.

Lately, I noticed that my bowel movements had changed. They had become narrow in size and a darker color. There were smeared with mucus, and I detected blood spots on the toilet paper. It was a textbook symptom of a colon cancer. I alerted the PA and the doctor at Bryan Medical Clinic. Without regard to the early signs and symptoms of potential colon cancer, they assured me that I should not worry about it and, furthermore, informed me nothing was wrong.

When the clinical symptoms had progressed for four months, I demanded a colonoscopy. Regardless of my explanation that I was an American board-certified oncologist, they attempted to persuade me that I read too much. You are healthy, they insisted, and nothing is wrong with you. The medical team did not pay any attention to what I was saying.

At the time, Bryan Federal Camp was being investigated for sexual scandals. One handsome physician's assistant (PA) was handcuffed and carried out by a marshal. Concurrently, the inmate who was involved in the scandal was quickly transferred to another facility. Something had hit the fan. Soon after this sexual scandal had spread, the doctor at the medical clinic was also carried out, and one of the kitchen officers was indicted. Through the grapevine, we heard that another officer in the kitchen had resigned.

Six months passed. My rectal bleeding was getting worse. Despite my progressing symptoms, the medical clinic did nothing. The director of the medical clinic explained that I had to wait for the region's permission to consider a colonoscopy after October, which ended the fiscal year.

Eight months passed, and I began to complain to everybody, including the assistant warden, the warden, the CMC, the psychologist, the case manager, the unit manager, the pastor, and other staff members. The warden recommended that I file an "eight and a half form" to seek an in-house resolution. I submitted the eight and a half to the counselor, saying that my symptoms and bleeding are getting worse. In-house resolution requests were to be responded to within thirty days. I received no response.

The counselor had no sympathy, was insensitive and disinterested, and appeared to have no regard or concern for the lives or deaths of the inmates. A simple colonoscopy would have diagnosed my colon cancer early, and it could have been cured. Instead, the clinic did nothing about my numerous requests. I was like a yo-yo, knocking on the door to have colonoscopy, and being snapped away. Grievously, my counsel got rid of the eight and a half resolution.

When I asked her, for the answer to the in-house resolution regarding my request for a colonoscopy, she said, "It is already four months old." She was not going to give me an answer because the request was "too old."

I requested another eight and a half form to file again; she would not give it to me. As time went on over the next fourteen months, my bleeding became severe. My rectal bleeding filled the toilet bowl as if I were menstruating. Several inmates witnessed this and advised me to report to an officer. The agent on duty freaked out and refused to see it.

Blood clots and bleeding on a pad were saved to show a PA for evaluation. Instead, one of the unit officers attempted to give me an incident report for saving an unsanitary bloody pad. Later, the director of the clinic explained to the officer that the specimen was required to evaluate the degree of the underlying condition. The incident report was then waived.

I started to become sick and weak. I went to triage at the medical clinic and lost consciousness, collapsing on the floor. The clinic must have called a paramedic, and an ambulance took me to the Regional ER. A few hours later, I woke up after a CT scan had been done at the ER. Undoubtedly, my cancer had spread to my lymph nodes, but there was no visible tumor in my liver. I received fluids without a blood transfusion, despite my blood counts having bottomed out.

When I had returned to the camp, the designated PA performed a rectal examination, and fresh blood covered his gloved finger. Consequently, the PA resigned. Finally, the clinic scheduled me for a colonoscopy, which confirmed a large cancer from the biopsy on the pathology report. Subsequently, the director of the clinic wanted to transfer me out in a hurry to Carswell Medical Center. If I agreed to her plan, then the surgery would be delayed. I told her that I needed surgery ASAP before the cancer spread to my liver or to another organ. Once colon cancer spreads to the liver, the average life expectancy is six months to a year.

I repeatedly refused to go to Carswell until my surgery was done. The director said that Bryan Clinic did not have colostomy bags, and no nurses were trained for the wound care I would need. I insisted that my tumor must be surgically removed at once.

There was a two-week delay before my surgery. Favorably, I had an excellent surgeon, and we discussed options of laparoscopic sigmoidectomy to avoid surgical scars. Thanks be to God! The bulky tumor was located at the end of the colon. I did not need to have a colostomy bag.

I was scheduled at 8:00 a.m., but the surgeons got busy that day, and it was delayed until 8:00 p.m. I had not eaten or drunk since the night before, yet I was not hungry; nor was I nervous about the surgery.

"Do you have so many patients scheduled for surgeries that you're still performing them 8:00 p.m.?" I asked the surgeon.

"I had an emergency appendectomy, and all the scheduled surgical patients were delayed," the surgeon explained.

After two days of post-op recovery, I was discharged from the hospital on the third morning.

As soon as I returned to the camp—though I had a wobbly gait and limited physical movement—the unit officer demanded that I pack my belongings within two hours. I was being transferred to Carswell Medical Center. Due to my illness and hasty transfer, I was unable to finish two remaining subjects in the Blinn College program.

Carswell FCI was quite different from Bryan Camp. The place consisted of several high-rise buildings, was larger bigger than Bryan, and was filled with scary vibes. Deplorably, the medical center was located next to the FCI.

I was assigned to the fourth floor of the medical and surgical unit. The room was large with a view of Fort Worth and had a private bathroom and shower along with a remote-controlled bed. My room was next to the nurses' station.

There were several inmate nurse's aides (INAs) who cleaned the room, brought meals, and assisted the nurses with patients' care. Doctor rounds daily, and an outside doctor covered nighttime emergencies. My chemotherapy was given outside the prison at a cancer center. I had a total of twelve cycles of treatments from January until July 2013. Luckily, I was able to treat myself as I had my own patients.

The doctors and the nurses at the cancer center recognized my medical background and the fact that I was a licensed medical oncologist. Thus, I was able to adjust my own chemo drug dosages based on toxicity of the drugs and my clinical symptoms. The assigned oncologist agreed to my request of adjustment based on my tolerance. The main chemo drugs were infused, followed by my requesting that the nurse give me antiemetic medications before they connected a portable continuous 5FU infusion via a tiny machine.

The second day, the 5FU infusion device was disconnected. I had a private room at the cancer center and was able to rest for two hours while receiving a bag of saline and antiemetics before I return to the medical center. My family cried over the phone; they could not understand my tumultuous destiny. I was not nervous. Nor was I sad. I believed that neither life nor death were in our control. We were born without our will, and we would each die like everybody else, which was life's inevitable process.

Learning was my pleasure. I decided to study during the chemotherapy. My plan was initially to get a Master of Science in business administration through the correspondence school of Southwest University in Louisiana. I had a hard time walking, as the chemo drugs had induced nerve damages, but I overcame this by walking exercises every day. My hair was pretty much spared. No symptoms were acquired, including pain, nausea, vomiting, and neuropathy. Chemicals were my least favorite medications, as they eventually create problems in our systems.

I had met Lacy in Tallahassee, and she arrived at Carswell two weeks after I was transferred there. We had been transferred together to Waseca and had worked at the library. Lacy had shaved her head, and she did not look good. We were reminiscing about the old times in Tallahassee. She informed me that Dr. Stile, who all the inmates respected because he was altruistic and genuinely cared for us, had been promoted and had become a general counsel at the Washington office. I had already learned the news.

As the head of the department, he had visited Waseca to evaluate the accreditation of the Waseca Institution. It had been my pleasant surprise to see him at the entrance of the Waseca cafeteria. I distinctively remembered that he was extremely glad to see me, and he stretched out his hand to me in front of many official members of the prison. The captain, warden, and prison staff watched us as we shook hands. I asked him whether he would be involved in inmates' education again.

He said, "I don't think so. I have many different responsibilities now in Washington." He then advised me to do something productive and not waste my time while serving my sentence. "I am awfully glad to see you," he added.

Being an inmate, I was not allowed to talk with outside dignitaries, not to mention shake their hands (this was strictly prohibited). The captain's eyes got bigger and he stared at me in silence. He could not restrict me from talking to Dr. Stile. My conversation with him was brief, but it made my day.

Lacy had also seen him when he had walked through the library. Lacking teeth, she had a hard time chewing, and Dr. Stile had arranged for a Waseca dentist to provide Lacy with dentures. After his visit, Lacy got a set of dentures, was able to eat better, and even looked prettier with the teeth.

Now what had happened to her? Suddenly, Lacy had appeared with a bald head at Carswell Medical Center.

"I was just diagnosed with aggressive lung cancer; I'm here from chemotherapy," she told me.

My port-a-cath had been effectively placed at a fancy private Methodist hospital. Lacy, on the other hand, had a temporary catheter inserted at a doctor's office. which did not work. She was not able to receive chemo drugs through the line. Poor Lacy! She had many problems, and many nurses had started her IV-line numerous times before her chemotherapy.

A few weeks later, Lacy was released by reason of her hopeless prognosis. She died two weeks after she was discharged. After ten years of prison life, she died soon after she had gone home. It was beyond sad. Life is unfair, and we all die.

A Bryan inmate, Sharan, was transferred a few days later. She knew me well, yet it took me a while to recollect my memory. She was a pretty and pleasant young lady. She accidentally bumped her left breast, and it rapidly increased in size. A biopsy report confirmed that she had breast cancer. She was physically active, and her chemotherapy, to be given in three cycles, started. Within two months, Sharan was found dead on her bed by an inmate nurse's aide (INA).

Another young female, Lynn was diagnosed with Stage III sigmoid colon cancer, which was the same as my cancer. I met Lynn at the medical clinic. Lynn received the same chemo regimen as mine. Obviously, her chemotherapy drugs were not adjusted, and she got extremely sick and was placed in hospice care for months. She had supposedly recovered before I completed my chemotherapy. I was informed that Lynn had died right before she was supposed to go home.

Henrietta, who had chronic hepatitis C and who I had also known at Bryan Camp, developed liver cancer. Soon after she was diagnosed, she was sent home and died.

These tragic stories broke my heart.

Inmates' corpses were carried out frequently while I was on the med-surg floor at Carswell. I could have easily gotten sick and died if I had not asked my oncologist to adjust my chemotherapy drug dosages based on my tolerance.

I did for myself exactly what I had been doing for my patients. I adjusted the chemo dosages based on individual tolerance. I had to save my own life. Fortunately, the medical team followed my suggestion.

Here I was sitting in the prison, and I could not do much for other sick inmates.

I could not fathom that using the appropriate dosages of lifesaving drugs was why I was here—the reason I had been made into a villain and painted as a criminal. I was a doctor and had taken the Hippocratic oath, and I applied its principles to my practice, with special attention to the following precepts:

1. I will apply dietetic measures for the benefit of the sick according to my ability and judgment; I will keep them from harm and injustice.
2. Neither will I give a deadly drug to anybody who asks for it, nor will I suggest such a drug be used.
3. I will care for the sick, remaining free of all intentional injustice.
4. If I fulfill this oath and do not violate it, may it allow me to enjoy life and art, being honored with fame among all men for all time to come; if I transgress it and steer falsely, may the opposite of all this be my lot.

I believed that I had accomplished my lifetime commitment and mission to restore patients' health, to remove their ailments, and to save lives—even those who had been diagnosed with a "hopeless" terminal cancer.

The eyes of the law focused on overfill discrepancies, which overweighed true facts. Conspirators and perpetrators had turned saving lives into something as petty and menial as Medicare fraud.

It was distinctive evidence that money is truly the root of all evil. Everyone had their hands out—the lawyers, my husband, and the government.

Within a week after my chemotherapy treatments were completed, I was transferred to Carswell Camp. I was blessed not to be placed at the FCI, which had frequent fights because the inmates were less disciplined. The Carswell Camp had been converted from an old Motel 6. The rooms had a door, a kitchen sink, a bathroom with a door, and a bathtub and shower in each of the four to six-person rooms. Each room had its own air conditioner and a ceiling fan; however, the place was exceedingly dilapidated.

The camp population was limited to 260, but occasionally slightly over 300 inmates were housed there. There were no microwaves and hair dryers, as inmates had broken them time and time again. Two TV rooms, both with wet, smelly carpet stained with dark spots and an unhealthy feel, were situated in each wing. The educational department and library were small. The leisure library and indoor recreation were in the last building. There were several exercise and CD music rooms upstairs. No one really used the CD music room, which looked haunted. Parts of the wallpaper had come loose over the months and years without repair. When I first went there, I came out of the room as quickly as I had gone in.

Later, though, the CD music room became my study room, and I got used to looking out at the nice lake view through the dusty windowpane. The view was lovely. When the sun went down, the shimmering water changed colors, sparkling in the sun's reflection. Several fawns would often rest next to their mother along the edge of the lake view and seeing them there was magnificent. I studied in that indoor recreation room often, listening to music in solitude—until fleas infested it.

After that, I discovered an outdoor bench where I could see the lake view through the small pathway between buildings. The view of the cafeteria was in the best part of the camp. An open picturesque lake scene could be seen through the surrounding large windowpane, and watching the seagulls was delightful. I begin to appreciate the beauty of nature, the masterpiece of God's creation, more deeply than ever. To think of the wild animals running through the surrounding fields gave me joy, peace, hope, and faith. Every afternoon, I could see flocks of snowy seagulls flying in one direction or another.

Numerous birds covered nearly a third of lake space. I enjoyed watching geese and flying blue herons on the other side of the lake toward the woods. Behind the indoor recreation area was an empty field next to the woods. Dozens upon dozens of deer roamed and grazed on the field in the early evening under the dim light. On the shallow lake, ducks would glide and dance over the twinkling, shimmering, colorful water of sunset.

Every morning when I exercised on the track next to the lake, I enjoyed feeding the wild geese. Soon the geese followed me everywhere. At night, I saw foxes with bright shining eyes like flashlights. They came closed to the dorm in the night and waited for us to throw some food. Raccoons were also searched for food; overweight and clumsy, they tried to come inside the room through the open windows. One inmate, who reacted by screaming her lungs out and running for her life in her bare foot, entertained the others.

One day, I threw holiday peanut brittle to a raccoon. It gathered the brittle and acted like a greedy child, wanting all for itself.

In spring I saw a variety of birds. I loved nature and wild animals. My body was captured in prison, but my spirit was in heaven beside God's masterpiece of creation. I only stayed inside the dorm to sleep and would go out early in the morning. I continuously studying for my Master of Science in business administration at the metal table attached to the bench and appreciated the blue lake view through the small pathway.

Texas had mostly hot weather throughout the seasons and experienced four seasons a day in the form of different temperatures between morning and night. I used an umbrella as a parasol to create some shade. There were holes on top of the table attached to my outdoor metal bench. I designed an umbrella holder using a creamer container placed inside my water mug and fastened the two items together inside a long sock. Several long shoelace ropes were sewn to the top of the sock and held the umbrella up by securing the holder through the holes.

The lake breeze and shade help me study without air-conditioning. On the other hand, sudden winds often flipped my umbrella, which, made in Taiwan, was delicate and sensitive, broke frequently, and did not last long. The cost of the umbrella was five dollars, and I purchased at the least twenty-six umbrellas before I finished my MBA studies. My nickname became Mary Poppins. Later, I protected the top of the umbrella with long shoelaces to prevent it from flipping in the winds.

On rainy days, I moved to the back of the kitchen building under the roof, where there was a beautiful open lake view. I tied boxes together to create a portable desk, used a room chair, and read with a book light. There was an exquisite charm in a rainstorm next to the lake and woods. The pouring rain under the streetlight on the track glistened, giving me a sense of Mother Nature's serenity.

One downfall to the beauty of nature at Carswell Camp was the many vicious Texas mosquitoes. I cut the toe section of socks and wore them as long gloves. Dryer sheets were used as mosquito repellent. I would sew the Bounce sheets together and wear them as a fashionable scarf around my neck, which coved most of my exposed skin.

The chemotherapy had induced serious nerve damage, and I could not walk for long periods and, in addition, experienced intermittent falling. On one such fall, my right knee was cut deeply, and the hanging tissue bled profusely and revealed its inner structure. The camp officer took me into the emergency, and it took many stitches to close the wound. I did not damage my kneecap. Nor did I break the bone, through God's grace. I stayed overnight.

The following morning, I was discharged with a full-length splint to immobilize my leg. Soon after I returned to the camp, I took off the splint and gave it to the medical clinic. I walked without it. Looking in the mirror, I saw a surgical wound that had not healed; a protruding port-a-cath; abdominal scars; and now, a stitched, swollen knee. I looked like an alien from another planet with an ill-fated destiny.

Time heals all wounds. The port-a-cath was removed, all my scars faded, and I could walk and even jog.

I received my MBA and graduated with higher honors in January 2015, registered as a member of the Honor Society at Southwestern University. I promptly enrolled for a second Masters of Science in criminal justice at Southwest University.

During my criminal justice course, I would dive into recycling bins to collect numerous newspaper articles for my assignments. A few inmates and officers were disturbed by my eagerness and audacious ambition to learn. I paid them no attention and accepted my current difficult situation and living in prison without any retaliation.

CHAPTER 38

We Thought You Were Dead (Coming out of a Fiery Furnace without a Burn)

I was transferred to Bryan Camp in October 2016. There, I was able to complete my second master's degree, this one in the science of criminal justice in December 2016. Bryan Camp did not have a lake view. On the other hand, it did have a study room and was much cleaner than Carswell Camp.

My efforts were not wasted, and I once again graduated with higher honors. The school recognized my academic achievements and registered my name in the honor society for both the MBA and the criminal justice degree at Southwestern University.

I did not want to return to Bryan Camp since I cherished living in a place surrounded by nature and had adored the wild animals at Carswell Camp for four years. But I did not require any further treatment, and Bryan was designated as my parental prison. Abruptly, Carswell gave me two hours to pack my belongings and informed me to be ready for transportation. I was assigned to the same dorm, across from officers' station, that I had previously occupied at the Bryan camp.

In December 2012, Officer Mollien had taken me to Saint Joseph Hospital for my surgery. Four years later, I appeared and standing up for the count, and Miss Mollien was counting. During count time, she passed by my room and then came back and stared at me. "Are you Victoria Gates?" she asked. "We thought you were dead."

After the count, the officer returned to my room. She was astonished to learn of my recovery. The second day, the night officer who had freaked out and refused to see my rectal bleeding in the toilet bowl many years earlier, stared, her wide-open eyes fixed on me. She had a stoic character but appeared to be scared. The next day, she again stared at me for a long time. Then after I had used the restroom around 2:00 a.m. one night, she beckoned me with her hand and pointed to her office.

When an officer calls an inmate into her office, it is usually not a good sign. I initially thought, I had done something wrong.

As I entered her office, she said to me, "Are you a ghost? We thought you were dead."

"I am not dead," I assured her. "And yes, I am Victoria Gates."

On Monday morning, I saw the nicest officer I had met. Ms. Walker had stayed with me when my surgery had been delayed for almost twelve hours. At the time, she had been a unit officer, and now she was the unit counselor. I was elated to see her and glad she was my counselor at this time. My previous consular was wicked and malicious. She had disposed of the eight and a half form I had filed and refused to do anything about the in-house resolution I'd requested when I had been deadly sick. Ms. Walker, on the other hand, was a Christian, and she was beautiful and intelligent. She could not believe she was looking at me.

"Are you Victoria Gates?" she asked me.

"Yes," I told her, adding, "I'll never forget you were praying for me when I was admitted to the hospital before my surgery."

She picked up a Kleenex and wiped her running tears. She kept saying, "We thought you were dead. How nice to see you again!"

At that very moment, I felt the rest of my time served would be much better than the time before. Many of the same inmates were still at Bryan Camp, and they had also thought I was dead. Another officer wanted to pinch me to see if she was seeing a person or a ghost in the cafeteria.

I continued to make the best of my time by studying, and in May 2017, I successfully completed Blackstone's paralegal program after being transferred back to Bryan. Everybody loves money. My unit manager, Ms. Hermon, contacted the department of justice in Washington to verify my restitution. She gave me a copy of the faxed inquiry report from the DOJ, dated September 12, 2006, which showed the transaction and the payment the DOJ had received.

After a brief discussion regarding my compassionate release with the unit manager, Ms. Hermon informed me that my presentencing report (PSR) revealed many patient victims. In January 2017, I requested the entire history of my malpractice record, which came back showing zero malpractice settlements. There was no evidence that I had patients who were victims.

One of my patients, Calvin, had initially sued me for $11 million. However, later, his claim had been dismissed by the state court judge, and there was no settlement. Calvin worked for a federal office, and a TBI agent had convinced him to file the civil suit. When Calvin had first come to me, he had been given less than six months to live. Under my care, he had achieved a durable remission that had lasted for seven years after chemotherapy. In any event, I saved his life, and he had disrespectfully turned around and sued me. But the suit had not been successful.

At the same time, the cases of my patients Jack and Sheila were dismissed, and there was no evidence of a victim in either, other than assumptive allegations by the prosecutor before my trial. My patients did not have injuries; nor were they harmed under my treatments. At no time did I ever show men's rea (the knowing or intention of wrongdoing), which is an element that is required for a crime to have been committed. Nevertheless, to reflect the seriousness of the offense, my case was filed as fraud related to medical billing, and I was found guilty by a jury for health care fraud.

There was no form of injury or damage in my practice. Yet I had been punished and sentenced as if I had purposefully injured my patients. Once again, the result was the expression of a fixed view, based on a presentence report (PSR) made prior to a hearing, which was inconsistent. Texas law held that the mistaken recording of my patients as victims on the PSR should be corrected and that such correction could take place at any time.

On March 1, 2017, I submitted a motion to amend my PSR in Nashville Federal Court. My motion was swiftly denied without material facts, as if the government's decision to punish me was set in stone. My prosecutor responded that the PSR was too old to be corrected. My PSR falsely showed more than ten patient victims. There were zero victims. The PSR was required to be corrected under the rule of law.

Additionally, I filed a motion saying that the stipulation that the court had collected victim restitution revealed significant discrepancies between the federal court in Nashville and the report of the department of justice in Washington. I requested that a transaction account with the Nashville courthouse be handed over to me. Nonetheless, the prosecutor failed to provide me with any documents related to the transaction. I received only a brief response in the smallest font, stating, "Sorry. There are no payment reversals."

The court collected patient victim restitution. My sentencing judgment ordered a total restitution of $432,238, which I had paid in full.

On August 11, 2009, my criminal judge orchestrated a further removal of my monies and became involved in my divorce proceedings (and the funds involved), as well as a civil action against me (for triple monetary damages) that had been dismissed by another judge in 2006 at the Nashville federal court. He ordered the funds that I had owned solely to be transferred to my divorce account in Oklahoma—against Wisconsin sovereignty. My bank account in Wisconsin had nothing to do with Tennessee, as I had earned the money held there outside the state of Tennessee.

On December 4, 2009, after my divorce was completed in Oklahoma, the Nashville federal court garnished another $719,615.68. Meanwhile, Medicare and TennCare still owed me nearly $80,000. Consequently, the court collected improper restitution. Additionally, it added an assumptive loss without correctly calculating for $1,295,653.36 and claimed it as intended loss.

Thus, the district court not only improperly collected $863,415.30 but also handed me an enhanced sentence, sixteen levels up. The level of ruling in the federal court, by far and away, favors the government. I believe that true justice had been overshadowed when I had been given a nearly two decades-long sentences for an alleged crime that I did not commit.

As a doctor, I did things right. However, I received the wrong outcomes under the eyes of the law, which resulted in a high-priced punishment. The indictment alleged an attempt to defraud the US benefit program and conspiracy to defraud, and these charges should have been dismissed. The rule of Medicare law states that, if there was no violation resulting in serious bodily injury, the defendant should not be imprisoned for more than ten years. I did not have any patients who had been injured; yet I was sentenced to serve 188 months. There was no victim except for the ghost victims planted by the prosecutor.

I am convinced that my sentence was unconstitutionally enhanced with presumptive prejudice. Attention had been shifted from the goal of finding truth to effectively playing the game by "winning."

Undeniably, I had been living in the gut-churning bureaucracy of reality. My colon cancer should have been cured when I had asked for colonoscopy before it spread to my lymph nodes and other tissues. After nearly a year and a half of my begging to be seen, the delayed diagnosis revealed end-stage IIIB cancer.

Time passed, and five years after my treatments, there were significant spots in my thyroid, the right upper lung, and my right pelvic area. However, those spots had not increased in size for one and half years. I was then considered to be in clinical remission.

Having been in prison for close to twelve years, I had grown older and was eligible by law for the nonmedical elderly second chance act. A year and a half prior to fulfilling my time served, I was permitted to go home. I was excited and packed all my belongings, mailing some out and giving many items to inmates. Ten months later, my early release arrangement was cancelled. As of a result, I repurchased daily use items.

Everything happens for God's purpose, and God sends only what we can handle. I had gone through many trials, and it was not easy to bear it all. Sometimes, I wondered why I had to go through this pain and endless torment. But my faith began to grow like a sprout budding from the ground, preparing to one day produce abundant fruit.

I could not see God's light at that time. Today my light began to shine. I experienced that I had burned down to ground and God had rebuilt me for a brand-new purpose. Once I let go of myself, God's love could shine through like a light in the dark. Life is a learning process, and I have so much more to learn about God's true love.

"Love strengthens me. The greater love I experience and express, the greater is all power of the universal happiness. Accepting the creative power of my thoughts and feeling in my path to freedom, inner power, and peace.

I am happy only when I judge not and condemn not. I am not here to edit God's creation." (GPS)

When I had possessed wealth and fame, I had thought I was successful, but I was only lured by a mirage of success. Success did not occur without failure. I understood that the hard times were what made me stronger and enabled me to grow so I could see the true purpose of life.

What else was new in prison life? When it rained, it poured. Inmates made so much noise they could wake the dead. Approximately six years ago, I had taught GED students and 99 percent of my students had passed the tests and obtained a degree. At the time, I had persuaded male warden to provide us study rooms. Before he retired, he gave us a study room for each dorm.

The wonderful counselor, Ms. Walker, controlled and restricted the use of the study room and ensured it was only for study. The room became a quiet place; studying was my peaceful time. I had new goals. I decided to study advanced civil and criminal law before I attended law school. It did not matter whether I was in prison or outside; my mind and my heart were already free. In a moment of stillness, I heard God's voice and his presence was felt. I was able to shift my focus in my quest for happiness, peace, and freedom. I began to understand that everything came from within myself—never from outside my mind.

To this day, I still rack my brain to understand why I developed colon cancer, without a family history of cancer. Generally, colon cancer runs in a family. I achieved remission, but many questions remained. I wondered if my colon cancer had been caused by drinking poisonous bleach in Crossville. The chlorine in bleach causes irritation to the nose, throat, and lungs and can result in seizures; in addition, it can also cause cancer. In my experience, the etiology of my cancer begged a quest for further research. God created a remedy for all illness. However, sometimes we cannot discover a panacea.

Prison taught me how to deal with different characters and to develop interpersonal relationships. My experience taught me that we must respect one another and that the value of understanding an individual's struggles and of learning to tolerate differences was high. I learned that forgiveness and kindness cultivate human connection. And anger is a superficial expression of emotional stress, and it leads to hatred. Hatred will lead to destruction without solution. However, love conquers all.

I hope that writing this book serves a humanitarian purpose. Together we can weave a colorful tapestry of unity and strength. Sometimes, I believe it would be nice if we could all become like a malleable Gumby to adopt and accept undesirable circumstances without vengeance.

No matter what happens to us, we should learn to focus on God and be still to receive his unconditional peace, joy, hope, and faith. Good decisions, perseverance, and wisdom will help to overcome our obstacles. I believe the Holy Spirit will guide me through my future missions and allow me to help others with God's Grace.

Ask, will receive it.

Seek, will find it.

Knock, the door will open.

I do not grieve for my ill-fated past, but joy for what I can do presently.

I will hold to my aspirations, no matter what is going on around me.

The greater the difficulty, the more glory in surmounting it. Skillful pilots gain their reputation from storms and tempests. Difficulty shows what we are." -Epictetus

If we realize that all things change, there is nothing we will try to hold on to. If we are not afraid of dying, there is nothing we cannot achieve." - Lao Tzu, Tao Te Ching

Time to involve myself with the battlefield of the pandemic virus which compels me to rejoin my medical training and help others.

This book is a true account. The names have been changed to protect the innocent and the guilty. My wishful dream is to build a cancer center and a free medical clinic to help patients.